A History of the Hull and Scarborough Railway

John F Addyman, John Farline, Bill Fawcett,
Nicholas P Fleetwood, David R Smith and John G Teasdale.

Edited by John F Addyman and Bill Fawcett.

NORTH EASTERN RAILWAY ASSOCIATION

Published by Kestrel Railway Books, 2013.
Kestrel Railway Books Website : www.kestrelrailwaybooks.co.uk

ISBN 978-1-905505-30-2.

Typeset by John G Teasdale.

Printed in Great Britain by The Amadeus Press, Ezra House, West 26 Business Park, CLECKHEATON, BD19 4TQ.

The North Eastern Railway Association

Formed in 1961, the NERA caters for all interested in the railways of north-east England, with specific focus on the North Eastern Railway, its constituents and successors, from their early history down to the present day. This also extends to the many industrial and smaller railways that operated alongside them. Interests range over all aspects of development, operation and infrastructure of the railway, including such diverse activities as locomotive history, rolling stock, train services, architecture, signalling, shipping, road vehicles and staff matters – both for the general enthusiast and model maker.

With in excess of 700 members, regular meetings are held in York, Darlington, Hull and London. A programme of outdoor tours and walks is also arranged.

Members receive a quarterly illustrated journal, the *North Eastern Express*, and a newsletter covering membership topics, forthcoming meetings and events in the region. Over 200 issues of the *Express* have been published to date.

The Association owns an extensive library of books, documents, photographs and drawings; these are available for study both by members and non-members alike. The Association also markets an extensive range of facsimiles of railway company documents, including diagram books, timetables and other booklets, while at the same time it is developing an expanding range of original publications, available to members at discounted prices.

For a membership prospectus, please contact:

Mr K Richardson, 7 Grenadier Drive, NORTHALLERTON, DL6 1SB.

A sales list of other NERA publications can be obtained from the Publications Officer:

Mr DJ Williamson, 31 Moreton Avenue, Stretford, MANCHESTER, M32 8BP.
(Please enclose a stamped addressed 9" x 4" envelope with your enquiries.)

NERA Website : www.ner.org.uk

Front cover photograph: Ex-LMS Black 5s dominate this photograph of the Scarborough end of Bridlington station in the early 1960s. Nearest the camera are at least three locomotives coupled together. A possible reason for this may be that they are waiting to travel to Filey Holiday Camp to turn on its triangle as Bridlington's turntable was unavailable at this time; on at least one occasion (D49 No 62703 'Hertfordshire' on 28 May 1958) a locomotive ran into the turntable pit, rendering it unusable until recovery could be effected. (Colour-Rail.com / Reference No 304603)

Title page photograph: The generally flat terrain negotiated by the Hull and Scarborough Railway resulted in a large number of level crossings. This is Royal Oak Crossing, seen from the railway on 3 September 1977. The handsome gates and the signal box would be replaced by Automatic Half Barriers and CCTV on 12 June 1983. (CJ Woolstenholmes / NERA Collection)

Rear cover photograph (top): Class 47/4 No 47442, built as No D1558, approaches Filey with a passenger train from Scarborough on 3 September 1977. Although the level crossing remains in use, the signal box has since gone; Automatic Half Barriers were installed, controlled remotely by CCTV, in June 2000, and the redundant box was demolished the following year. (CJ Woolstenholmes / NERA Collection)

Rear cover photograph (bottom): A Class 158 Sprinter leaves Beverley as it works a Scarborough - Sheffield (via Hull and Doncaster) service. Currently the train operating company Serco-Abellio has the Northern Rail franchise which includes the Hull and Scarborough Railway. (John Furneval)

Contents

Introduction

Some ten years ago I started a project to write about the railway at Bridlington and its adjoining stations with a view to having it published in the *North Eastern Express*, the quarterly journal of the North Eastern Railway Association. I was very conscious that although the North Eastern Railway historian, the late Ken Hoole, had commuted during his school days from Bridlington to Hull, he had never gone further towards a history of the branch than a few references in some of his books or articles. As the information from my research amassed, discussions with John Addyman and Bill Fawcett suggested that we extend the scope to cover the whole of the line between Hull and Seamer. The north end, from Seamer to Scarborough, has been adequately covered in Bill Fawcett's *A History of the York - Scarborough Railway* (1995) and Hull itself in Mick Nicholson and the late Willie Yeadon's two volumes *An Illustrated History of Hull's Railways* (1993-5). The railways along the Yorkshire coast north of Scarborough have been covered in a number of works making this volume essential to fill in the final section southwards to Hull.

From 1845 to the present day the Hull & Selby, York & North Midland, North Eastern, London & North Eastern, British Railways, Railtrack and Network Rail have all made their mark on the services and/or infrastructure of the line. This rich history, and the line's changing fortunes from Nineteenth Century success to near closure and its current revival are recorded in detail within the pages of this new book.

John Richardson, President North Eastern Railway Association, March 2012.

Acknowledgements

The authors wish to acknowledge the help given by the following individuals both in providing information and photographs: WF Astbury, R Bastin, J Bennett, J Buckman, P Chancellor (Colour-Rail.com), P Crossland, R Coulthard, F Dean, M Dixon, TJ Edgington, CB Foster, G Foster, J Furneval, D Harrison, M Lake, JR Lidster, P & A Los, N Mackay, J McCrickard, S Metcalf, J Midcalf, T Morrell, M Nicholson, G Oliver, Pat Pinder, A Porter, the late J Proud, the late P Robinson, R Pulleyn, A Ross, C Ryder, J Sadler, A Stanyon, DL Stephens, A Turner, J Walker, F Walkington, the late J Ward, S Watson, IK Watson, D & C Williamson, HGE Wilson, M Wilson, AE Young, and C Wright former harbourmaster at Bridlington. Leona White-Hannant, curator of the Ken Hoole Study Centre, Sarah Hutchinson and the staff of Bridlington Library, the staff of East Yorkshire Archives, the National Railway Museum and The National Archives have also been most helpful.

Particular thanks are due to Neville Stead for making his large selection of photographs available.

Class B16 No 61472 is seen at the south end of the line on 7 September 1963 about to haul the last ever steam-worked Hull to Edinburgh express over the first leg of its journey. (Ian K Watson)

At the north end of the line, passing Seamer West cabin, we see Nos 62381 and 43096 hauling special No 238 to Liverpool on to the branch on 13 September 1957. (Neville Stead)

***Map**, showing the Hull and Scarborough Railway and its immediate connecting lines in heavy red lines. The bus services in operation before 1914 are shown as fine red lines. (The lines shown purple represent the Hull & Barnsley Railway.) Other parts of the map are colour-coded too: dark blue (Bridlington, Hornsea and Rye Hill) represents sand and gravel deposits; light blue represents stands of round timber; white (Hunmanby and Hessle) represents deposits of limestone; orange represents moorland and hill pasture; off-white represents agricultural land, including that used to raise livestock. A superimposed X marks the location of a level crossing. (Private Collection)*

Chapter 1 : Hull to Scarborough Railway

Bill Fawcett

Introduction

Individual railways convey different identities to different travellers. This was particularly evident in the heyday of the Hull - Scarborough line. For denizens of the industrialised West Riding and further afield, it was the holiday line which took them to the bracing breezes of the Yorkshire Coast: to resorts such as Filey and Bridlington or Sir Billy Butlin's Filey Holiday Camp, served by its own branch line. Country folk knew it as the means of getting to market or shops in towns such as Driffield and Beverley. Numerous people working in Hull found that it gave them the opportunity of living further afield and commuting by train from as far off as Bridlington. A further dimension was provided by the creation, in 1889, of the East Riding County Council, with its headquarters at Beverley.

Even today, Bridlington is a transition point on the line. There is a more frequent service southwards, to Hull and beyond, than north to Scarborough. It also sees the line leave the flat coastal plain, which has made the going very easy all the way from Hull, to climb north over the tail end of the Yorkshire Wolds, the great chalk uplands, as they roll down to the sea. The town was also, at the very beginning, the meeting point of the two railways which promoted the route: the Hull & Selby (H&S) and the York & North Midland (Y&NM), the latter chaired by George Hudson, the first 'Railway King'.

Before the railway came, transport locally was by road and water. The township and turnpike roads carried a network of services intended primarily for goods and provided by local carriers, which continued to develop after the appearance of the trains. Coaching options were much more limited, as can be seen from the entry for Driffield in Baines's Directory of 1822; this records a daily coach serving the town on a Hull - Bridlington - Scarborough service in summer, reducing to thrice weekly in winter.(1) Beverley, served also by coaches on the road to Market Weighton and York, was somewhat better off as can be judged from Table 1.1. For a map of the area, see page 5.

Table 1.1.

Extract from the Beverley entry in *Baines's Directory* of 1822. In addition to these operators Baines listed 61 country carriers operating scheduled services between Beverley and various towns and villages.

COACHES

From Robert Clark's, Pack Horse, Market Place
The HIGHFLYER on Tuesday, Thursday, Friday and Sunday, to Hull at 8 morning returns 7 evening.
ACCOMMODATION from Hull on Monday, Wednesday, Thursday, Saturday and Sunday at $^1/_2$ past 10 morning returns 5 evening.

From Nathaniel Dalby's, Beverley Arms, North Bar Street Within
BRITISH QUEEN to Scarborough daily during summer, in winter three days per week, depart $^1/_2$ past 7 morning return at 1 afternoon.
ROCKINGHAM from Hull to York at 11 morning return at 3 afternoon.
TRAFALGAR from York to Hull at 11 morning return at $^1/_2$ past 3 afternoon.

From Charles Greenwood's Tiger Inn, North Bar Street Within
ROYAL MAIL from Hull to York at 4 in the afternoon return 5 morning.
TRAFALGAR from Hull daily at 7 morning return $^1/_2$ past 6 evening.
WELLINGTON TO Scarborough daily during summer at 8 morning return at 2 afternoon, in winter three days a week.

LAND CARRIAGE

John Botterill, *Valiant Soldier*, Norwood, to the *Three Crowns*, Market Place, Hull, on Tuesday and Friday at 7 morning, return 9 evening.

Samuel Fenteman, *Gardham's Yard* to the *Blue Bell*, Market Place, Hull, daily at 9 morning, return at $^1/_4$ past 8 evening.

James Swaby, Walkergate to *Rein Deer*, Market Place, Hull, daily 9 morning, return at $^1/_4$ past 8 evening.

Widow Wilson, from the *Green Dragon* to Hull Mondays and Thursdays; to Market Weighton and York every Wednesday and Saturday.

John Cockburn, to Hull every Monday and Thursday; to Market Weighton and Pocklington every Tuesday and Friday.

Thomas Newcombe, to Hull Monday and Thursday; to Market Weighton and York every Tuesday and Friday.

Water transport was important. Only very small boats could be beached at Filey, while Flamborough had just two 'landings' for fishing boats, but Bridlington boasted a proper harbour, recorded as importing six thousand chaldrons (almost 16,000 tonnes) of coal from the Tyne in 1820; this clearly supplied quite a large hinterland.(2) Of great value to the communities between Driffield and Beverley was the system of inland navigation based upon the River Hull.(3) The river originates as a pair of trout streams, springing at the foot of the Wolds not far from Driffield, where they join forces and head south to the mighty Humber at Kingston upon Hull. Beverley lies a mile west of the river, to which it is linked by the Beverley Beck. This has been a trade route throughout recorded history, and for most of this time the responsibility for managing and improving the navigation lay with Beverley Corporation, who recorded coal traffic of about 15,500 tonnes in the year ending 1 March 1847. Upstream of Beverley, the wandering course of the River Hull was gradually improved by the Driffield Navigation, set up by an Act of Parliament in 1767. Coal was again the major cargo, with about 25,000 tonnes being recorded in the year ending 1 April 1825.

Railway Proposals

The earliest proposals for railways to serve this area date from the 1830s. The enterprising folk of Whitby set an example, securing an Act for their railway to Pickering in May 1833, and later that year there was much discussion in and around Hull of possible railways. The arguments for a line up to Driffield by way of Beverley were ably expressed in a letter from an un-named Driffield citizen published in the *Hull Packet* of 28 February 1834 and reproduced here. However, a significant number of people felt that both Driffield and Bridlington would be better served by a line heading inland across the Wolds to Leeds and York. The latter view prevailed to the extent of commissioning a survey from Sir John Rennie, who came up with a route crossing the Wolds via North Dalton and Warter.(4) However, this was a very ambitious project for the time and quickly faded away, though the underlying ambition remained.

Plate 1.1. *Driffield : a modern view of the Riverhead, retaining a wharf crane of the type also found in the railway goods yards. This is the head of the navigation, fed by the Driffield Beck, not the River Hull which lies a third of a mile to the south. (Bill Fawcett)*

To the Editor of the Hull Packet.

SIR – Amidst the various schemes for railways, &c. I have been much surprised that none of your correspondents have noticed the hint in your paper, three months ago, of the utility of a railway from Hull to Driffield: as very few places afford easier, or less expensive methods to an accomplishment, or a greater traffic on the whole line of road. One great object would be accomplished by the expeditious conveyance of the post to and from Driffield, Burlington, Hunmanby, Scarbro', &c. as, at least two hours would be saved each way, thereby enabling the inhabitants of Bridlington, Scarbro. &c. to answer any south correspondents a day sooner than at present. The line of road would be three or four miles shorter than the present turnpike, the heavy tolls on which, cause many per-sons to go, round still further, by way of Holderness, to save the expense. Many articles coming up the navigation, are so long delayed, as to cause great disappointment, not to mention the very heavy dues on corn, viz. 8d. per qr. on wheat and beans, and 6d. per qr. on barley and oats. These commodities would be taken on the railway as cheap as by water. There are also large quantities of live stock, which cross over at Hessle, the owners of which would prefer this new road: and there is no doubt the number of passengers would be increased greatly, for various reasons. I will now sketch the line of road, hoping a commodious station might be got near the New Dock, so as to have an open and immediate intercourse with the Humber. From thence, the road might proceed near the Botanic Garden, to the right of Cottingham, crossing the street at Beverley, a little below the Minster, then crossing the present turnpike, betwixt Leconfield and Scorbro', leaving Lockington and Kilnwick on the left, by Burn Butts, Southburn, Eastburn, &c. and have a large and commodious station on the south east of George-street, Driffield, where some very convenient building ground is now on sale, and where coaches might be waiting to take passengers to Burlington, Scarbro', Malton, Yedingham Bridge, and Pickering. This would meet the views expressed at the meeting of the Guardian Society in your town last week, and thereby take the line round by way of Hull, to the West Riding, both from Bridlington and Scarbro'.

Hoping this matter will be taken up by abler hands,

I am sir, your obedient servant.

Driffield, Feb 10, 1834. A.B.C.

[Verbatim from the *Hull Packet*, 28 February 1834.]

At no stage, evidently, was serious consideration given to the alternative route from Beverley to Bridlington via Hornsea and the coast. This could have served Leven, which had its own canal from the River Hull, and would have given a comparable route mileage to that via Driffield. However, quite apart from the influence of the latter town, the inland line stood to benefit both the eastern Wolds and the arable flat-lands bordering the River Hull. Hornsea had to wait for the arrival of its very own railway in 1864.

The catalyst for making the Bridlington line arrived on 1 July 1840, with the formal opening of the H&S. This was the eastern link in a route across England created by the Liverpool & Manchester (1830), Leeds & Selby (1834) and Manchester & Leeds (M&L: 1839-41) Railways, whose final section would open to the public nine months later. Speculation soon began about possible branches from the Hull & Selby, the strongest contender being an extension to Beverley, although there was also talk of a branch from Brough to Market Weighton, a small agricultural centre nestling below the western escarpment of the Wolds.

Initially, the H&S directors, most of whom were leading members of Hull's mercantile and banking community, were more concerned with consolidating the operation and traffic of their new line. Their attention then turned to the idea of a merger with the M&L. This may seem strange, since their obvious partner was the Leeds & Selby. However, George Hudson had secured a lease of that line in November 1840 for his Y&NM; in any case through traffic from the M&L had to pass over the Y&NM main line from Normanton since the Selby line had no links to other railways at Leeds. From the start of 1844, the Hull and Manchester companies were operating under a joint working arrangement and it seemed the merger would proceed, but some Hull shareholders were dissatisfied with their proposed share of profits in the merged company. The growing number of dissenters approached Hudson, who made an offer to lease the railway, on behalf of his Y&NM, for a rental of 10% of its capital. This won the day, and the H&S was leased out from 1 July 1845, an Act of Parliament being obtained the following year to sanction this in perpetuity. The Act also allowed the M&L an equal share in the lease, but the option was never taken up. It was against this background that the coast line finally emerged.

Making Headway to Bridlington

The first step was taken in the summer of 1844, when the H&S Board asked their resident engineer and surveyor, William Bailey Bray, to carry out a survey for a line to Beverley, resolving on 1 July that once this was completed he should negotiate 'conditional purchases' of the land which would be required.(5) Shortly afterwards, he was requested to make a 'cursory' survey of a continuation to Driffield and Bridlington. At this stage, the directors were debating the merits of forming a separate company to undertake the line but eventually they decided to apply to Parliament for powers for the H&S to make the line and raise the extra capital required for this. Accordingly, Bray organised a detailed survey and the preparation of plans for the Parliamentary Bill, which were deposited with the requisite authorities on 30 November 1844.(6)

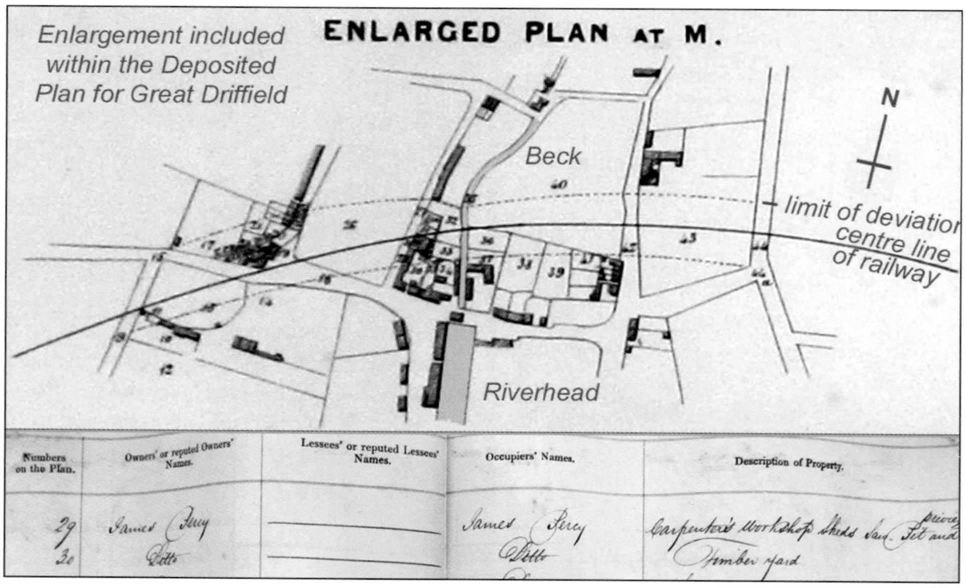

Figure 1.1. Driffield: a portion of the H&S Deposited Plan showing the Riverhead and the area to the north-west which would be developed for the passenger station. The extract from the accompanying Book of Reference details land owner, occupier and usage, from which we see that James Percy would have to move his carpentry business to make way for the railway. Apart from this, the railway would make its way through open land, with the town centre lying just off the plan to the north.

Bray's role is intriguing. He had been an assistant engineer on the construction of the line from Hull to Selby under James Walker, one of the leading civil engineers of his day, who also built the Leeds & Selby and carried through an extension of Hull docks. In this role Bray was answerable to John Timperley, Walker's resident engineer. Bray went on to serve the H&S for a while after its opening, but was then dispensed with when they economised by placing all engineering maintenance under their locomotive superintendent, John Gray. Much to Gray's chagrin, Bray was re-engaged in October 1843 as 'resident engineer', with the proviso that he could only perform work outside the company with the consent of the chairman or his deputy.(7) The line from Hull to Bridlington follows the route he determined but supervising its construction was apparently earmarked for Timperley; what actually happened is confused by the Hudson lease, which transferred the final responsibility to the Railway King's engineer, Robert Stephenson.

The chosen route was an incredibly easy one, keeping to the flat country at the foot of the Wolds and involving nothing significant in the way of earthworks and just one modest river crossing. Bray estimated the capital cost, including land purchase, at just £190,000 for a single-track line of some thirty-one miles.(8) This is a long way below the average for railways of the period.

The H&S directors prepared the ground for their Bridlington Branch Bill thoroughly. In August 1844, the company secretary and operating superintendent, George Locking, was despatched to Driffield and Bridlington to obtain the views of local people and stir up support. One outcome is the requisition from sundry inhabitants of Bridlington, received in October and stating what a great benefit such a railway would be.(9) This will have helped in securing the backing of the railway's own shareholders, who, promised a return on investment of at least 11%, endorsed the scheme at a meeting on 30 October which cleared the way for an application to Parliament.(10) Meanwhile, the directors had been discussing things with local landowners, most of whom were strongly in favour of the venture, seeing it as something which would enhance the value of their agricultural properties. Typical of these was Beaumont Hotham (1794-1870), third Baronet Hotham, of South Dalton, who owned property through which the line would pass for some $3^1/_2$ route miles in the parishes of Scorborough, Lockington, Kilnwick and 'Hutton cum Cranswick'. He was also Member of Parliament for the East Riding (1841-68) and in January 1845 agreed to take charge of introducing the Bill into the House of Commons.

The H&S Bill had an easy passage.(11) It was introduced into the Commons in February 1845, receiving its formal second reading on the 24th and then being referred for scrutiny by committee some months later. A number of objectors were heard, of which more later, but it passed the House on 5 May. By this time just two objectors remained: Thomas Denton, a Beverley landowner with whom agreement was reached just before the first day of the Lords committee hearing, 18 June. That left the Commissioners of Bridlington Pier & Harbour. The committee declined to hear evidence on their behalf and the Bill went on to receive the Royal Assent on 30 June. It allowed the company to raise £216,000 in capital with the usual borrowing powers for a further third.

Most of the people petitioning against the Bill were not against the principle of the railway but did so in order to safeguard specific interests which could easily be resolved by minor amendments as it made its way through the Commons committee. That category covers William St Quintin, of Scampston Hall, a major landowner who owned about three miles of the route, between Nafferton and Burton Agnes. The navigations were not a problem: Beverley Corporation was firmly in favour of the scheme, while the railway's deputy chairman Joseph Robinson Pease (c1789-1866) was not only a leading Hull merchant and banker but also a trustee of the Driffield Navigation and one of its major creditors.(12) The Commissioners of Bridlington Pier & Harbour proved the most obdurate, seeking provisions for compensation, but Parliament was not impressed. Turnpike road trustees could hardly, as a body, have endorsed the railway, though as individuals they no doubt welcomed its benefits. Two petitioned against, the trustees of the Hull & Kirkella and Hull, Hessle & Ferriby turnpikes, but their concern was at the prospect of level crossings on two busy roads on the (then) outskirts of Hull.

Road crossings were an object of general concern, and on 8 May, while the H&S Bill was proceeding through Parliament, an Act received the Royal Assent which specified that 'turnpike roads and public highways' should be bridged unless provisions were made in individual Acts to permit level crossings at specified locations.(13) In the case of the Bridlington Branch, running on a level with the surrounding land, bridges made no sense in the age of the horse and cart. No-one welcomed the idea of spoiling flat roads with the gradients required to climb up and down from railway bridges, however it was necessary for the Lords and Commons committees to work through the road crossings and in each case record the justification for employing a level crossing. Interestingly, Bray does not seem to have been called on for evidence. Instead, the Secretary, George Locking, gave the bulk of the detailed evidence while Robert Stephenson, Engineer-in-Chief of Hudson's various railways among many others, served as expert witness on the principle involved.(14)

Before losing their independence to George Hudson, the H&S directors were becoming quite enthusiastic about promoting new lines. The Bridlington Branch was the only one for which they actually sought powers, but on 27 March 1845 Pease and Locking attended a public meeting at Market Weighton regarding a line from Beverley to York. Hudson was also there, on behalf of the Y&NM, but Pease set out 'the claims of the Hull & Selby company to make such lines as are required for the East Riding of Yorkshire.' This was followed up by engaging Timperley to survey the route from Beverley to Market Weighton, despite which the directors reassured one enquirer that this did not mean abandoning the idea of a line from Brough: 'it is probable that both the lines … will be made'.(15) Given this display of ambition it is no wonder that Hudson acted quickly to take the railway over and make the East Riding his own fiefdom instead.

Bridlington to Scarborough

By the summer of 1844, George Hudson was chairman of three railway companies: the Midland, the Newcastle & Darlington Junction, and the York & North Midland. The latter had been his first venture, originating as a modest 21-mile link in the main line from London to York (then routed from Euston station via Derby and Normanton). In July 1844 it obtained an

Act for its first extension: from York to Scarborough. The forty-mile route was completed with amazing expedition, having its formal opening just a year later, on 7 July 1845. In anticipation of this, and perhaps also to put pressure on the H&S shareholders, Hudson promoted a Y&NM branch from Seamer, on the Scarborough line, to Bridlington, where it was to make a direct junction with the H&S. In a characteristically flamboyant gesture he announced at the opening of the Scarborough branch that the savings made during the building of that line would pay for the Bridlington branch, but this was, to say the least, misleading.(16) The Scarborough line had been made with commendable economy but the formation was only of single-track width, and Hudson had already instructed that the route be doubled, something likely to eat up all the vaunted saving.(17)

Robert Stephenson had overall responsibility for the Y&NM Bridlington Branch, but the surveys and supervision were carried out by his trusted assistant John Cass Birkinshaw (1811-67), who was already looking after the Scarborough line and would do the same for the Y&NM's later branches. The twenty-mile route from Seamer was more demanding than the line from Hull. It shared the latter's very easy gradients on its initial push to the coast, at Filey, but the deposited plans show these steepening to 1 in 91 on the climb over the tail of the Wolds and 1 in 86 on the descent to Bridlington.(18) These made for a significant hump in the days of steam traction, while the topography is also reflected in the provision of bridges for many of the road crossings between Filey and Speeton.

The Y&NM Bill was introduced into the House of Commons by the members for York: John Henry Lowther, Hudson's Tory protégé, and the Whig, Henry Redhead Yorke. Petitions in favour had been organised from the main places on the way: Filey, Hunmanby, Bridlington and Bridlington Quay. Opposition was modest, though once again the Commissioners of Bridlington Pier & Harbour were in evidence. The Commons committee reported in favour of the Bill on 9 May, with a few amendments, and it came to the Lords committee on 16 June, two days before the Hull & Selby's Bill.(19)

By then Hudson had sorted out all the opposition and the scheme was unopposed, but even so the committee were treated to a disquisition by the Railway King, appearing not just as promoter but as a local landowner; he owned property near Hutton Cranswick on the Hull route, purchased from the Duke of Devonshire. His evidence was cogent but not always sound, as, for example, when he spoke of Flamborough as 'a fishing town also of very great importance, very great.' If they ever got to hear of this, the few inhabitants of that modest village must have wondered what the great man had in mind for them. Birkinshaw gave the engineering evidence, and the capital cost was estimated at £87,000: slightly more than the notional cost per mile of the York - Scarborough line but well below Bray's estimate for the route from Hull. The discrepancy cannot just be put down to land values since Bray estimated the actual construction cost at £160,000, or £5,300 per mile as against Birkinshaw's £4,350.

Plate 1.2. *The steep climb north from Flamborough is emphasised by this view of a summer Saturday excursion from Ashton under Lyne to Scarborough approaching Buckton Lane crossing on 15 August 1959. Leading is No 62770, 'The Puckeridge', one of the Gresley Class D49 4-4-0s commonly employed on the coast route. It is helping out No 43057, a Selby-based Ivatt 2-6-0. (Neville Stead Collection)*

The Y&NM Bill received the Royal Assent on 30 June 1845 but arrangements with one of the landowners at the Seamer end required the sanction of a second Act, passed in 1846, allowing a modest deviation in the route.(20) 1846 also brought the passing of the Hull & Selby Railway Purchase Act (Royal Assent 27 July), which allowed the Y&NM to lease that railway indefinitely, in concert with the Manchester & Leeds company, and also gave them the option of purchase. In the event the Y&NM and its successor, the North Eastern Railway, remained sole lessees and the option to purchase was not taken up until 1872. Despite this, the entire Hull - Seamer route was operated and developed by the Y&NM and NER as an integral part of their system.

The Purchase Act also increased the powers to raise capital for the Hull - Bridlington line, parts of which were by then nearing completion.(21) The 1845 Act had sanctioned a share issue of £216,000 plus borrowing powers for £72,000 but the total required was now stated to be £350,000. Part of the difference can be ascribed to the entire route being built as double track, whereas Bray had costed for single. However, another cause specifically related in the Act was the stations being on a much more substantial scale than those originally envisaged by Bray, who had probably made next to no allowance for them. The stations were indeed of a quality which the H&S could not have envisaged but one may suspect that Hudson was also looking for spare cash to help with Y&NM expenditure. Raising the extra money should have been easy since, once the Bridlington Branch opened, the H&S £25 'half-shares' issued for its construction would earn the same generous 10% from the Y&NM as the company's original capital.

Endnotes:

1. Edward Baines, *History, directory & gazetteer of the County of Yorkshire volume 2 : East & North Ridings,* 1823.
2. Baron F Duckham, *Yorkshire ports and harbours : a short historical guide,* Dalesman, 1967.
3. Baron F Duckham, *The Inland Waterways of East Yorkshire : 1700-1900*, East Yorkshire Local History Society, 1972. See also Victoria County History: *East Riding volume 6* and Stephen Harrison, *The History of Driffield*, Blackthorn Press, 2002.
4. Reported in the *Hull Packet* and other local newspapers.
5. TNA (The National Archives, Kew) RAIL 315/10 H&S Board 1 July, 12 and 20 August 1844.
6. ERA (East Riding Archives), Beverley QDP 133 Deposited Plans for the Hull & Bridlington Branch Railway.
7. TNA RAIL 315/9 H&S Board 7 October 1843.
8. TNA RAIL 315/10 H&S Board 28 October 1844.
9. *ibid.* 12 August and 10 October 1844.
10. *Hull Packet & East Riding Times,* 1 November 1844.
11. Parliamentary Archives: *House of Commons Journal*; *House of Lords Journal*; HL/PO/PB/5/11/1 Record of evidence before the Lords committee.
12. Duckham, *op. cit.* note 3.
13. 8 Victoria *cap.* 20, clause 46.
14. *Railway Chronicle,* 10 May 1845, page 544.
15. TNA RAIL 315/10 H&S Board 28 March, 11 April, 30 May 1845. 4 June 1845 resolved to complete the survey to York with a view to an application to Parliament in the next session.
16. *York Courant*, 10 July 1845.
17. For the widening, see Bill Fawcett, *A History of the York - Scarborough Railway,* Hutton Press, 1995.
18. ERA, Beverley. QDP134: Deposited Plans for YNM Seamer to Bridlington Railway, with both Robert Stephenson and JC Birkinshaw named on the cover. QDP133 is the Hull - Bridlington line.
19. Parliamentary Archives: *House of Commons Journal*; *House of Lords Journal*; HC/CL/PB/2/11/101 Record of evidence before the Commons committee; HL/PO/PB/5/11/1 Record of evidence before the Lords committee.
20. ERA, Beverley. QDP136: plan for the deviation of the YNM branch within the parish of Seamer, deposited 4 August 1845.
21. Parliamentary Archives: HC/CL/PB/2/12/84 Record of evidence before Commons committee on the Hull & Selby Purchase Bill begins at 17 June 1846.

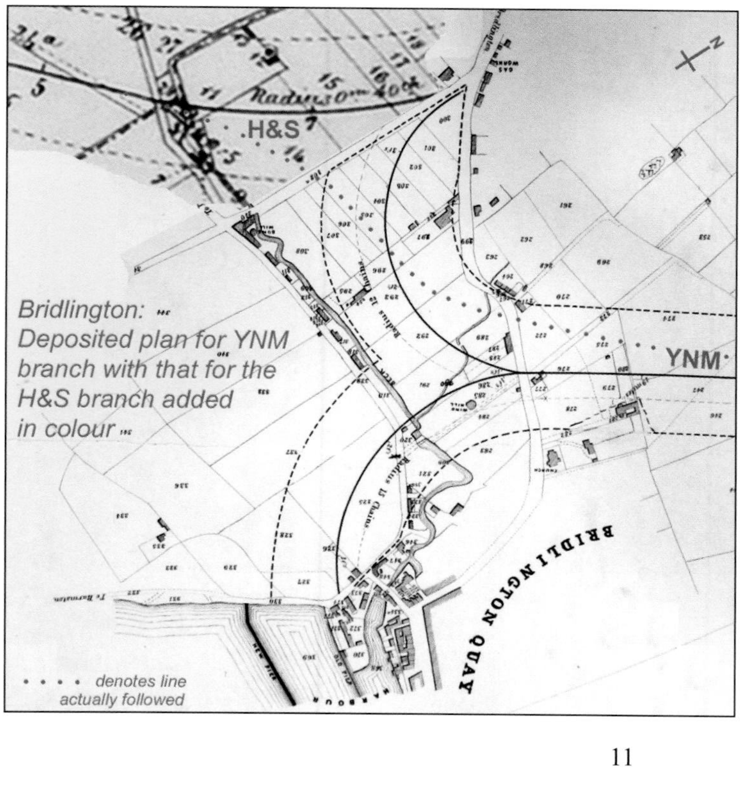

***Figure 1.2.** Bridlington: this YNM Deposited Plan shows the route forking, with one line serving the harbour and the other swinging round to a terminus midway between Bridlington Quay and the Old Town. Superimposed on this is the H&S Deposited Plan with its line ending just across the road. In the event, the railway was built along the route indicated by the dots, where there was plenty of open land on which to build the station. It can be seen how this exploited to the full the limits of deviation permitted by Parliament.*

Chapter 2 : Construction and Route

Bill Fawcett

Introduction

By the end of June 1845, both companies, the Hull & Selby (H&S) and York & North Midland (Y&NM), had acquired Parliamentary powers to raise capital and build their Bridlington branches. Work began first on the line from Hull, the contracts for the YNM branch being delayed until February 1846. Rapid progress was made with most of the route, the sections from Hull to Bridlington and Seamer to Filey being opened in October 1846; the intervening stretch, crossing the tail of the Wolds, was completed a year later. The engineering works were generally modest, and the chief features of interest were the buildings, designed by Hudson's friend George Townsend Andrews (1801-55) and including some of his most handsome stations.

Building the Line : Hull to Bridlington

The Hull & Selby directors were in a curious position. Under the lease, which took effect from 1 July 1845, they no longer had any role in the operation of their railway; it was just a matter of collecting the rent and paying the dividends. However, they remained responsible for constructing the Bridlington Branch and raising the share capital required; under the lease they would receive a 10% return on this only when the line was completed. The issue was addressed by setting up a committee of six directors, three H&S and three Y&NM, to oversee the building of the branch and sanction expenditure on it. The Hull company immediately nominated its chairman and deputy chairman: Richard Tottie and Joseph Robinson Pease, together with Thomas Mayelston. The Y&NM waited three months, until October, to appoint Hudson, along with his deputy chairman (and lawyer) James Richardson and Sir John Simpson, another prominent York figure.(1)

The H&S had been making provisional agreements for land months before their Act was passed, engaging a Hull surveyor, LB Earnshaw, to negotiate and value property. The major landowners were generally helpful, with prices typically in the range £65 to £75 per acre being agreed for ordinary agricultural land.(2) Things could be more problematic in the towns, as with Thomas Denton, whom we encountered in Chapter 1 and whose opposition to the Bill was overcome by an arbitration agreement. The Act enabled the company to enter land prior to a final agreement on price, so that some conveyances were still being made after the line had opened, but only one disgruntled party chose to take the company to a jury, the final recourse, in the hope of being awarded a high price.(3) Land purchases sometimes involved special provisions, as with Baronet Hotham, who required a station at Lockington, where a horse box and carriage truck should be kept to accommodate his lordship and friends.(4) In addition, it was stipulated that the H&S should not 'interfere' in the sale of coals at Scorborough, Lockington and Hutton Cranswick, from which it seems that Lord Hotham, a strong supporter of the railway, had a vested interest in coal traffic up the navigable Aike (Coal) Beck, a family venture, to a wharf just east of the site chosen for Lockington station.

The route approved by any railway Act is a very narrow corridor, specified by a centre line and limits of deviation. For the Bridlington line the limits were plus and minus 5 chains (110 yards or 100 metres) in the countryside, narrowing down considerably in towns and villages. John Timperley was therefore engaged to survey and stake out the exact route, work which seems to have been completed sometime in October 1845.(5) The next step was to let the construction contract, but

Plate 2.1. *The view north at Milepost 23 (north of Nafferton), 2 May 1960. This stretch of the present day Hull & Scarborough Branch was constructed as the Bridlington Branch of the Hull & Selby Railway; note the flatness of the terrain. Note too the field crossing in the foreground, and the flat-bottomed rails on the Down line (on the left) and the bull-head rails on the Up. (John F Mallon / Joint NERA - Ken Hoole Study Centre JF Mallon Collection)*

here Hudson over-reached himself. As usual, competitive tenders were invited for this, and an advertisement appeared in mid-October 1845, above his name alone, inviting tenders for the stretch from Hull to Driffield. This was not to the liking of the Hull directors, who were equally responsible and who wished the whole line to progress simultaneously, therefore a second notice appeared a fortnight later, coupling Hudson and Tottie and specifying the full route from Hull to Bridlington.(6)

The route was divided into three contracts (Beverley, Driffield and Bridlington) and tenders were considered at a meeting of the joint committee at York on 24 November, all three being awarded to the experienced partnership of Thomas Jackson and Alfred Bean, who had built two sections of the Birmingham & Derby Junction Railway, for a total price of £93,534.(7) At the H&S Board meeting which ratified this, a week later, the directors agreed to make a first call, of £5, on the £25 shares created to finance the line. They also sought to improve their cash flow by offering 4% interest to any investors who chose to pay up their shares in full and equal interest to any landowners who would accept deferred payment of their purchase money. In practice the H&S had no problem finding takers for its shares; the financial bubble known as the Railway Mania was now in full swing and the Y&NM's 10% rental made these shares a very attractive prospect anyway, so long as there was no serious cost overrun in building the branch. In the event, the company took up the £72,000 borrowing powers, granted by the Act, in September 1846.(8)

The engineering requirements of the line could not have been more modest; much was laid on the level of the surrounding land, there were no road bridges and only one significant waterway: the infant River Hull, crossed at Driffield by a low, four-arch viaduct (Plate 2.2). Robert Stephenson was given responsibility, as Hudson's engineer, but he passed it on to his trusted assistant, John Cass Birkinshaw, aided by a younger brother.(9) Birkinshaw had already supervised the Y&NM Scarborough Branch and was still engaged with that line, attempting to expedite a doubling which entailed the widening of its formation and occupied his attention until early 1846.(10)

By April 1846, work was sufficiently advanced for contracts to be let for the stations and other buildings. Again, these were divided into three sections, and they went to three different contractors: the Hull firm of Simminson & Hutchinson, who had built the first Hull terminus; Brown & Hall; and Samuel Atack, of Leeds.(11) The total cost was £73,580, just 21% under the contract price for building the line. On 2 June the joint committee made an inspection of the works, and found the buildings progressing less rapidly than they had hoped.(12) Pease confided to his diary that there was 'much to annoy us at Driffield and the Quay [Bridlington], we put spurs into the builders and did good.' The chief laggard seems to have been Atack, who was served with a formal notice six weeks later, specifying the extra men whom Andrews, the architect, required him to take on to expedite the work.(13)

The H&S directors hoped to open the line in the course of the summer, but did not quite manage this. The obstacle was said to be a shortage of rails for the permanent way, no surprising thing given the enormous railway mileage under construction at this time.(14) In mid-August they made a further inspection, noting that one line was laid throughout but only a third of the second track had been laid and they had only 13 miles of rails in hand for an outstanding distance of 20 miles.(15) The work was inspected for the Board of

Plate 2.2. *Driffield: the view from the south-east of the viaduct over the River Hull, situated where the channel temporarily splits a quarter mile upstream of Bell Mills. (John F Addyman, 2012)*

Trade on 3 October 1846 by Major-General Pasley, of the Royal Engineers, and passed for passenger use, clearing the way for a grand opening three days later on 6 October, when a 'monster train of 66 carriages, drawn by three engines, left Hull.(16) At Bridlington, the directors [Y&NM and H&S] and their guests, numbering upwards of 900, partook of a sumptuous lunch in the goods station; and in the evening there was a grand banquet at Hull'.(17) This was presided over by Hudson and included a civic party from York. Amongst all the vacuous speeches customary at such events, Hudson had the grace to draw attention to the navvies who had built the line, and their behaviour, largely free from those incidents which provided horror stories for Victorian newspapers. Public traffic began the following day.

Building the Line : Seamer to Bridlington

Negotiations for the land between Seamer and Bridlington should have got underway at an early stage. However, Hudson delayed letting the construction until 2 February 1846, more than two months after the H&S branch.(18) The work was divided into two contracts: Seamer to Filey and Filey to Bridlington, which were awarded to Joseph Crawshaw (1803-56) in partnership with his brother Richard (c1804-57). Their previous works included parts of the original Y&NM main line as well as its Scarborough Branch. The contract prices were £31,227 and £90,669, which work out at about £5,100 and £6,700 per mile respectively, not a big difference bearing in mind the heavier works on the latter section. The notable discrepancy is between these figures and Birkinshaw's £87,000 (£4,350/mile) Parliamentary estimate.

The Builder of 3 January had carried an advertisement for these works but Hudson may already have earmarked Crawshaw as his preferred contractor. His widening of the York - Scarborough line was nearing completion in February 1846, and it looks as if Hudson deferred the contract to ensure this was out of the way first. It also seems as if Hudson fudged the timing of payments to Crawshaw, who, after the Railway King's downfall, pursued with partial success a costly claim against the Y&NM for money due in respect of the Scarborough doubling.(19)

The work was supervised by Birkinshaw with the assistance of Alfred Lamerte Dickens, younger brother of the famous novelist, who had already played this role on the Scarborough Branch.(20) Hudson took the opportunity to let the contract for the buildings at the same meeting, 6 April, which dealt with those from Bridlington southwards, the work going to Samuel Atack for £13,167. This is a very small amount compared with the Hull - Bridlington line, reflecting the fact that there were just two major buildings, the Filey goods and passenger stations, and a lesser density of gatehouses.

Work proceeded briskly on the stretch from Seamer to Filey, which was formally opened on 5 October 1846, the day before the line from Hull. However, Hudson's customary vigour is not evident in his approach to the line from Filey to Bridlington; perhaps he was husbanding his cash flow. Birkinshaw later admitted that Crawshaw had been delayed five or six months by Y&NM sluggishness in completing land purchases.(21) By April 1847 it had become evident that the remaining mileage would not be open in time

Plate 2.3. *Bridge No 29, situated to the west of Speeton on that part of the Hull & Scarborough Branch built by the York & North Midland. Built on the skew, the bridge was the largest over-track structure when the line was constructed. It carries the Grindale - Reighton road across a cutting laboriously dug through the local chalk. The track here was singled in 1973 as part of the scheme to single the track between Bridlington and Filey; new rails were laid in the centre of the formation. Prior to 1970, the heavy trains running then were wearing the rails at the rate of 1lb/yard in ten years. With today's light DMUs, these new rails could last 200 years! (John F Addyman)*

for the summer season, and on the 22nd the local firm of Rycroft & Nicholson was given the exclusive right to run coaches between Filey and Bridlington stations, pending completion.(22)

The delayed start to this final stretch was unfortunate as it involved cuttings, averaging more than a hundred thousand cubic yards per mile through very hard chalk, between Bridlington and Hunmanby.(23) A first inspection for the Board of Trade was made on 30 September 1847 by Captain (later Field-Marshal Sir Lintorn) Simmons, who remarked approvingly on the steep-sided cuttings, which he reckoned 'should stand well' but pointed out that one of these was still incomplete as was the permanent way; presumably space had been made to lay just one of the two tracks. Captain (later Lieutenant-General Sir Robert) Laffan did the re-inspection on 16 October, noting that the cutting slopes needed to be cleared of loose fragments and stipulating the removal of 'large masses [which] had been left standing nearly perpendicular within a few feet of the outer rail'; these had become fissured in the course of the work and were liable to collapse so Birkinshaw promised to deal with them.(24) The line finally opened to the public on the 20th. The only report we have of the navvies is their striking in December 1846, because Crawshaw 'refused to maintain the present rates of pay'; the one-day strike and parade through the streets was enough to ensure a resumption of their former pay.(25)

Plate 2.4. *The view west through the cutting which takes the line through the chalk Wolds south of Reighton. At this point the line has climbed to 300 feet above sea level. The bridge, adjacent to Eastfield Farm, is the tallest on the branch and given a slightly more formal treatment than the others. (Bill Fawcett)*

Plate 2.5. *The view from the south-east of the bridge east of Hunmanby which retains its original cast-iron facing girder and parapet. (Bill Fawcett)*

Engineering Works

The route left the Hull & Selby main line a mile and a half short of the original terminus on the west side of the Humber Dock. From May 1848 this was supplanted by GT Andrews' splendid new Paragon Street station, access to which was by a pair of loops from the Bridlington Branch accompanied by an additional west curve at the original junction. From here as far as Bridlington, the only original engineering feature to note was the diminutive viaduct at Driffield, already mentioned. Leaving Bridlington, one encountered the first of seven brick overbridges. Their type is seen to best advantage where the line passes south of Reighton village. From a bridge of three segmental arches carrying the lane to Grindale (GR TA129738) (Plate 2.3), one gets a fine view west along the steep-sided cutting to a single, tall arched span bearing another lane (Plate 2.4). The tall abutments of this simple bridge give it a very handsome air, unmarred by the cast-iron bracing which looks to have been introduced at a relatively early date. A nice detail of all these bridges is the bold sandstone roll-moulding below the parapet; the Driffield viaduct employs a visually less-effective Grecian cornice instead.

Beyond Hunmanby station the line skirts the village on a low embankment pierced originally by a pair of cast-iron road bridges and seven cattle creeps. One bridge crosses a minor lane (GR TA103773) with a span of 27 feet (8.2m), and retains its original appearance, with attractive cast-iron facing girders and parapet, although the deck is a North Eastern Railway (NER) replacement (Plate 2.5). The second is a skew span of 46 feet (14m) crossing a main road (GR TA104777), which has been twice renewed. Originally it comprised three cast-iron girders at $10^1/_2$ feet centres, with each track borne by a 9-inch thick timber platform resting on their bottom flanges.(26) Each girder was cast in two sections, jointed at the middle with the aid of wrought-iron clips. Captain Simmons' description of these is a little ambiguous and could be construed as one of Robert Stephenson's trussed girders, such as he had employed for the Scarborough Branch Bridge over the River Ouse at York. The NER replaced these with a plate-girder bridge on the original abutments but a recent rebuilding has substituted a steel span with a rather ungainly raised footway. Alongside is an example of one of the 12-feet span plain brick-arched cattle creeps provided for farm use (Plate 2.6). Beyond this point, the line resumes an uneventful course through Filey and then along the northern slope of the shallow valley of the River Hertford (a glorified land drain) before joining the Scarborough line half a mile south of Seamer station. The only original structures on this latter stretch crossed drains and streams and comprised timber waybeams of twelve-feet span borne on timber piles.(27) These were likely to be temporary structures to get rid of standing water that had built up during the construction of the embankment.

Plate 2.6. *This underbridge east of Hunmanby (GR TA105780) is typical of the 'cattle creeps' provided to accommodate farms split by the railway. Just to the right lay the junction of the south curve into Filey Holiday Camp station. (Bill Fawcett, 2012)*

Endnotes:

1. TNA (The National Archives, Kew) RAIL 7702 YNM Board 9 July 1845 for notification of the H&S nominees; 8 October 1845 for appointment of the YNM members.
2. TNA RAIL 315/10 H&S Board 5 March 1845 read and approved an agreement for land to be purchased near Arram from Col. Wyndham at £65/acre including severance. Dyas Lofthouse, a shareholder, was offering a site in Cottingham, considered suitable for the station, at £210/acre plus £900 for the existing house; Tottie and Pease were deputed to examine the site. 28 March 1845: Earnshaw had seen Marmaduke Langley's agent re land at Driffield and got offers from him and other proprietors there and at Burton Agnes; prices around £70-75/acre were quoted.
3. *Hull Packet,* 22 May 1846. The land was some 5 acres of potential building ground near Eastgate, which John Oxley and his wife had purchased as an investment; the company appears to have offered £3,500 at some stage whereas the jury award was just £3,000.
4. TNA RAIL 315/10 H&S Board 5 & 6 March 1845.
5. *ibid.* 27 September 1845 Read Timperley's survey of the line to Bridlington; he was probably assisted in this by his son John, a surveyor.
6. *Hull Packet,* 17 and 31 October 1845.
7. TNA RAIL 315/10 H&S Board 1 December 1845. The breakdown was: No 1 Beverley Contract £22,816; No 2 Driffield Contract £36,718; No 3 Bridlington Contract £34,000.
8. *ibid.* 17 September 1846.
9. TNA MT6/3/67 Board of Trade inspection report of Major-general Pasley mentions the 'younger brother' but does not name him.
10. See Bill Fawcett, *A History of the Hull - Scarborough Railway,* Hutton Press, 1995. TNA RAIL 770/2 YNM Board 8 October 1845 instructed Birkenshaw to reside near the Malton-Scarborough line to expedite the doubling, of which 6 weeks work remained outstanding in early February 1846.
11. TNA RAIL 770/2 YNM Board contains a minute of the joint committee meeting on 6 April 1846 which let the contracts for buildings, designated Nos 7, 2 and 3. The prices were: 7: Simminson & Hutchinson £22,000; 2: Brown & Hall £26,000; 3: Samuel Atack £25,580. A separate minute book does not survive for the joint committee.
12. JD Hicks, *The Journal of Joseph Robinson Pease,* East Yorkshire Local History Society, 2000.
13. TNA RAIL 770/107 Draft formal notice to Atack, dated 20 July 1846.
14. *Hull Packet,* 21 August 1846, reporting Richard Tottie's report to the H&S half-yearly meeting.
15. *ibid.*
16. TNA MT6/3/67 Letter from Pasley to Board of Trade. This is wrongly dated 3 August but a report of his Seamer - Filey inspection, which he points out was made the same day, is correctly dated 3 October; Pasley was clearly suffering from jet-lag as he zipped round a succession of new lines in the course of the day.
17. James Joseph Sheahan, *History of the Town and Port of Kingston upon Hull,* second edition, John Green, Beverley, 1866, pages 214, 679. *Hull Packet,* 9 October 1846.
18. TNA RAIL 770/2 YNM Board 2 February 1846. *Doncaster, Nottingham & Lincoln Gazette* had already on 2 January reported the start of works on this line but perhaps that was staking out.
19. TNA RAIL 770/12 MSS Evidence to YNM Committee of Investigation 16 August 1849 Evidence by John Cass Birkinshaw reveals Crawshaw's original claim as £156,000 in respect of the York-Scarborough and £38,000 for Seamer - Bridlington. The claims were excessive, and Birkinshaw negotiated them down to some extent before they went to arbitration. TNA RAIL 770/5 YNM Board 8 May 1852 The Court of Queen's Bench had confirmed the referee's award to Crawshaw of £34,176-2-8; 22 September the directors agreed with George Leeman (Crawshaw's lawyer) to settle any outstanding items with a payment of £2,500.
20. This emerges from Pasley's inspection report on the Seamer - Filey stretch (TNA MT6/3/66).
21. Birkinshaw *op. cit.*, note 19.
22. TNA RAIL 770/3 YNM Board 22 April 1847. Rycroft & Nicholson were required to provide 'sufficient accommodation for traffic to the satisfaction of the Directors.'
23. TNA MT6/4/65 Board of Trade report by Captain Simmons, inspecting the line on 30 September 1847.
24. TNA MT6/4/73.
25. *Yorkshire Gazette,* 12 December 1846.
26. Captain Simmons, *op. cit.*, note 23.
27. General Pasley, *op. cit.*, note 20.

Chapter 3 : Buildings

Bill Fawcett

Introduction

Given the lack of significant engineering features, the most interesting aspect of the line's infrastructure is the variety of handsome buildings, ranging from original ones designed for George Hudson to the spacious 1912 station at Bridlington. There are obvious comparisons between this route and the York - Scarborough line, completed in 1845. Both pass through similar agricultural landscapes for much of their length and were equipped with stations at intervals of about three miles. Similarities will be found in the design of station buildings but different strategies were adopted with regard to coal and goods traffic.

All but two of the Scarborough line stations were provided with coal depots of the classic North-East form, with tracks running over brick-walled cells served by bottom-door wagons. By contrast, there were few coal depots outside the towns on the line from Hull to Bridlington, although all but two of the stations between Bridlington and Seamer had them. This seems to reflect a difference in outlook between the YNM and H&S directors as well as the restrictions imposed by some landowners, such as Baron Hotham, who deterred the H&S from providing coal depots at Lockington and Hutton Cranswick in order to protect his canal investment. Before many years had passed, the North Eastern Railway (NER) was handling coal traffic at virtually all the stations but with inadequate facilities. Where there was no depot, coal would have been supplied in side-door wagons and simply shovelled out into a heap. If traffic was slight this would not matter, and indeed the NER eventually abandoned two of the original coal depots: at Bempton and Speeton.

Most of the coast line stations will have begun life with a siding to handle goods and livestock traffic but very few were equipped with goods sheds, whereas the Scarborough line had goods sheds at more than half its stations: relatively few at the York end but at all locations east from Malton. The coast line had goods sheds at just seven of its original seventeen stations, although these were conceived on a much larger scale than the standard Scarborough branch design. So far as the general run of goods traffic is concerned, this proved to be a sound choice but the YNM was soon obliged to provide additional warehousing for individual traders: usually grain, seed and manure merchants. This was done on the basis of the trader guaranteeing a rent based on the capital cost of the building.

The Architect

The handsome buildings designed by the York architect George Townsend Andrews (1804-55) formed the most distinctive feature of the line, and most survive, many in a very respectable condition.(1) Andrews was a close friend of George Hudson, and the eighteen-forties saw him at the height of his powers, the designs for this line being carried through at a time when he was also busy with such prominent York buildings as the collegiate-gothic St John's College and Yeoman School (1845-7, now York St John University) and the Italian renaissance palazzo of the Yorkshire Insurance Head Office (1846-7). He had developed an expertise in the requirements of railways with work on the original YNM main line and Scarborough Branch, the Great North of England Railway (GNE, opened 1841) and Hudson's Newcastle & Darlington Junction Railway (NDJ, opened 1844).

Plate 3.1. *Bridlington coal depot looking towards the Station Road bridge on 10 June 1960. Like those at Beverley and Driffield, it was conceived on a grand scale and had 19 cells, each served by three tracks. The NER's 1922 'Appendix to the General Rules and Regulations...' stated that each of the tracks at Bridlington had a weight limit of* $17^1/_2$ *tons per cell. This was subsequently increased to 33 tons in order to allow large-capacity wagons to be used; this is reflected in the wagons seen here, which are, from the left: 13 ton LNER Dgm 137 (BR Dgm 1/140, approximately 20 tons gross weight); 13 ton LNER Dgm 193; 13 ton BR Dgm 1/142; 13 ton LNER Dgm 193. (JF Mallon / Joint NERA - Ken Hoole Study Centre JF Mallon Collection)*

The later development of the more important buildings is considered in subsequent chapters dealing with various locations, however it is convenient to look at the principal common design features at this stage. This is done by dividing the buildings into four main functional groups: the larger passenger stations, goods sheds, wayside stations and gatehouses, of which there were a considerable number.

The Larger Stations

This group embraces just four buildings: Filey, Driffield, Bridlington and Beverley. They share the form of a one-storey office range fronting a hipped-roof trainshed, covering two platforms and framed by light wrought-iron roof trusses of the type introduced into railway usage at Euston station, planned by Robert Stephenson and opened in 1837. One of Andrews' achievements was to harmonise the scale and treatment of shed and offices so that both play an equally effective visual role in the design.

Filey and Driffield began life as identical designs, except that the Filey station house was a separate building tucked away behind the station whereas the Driffield house forms part of the station frontage, though distinct from the offices to which it was linked by a screen wall. The office range is based on a design used for the 1844 terminus of the NDJ Durham Branch, where it was built in sandstone ashlar. For the coast line, Andrews increased the passenger accommodation and refined the proportions to suit a building carried out in brick with sandstone dressings. The result is both dignified and welcoming, with carefully-observed details such as the finely-jointed gauged-brick lintels and arches, the latter matched inside by curving, panelled window reveals. The plan of Filey reveals a modest degree of segregation, with the general accommodation to the left of the entrance and the refreshment room, together with First Class and Ladies' waiting rooms to the right. (For Filey, see Figures 3.1 and 3.2, Plates 3.2, 3.3 and 3.4.)

The trusses bearing the hipped ends of both sheds were borne on a wrought-iron girder peculiar to Andrews, a form of lenticular truss fabricated from wrought-iron sections in which a web made up of flat bars is braced by a pair of gently-curving L-section bars. These compose well in the end view of the shed, whose walls were crowned by a plaster coving which makes them read as classical antae or piers, formally framing the trains. Lighting was by tall windows in the rear wall, equipped with small-paned cast-iron frames, and a ridge skylight raised up on ventilating louvres. Large doorways were also provided in the rear wall to facilitate vehicle access to the platforms, which were formed of 'Elland landings', large slabs of sandstone, about $2^{1}/_{2}$ inches (6cm) thick, laid on low brick walls. Engines were expected to stand just outside the shed, where a dignified little water tower was placed to replenish the modest tenders of the early years. A convenient trick was to place the men's toilet in the building under the tank, which was built up from standard cast-iron panels. 4-feet square plates, giving a capacity of 3,000 gallons, were used at Beverley and Driffield but for Bridlington and Filey, with an interim role as termini, this was raised to 4,500 by employing the same number of 4 feet 6 inch panels.

Filey remains a very good example of Andrews' work, thanks in part to work by British Rail in the nineteen-nineties, which restored the trainshed and reinstated the vanished end bays. The frontage has also worn well, although some of the original details have been obscured by the NER, which inserted new doorways and added a cantilevered glass awning. The building is listed grade II*, which recognises its

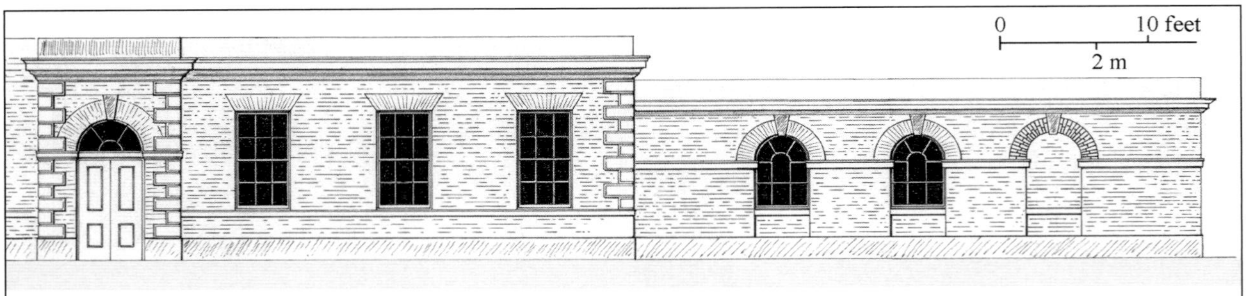

Figure 3.1. *Filey station : front elevation of the office range. (Bill Fawcett)*

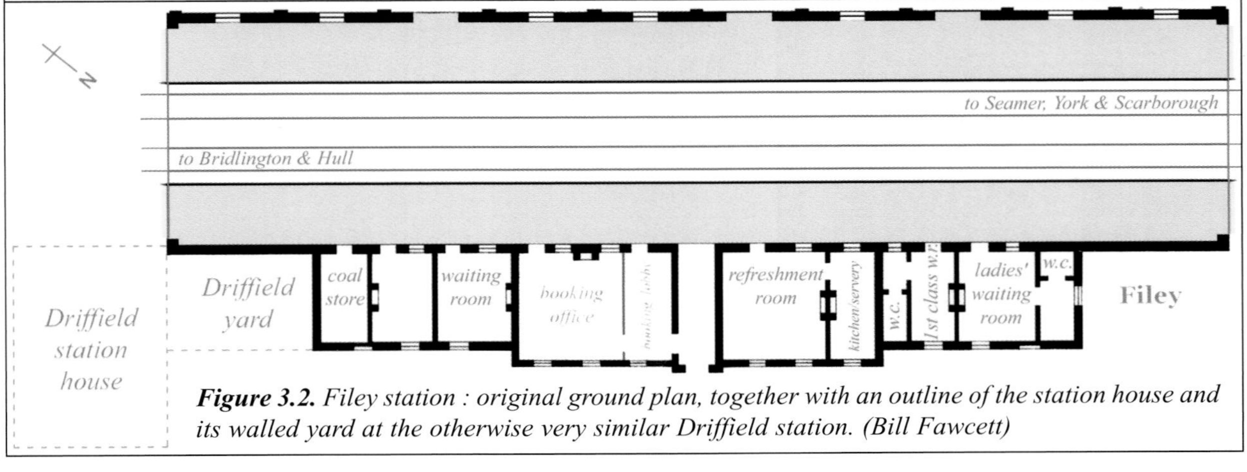

Figure 3.2. *Filey station : original ground plan, together with an outline of the station house and its walled yard at the otherwise very similar Driffield station. (Bill Fawcett)*

Plate 3.2. *Filey station : a modern view from the north, showing the relationship between the trainshed (restored from 1990 onwards) and office range; the details of the latter are partially obscured by the prominent cantilevered canopy which the NER added in 1910. The stationmaster's house is off the picture to the right, on the far side of the tracks. (Bill Fawcett, 2010)*

Plates 3.3 and 3.4. *Filey station : left, a view of the east (Hull) end in about 1970, showing GT Andrews' original lenticular truss and the plaster eaves coving which crowns the trainshed walls, together with the fine NER cast-iron railings re-sited here in the 1940s. On the right is a modern view showing how the NER was able to squeeze a standard footbridge into the station. (Bill Fawcett)*

national significance. Driffield has fared less well, with first the extension of the trainshed and then its unroofing, coupled with alterations to the office range. However, it still retains many features of interest, not least the well-preserved station house (see Plate 3.5).

Plate 3.5. *Driffield stationmaster's house stands at the north end of the station frontage, and resembles the one Andrews had provided the previous year (1845) at Malton. Note the subtle use of materials, with gauged brick lintels and carefully-profiled sandstone cill-bands. This detailing has been maintained in the right-hand wing, added by the NER to provide extra accommodation including a bathroom, a feature which was absent from all the original railway houses. (Bill Fawcett, 2012)*

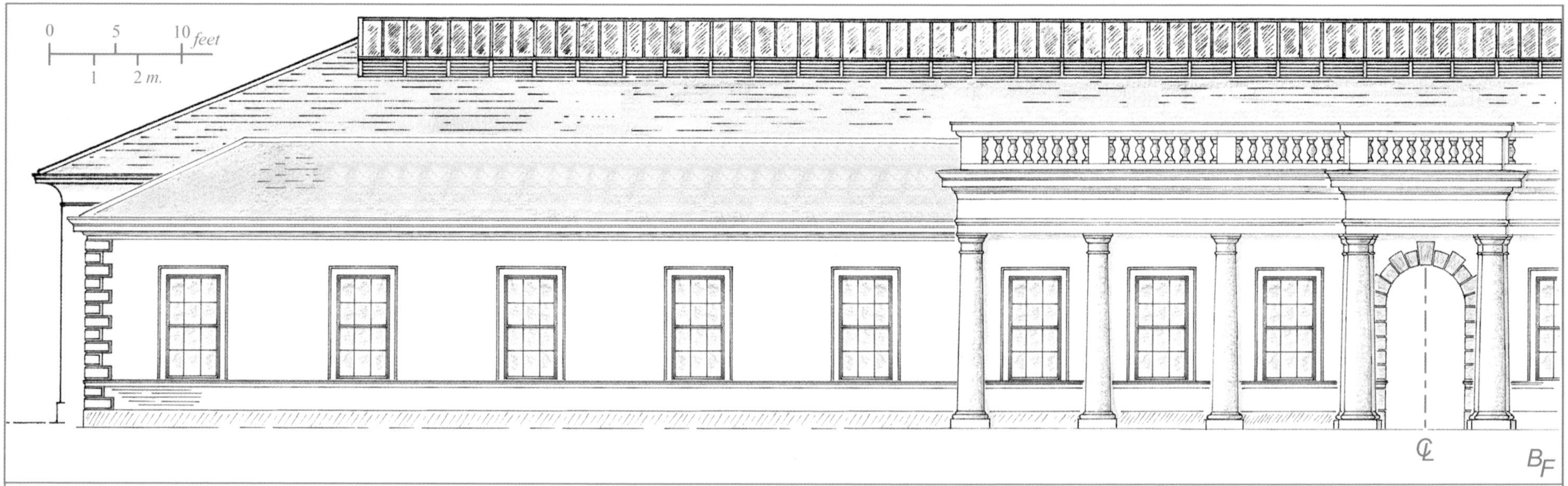

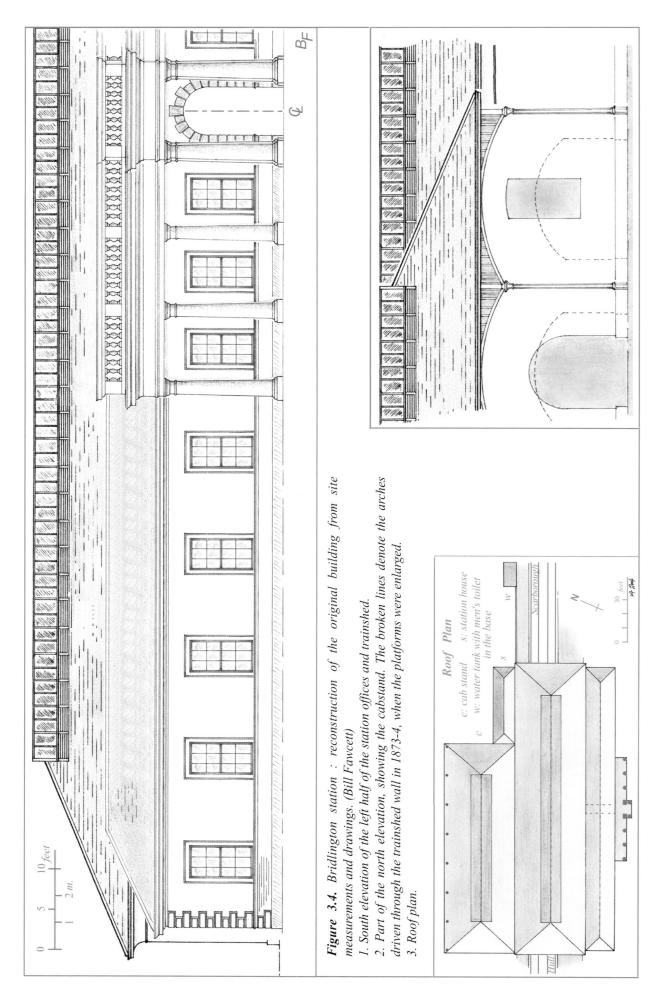

Figure 3.4. *Bridlington station : reconstruction of the original building from site measurements and drawings. (Bill Fawcett)*
1. South elevation of the left half of the station offices and trainshed.
2. Part of the north elevation, showing the cabstand. The broken lines denote the arches driven through the trainshed wall in 1873-4, when the platforms were enlarged.
3. Roof plan.

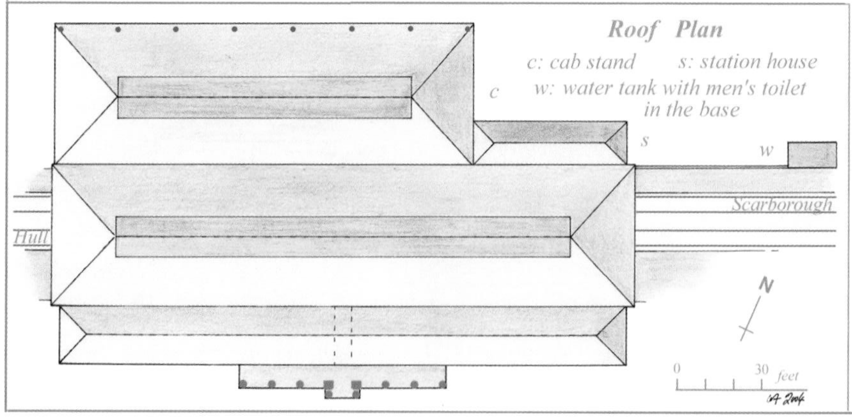

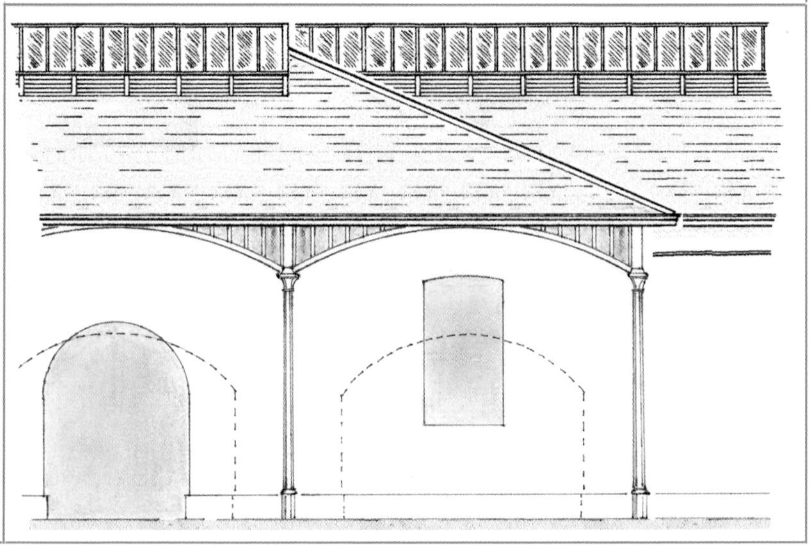

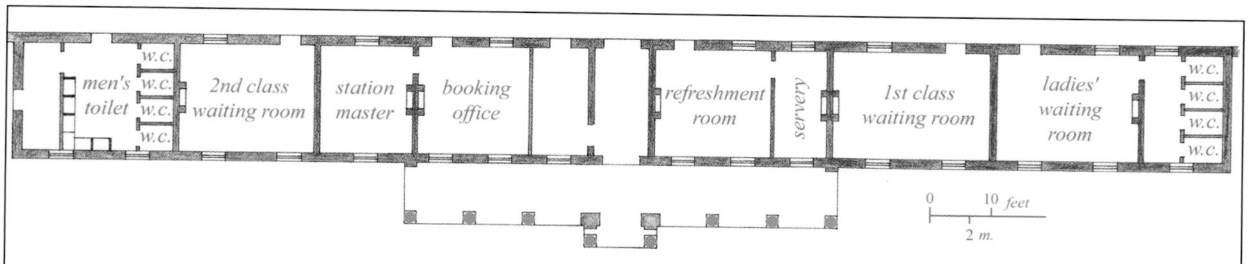

Figure 3.3. *Bridlington station : reconstruction of original office plan. (Bill Fawcett)*

Bridlington was a larger station, comprising a trainshed 200 feet long and 44 feet wide, as at Filey, accompanied by a shorter second span attached to the rear wall and forming a covered cab-stand (see Figures 3.3 and 3.4). This adjoined the Down platform, serving trains from Hull, which was conceived as the 'arrival' side of the station. The opposite platform, serving trains to Hull, was treated as the 'departure' side, with the offices placed alongside. The office range was more extensive than at Filey, indeed it was loosely modelled on that at Scarborough station (1845). Both were dignified by Tuscan colonnades, the actual entrance at Bridlington being emphasised by setting forward the middle pair of columns. The station was much extended over the years to cope with holiday traffic but has been pruned in recent decades, so that little survives of the original building, and traffic is now dealt with at platforms added in 1912 and accompanied by a concourse and platform roof which are themselves fine examples of that period.

Beverley is the most important town along the line, and the station was given added significance by Hudson's decision to have the YNM implement the H&S proposal for a direct line from there to York via Market Weighton. Thus it was given unusually broad platforms although, in the event, the York branch did not reach Beverley until 1865. These required a trainshed sixty feet wide, which Andrews chose to roof in two spans, so as to keep it in visual balance with the office range (see Figure 3.5). It read as a smaller edition of the surviving two-span Scarborough station roof, the hipped ends being borne on a cast-iron arcade of similar design to the internal one supporting the junction of the spans. The office range is a richly detailed and carefully composed design, which will be considered more closely in the appropriate chapter. However, its visual relationship to the trainshed was upset by the re-roofing of the latter in 1908 as a single span crowned by a prominent ventilator cowling (see Plate 3.6).

Goods Sheds

The large, hip-roofed goods sheds, with which Andrews endowed the railway, remind one of the trainsheds although their construction is less refined: with traditional, hefty, timber queen-post trusses being employed for the roofs. These were provided in the towns and at selected wayside stations, such as Nafferton, which boasts the best surviving example. Having experimented with some curious designs a few years earlier, such as the two-storey transhipment sheds of the GNE, Andrews settled on a simple, practical design for the coast line, with a one-storey shed housing a wooden platform with a railway line running through on one side and cart docks set into the other. Other railways had arrived at the same solution, but a distinctive feature was the continuation of one end of the hipped roof beyond the shed walls to form a covered loading area. These 'extensions' were borne on cast-iron columns and provided with a limited amount of timber side-cladding just below the eaves.

In his next generation of goods sheds, as on the line which was actually built from York as far as Market Weighton, Andrews would abandon the cart docks in favour of a through roadway, parallel to the railway track. In line with common practice, each shed was equipped with a crane with a fixed jib arching out from

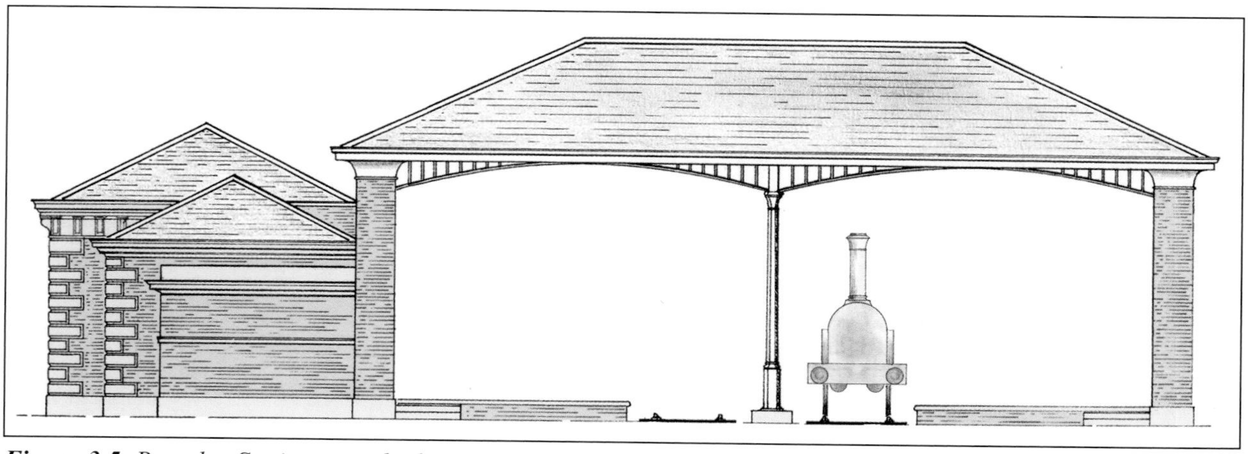

Figure 3.5. *Beverley Station : south elevation of the original trainshed. Depicted in profile at the Hull platform is the York & North Midland locomotive 'Antelope', one of three engines employed at the formal opening in 1846. Note the much lower profile of this roof than the present trainshed and the very modest platform height. (Bill Fawcett)*

a vertical post which could swivel on bearings attached to a roof truss and the platform. Nice visual touches are the deeply overhanging eaves and the semicircular Diocletian windows, resting on continuous stone cill bands, which are out of reach of prying eyes yet give these buildings something of the air of Palladian country-house stables.

Goods sheds of this type were built originally at Cottingham (the only one not to have an extended loading area), Beverley, Hutton Cranswick (where Hudson was a landowner), Driffield (Plate 3.7), Nafferton (Plate 3.8), Bridlington and Filey. Beverley and Bridlington boast two cart docks, whereas the others had just one; the lengths of these buildings varied according to the perceived traffic. Within a short time, the YNM felt a need for warehousing at other stations, built in response to requests from merchants, who would guarantee a rental for at least seven years. An early example is Burton Agnes, built in 1851 in return for an annual rent of £20; this gave a yield of almost 8% on the contract price.(2) Others include Lowthorpe (1853) and a pair at Hunmanby (1853 and 1854).(3) In the climate of economy which followed Hudson's downfall in 1849, these were designed by Thomas Cabry (1801-73), who had been the YNM Resident Engineer, responsible for maintaining the works, and was now its Engineer-in-Chief. They were competently drab buildings, smaller than the original ones and with thin brick walls strengthened by external pilaster strips. Cabry also designed a two-storey grain warehouse to be added at Burton Agnes in 1854 but its present form suggests significant intervention by Thomas Prosser, the first NER Architect, who was appointed late that year.

Most of Andrews' original goods sheds survive, though they had generally lost the 'extended' roof, as a maintenance economy or otherwise, prior to falling out of use, The only one to now retain this is Nafferton (along with Thorp Arch on the former Harrogate Branch). These buildings naturally lend themselves to commercial re-use, but Hutton Cranswick provides a splendidly sensitive example of conversion into a dwelling.

Plate 3.6. *Beverley station : a modern view of the restored frontage, showing how the trainshed now dominates the building. The chimneys are all in altered form. (Bill Fawcett)*

Plate 3.7. *Driffield goods yard seen in 1995. At far left is the former mill of the East Riding Pure Linseed Cake Company, with its prominent cupola and clock; next comes the original goods shed followed by a hip-roofed version of Thomas Cabry's YNM warehouses and the 1857 water tower, bereft of its 11,000 gallon tank. The number plate 14 refers to the bridge over the Driffield Beck. All these buildings have been demolished. (Bill Fawcett)*

Plate 3.8. *Nafferton goods shed in the 1970s. Originally the timber cladding at the far end only comprised the six broad planks below the eaves. Beneath these the loading area was open sided with its cast-iron columns on show; the later boarding was done to increase the secure storage capacity. (HGE Wilson)*

Wayside Stations

The wayside stations largely conform to three basic patterns established on earlier lines, though the stretch from Filey to Bridlington sees a couple of departures from these: at Flamborough and Hunmanby, while Cottingham is an 'in-between' design, more like a town station which never got its trainshed.

The most formal buildings are to be found at Bempton, Nafferton (Plate 3.9) and Lockington, the latter provided to demonstrate especial favour towards Lord Hotham. As at nearly all the wayside stations, other than Cottingham, the main building is placed in the angle of railway and road alongside a level crossing. In a design originally employed in 1840 at Shipton, on the Great North of England Railway, it comprises a two-storey house presenting a formal three-bay frontage towards the road. This is built of common brick but has lintels of finely-jointed orange gauged brick, while the floors are separated by a deep sandstone plat band. The distinguishing feature is a graceful portico, employing slender stone piers, which masks the fact that the building has two entrances: a private one into the house and a public one into the booking lobby. The platform frontage comprises the gable end of this block, whose shallow roof pitch conveys a somewhat Italian air, accompanied by a one-storey waiting-room range whose roof is continued down onto slender cast-iron columns to provide a shallow, sheltered area of platform. The opposite platform was given a timber waiting shed with a pent roof sloping up from back to front (Plate 3.10);

Plate 3.9. *A modern view of the well-preserved Nafferton station. (Bill Fawcett)*

Plate 3.10. *Hutton Cranswick Up platform, showing how the waiting sheds were generally extended by the NER. The view of Flamborough, Plate 8.14 on page 101, gives an idea of their original appearance, with cast-iron columns visible at the front corners. (John M Fleming, 1967)*

all of these have vanished from the line, although an extended example can be found on the long-closed railway from Malton to Pickering (1845) at Marishes Road.

The second design derives from one originally used on the Newcastle & Darlington Junction Railway but seen in a mature form on the Scarborough Branch, where a particularly good example survives at Haxby. This lacks the Lockington portico and instead features a slab-like stone doorcase, of Italian Renaissance inspiration, as the centrepiece of the road frontage (see Hutton Cranswick, Plate 3.11). At Haxby this gives access to the house, so that the symmetry of the design must be upset to accommodate a relatively inconspicuous public entrance as well. Used at Cayton, between Filey and Seamer, it was turned round to face the platform so this main door became a public one.

Plate 3.11. *Hutton Cranswick station in 1972. On the right is the gable end of offices added by the NER, whose cleaner patch of brick reveals the outline of the vanished original platform verandah. (Bill Fawcett)*

The second design was developed into the third by re-arranging the plan to place the booking office in a one-storey wing projecting from the road frontage of the house; the formal entrance is then situated on the gable end of this wing. This gives a more practical layout coupled with a picturesquely informal visual composition. A characteristic feature in all three designs is the canted bay window on the platform frontage, which lights the stationmaster's office in designs one and two and the waiting room in design three, which first saw the light of day at Kirkham Abbey (1845) on the Scarborough Branch and appears at Hutton Cranswick and Burton Agnes.

Hunmanby and Flamborough are one-off designs in which the station is treated as a little hip-roofed villa, drawing on elements from a variety of earlier stations. Flamborough is dignified by shallow giant pilasters and formerly enjoyed a portico of the Nafferton sort (see Figure 3.6). This largesse was evidently aimed at the Yarbourgh family of nearby Sewerby Hall, rather than tourists visiting the spectacular cliff scenery of Flamborough Head. Hunmanby is less formal and boasts a platform awning whose chunky woodwork is reminiscent of Andrews' contemporary station at Thorp Arch, though that is a much more sophisticated gothic design. In total contrast to these buildings is the modest affair originally provided at Carnaby. This amounted to little more than a one-storey crossing house, yet it had to serve until 1909, when it was remodelled to provide more office and waiting accommodation while the stationmaster moved to a new house a little way off.(4)

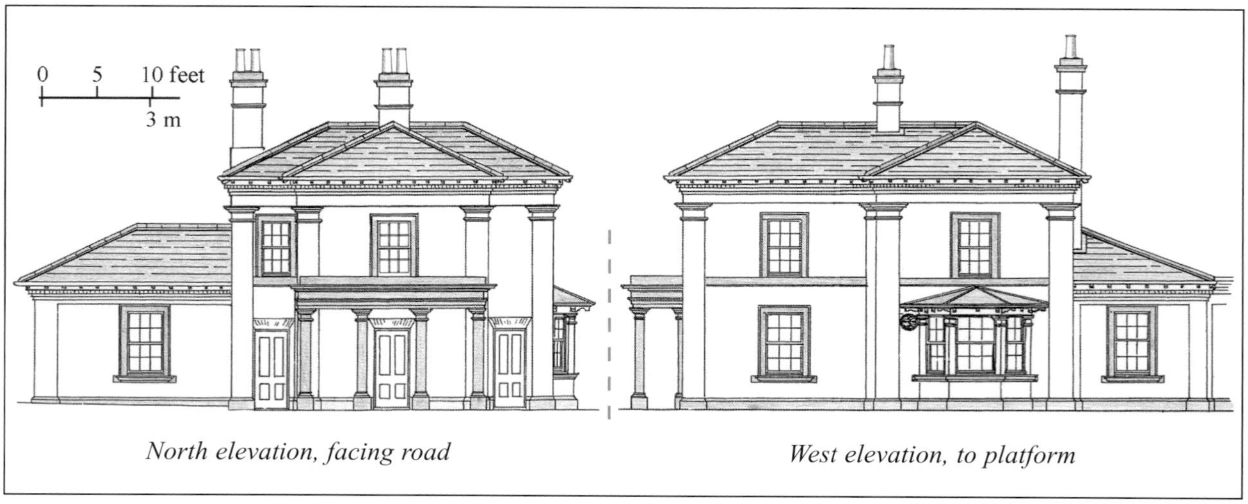

Figure 3.6. *Flamborough station in its original state; the panelled wall on the right screened the house yard. In recent years the house has been carefully extended to the rear but lacks the portico, which was removed many years ago. (Bill Fawcett)*

The latter is characteristic of the work of William Bell, NER Architect from 1877 to 1914, who had provided a new house and offices for Gristhorpe station a decade earlier, in 1897.(5)

Cottingham could never decide whether to be a small town or a very large village, an ambiguity reflected in its station. While this has always lacked any platform roofing, it boasts a handsome stationmaster's house of the sort found at Driffield along with a separate office range, like a smaller edition of the rather plain ones at Malton and Pickering. The goods shed is somewhat puzzling, with a variety of supplementary openings on the rail frontage, which are clearly early and hint at part of it having been appropriated for separate warehousing.

Gatehouses

The proliferation of manned level crossings means that the line is well blessed with gatehouses. On the first stretch, from Hull to Bridlington, these generally take the form of one-storey dwellings, built in pairs on an H-plan and characterised by low-pitched roofs, arched chimneys, canted bay windows and flat timber door-hoods borne on curved brackets. The disposition of these features is varied a bit, to avoid dull uniformity, but the overall effect is to provide the railway with a recognisable 'house style'. The dwellings were normally occupied by platelayers, engaged in the maintenance of the permanent way, which required about one man per route mile. One man would pay rent for his house while the other would enjoy it rent-free in return for ensuring that his family looked after the crossing. A small number of crossings, at Cottingham and Beverley, were provided with a single, two-storey house. Beyond Bridlington Andrews introduced a two-storey cottage-pair design which is remarkable for the generosity of its provision, by the standards of the time, each house having three bedrooms upstairs and two rooms below.(6)

In the eighteen-seventies the NER finally bowed to Board of Trade pressure and introduced block signalling throughout the system. This brought an enormous increase in the number of signalmen and a requirement for additional housing. In 1875 this line received its new housing, which generally took the form of paired houses of the sort which survive at Burton Agnes, built to the type 2a design of the company's then architect, Benjamin Burleigh.(7) These look rather cheerless compared with Andrews' work and are in fact smaller than his two-storey houses though still managing to fit in three bedrooms.

Endnotes:

1. Bill Fawcett, *George Townsend Andrews of York : The Railway Architect,* Yorkshire Architectural & York Archaeological Society and North Eastern Railway Association, 2011.
2. TNA (The National Archives, Kew) RAIL 770/5 YNM Board 9 April 1851 Min. 283 agreed to build a small warehouse for Jeremiah Julian to rent for 7 years at £20 *p.a.*; 7 May Min. 360 let work to William Hall at £256-10-0.
3. TNA RAIL 770/5 YNM Board 2 March 1853 noted completion of the first warehouse at Hunmanby and its letting to Dawsons [of Driffield] at £25 *p.a.* from 15 March, also agreed to build a second warehouse there and one at Lowthorpe; 23 March considered tender brought by Cabry for

Plate 3.12. *Sewerby Gates level crossing, protected by the rotating board signal seen behind the crossing keeper's cabin. Note the crossing house, designed by GT Andrews somewhat in the manner of his Flamborough station. Typically the head of the family living in such a house would be a platelayer, whose wife would man the crossing in lieu of rent, though for this posed photograph he is shown wielding the flag. (Ken Hoole Study Centre Collection)*

the Hunmanby and Lowthorpe warehouses and agreed to let the contract for both to Mr Hall; 23 March confirmed a price of £575 total for the pair.
4. TNA RAIL 527/49 NER Way & Works Committee 15 October 1908 Accepted Traffic Committee recommendation for new house etc at Carnaby; 11 March 1909 min. 18204 let work to Frederick Thornton of Driffield at £447.
5. TNA RAIL 527/43 NER Way & Works Committee 11 February 1897 Min. 10624 let the Gristhorpe buildings to A Lyons of Malton at £495, subsequently revised to £515 12 16.
6. Bill Fawcett, *op. cit.* note 1, page 200 gives plans, elevations and section of the two-storey design.
7. TNA RAIL 527/31 NER Locomotive & Works Committee 25 February 1875 min. 15124 let the building of 34 cottages to J Broadley of Northallerton for £6,402-1-0. One was at Wilmington (Hull) and not actually on the line. There were 7 between Hull and Driffield and 27 between Driffield and Seamer.

Plate 3.13. *Bridlington: the original water tower and standard NER water cranes at the east end of the station frame this view of Class B1 No 61013 heading an excursion from Bradford around 1955. The water tank, originally just one line of plates, had been doubled in capacity by the NER. See also Figure 3.7 below. (Neville Stead Collection)*

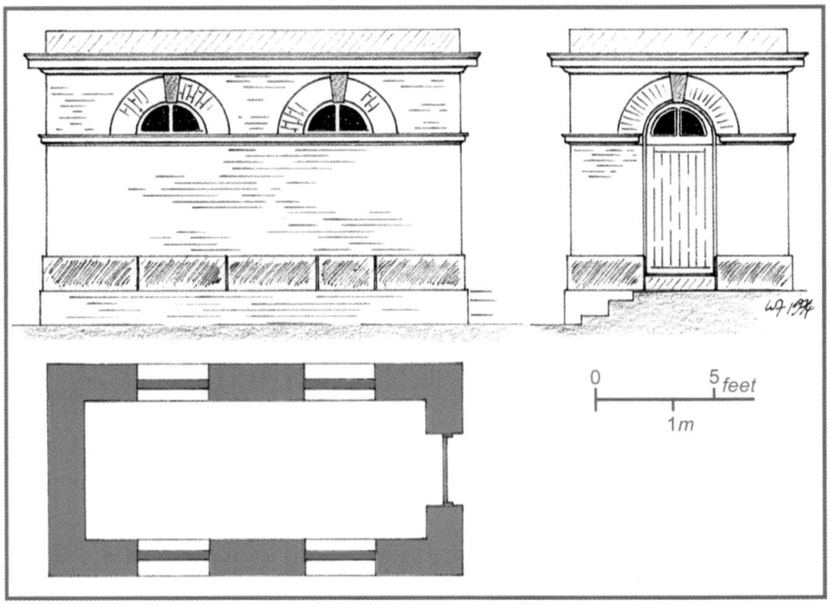

Figure 3.7. *Bridlington station water tower. Surveyed in 1974, by which time the tank had gone. (Bill Fawcett)*

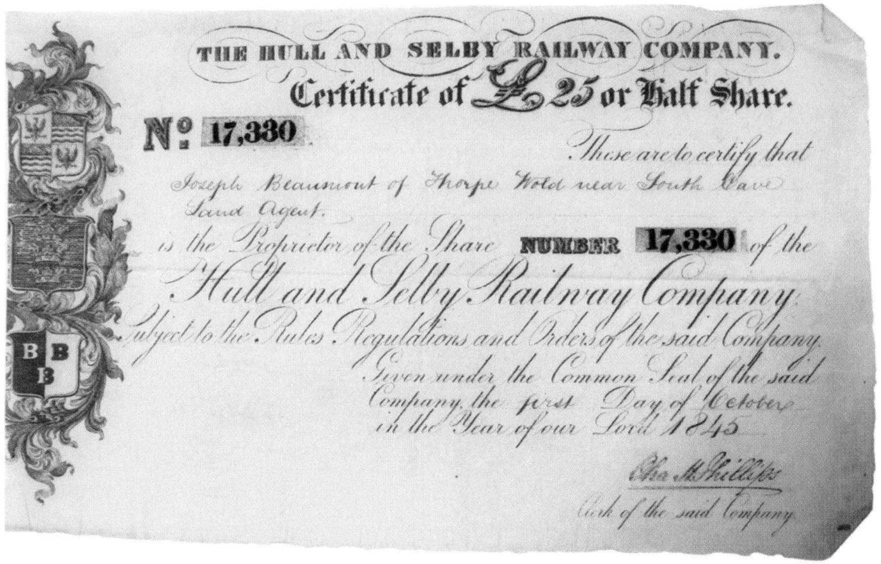

Colour Plate 1 (left).
Hull & Selby Railway certificate for a £25 share issued on 1 October 1845 to finance the Bridlington Branch; since the original H&S shares had been for £50 each, this was known formally as a half share. (Reproduced at 50% of original size.) (Bill Fawcett Collection)

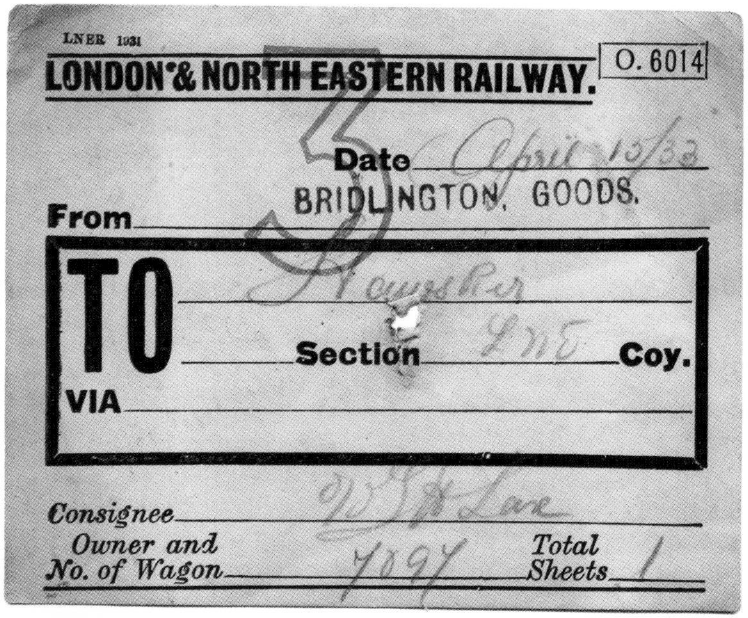

Colour Plate 3 (above).
A London & North Eastern Railway wagon label used for conveyance of goods from Bridlington Goods to Hawsker on 15 April 1933. The classification '3' was for goods other than coal and minerals. (Reproduced at 80% of original size.) (JG Teasdale Collection)

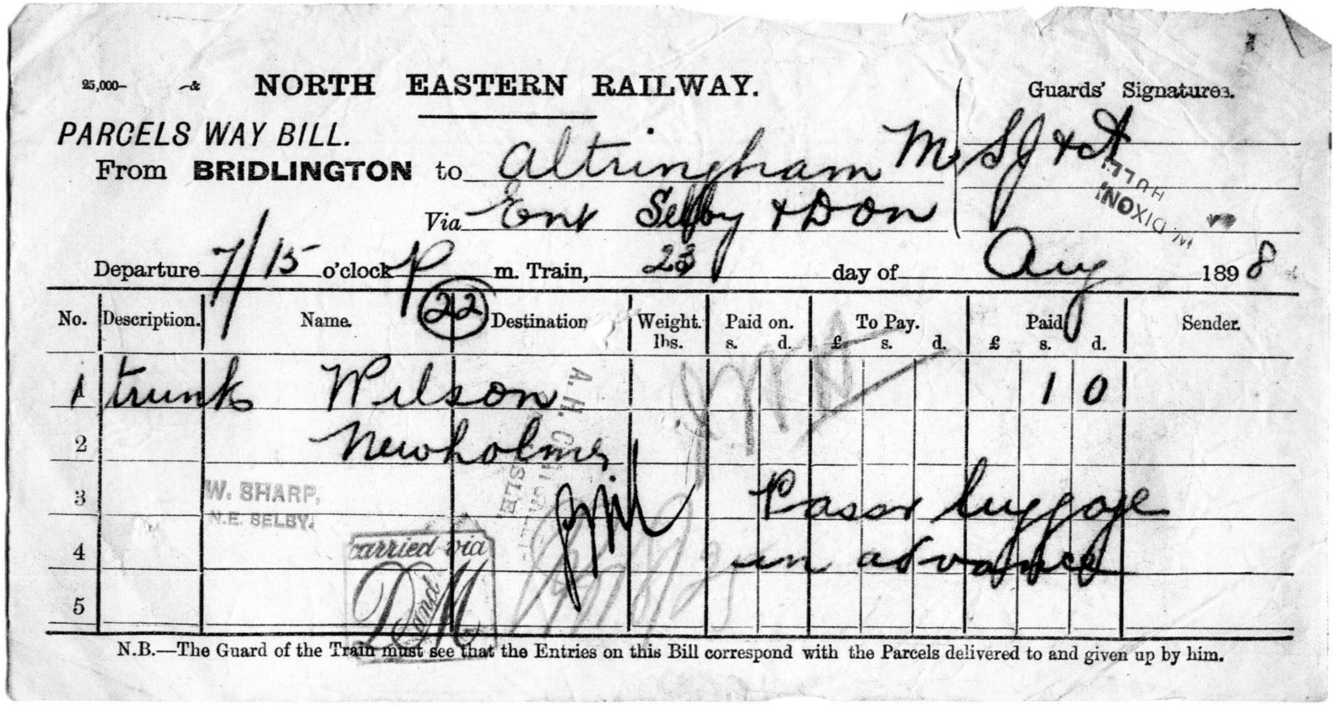

Colour Plate 2 (left).
A North Eastern Railway Parcels Way Bill, pre-stamped Bridlington and used for the conveyance of a trunk as Passenger's Luggage in Advance to Altrincham on 23 August 1898. (Reproduced at 80% of original size.) (JG Teasdale Collection)

Colour Plate 4 (Left). *The interior of the 1922 Bridlington station Second Class refreshment room, as photographed in 2003. (John F Addyman)*

Colour Plate 5 (below). *The interior of the 1912 concourse at Bridlington station, as photographed in 2003. (John F Addyman)*

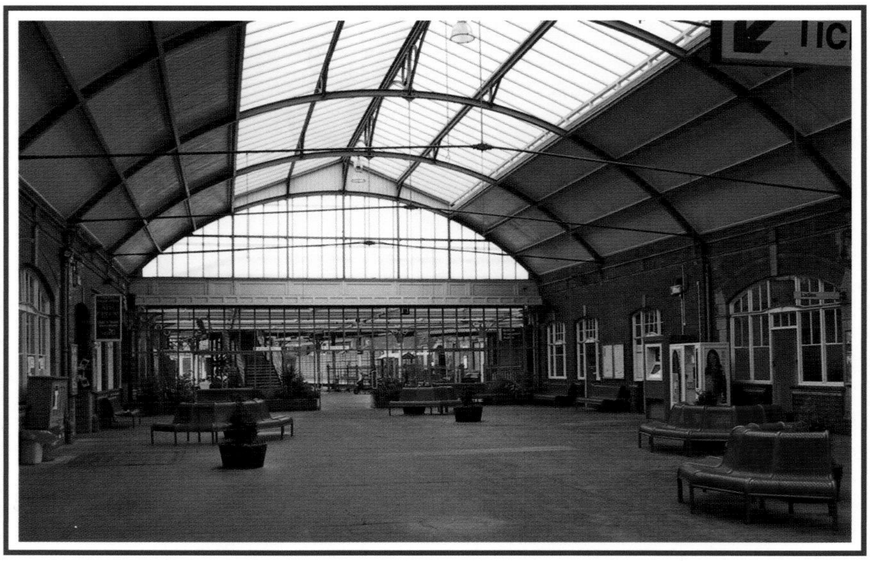

Colour Plate 6 (below). *An 1878 scheme to develop Filey as a fishing port (page 75) envisaged building a harbour to the north of the church ravine served by a branch railway which would have required a total remodelling of the NER's goods facilities.*

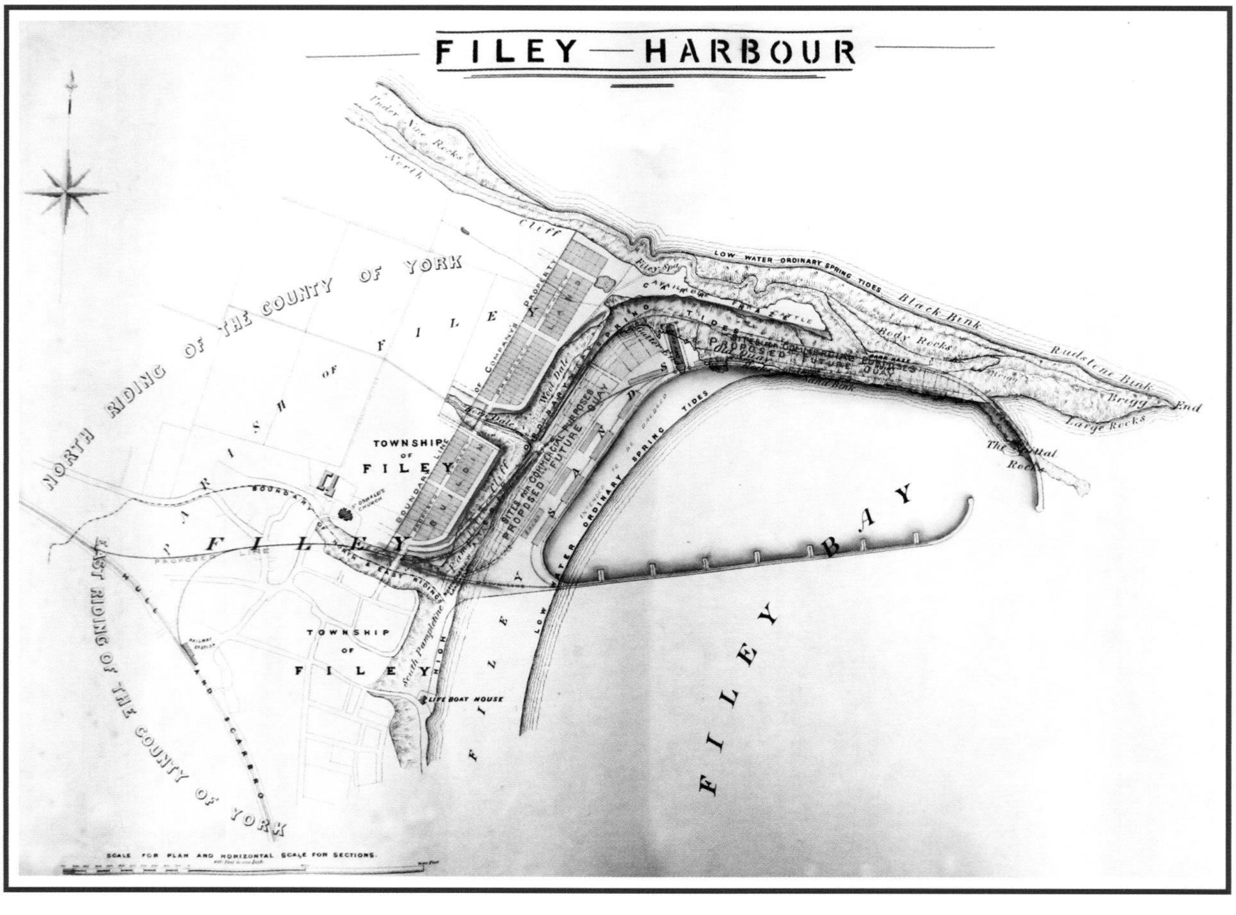

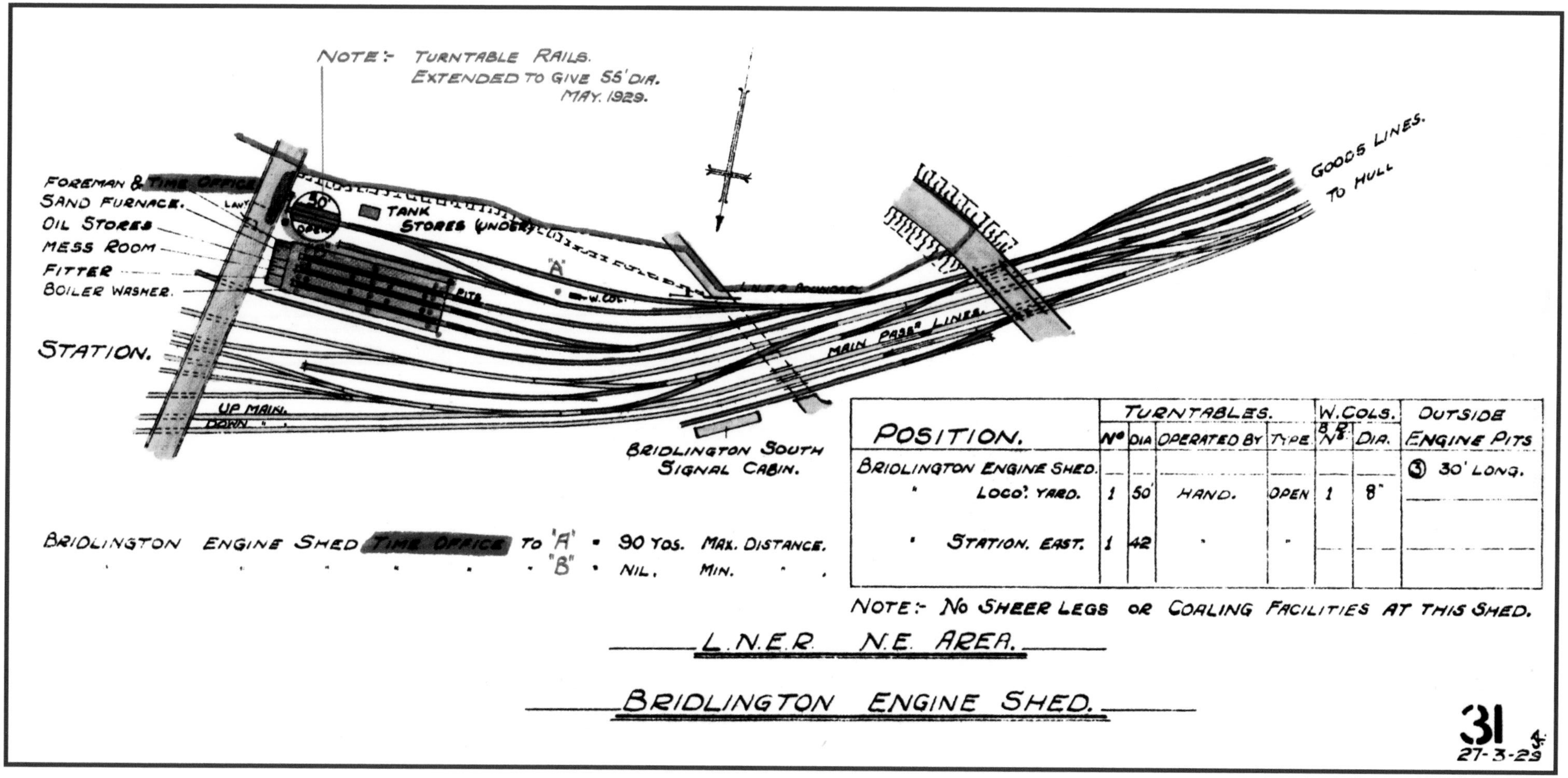

Colour Plate 7. *The LNER's 1929 diagram of Bridlington engine shed. (LNER)*

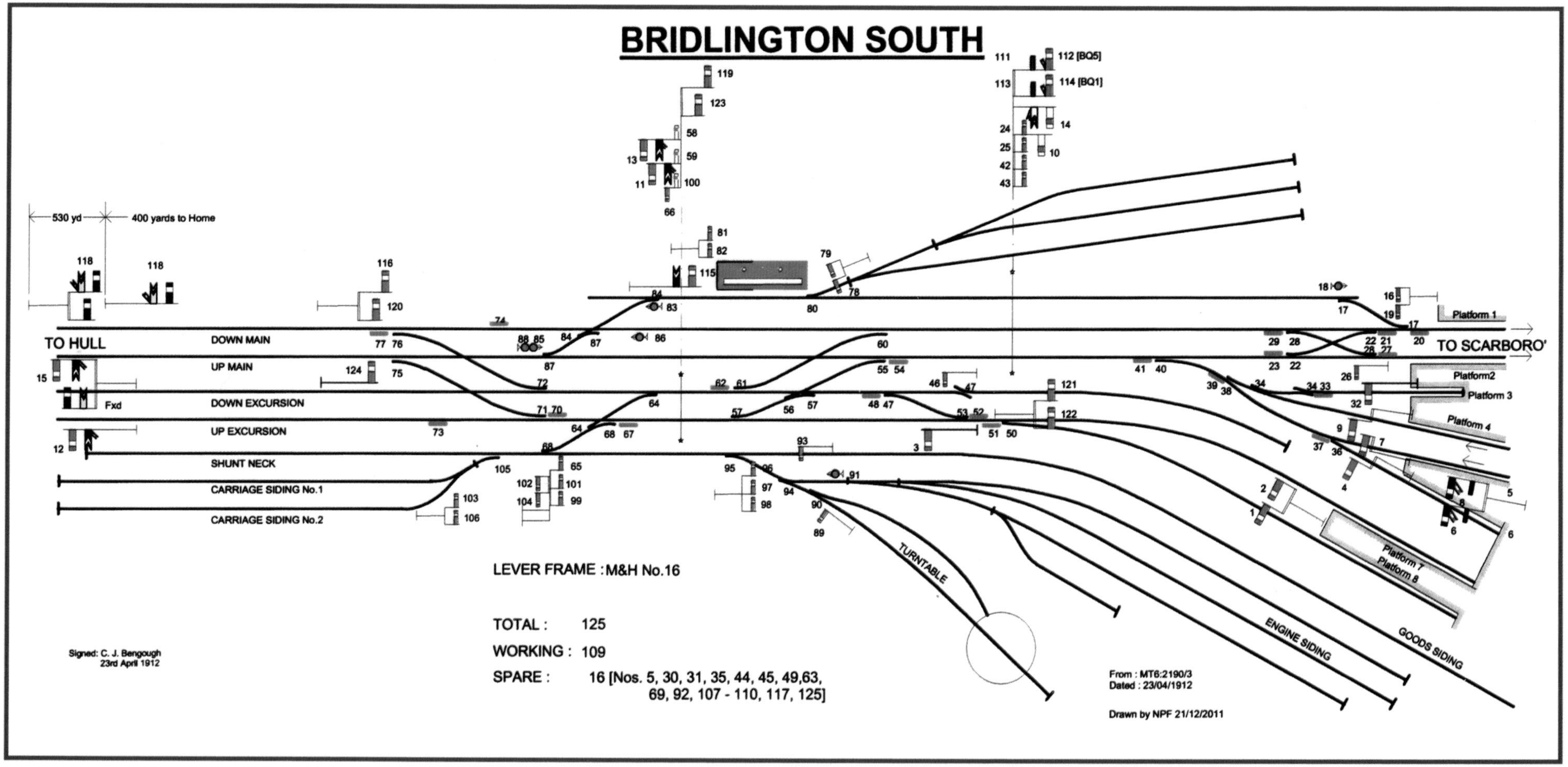

Colour Plate 8. *The signalling diagram for Bridlington South, dated 23 April 1912. (Nicholas P Fleetwood)*

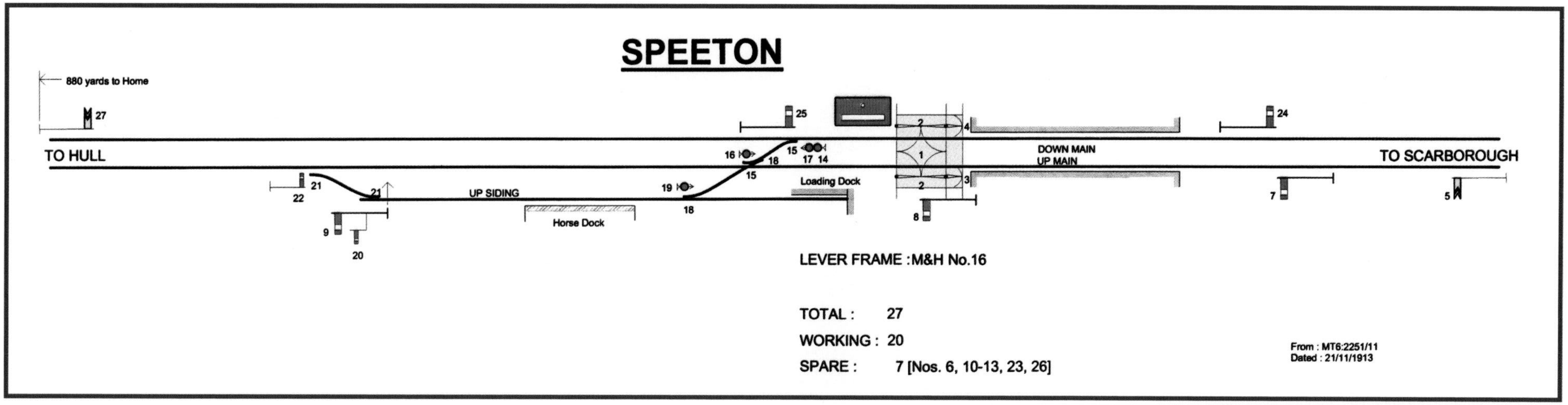

Colour Plate 9. *The signalling diagram for Speeton, dated 21 November 1913. (Nicholas P Fleetwood)*

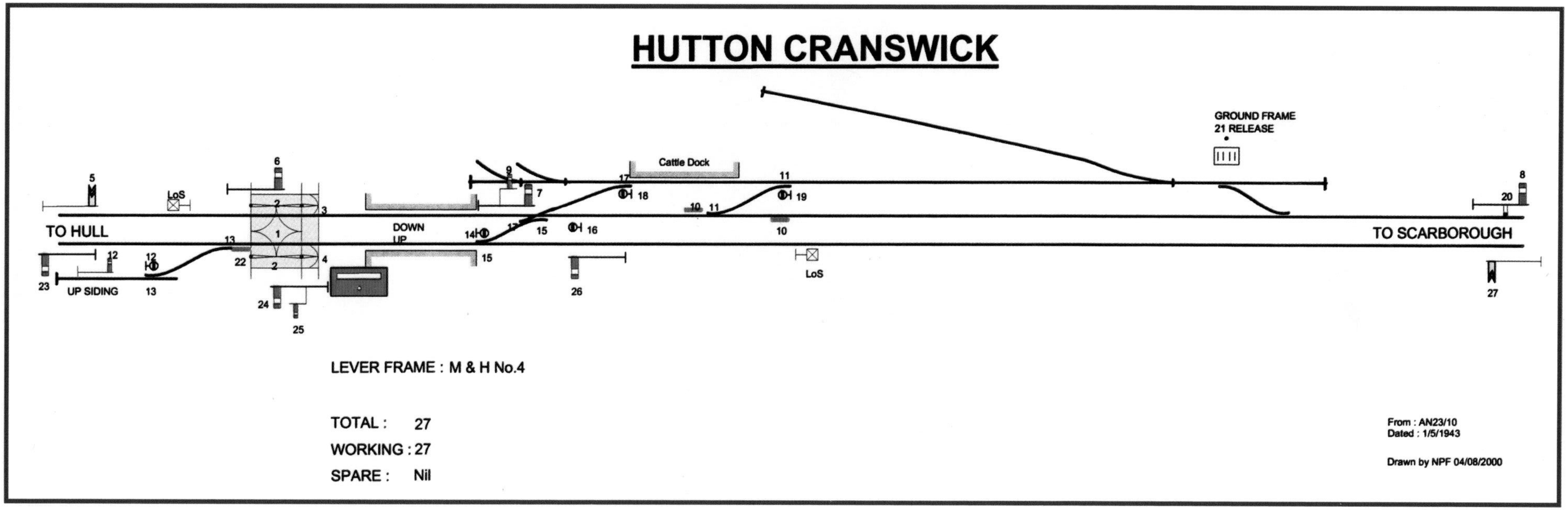

Colour Plate 10. *The signalling diagram for Hutton Cranswick, dated 1 May 1943. (Nicholas P Fleetwood)*

Colour Plate 11. *The use of photographs in railway company advertising posters in the 1930s was not common, so this photograph of the very popular singer and entertainer Gracie Fields is unusual. Indeed, this may be the first time that a star of stage and screen appeared on a railway poster; it is a little surprising, perhaps, that the LNER should have engaged a Lancashire lass for its East Coast advertising. The photograph was taken on the sands at the north end of Filey Bay, and the poster was issued in 1935. (LNER / J Robin Lister Collection)*

Chapter 4 : Beverley

Bill Fawcett

Introduction

Beverley contends with Bridlington for the title of largest town along the way, with a population of 29,110 in 2001; by then Bridlington had overtaken it with 33,837. It is also the urban showpiece of the East Riding: one of England's finest country towns, which has managed to retain its historic character while serving as a modern administrative centre for the county. Approaching from Hull, we leave the conurbation behind at Cottingham and cross a corner of the Holderness Plain long known for its market gardens. Beverley itself is sited where the chalk downs rise gently from beneath the boulder-clay of the plain, and the grassy downland extends close to the town centre in the form of the common pastures of Westwood and Hurn. The latter is home to Beverley racecourse, a reminder that the town was traditionally a social centre for the East Riding gentry. Indeed, it was in many ways a microcosm of York itself, a resemblance heightened by Beverley's lofty Minster, whose twin-towered west front reminds one immediately of its big cousin.

Plate 4.1. *This High Speed Train was a rare visitor to the line, speeding south towards Beverley Parks crossing on 13 July 1991, with the Minster in the background. An HST had been employed on a return summer Saturday working from Glasgow to Scarborough, but in 1991 the experiment was tried of extending it through to Hull. This meant it could not perform the return leg so it was used (probably on the Monday) on a working from Hull to King's Cross while an HST which had come from London to Hull made the journey on to Glasgow. The idea was not repeated in later years. (Neville Stead)*

Down to the nineteen-seventies, Beverley also boasted a significant amount of industry, mainly located in the south-east corner of the town and the area around the Beverley Beck. This navigation had been critical to the town's medieval prosperity, based on the wool trade; that ebbed away in the Sixteenth Century but Beverley's Eighteenth Century evolution into a smart social centre was followed by growth in several industries, notably tanning, milling, ironfounding and the manufacture of agricultural implements, and even shipbuilding.

An obvious locus for industry was the beck; by the early Nineteenth Century its upper reach was lined with warehouses, coal-yards, a linseed oil mill and a couple of whiting works, the latter grinding and washing local chalk to produce a powder widely used as a filler and white pigment in paints as well as a filler in putty.(1) In the angle of the beck and the River Hull is Grovehill, which was home to shipyards, launching into the Hull, and a large manure factory run by Pennock Tigar, who was a strong advocate of the railway, even though his own business would continue to depend on water transport. Nearby was the flour mill of Crathorne & Sons, which was the last survivor of several when it burned down in 1907; like Tigar's this would have been wholly reliant on the beck. The largest of several tanneries was Hodgson's, located at the west end of this industrial corridor, on the north side of Flemingate, close to the town centre. This was some way from the head of the beck but proved a convenient location, not far from the goods yard, once the railway arrived. During the second half of the Nineteenth Century, Hodgson's premises more than doubled in size and they became the town's largest employer, also maintaining a fleet of barges on the beck. They and other local industries moved with the times, and by the eighteen-eighties the Grovehill shipyards were building iron-hulled steam trawlers for the Hull deep-sea fleet.

Thus, even with a railway, the beck retained a distinct role, well-suited to handling bulk commodities for transhipment at Hull. The gasworks, established nearby in 1824, remained there and continued to draw most supplies in by water. As well as coal, hides, leather and tanning materials, the navigation handled commodities such as bricks, gravel, and chemical fertiliser. The total freight tonnage actually rose from 31,185 in 1838 to 51,578 fifty years on, of which about 40% was coal. Exceptional figures at the turn of the Twentieth Century, such as 101,540 tons in 1905, were not matched by trends in net income but that was not an issue so long as Beverley Corporation, the proprietor, secured a sufficient balance to keep the waterway in good repair.(2) Their last major investment was the reconstruction of the lock at Grovehill in 1958. Commercial traffic died out during the nineteen-eighties, at the end of a decade which brought the demise of most of the town's traditional industries, and the beck is now used for leisure boating.

The Railway Goods Premises and Traffic

The Hull & Selby company was fortunate in being able to find a route which took the railway close to the town centre with enough space for a large passenger station and coal depot without having to demolish much in the way of existing property. The key to this was a predominantly open area known as the Trinities, once the property of the Knights of St John of Jerusalem. However, the goods shed was not sited here; instead it was built some way south of the station in a location more convenient for the industries of Flemingate and the beck side.

The goods shed was the standard GT Andrews design for the line, built on the same scale as Bridlington, with two cart docks. It occupied a narrow plot on the west side of the railway (Figure 4.2, D), and when further accommodation was required the YNM built a one-storey warehouse to Thomas Cabry's design on the opposite side of the tracks (Figure 4.2, E). In 1874-5 the NER added a two-storey grain warehouse at the south end of Cabry's building, leasing this to Mr Marshall of York, who had agreed to pay an annual rental of 7% of the outlay; at a contract price of £850 this would yield almost £60 *per annum*.(3) Designed by the railway's Southern Division architect, Benjamin Burleigh, it typifies these buildings, with its sack-hoist housed in a wooden gable above the eaves (Figure 4.2, F).

The coal depot lay on the west side of the line, just beyond the station, and was conceived on a grand scale, with 19 cells, each served by three tracks. For several decades, the majority of coal merchants were still based down by the beck, and the figure recorded by the NER for 'coal, coke, lime and limestone' (both inward and outward) averaged only 7,208 tons a year for 1885-9 compared with over 13,200 tons at Driffield. However, the Beverley figures climbed rapidly from the late eighteen-nineties and the average for 1910-15 had reached 24,817.(4)

A little further on, just east of the line, is the site of the East Riding Maltkilns. These were built in 1873-4 by William Glossop, a prominent Hull brewer, later trading as Glossop & Bulay and continuing under that name after the firm sold its licensed premises to the Hull Brewery Company.(5) The building had a frontage of over 400 feet to the railway and was served by a siding connected in at both ends and provided at the joint expense of Glossop and the NER, which was allowed to use it for wagon standage when not fully occupied by brewery traffic.(6) In later years part of the building was used as a beer store, giving the railway a three-way traffic: grain coming in from a number of railheads, malt heading out to the brewery in Hull, and cask and bottled beer returning from Hull. Further north, beyond Cherry Tree crossing, was another rail-served malting: the much smaller premises of the local *Golden Ball* brewery.

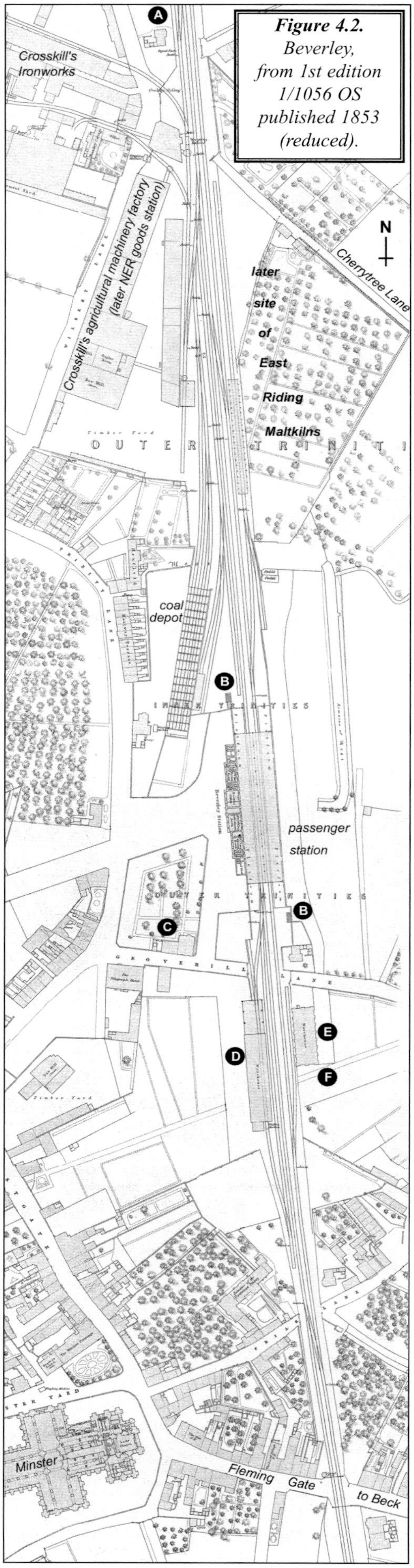

Figure 4.2. *Beverley, from 1st edition 1/1056 OS published 1853 (reduced).*

Figure 4.2. *Key to identifying letters not mentioned in the text: A - Cherry Tree crossing house; B - water towers; C - stationmaster's house.*

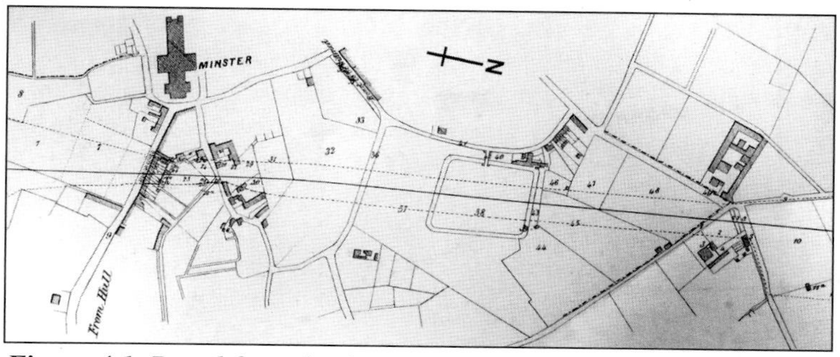

Figure 4.1. Detail from the deposited plan for Beverley, showing how the railway would be taken through largely unbuilt ground except for some premises on and near Flemingate (shown as the road from Hull).

Plate 4.2. The original Beverley goods shed, seen from the north-east, probably circa 1960. This end originally continued as the open-sided section. The rail entrance into the gable would have been closed up when the building was adapted as the NER motor garage in 1910 but the adjoining lunette retains its characteristic Andrews pattern of staggered glazing bars. (John F Mallon / Joint NERA - Ken Hoole Study Centre JF Mallon Collection)

Plate 4.3. View north from Chantry Lane footbridge circa 1970. The 1846 goods shed is on the left, then the passenger station and its footbridge. After that we see a corner of the Cabry goods warehouse followed by the 1875 grain warehouse with its prominent transverse timber gable for the sack hoists. At far right is one of the original two-storey gatehouses provided at Beverley and Cottingham, with modern blocking of the upper window. (Bill Fawcett)

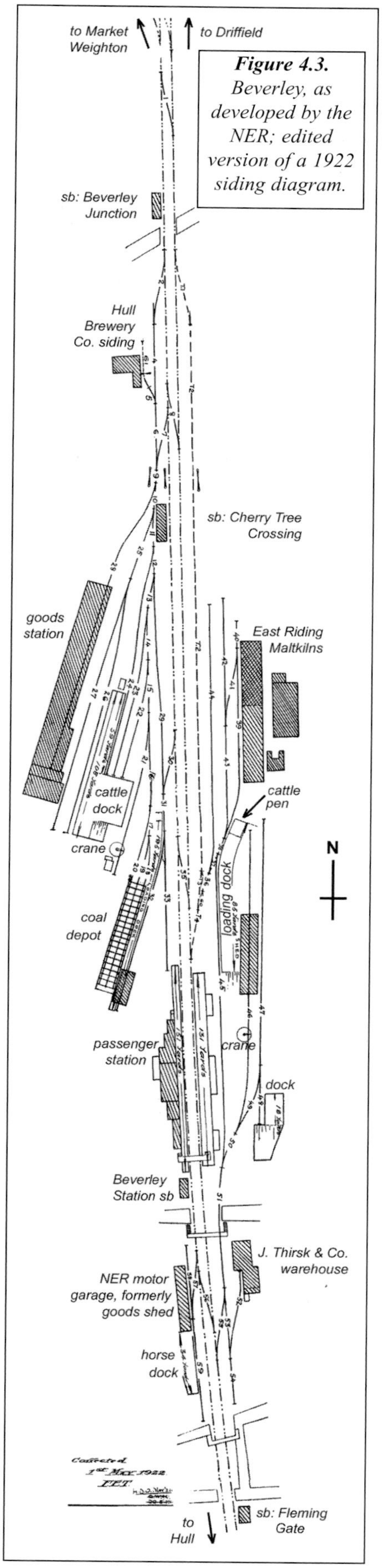

Figure 4.3. Beverley, as developed by the NER; edited version of a 1922 siding diagram.

South of Cherry Tree crossing and across the line from Glossop's malting were the premises of Beverley's leading early-Victorian entrepreneur, William Crosskill, ironfounder and inventor. He had been very keen to get the railway to Beverley, giving evidence in the House of Commons and receiving expenses of 3 guineas a day.(7) The town had several foundries but his was the most notable, established in the eighteen-twenties and soon developing an innovative range of agricultural machinery, notably *Crosskill's Clod Crusher*; by mid century he was the town's largest employer. The foundry lay on the west side of Wilbert Lane and in 1847 he took advantage of a strip of land left stranded between that road and the railway to build a new factory for agricultural implements, engaging GT Andrews as his architect.(8) All these premises were rail-connected.

Unfortunately, this expansion left Crosskill over-extended financially at a time when the British economy was running into trouble. In 1855 his lenders, the East Riding Bank, foreclosed on their mortgage although the business was kept going, initially by creditors and from 1864 as the Beverley Iron & Wagon Company, until 1878, when it went into liquidation and

Plate 4.4. *View south from near Cherry Tree crossing in LNER days. On the left are the East Riding Maltkilns, the near end of which has already been abandoned and partly demolished. To its right we glimpse the steel transhipment shed built over part of the goods and livestock dock line at the back of the station. Further right is the access to the coalyard and the dock added in the 1890s. (Dennis L Stephens Collection)*

Plate 4.5. *Taken circa 1960, this view shows the area to the right of that seen in Plate 4.4. From 1910 this served as the main goods yard, with the buildings of Crosskill's factory adapted as the goods shed. This is seen with a new gable end (far right), having been pruned back by BR. The yard was busy enough to warrant providing numerous electric lamps perched on tall timber poles. (John F Mallon / Joint NERA - Ken Hoole Study Centre JF Mallon Collection)*

the site was sold. The NER was among the creditors but there was a silver lining in that the railway was able to purchase the 1847 premises; five years later the properties between these and the railway coal yard came up for sale, and the NER bought these as well.(9)

The long-term strategy was to build a new goods station on the site, and in the interim the NER used part of the factory premises as warehousing, leasing out the rest. Thus the south end of the factory became a gymnasium. In August 1894 Beverley played host to the annual Yorkshire Agricultural Show, which was then a peripatetic event. This meant a lot of extra traffic in a short period, to handle which the railway built extra siding and dock accommodation between the Crosskill building and the line to the coal depot while further sidings and a dock had already been provided behind the passenger station.(10) Both were permanent facilities, the latter being used for livestock traffic, a significant business averaging an annual total of over twenty thousand heads (in and out) in the period 1885-1909, though this is little more than a third of the comparable figure for Driffield.

In 1903 the NER launched its first road omnibus service (see Chapter 12). This ran from Beverley via Brandesburton and North Frodingham to Beeford, serving the area between the railway and the coast. The need to find permanent stabling and maintenance facilities for the vehicles was a modest prompt towards the re-arrangement of Beverley goods station which finally took place in 1910.(11) The original goods shed was adapted, with only modest surgery, as the bus garage while the northern range of the Crosskill building was altered to become the new goods station, served by a single track entering from the north end. This gave an increase in floor area of 75% over the older building, whose loading area had been walled in with timber in 1883 to enlarge its secure capacity. In addition, a steel-framed loading shed was built over one of the sidings at the back of the station.

At about this time, Gordon Armstrong began making a few cars at his premises in Beverley. Like similar ventures elsewhere this was halted by the First World War, after which he moved into car shock absorbers, becoming one of the town's major businesses and building a factory which stretched from near the old goods station as far west as Eastgate. This meant traffic for the railway but was also a pointer towards a different world. Average tonnages for goods forwarded and received remained at or above pre-war levels in the nineteen-twenties but the next five years witnessed a sharp fall in received goods, from 37,060 per year in 1925-9 to 25,659 in 1930-4; forwarded goods fell less: from 21,638 to 16,954. A major element in this was the Depression but road traffic was already beginning to nibble at the railway's heels.

After an upsurge in traffic during the Second World War, road haulage began making serious inroads, while the railway's use of motor vehicles for local collection and delivery greatly increased the radius which an individual goods station could economically serve. This was reflected in British Railways' Modernisation Plan, which sought to reduce the number of railheads handling sundries traffic to just thirty in the North Eastern Region. Under this plan Driffield and Bridlington would retain their goods stations but Beverley would be served from Hull while keeping its coal depot and other siding facilities.(12) It may be in this context that the 1910 goods station was cut back to about half its original length.

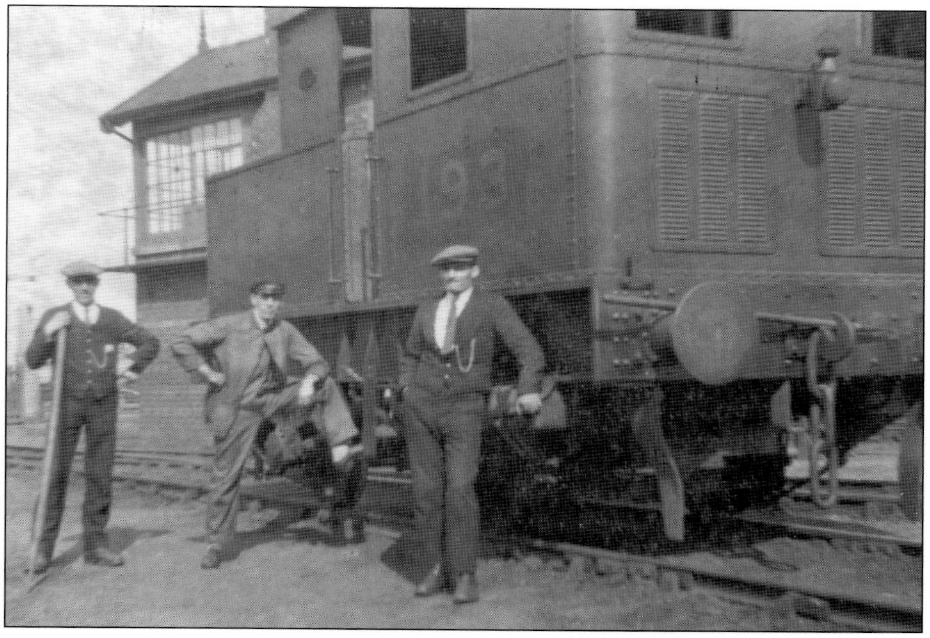

Plate 4.6. *From the 1930s, the LNER based a number of Sentinel shunting locomotives at Hull, and one of these spent the day at Beverley, working the goods yard and sidings. Class Y3 No 193 is on the tracks leading into the yard, with Cherry Tree signalbox in the background; the date is before December 1946, when the locomotive would be re-numbered to No 8158. The railwayman at the far left is Joseph Harold Stephens. He had previously worked at Sandholme on the former Hull & Barnsley Railway, but his post had been abolished when traffic decreased in the aftermath of the General Strike in 1926. However, the LNER had offered him a post at Beverley, 16 miles from his residence in Sandholme. Stephens had taken up the new post, cycling each day to and from work. He hoped that one nearer home would subsequently become vacant, but it never did, and he cycled 32 miles a day for 25 years. (As well as working as shunter and being a prime mover in the planning and care of Beverley station gardens, Stephens also farmed a smallholding at Sandholme, so removal closer to Beverley was not an option.) (Dennis L Stephens Collection)*

The BR freight strategy was overtaken by a number of events. The ill-fated creation of National Carriers, intended to establish a road/rail partnership in the handling of sundries, simply led BR to lose this traffic altogether. Livestock had become an inappropriate traffic for the railway, involving short-haul movements which could more sensibly be handled throughout by road, and BR moved out of this in the nineteen-sixties. Wagon-load traffic persisted longer but the customers themselves began to wane; the East Riding Maltkilns closed in 1963 and a clear-out of the town's industries began a decade later in the aftermath of the 1974 Oil Crisis.

Even coal lost its position as a domestic and industrial staple, with the move to electricity (largely generated using coal) and natural gas. The response to this was to concentrate coal deliveries at a limited number of railheads, something which led to the withdrawal of facilities from wayside stations but did not immediately affect places like Beverley. Coal traffic survived into the nineteen-eighties, served by a goods train from Hull to Bridlington, calling also at Driffield. 1985 brought an end to goods facilities at Beverley and Driffield, Bridlington having already fallen by the wayside, and on 17 May BR closed Cherry Tree signalbox, which controlled access to Beverley's coal and goods yards. Since then, all the railway buildings associated with the goods business have vanished and most of the coalyard, dock and siding areas have been converted into car parks.

Passenger Facilities and Traffic

Beverley station is a handsome and dignified building, well-matched to its town, even if we see it today in a rather different state from the original. As noted in Chapter 3, it was built on a larger scale than the line's other town stations, with a trainshed 280 feet long and 60 broad compared with their 200 by 44 feet. This housed just two tracks, but the platforms were much wider than usual, perhaps due to the prospect of becoming a junction for the line through Market Weighton to York. The YNM got an Act for this in 1846 but Hudson first let the contract for the easy stretch from York to Market Weighton, deferring work on the line through the Wolds. This first part opened in October 1847, by which time Hudson had eaten up the remaining capital to swell the company's dividends, and the state of the markets would not let him raise any more. His successors were unwilling to incur any capital expenditure which might be avoided, and the scheme was allowed to lapse. It was eventually revived by the NER, who opened the line to a junction a thousand yards north of Beverley station, just beyond Hull Bridge Road level crossing, on 1 May 1865.

Plate 4.7. *View north from Beverley station, with the goods yard and Cherry Tree box on the left. Stanier 'Black Five' No 45208 is working the return leg of a summer excursion train which conceals any truncated remnants of the former East Riding Maltkilns. (Neville Stead Collection)*

Plate 4.8. *The north end of Beverley station circa 1960. On the left is the lengthy dock originally built to handle horses and livestock; on the right is the 1846 water tower. Its counterpart at the south end of the Up platform will have been removed to accommodate the 1884 footbridge. (John F Mallon / Joint NERA - Ken Hoole Study Centre JF Mallon Collection)*

The biggest change to the station since 1846 is the trainshed roof. Originally this was a smaller version of Scarborough, with two 30 feet spans, returning across the ends to create a hipped outline. During its first sixty years, the only significant changes seen within the shed were a lengthening and raising of the low platforms, which were brought up to 2 feet 6 inches in 1883.(13) However, in August 1908 the NER architect William Bell presented his directors with the news that the roof was 'worn out' and must be replaced as a matter of urgency. Given the longevity of other Andrews' shed roofs this is surprising but Bell must have cleared the matter in advance with the chairman of the Way & Works Committee, for he came armed with tenders for the new steelwork, which was let on the spot.(14) The new roof is a very practical one, which spans the original shed walls, raised slightly, in a single leap. Broad bands of glazing make for a light interior and the hipped profile defers to the style of the office range but its scale does not. Inevitably, the single span crowned by a prominent ventilator cowling, such as Bell favoured at the time, dominates the front building in a way the original roof did not.

The office building is a carefully composed design in the Italian palazzo manner, building up in three stages. Low arcaded walls either end, like those at Filey and Driffield, originally screened toilets and yards. The wall then steps forward and up for the start of the office range, with windows set into sunk panels and resting on continuous sandstone cill bands. Finally, the central section breaks further forward and upward, given an enriched treatment with the cornice borne on shapely brackets. The focal point is a central doorway, emphasised by a rusticated arch framed by Ionic columns, though the present columns, reinstated by BR, do not look quite bold enough for the job. Andrews' original intention may be better judged from the contemporary entrance to his Yorkshire Insurance

Plate 4.9. *No 61800, the first of Gresley's Class K3, heading north through the station in 1958 with a train of empty flats. Hull Dairycoates shed had a considerable number of these engines in BR days, and they were a common sight on the line, engaged in both passenger and freight duties. (Neville Stead Collection)*

Plate 4.10. *York-based BR Standard 3MT No 77012 has brought the North Eastern Region's Chief Operating Officer's inspection saloon into the south end of the station. Originally numbered 305, this had been built by the NER in June 1903 for use by the General Superintendent; leading a cosseted existence, it would remain in service until 1969, and then passed in to preservation. The photograph also gives a good view of the Edwardian roof structure at Beverley station: a Polonceau truss built up from flat steel strip and angle. (Neville Stead Collection)*

Head Office in York. The articulation of the facade is not just for show; it also reflects an internal hierarchy, with booking office, lobby and refreshment room in the middle section; First Class waiting rooms in the right-hand wing and Second Class in the left. An 1852 tenancy agreement for Francis Riggall, innkeeper, refers to two refreshment rooms, though only one can be traced in the original layout, and provided for their opening every day, including Sunday; the times being from half an hour before the first train to half an hour after the last.

The office range underwent successive bits of surgery at the hands of the NER, the problem being to adapt the building to the increasing demands of the railway and its passengers. In 1864 Beverley Corporation made a formal approach, asking for the platforms to be raised and a covered cabstand provided at the entrance. Nothing happened about the cabstand but they returned in 1871, adding in a request for better access between platforms, namely a footbridge, because 'the frequent shunting of goods trains up and down the station is attended with great danger to passengers having to cross the line.' As a result, Thomas Prosser, then company architect, removed the entrance columns and attached a glass awning to the front wall, cantilevered out on cast-iron brackets.(15) At the same time, the 'current of wind' which blew 'almost constantly' through the station was tackled by providing glazed screens at each end of the shed. Access between platforms had to wait until 1884, when the station was equipped with one of the first cast-iron footbridges to be built to a standard design recently approved by the company.(16) These were to become a characteristic feature of the NER. The restricted height of the trainshed meant the bridge had to be built just outside, at the south end, but six years later it was covered in with the present roof, linked in to the trainshed end screens. One reason the footbridge was needed is that the booking office was on the Down platform while the bulk of passengers would be heading for Hull and leaving from the opposite side.

By 1890 Beverley was booking over 140,000 passengers a year (about 60% more than Driffield), bringing in revenue of almost £11,000, while parcels generated around £2,000. By now, the NER was on the verge of giving up the fight to maintain a niche for Second Class travel, and most people were travelling Third Class, with those who wanted something more exclusive going First. This meant reorganising station offices to provide larger 'general' waiting rooms, as done at Beverley in 1890.(17) The growth in parcels traffic, conveyed by passenger train, put pressure on booking offices, wherever no separate parcels office was felt necessary, leading to work carried out in 1897 and, in a more drastic fashion, 1909.(18) This saw entrance hall and lobby united to create a larger booking hall, which was fair enough, but the facade was mutilated to accommodate a new entrance, wide enough to cope with parcels trolleys. This was in the bay to the left of the original doorway, which was rebuilt on a smaller scale, without its stone arch. This left the facade a bit of a mess, although this was partially masked by the 1909 replacement for Prosser's cab awning, the new brackets being an essay in curly ironwork.

Plate 4.11. *A detail of Beverley station frontage circa 1970, showing one of the frilly brackets of the 1909 verandah. The contemporaneous shed roof had lost its prominent ridge cowling but this would be reinstated as part of the 1990 restoration scheme. At far right we glimpse the gable of the Grovehill Lane crossing house. (Bill Fawcett)*

Plate 4.12. *A modern view of the restored station. (Bill Fawcett, 2010)*

As well as sorting out the station, the NER was obliged to address the problems caused by Beverley's numerous level crossings.(19) Cherry Tree was a particularly awkward location, where the railway was crossed by two public roads and a private drive; this placed the Cherry Tree signalman in charge of three gates on the eastern boundary and one on the west. This was resolved by building a short link road along the east side of the line and diverting Cherry Tree Lane along it. Immediately south of the station, at Grovehill Lane, pedestrians, waiting impatiently whilst wagons were shunted back and forth, were provided with a footbridge on the south side of the road, since removed. The next crossing south, Chantry Lane, was closed and replaced by a footbridge and a link road down to the crossing at Flemingate. All these works were authorised in the company's 1909 Act and carried out soon afterwards.

A feature of Beverley, Driffield and Filey was the provision of ticket platforms. In the days before corridor and saloon carriages became commonplace, trains could be stopped at these narrow wooden platforms for a team of inspectors to check and collect tickets before drawing into the station. This would ease congestion within the station at peak periods and was probably just adopted on the coast line at summer weekends and special events. The platforms were originally ordered in November 1862 and survived at least into the eighteen-nineties.(20) By then the Beverley ticket platforms were 300 feet long (the station platforms being about 350) with the Down platform situated in front of the original goods shed and the Up platform ending about 200 feet north of the station.

The borough had seen steady population growth from 7,574 in 1841 to 13,654 in 1911. This year provides a useful snapshot of the Edwardian era, with Beverley booking 167,616 passengers, a third more than Bridlington and just over half the figure for Scarborough, although those much larger stations also enjoyed an enormous inward traffic in holidaymakers and day-trippers. By 1914 the figure had reached almost 208,000 and, after the disruption of the

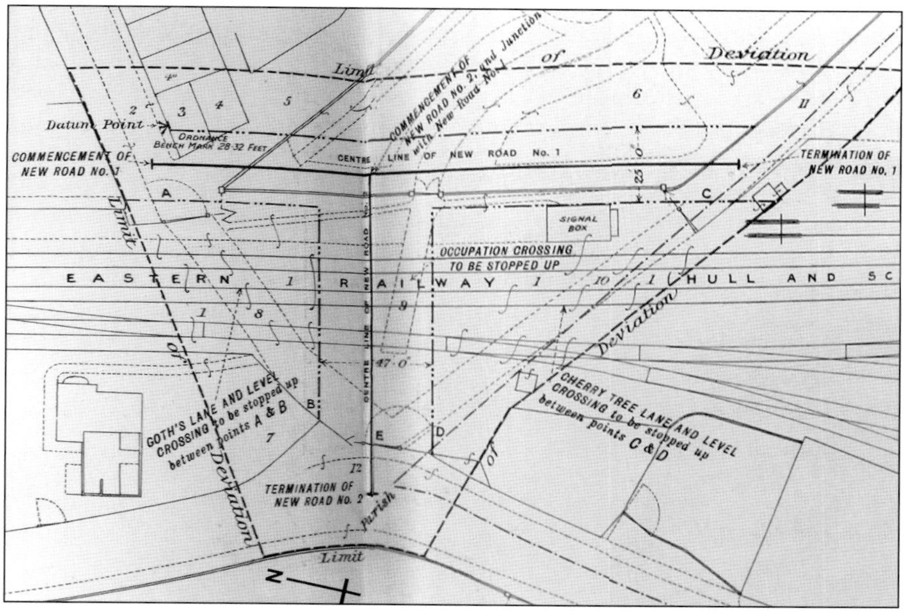

Figure 4.4. *Part of the deposited plan for the alterations at Cherry Tree crossing, authorised by Parliament in 1909. The bold lines indicate the new roads and limits of deviation; the thinner lines are the layout then existing. At bottom left is the 1846 gatehouse, unaffected by these works, while the signalbox would be re-sited from the east side of the line to the west.*

Plate 4.13. *View north over Cherry Tree crossing circa 1960. On the left are the tracks leading into the goods station, together with one of the neat lineside huts made up from prefabricated concrete components. These were designed in the latter years of the LNER and also used extensively in early BR days. Behind the signalbox looms the former malting originally built for the Golden Ball brewery. It has since vanished, together with most of the railway features other than the running lines and a modernised crossing. (John F Mallon / Joint NERA - Ken Hoole Study Centre JF Mallon Collection)*

First World War, it would return to this level for 1920. However, numbers then declined steadily, averaging 157,265 annually in 1926-30 and only 96,223 in 1931-5. In part this reflects the Depression but the fall is much larger than that seen in goods tonnage and clearly motor buses were making serious inroads, although the figures for 1933-5 hint at a slight recovery.

By the nineteen-sixties, though the future of the line was being called into question, Beverley's passenger traffic was holding up, with a solid base of commuter business to Hull. Closure of the Market Weighton route, in November 1965, deprived the town of a direct route to York but probably had little other impact. However, by the nineteen-eighties a frequent train service meant that a comprehensive range of waiting rooms was no longer required nor was there any real need for a cab shelter. This paved the way for an enterprising piece of work in 1990 in which British Rail restored the station frontage to approximately its original appearance. Nowadays Beverley retains a manned booking office but redundant space within the office range has been exploited by letting the area to the right of the entrance as a smart restaurant and adapting the extreme right-hand wing as public toilets. The area in front is a landscaped car park, part of it occupying the site of the stationmaster's garden and dwelling: 'Station Villa', a typical GT Andrews' essay which seems to have vanished in the nineteen-seventies.

In contrast to the lone person staffing today's booking office, the extensive workforce and traffic in NER days warranted two Assistant Stationmasters, as in 1905 when Charles Frank and Fred Ramsey were ASMs, with Anthony Newton presiding overall. Newton would have been a pillar of the local community, in contrast to the earlier Stationmaster King, who was hauled before the directors in 1865 for being 'somewhat intoxicated whilst on duty'. Their first reaction showed understanding: he was to be sent to another station, but a second complaint of insobriety and impertinence brought dismissal.(21)

The responsibilities of the Beverley post were recognised by an annual salary of about £400 during the first half of the Twentieth Century (down to 1944), which was the same level as that of Bridlington's stationmaster and about 20% more than the Driffield post attracted. However, coal sales at Beverley were entirely in the hands of local merchants and brought the stationmaster no extra revenue, unlike his Driffield counterpart whose salary was significantly boosted by the sales handled on his own account at the coalyard. This was a traditional and highly-welcome perquisite of the post for most NER stationmasters and continued under the LNER and BR.

Plate 4.14. *For several decades, a mainstay of routine passenger services on the line was the Class A8 tank locomotive, and we see No 9885 standing at Beverley in 1947 with the 2.25 pm train from Scarborough to Hull. These originated as the NER's largest passenger tank engine, designed by Sir Vincent Raven with a 4-4-4 wheel arrangement, but rebuilt by the LNER as 4-6-2 to give better stability and traction. Taken from Grovehill Lane footbridge, since removed, the scene was still dominated by classic NER features including the slotted-post starting signal and the revolving-board crossing signal alongside. (Neville Stead Collection)*

Plate 4.15. *NER Atlantic No 2993 began life in 1917 hauling expresses on the East Coast Main Line. Many of the class (LNER C7) ended their days based at Hull and Scarborough, and this shows the 5-35 pm Hull to Scarborough approaching Beverley in 1947. The train is composed of a mixed collection of stock: the leading carriage is an ex-NER Third to Diagram 14; the second may be an ex-Great Central Brake Third; the third is an ex-NER Brake Third to Diagram 76; the fourth is an ex-NER elliptical roof Third; the fifth is a Thompson Lavatory Composite; the last two carriages cannot be seen clearly enough to identify. Note the tablet number on the locomotive's front right lamp iron; such was the volume of traffic out of Hull, these were carried by service trains as well as excursions until, it is thought, the late 1950s. No 2993 would be withdrawn in March 1948 and the entire class would vanish by the end of the year. (Neville Stead Collection)*

List of NER and LNER Stationmasters

Note: years in round brackets denote birth and death where known; square brackets enclose the time in post; if the first year is preceded by a dash this indicates that he (they were all male) was in post by then but may have started earlier; a dash following the final year means that he may have left after that. The list makes no claim to be exhaustive.

George Beauchant [-1848-1851-]

Benjamin Robinson [-1855-]

H Morrell [-1867-]

- King [-1865]

Edward Render [-1887-1900]

Anthony Newton [-1901-1913-]

Robert William Charlton (1865-1926) [November 1919-retired 31 December 1924] moved from Signal Inspector, Hull.

Frederick Winn Cooper (-1944) [March/April 1925-retired 30 August 1941] moved from SM Monkseaton.

JT Batty [February/March 1942-retired 30 September 1944] moved from SM Driffield.

J Dennis [December 1944-1946-] moved from SM Driffield.

Plate 4.16. *An LNER view at Cherry Tree, with Stationmaster Frederick Winn Cooper standing by one of the flowerbeds which made an attractive feature of otherwise waste ground and earned him and his staff seven prizes in 16 years in the company's annual competition for best kept station. (Dennis L Stephens Collection)*

Endnotes:

1. Directories and 1/1056 OS, surveyed in 1853.
2. Baron F Duckham, *The Inland Waterways of East Yorkshire: 1700-1900,* East Yorkshire Local History Society, 1972; VCH: *Yorkshire East Riding volume 6,* 1989.
3. TNA (The National Archives, Kew) RAIL 527/31 NER Loco & Works Committee 10 September 1874 Min (Minute) 14506; 8 October Min 14596 let the contract to J Barnes at £850-0-7.
4. Sources for traffic figures include TNA RAIL 527/2142 and 527/2179.
5. *Hull Packet* 13 June 1873 reported Beverley Sanitary Committee sanctioning Glossop's scheme.
6. TNA RAIL 527/67 NER Traffic Committee 4 January 1877 Min 11373; 2 August Min 11605.
7. TNA RAIL 315/10 Hull & Selby Board 21 July & 15 August 1845; he had wanted 5 guineas.
8. East Riding Local History Society *Bulletin No. 26*, 1982; VCH *op. cit.* Note 2; Bill Fawcett, *George Townsend Andrews of York,* YAYAS & NERA, 2011, page 207.
9. TNA RAIL 527/37 NER Way & Works Committee 26 July 1883 Min 611.
10. TNA RAIL 527/73 NER Traffic Committee 28 February 1895 Min 18727; 19 March 1896 Min 19144 re retention of these facilities. Recorded for first time on OS 1/2500 revised 1908.
11. TNA RAIL 527/649 NER Contract Summaries.
12. TNA AN 92/42 British Railways Modernisation Plan: report on progress of NER Traffic Plan, 1961.
13. TNA 527/36 NER Way & Works Committee 11 October 1883.
14. TNA RAIL 527/49 NER Way & Works Committee 13 August 1908 Min 17981; 24 September Min 18012.
15. TNA RAIL 527/1649 Memorial from Beverley Corporation; 527/29 Loco Committee 5 May and 1 August 1871.
16. TNA RAIL 527/36 NER Way & Works Committee 11 October 1883 Min 760; 20 December Min 1010; 5 September 1889 Min 5065 re covering in.
17. TNA RAIL 527/40 NER Way & Works Committee 1 May 1890 Min 5547; 3 July Min 5684.
18. TNA RAIL 527/73 NER Traffic Committee 17 December 1896 Min 19392; 527/49 NER Way & Works Committee 11 March 1909 Min 18178; 22 April Min 18262.
19. TNA RAIL 527/1876 NER correspondence and papers re crossings and footbridges at Beverley, 1908-13.
20. TNA RAIL 527/26 NER Loco Committee 21 November 1862 Min 5958.
21. TNA RAIL 527/64 NER Traffic Committee 7 July 1865 Min 6234; 18 August Min 6316.

***Plate 4.17.** This LNER motor horse box is a reminder of the role the railway once played in bringing equines to Beverley races, though after the First World War the East Yorkshire buses took on the mass transport of people to the event. The horse box, which first took to the road in 1939, is based on an Albion Valkyrie coach chassis; bodywork was provided by the coachbuilder Thomas Harrington. (NERA KL Taylor Collection)*

Chapter 5: Driffield

Bill Fawcett

Introduction

Each of the towns along the line presents a distinctly different character. Driffield looks the archetypal East of England market town, yet that is perhaps misleading. Despite an impressive medieval church, Driffield was really a large village until the latter part of the Eighteenth Century, with a population estimated at 742 in 1760 rising to 1,411 in 1801 and increasing steadily during the first eight decades of the Nineteenth Century to reach 5,937 in 1881. Bad harvests in the late eighteen-seventies combined with a massive increase in grain imports to usher in the Agricultural Depression, with Driffield, a centre for the corn trade, being badly hit. People sought jobs elsewhere and the town's population stagnated for half a century before resuming its upward course to reach 11,477 in 2011, making it almost twice the size of Filey but less than 40% of Beverley.(1)

Like Beverley, Driffield is situated at the boundary between the Holderness Plain and the Wolds. One consequence of this is that a number of streams rising in the lower slopes of the Wolds combine at and near the town to form the River Hull. The principal source is the Driffield Trout Stream which is, in effect, already the River Hull by the time it flows beneath the railway just south of the town. Paradoxically, the area of Driffield known as River Head is a distinct entity, the head of the Driffield Navigation, which is fed by the Driffield Beck and pursues an artificial course for $5^1/_2$ miles before meeting up with the meandering river.

The town's early growth was prompted by the opening of the canal to River Head in 1770, and that became the locus for industrial activities; quite a few warehouses and buildings from the Canal Age survive there, though in quite different use. A second centre is found a half mile away, by the river, where EB Bradshaw & Sons continue to mill a range of wheat flours at their Bell Mills. The history of their site gives an idea of the vicissitudes of Driffield industry in its early days. Thus it was established as a paper mill in 1754; forty years later it was rebuilt on a much larger scale as a textile and carpet factory, powered by the river. This ambitious venture was not a commercial success, and by 1812 the mill was producing a form of linen for packaging; this was followed by a brief venture into flax spinning before redevelopment in the late eighteen-twenties as a barley mill set it on its final course.

Population growth from 1841 to 1881 suggests that the railway played a crucial role in fostering Driffield industry; perhaps one should say railways, since the Hull - Bridlington opening was followed on 1 June 1853 by the locally-promoted Malton & Driffield Junction Railway, which finally realised the town's ambitions for a direct outlet to York and the West. 1890 brought a line branching off this route just outside the town and heading for Market Weighton. However, neither of these routes could be regarded as having a significant economic impact beyond the villages which they directly served, although the 1890 line provided an outlet to Selby and hence a direct route to the West Riding for holiday traffic to and from Bridlington. By the middle of Victoria's reign, Driffield's industry reflected on a smaller scale the pattern seen at Beverley, its most prominent symbol being the lofty premises of the East Riding Pure Linseed Cake Company, manufacturers of cattle feed, opened in 1862, located just along from the River Head and served directly by the railway. As well as other millers, local businesses included corn merchants, the usual ironfounders, specialising in agricultural implements, and a number of breweries.

Plate 5.1. *A Fletcher 2-4-0 posed on the viaduct over the River Hull with a train of 6-wheel carriages; this would have formed a typical train of up-to-date stock from the late 1870s. (Ken Hoole Study Centre Collection)*

The Railway Goods Premises and Traffic

From Beverley the railway is heading north as far as the river bridge; it then swings north-east to pass between the town centre and River Head, crossing the road to the latter just before entering the station. On departing, the line originally crossed another road, later blocked off to permit platform lengthening, before passing over the beck. The coal yard came immediately after this, on the left, and was laid out on a generous scale, with a line of fourteen cells served by three tracks;

access was from Albion Street past the customary weigh office and yard house. At first, the coal merchants still tended to operate from their traditional location at the River Head but the drift to offices nearer the railway happened more quickly than at Beverley. The new coal yard was slightly more convenient than the navigation for the gasworks, established in 1835 and sited about a third of a mile north of the railway; a location chosen to minimise the amount of gas main required for town lighting. A development which hinted at the future was the creation, evidently in the early Twentieth Century, of a small motor fuel depot, served by a dock and siding alongside the line to the coal depot. The dock proved a convenient place for handling sackloads going to and from various mills and maltings, and was eventually provided with a spacious steel canopy.

The goods yard lay on the opposite side of the tracks, with road access from Eastgate South. It began life with a substantial GT Andrews goods shed but from about 1851 this was augmented by one of Mr Cabry's modest brick warehouses, provided by the YNM in return for a guaranteed rental from Dawson & Sons, the leading local corn merchants. Already established at the River Head and also proprietors of the Poundsworth Mills, just upstream of the railway's River Hull crossing, they were quick to make use of the railway to consolidate their supply and distribution network, and got the YNM to build them warehouses at various stations: Burton Agnes (1851) and Lowthorpe (1853) were apparently built for Dawsons while the first at Hunmanby (1853) certainly was. Just behind the Driffield warehouse was stabling for the railway horses, used for local collection and delivery and, to some extent, for shunting the yard. The ensemble was completed in about 1875 by a locomotive water tower,

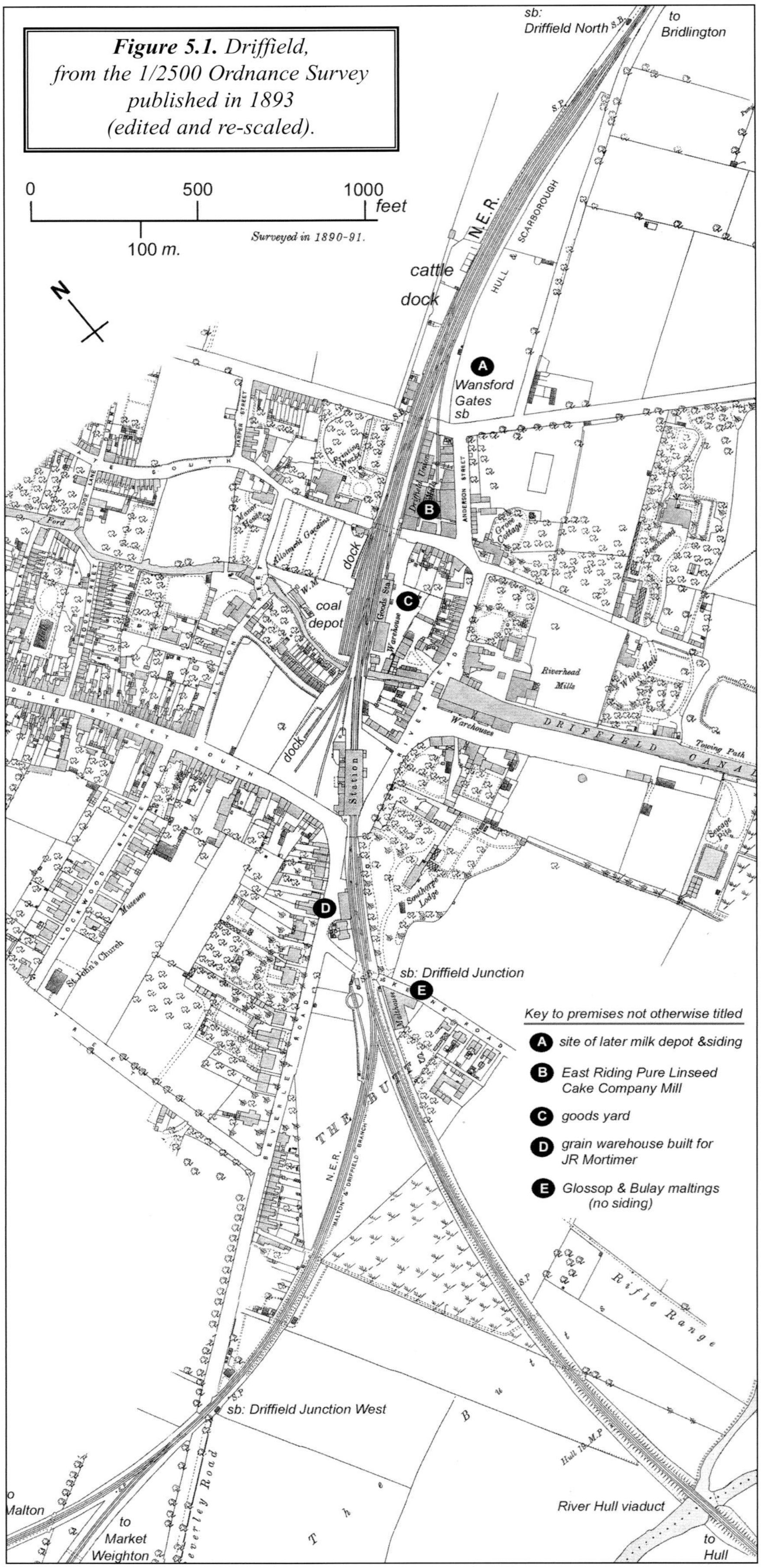

Figure 5.1. *Driffield, from the 1/2500 Ordnance Survey published in 1893 (edited and re-scaled).*

replacing a small one of 1846 on the Up platform, which was being displaced by station improvements.

As at Beverley, there was no space near the goods shed for any sidings, so early on a track was laid in at the front of the station, complete with crane, and this was gradually developed as a goods yard known as the 'Front Yard'. Late in 1863, the NER was approached by another merchant, John Robert Mortimer (1825-1911), seeking warehouse facilities.(2) He is known today as a serious amateur archaeologist, who founded his own museum in the town, but he made his living as a corn, seed and manure merchant. Initially, the NER considered building new premises for Dawsons and letting him lease their warehouse, however the railway was reluctant to build on the site Dawsons favoured, in the 'Front Yard', so they stayed put. Mr Mortimer was found a site just west of the station, squeezed between a siding and the Beverley Road, and in 1864 the NER built him a warehouse to designs by their architect, Thomas Prosser. It boasted a cellar as well as its two more obvious storeys and was given louvered windows with quarterlights at the top. There was no external sack hoist, instead access between floors was by the double-flap trapdoors commonly found in mill premises. In 1887 Mortimer became bankrupt and the warehouse was subsequently leased by JC Barker, operating in the same line of business.

Agricultural produce being railed from Driffield was dominated by linseed oil cake (9,034 tons in 1911) and grain (3,164 tons of barley and 1,085 of wheat in 1911). The largest of the town's cake mills was that of the Driffield & East Riding Pure Linseed Cake Company, founded in 1861. This was built just east of the goods yard, on the opposite side of Eastgate South, and was served by two railway sidings. One led into the heart of the mill complex from the opposite side of the Wansford Road level crossing while the other ran alongside the running lines as an extension of the track serving the original goods shed. To accommodate this, the railway's Eastgate gatehouse had to be demolished and replaced on the other side of the line.(3) The frequent shunting of wagons across must have made Eastgate a very tiresome crossing for road users, and it was eventually closed by British Railways, who provided the present pedestrian footbridge instead. The mill was largely destroyed in a fire which raged for three days in December 1887 and must have raised fears as to the safety of the NER goods premises nearby. It was promptly restored, however. Shunting operations there and at the goods yard had to be carried out either by train engines or else by locomotives based at Bridlington and despatched to Driffield for a few hours. From the nineteen-thirties to the fifties this task was performed by a Sentinel steam shunter making a daily (weekday) trip from Bridlington.

A considerable amount of grain dealing was carried on at Driffield's weekly market, and in 1866 the NER agreed to run a market train, leaving the town at 4-15 pm every Thursday for the accommodation of corn merchants and others residing in the Market Weighton district.(4) That market was of very long standing but successive attempts to set up a livestock market had failed until the arrival of the railway. A further try in 1847 succeeded, and the livestock market was held on alternate Wednesdays until killed off by the foot and mouth outbreak of 2001. This brought the railway a lot of traffic in cattle and sheep, and by 1861 the NER was running a regular cattle train from Driffield to Hull on market afternoons; additional trains would be provided as required. The market lay alongside Eastgate, a quarter mile north of the railway, and for decades the livestock must have been dealt with at the sidings in front of the station; it is noteworthy that there were still two fields adjacent to these in the eighteen-nineties. Later, a large cattle dock was built to the east of Wansford Road crossing.

Plate 5.2. *View north-east from Driffield station in May 1977. The wagons are standing on the coal cells while across the line we see the Cabry warehouse (far right) and the 1846 goods shed; originally the boarding down its left-hand side would have extended no further than that down the end. In the background is the former oil-cake mill, which has lost its siding though the awning for the trackside loading door remains. (HGE Wilson)*

Plate 5.3. *View north from Driffield station in July 1970. On the left is the motor fuel dock, with a road tanker standing under the steel awning which was a relatively late addition. To the right of that is the former gateman's cabin for the Eastgate level crossing, which was superseded by the adjoining footbridge, beneath which we glimpse Wansford crossing signalbox which controlled access into the coal and goods yards. At far right are the base of the 1875 water tower and a small building behind which lurked what appeared to be the former stable. (John M Fleming)*

Plate 5.4. *View south from Eastgate level crossing on 12 July 1959, with Class K3 No 61847, based at Hull Dairycoates, hauling the 1-20 pm train from Hull to Scarborough. Fish was conveyed from Hull in the vans marshalled in front of the passenger stock. On the right is the dock, which by then was handling general goods, while the line through the 1846 goods shed is filled to capacity. (Neville Stead Collection)*

For a couple of decades, the navigation continued to share in the town's growth but the eighteen-seventies saw the start of a steady decline: from a total of 35,654 tons despatched and received in 1871 to 24,117 in 1898. A brief upsurge early in the Twentieth Century was followed by a sharp fall after the First World War, with the tonnage down to just 4,672 in 1931. The last commercial vessel struggled up the weed-choked canal to Driffield in March 1945. In recent years, however, the moribund waterway has been brought back to life for leisure boating by the Driffield Navigation Trust.

Railway freight eventually went the same way. The first two decades of the Twentieth Century show a relatively static picture for outward goods, with an annual tonnage generally hovering between 17,500 and 21,000. The third decade brought a drop to 15,501 by 1927 and a steady decline to 9,517 in 1934.(5) This, of course, represented the height of the Depression but also marked the start of a steady fall in short-haul livestock movements by rail. Figures for inward goods were more robust, with tonnages generally in the range 20 to 25,000 for the first three decades; an exceptional figure of 40,749 for 1918 is probably explained by the construction and fitting out of buildings at RAF Driffield, which opened the following February. The airfield was dismantled in 1925 but was rebuilt a decade later, re-opening in 1936.

After the Second World War, the loss of goods and livestock traffic to road haulage accelerated. It made sense to use road lorries for short distances and British Railways themselves based a number of vehicles at Driffield, taking the opportunity to secure additional work for these through contracts for the local dairy factory, which also had its own siding east of Wansford Road.(6) Under the BR Modernisation Plan, adopted in 1955, Driffield was one of just thirty goods depots in the North Eastern Region scheduled to remain open as railheads for sundries traffic. In the event this idea was overtaken by the nineteen-sixties' flight from goods traffic and the declining coal trade. By 1981 most of the sidings had been removed, leaving the coal depot and adjoining fuel siding, together with the no-doubt disused line into the goods shed. The end came in 1985, with all connections being abandoned on 11 November except for that into the civil engineer's siding.

A symbol of change is the great oil-cake mill whose cupola and prominent gable-end clock used to dominate the scene east of the station. The railway's oil-cake traffic in 1923 and 1924 was little more than half the level of 1911 and about 1947 the building was converted into a sugar mill, continuing to provide some traffic for the railway; now just a melancholy fragment remains. Sadly, the same is true of the NER goods and coal yards. The Andrews goods shed and Cabry warehouse, the former still retaining its roofed loading area, were refurbished and pressed into use by the Red Arrow Garage. Despite enjoying an apparently secure future, they fell out of use in the nineteen-nineties and were demolished in 1998. The coal yard is still used by a local merchant and retains its

Plate 5.5. *View south past Mortimer's warehouse in 1933, with a couple of wagons standing on its siding as Class F8 No 1581 rattles past on a local train from Malton. Built in 1891, to a design introduced 5 years earlier, this was the regular engine on that service from the 1920s until its withdrawal in May 1935. (Tom Rounthwaite)*

Plate 5.6. *View north from Skerne Road level crossing in July 1970. On the left is a typical GT Andrews crossing cottage pair to the one-storey design used between Beverley and Bridlington. Next comes the grain warehouse built in 1864 for Mr Mortimer. The windows have glazing in the top third with wooden louvres below but the cellar is much less well ventilated and has a floor about 3ft 6in (1.1m) below rail level. There were two loading doors served by the vanished siding, and the far one boasts an awning not shown on the original drawing. (John M Fleming)*

original house and the brick division walls of the coal cells. The railway, rather impressively, boasts three tracks south from Wansford Road crossing, the third being a siding for permanent-way (PW) maintenance vehicles. From NER days into the first two decades of British Railways, track maintenance was a very labour-intensive business and a PW inspector was based in the town. West of the station, Beverley Road grain warehouse survives adapted as housing, with a curious piece of mock timber-framing at one end. Beyond this is the site of the junction with the Malton line, next to which the NER had provided a 45ft engine turntable in 1880.

Passenger Facilities and Traffic

Driffield station began life as an important stop on a railway which had few trains; the requirement was for a fairly imposing building with a quite simple role. A number of things combined to make life more complicated. The first was the arrival of the Malton service on 1 June 1853. Neither its passenger numbers nor its service of three trains a day (each way) will have placed much strain on the station's capacity, but in the early days a two-hour wait for the Hull connection from the mid-day train may have stimulated business at the refreshment room. A greater demand on that facility will have arisen from corn merchants attending the market. The start of middle-class commuting into Hull created a more serious pressure, largely, as at Beverley, due to the booking and waiting facilities being on the opposite platform to the Hull trains. Finally, the opening in 1890 of the Market Weighton line (linking through to Selby) will have generated some extra traffic although the trains ran through to Bridlington and relatively few people will have wanted to change between that service and the Hull trains. Nonetheless, the NER can be seen responding to these developments with two station improvement schemes: one in 1874 and the other in 1890. At the end of the day Driffield still had just two platforms but these had been doubled in length from their original size of just over 200 feet.

The first notable development was the provision of ticket platforms in 1862. Up trains were handled at one about 220 feet long situated opposite the goods yard, while down trains from Hull were dealt with at one south-west of the junction with the Malton line. In 1890 the NER decided to build a further pair of platforms but only one has been traced; sandwiched between the Down line and the siding serving the Beverley Road warehouse, this would have been enough to tackle trains coming off the new route from Selby.(7)

Plate 5.7. *Driffield Junction at the end of the 1950s, with the turntable site on the left and the station in the far distance. (John F Mallon / Joint NERA - Ken Hoole Study Centre JF Mallon Collection)*

Plate 5.8. *Driffield Junction in 1957, with BR Standard 5MT No 73169 heading onto the Malton line (and then Selby) with an excursion returning from Scarborough to Sowerby Bridge. The site of the turntable is just off the picture to the left. Glossop & Bulay's maltings form an impressive backdrop and have since been converted into housing. (Neville Stead Collection)*

Plate 5.9. *Driffield station in its original condition. This view, taken prior to 1874, shows the tall 'Station Signal' which read for both lines and replaced the original disc signal evidently during the 1860s. The two arms were placed high for sighting over the trainshed roof. The Down platform water tower, seen here, had a twin at the other end of the station. A surprising feature is the way in which, right from the early days, the station forecourt was commandeered for a goods siding and crane, forming the nucleus of the 'Front' goods yard. Somewhat truncated, the siding survives today as a berth for permanent-way maintenance vehicles while the front yard has become a car park. (Ken Hoole Study Centre Collection)*

Driffield station originated as a handsome building with a hip-roofed trainshed fronted by a one-storey office range, much as we see today at Filey except that the stationmaster's house formed part of the composition, located at the left-hand end of the frontage. As at Filey there was a refreshment room to the right of the entrance. In 1873 the NER appointed a committee to examine the improvements required at Driffield and Bridlington stations.(8) This implies that the natives were getting restless, and it is not difficult to divine their chief concerns. The main issue at Driffield was no doubt the facilities available to passengers bound for Hull, a need being seen for a wider Up platform accompanied by some waiting room and toilet facilities and, ideally, a footbridge. The latter may seem strange given the adjacent level crossing, but it must have been immensely frustrating to be prevented from getting from the booking hall to the opposite platform by passing trains and shunting movements.

Work began early in 1874, with the Up platform being widened by some fifteen feet. This involved punching a series of large arches through the rear wall of the trainshed but no-one seems to have anticipated the obvious outcome, namely wind and rain driving through these openings. Three years later that problem was addressed by building an outer wall with a pent roof over the exposed platform; the opportunity was also taken to provide toilets, a waiting room and a modest booking office for the Hull traffic.(9) The 1874 work also included extending the main office range at the right-hand (south-west) end to provide increased office and refreshment room accommodation.

At the end of 1883 Driffield was selected to receive one of the new standard footbridges but this never happened, and the next development came in 1890 with the provision of a further waiting room on the Up side and additions to the south-west end of the main office range, including new toilet facilities for men.(10) The two campaigns left the station frontage somewhat altered, with the station house now balanced visually by a longer two-storey range at the right-hand end, housing refreshment rooms, complete with beer cellar, and living accommodation. Though very much of its own time, the new block picked up some details, such as its roof massing and gauged-brick lintels, from the original station house. The former refreshment room, within the original station building, was adapted to provide an enlarged parcels and booking office.

The final public improvement came in 1891 when the station entrance was provided with the present cantilevered verandah, using some elaborate cast-iron brackets recovered from Stockton station, which was being rebuilt at the time.(11) 1904 brought problems with the roof trusses at the west end of the trainshed, so the last few bays running into the hipped end were rebuilt with new steel trusses finishing with a glazed gable, designed to lighten the interior.(12) Interestingly, the lenticular truss which had borne the original hip was retained as a feature.

By the early years of the Twentieth Century, Driffield station had reached its fullest extent. The same might be said of its passenger traffic, which peaked at 92,356 outward bookings in 1902.(13) The annual figures, averaged over five-year periods, remained in the range eighty to ninety thousand until 1925 but then slid to 57,414 per annum for 1926-30 and 38,572 for 1931-5 although they were actually showing signs of recovery towards the end of the latter period. As a consequence of fare increases, largely during the First World War, the revenue from passenger bookings was little altered, being £8,260 in 1935, compared with £8,238 in 1902, however, inflation meant that the real value of these earnings was much reduced.

Against a background of rising costs, falling patronage and static revenue, Driffield continued to employ a considerable number of staff. The station had a tradition of longevity, the pattern being set by Francis Warwick, stationmaster in 1851, who was still in post at the end of the eighteen-seventies. He combined the post with that of goods agent, as did his successor, Thomas House, who saw the railway through into the beginning of the Twentieth Century, while John Mais followed on into the First World War. After that terms in office were much shorter. Salaries in the early decades of the Twentieth Century were around £320, a fifth below Beverley, but stationmasters' coal sales were the highest on the line, with annual revenue averaging £208 in the period 1906-1920.

Plate 5.10. *Driffield station frontage in 1908, as work was ending on the enlargement of the stationmaster's house to provide a bathroom and other facilities; the scaffolding poles and new brickwork of this wing are clearly visible. At far right is the rather lumbering two-storey block of NER refreshment rooms and bedrooms. To the left of the 1891 entrance verandah we see one of the NER's Dürkopp motor buses. The NER's motor bus service to Driffield (from Beverley via Beeford) commenced on 1 December 1903, Thursdays only, though the bus seen here did not enter service until 1905. For further details, see Chapter 12. (Ken Hoole Study Centre Collection)*

Plate 5.11. *The early days of British Railways, with poster boards still proclaiming their allegiance to the LNER. Since 1908 the office facade has been disfigured by slapping through a shop frontage for WH Smith in place of the left-hand pair of windows. The trainshed roof is still there, but not for much longer, with glass missing from the left end of the skylight. (Ken Hoole Study Centre Collection, August - September 1948)*

All changed after the Second World War. The Malton line was weeded out in the early years of British Railways, losing its passenger service in 1950; Burdale Quarry, its main source of traffic, shut down in 1955 and the line closed altogether three years later. The branch to Market Weighton and Selby lost its local passenger service in 1954 though goods facilities were retained and the line continued to be used by holiday trains to Bridlington; however, the 1962-3 winter timetable shows just one regular passenger train in each direction, and total closure followed in 1965. The staffing economies eventually introduced by British Rail mean that Driffield station is now maintained by a peripatetic cleaning team and the booking office can be manned in one shift per day.

In 1949 the station trainshed was identified as being in need of further repairs so, to minimise future maintenance costs, it was unroofed and equipped with the present cantilevered steel awnings, which are serviceable if not elegant; the trainshed walls were also cut back at the west end. The office range has undergone some unfortunate surgery, having lost much of its slate roof and cornice in favour of ungainly cement cladding; this, however, could easily be remedied and the station generally presents a well-kept and inviting appearance, while the refreshment room block is let as a restaurant. A poignant reminder of the days when the forecourt was cluttered with sidings bustling with goods traffic is provided by the LNER pattern 'railhead store' which survives alongside the station car park. Built from pre-cast concrete panels and posts, it was one of many provided in rural areas for Silcocks, the cattle-feed manufacturers.

Plate 5.13. *John Fleming eloquently captured the railway scene in July 1970 with this view of the 1891 recycled Stockton verandah framing bicycles and one of BR's parcels delivery semi-trailer vans for use with the three-wheeled Scammell Mechanical Horse. The cast-iron brackets had probably been made for Stockton in the late 1870s. The poster on the right advertises bargain fares for shoppers travelling to Hull. (John M Fleming)*

Plate 5.12. *1970 view along the siding past a collection of period cars to the station house. At far right we see a pair of elegant windows, above which the station has lost its cornice and gained some corrugated cement roofing. (Bill Fawcett)*

Plate 5.14. *The Hull end of Driffield station circa 1908, showing the glazed gable which accompanied the modest trainshed extension carried out just 4 years earlier; the gate box looks as though it formed part of the same scheme. On the left is the refreshment-room block with the 1890 one-storey men's toilets in front. (Ken Hoole Study Centre Collection)*

Plate 5.15. *A view in the opposite direction to Plate 5.14, taken half a century later. Gresley Class V3 No 67663, a common sight on the route, heads into the station on 3 August 1959 with the 1-20 pm from Hull to Scarborough. We see the replacement platform roof, then just ten years old and made up from standard steel sections. That work may have been a spur for rebuilding the toilet block as the neat range which we see on the right but the platforms continued to be lit by gas. The poster informs us that 'There's no better job' than the police. (Neville Stead)*

List of NER and LNER Stationmasters

Francis Warwick [-1851-1879-]
Thomas House [-1887-1901-]
John Mais [-1905-1913-]
R Hinchcliffe [- retired 11 October 1919]
William James Chapman [1920- retired 1 September 1925] transferred from SM Market Weighton
EH Fowler [1925-1932] to SM Northallerton
T Allen [1932-1936] transferred to SM Bridlington
JT Batty [1936-1942] transferred to SM Beverley
J Dennis [1942-1945] transferred to SM Beverley
EW Hope [1945-]

Endnotes:

1. A valuable introduction to Driffield is provided by Stephen Harrison, *The History of Driffield,* Blackthorn Press, 2002. While its coverage extends to the end of the Twentieth Century, the focus inevitably becomes more selective after the mid nineteenth. Sources consulted for this chapter include Sheahan & Whellan, *History & Topography of York & the East Riding of Yorkshire volume 2,* 1856; directories; local newspapers and the ever-helpful large-scale Ordnance Survey, notably the 1891 survey at 1/500. The Navigation is covered in Harrison and also in Baron F Duckham, *The Inland Waterways of East Yorkshire: 1700-1900,* East Yorkshire Local History Society, 1972.

2. TNA (The National Archives, Kew) RAIL 527/64 NER Traffic Committee 6 November 1863 Min (Minute) 5529; 15 January 1864 Min 5613; 11 March Min 5671; 6 May Min 5745; RAIL 527/27 NER Locomotive Committee 3 June 1864 Min 6880. Contract let to Robson of Driffield at £679-7-9 and Mortimer to take it at a rent of $7^{1}/_{2}$% of this per annum. Drawings for the warehouse survive as Network Rail York 81/137.
3. TNA RAIL 527/26 NER Locomotive Committee 24 October 1862 Min 5914; 7 November Minute 5930.
4. TNA RAIL 527/64 NER Traffic Committee 16 February 1866 Min 6564.
5. TNA RAIL 527/2142 Station traffic annual totals 1902-35.
6. Milk siding put in during the 1930s but had been removed by 1981, with the traffic by then lost to road.
7. TNA RAIL 527/26 NER Locomotive Committee 21 November 1862 Min 5958; RAIL 527/40 NER Way & Works Committee 2 October 1890 Min 5848.
8. TNA RAIL 527/30 NER Locomotive Committee 27 June 1873 Min 13138; 19 September Min 13312.
9. TNA RAIL 527/67 NER Traffic Committee 11 May 1876 Min 11111; 8 June 1876 Min 11137; RAIL 527/32 NER Locomotive Committee 26 October 1876 Min 17211; 21 December Min 17350; 1 February 1877 Min 17460. Contract let for £444-2-6 to Henry Brown, of Malton, father-in-law of William Bell, who would become NER Architect from 1877.
10. TNA RAIL 527/37 NER Way & Works Committee 11 October 1883 Min 760 and 20 December Min 1010 for the footbridge. (RAIL 527/40) 5 March 1890 Min 5436; 19 June Min 5667 for the enlargement.

Plate 5.16. *A May 2010 view of the Up platform, showing the arches cut through for its widening in 1874; inset picture shows the NER fireplace surviving in the waiting room further along that platform. (Bill Fawcett)*

Plate 5.17. *North of the station, probably in early 1961, with a Hull - Bridlington train passing a recently-acquired Matissa track-recording vehicle. This is standing in the engineer's siding (still extant today) in front of the wall which bounded the coal cells. (Ken Hoole Study Centre Collection)*

Plate 5.18. *Class K3 No 61947 crossing Wansford Road with an excursion from Sheffield (Meadowhall) to Bridlington on 3 August 1959. Wansford box has deep windows at the far end, to give a good outlook along the road, and has been lengthened by one bay at this end, where its neighbour is the usual Andrews pair of crossing cottages. On the left is the siding into the former oil-cake mill, latterly used, in part, for the production of sugar cake decorations. (Neville Stead)*

11. TNA RAIL 527/40 NER Way & Works Committee 19 March 1891 Min 6251 William Bell reported that the verandah of North Stockton station had now been taken down and was authorised to re-erect it at Driffield. RAIL 527/644 Contract Summaries: work began on 4 May 1891 and the final cost was £63-14-5.

12. TNA RAIL 527/47 NER Locomotive Committee 3 March 1904 Min 15811; 28 April Min 15881. The firm of Andrew Handyside supplied the steelwork but the work seems to have been carried out by the staff of the southern division engineer, William John Cudworth, rather than being let out.

13. TNA RAIL 527/2142.

Plate 5.19. *Driffield Station Gates. (Ken Hoole Study Centre Collection)*

Plate 5.20. *View from Wansford box showing the milk works with a van standing on its siding, the rails of which are set, tramway fashion, into a road surface. Class B16 No 61411 holds centre stage, heading south. (John F Mallon)*

Plate 5.21. *The north end of Driffield, with Class K1 No 62007 heading an excursion train from Normanton to Bridlington past the cattle dock. Road access to this was round the back of Wansford signalbox, which can be glimpsed to the right of the signal. The date was 3 August 1959, and the engine was just ten years old. (Neville Stead)*

Chapter 6 : Bridlington

John F Addyman, Bill Fawcett and the late Ken Hoole

When the railway opened there were two distinct settlements linked by Quay Road: Bridlington Quay, beside the harbour, and Bridlington Old Town, situated around the ancient priory a mile further inland. There had been a harbour from the Eleventh Century, and by 1700 its usage had increased to handle malt, grain, wool, tea, salt, coal and, of course, local fish. In 1704, 48 out of the 833 ships used in the east-coast coal trade had Bridlington owners, and landed about 2,500 tons at the harbour – by 1820 this had risen to 16,000 tons. Nineteenth Century imports from the continent grew to include timber, bones, stone, bricks and foodstuffs, and its bay provided a 'harbour of refuge' for vessels to shelter from storms. By 1820 there were 145 Bridlington-owned ships, and the 1840s saw the completion of the protracted rebuilding of the harbour to accommodate them. However, the coming of the railway, in the same decade, and the growing facilities at Hull Docks meant that by 1872 their trade had seriously diminished with only one ship left.(1) The Harbour Commissioners had seen this coming and had petitioned Parliament, without success, against the railway Bill (see Chapter 1).

The combined population of the Old Town and Quay was 3,130 in 1801, and it saw a steady increase to 9,500 by the end of the Nineteenth Century. By 1900 the two towns were firmly joined, outlying villages were becoming engulfed, and the development continued apace during the Twentieth Century with the population reaching nearly 34,000 by 2001.(2) In 1932 the LNER had reported on Bridlington's traffic potential: 'There are extensive housing developments and the town is growing in popularity as a residential place'.

Between 1770 and 1820, Bridlington Quay had developed from an 'inconsiderable village to become a neat, lively and prosperous town', and seems to have provoked jealousy in the Old Town, which was resting on its laurels.(3) When the final route, to link up the two railways, became known in 1844 around 200 residents of the Old Town sent a memorial to the directors of the Hull & Selby Railway complaining that the proposed station was to be nearer to Bridlington Quay than to the Old Town, instead of midway between them – a variation of about 300 yards! They considered:

> The Town of Bridlington is the ancient and parent Town of the Parish, where the bulk of the inhabitants reside [Quay 1,800, Bridlington 4,000], and nine-tenths of the trade is carried on. That all the banks, the post office and the excise office are at the town. There the professions reside and there the Petty Sessions held. There is also the resort of the commercial travellers. The business of the markets, fairs and statutes is there carried on. There is the Corn Exchange where thousands of quarters of corn are sold throughout the year, and there the Town Hall for transaction of public business is situate.

They expected 'immediate compliance' but did not get it.(4) The growth of tourism, and not the position of the station, was to move the commercial centre away from the Old Town to the seaward side of the railway.

Plate 6.1. *A view taken prior to the First World War showing crowds of holidaymakers thronging Bridlington harbour.*

Table 6.1: showing a peak in tickets issued in 1920, but arrivals still increasing in 1935.(5)

Year	Tickets Issued	Passenger Revenue*	Tickets Collected
1885	72,597	£9,633	#
1890	85,687	£11,454	#
1895	95,189	£12,980	#
1900	119,573	£18,067	#
1905	119,800	£18,185	#
1910	124,983	£20,841	#
1915	103,661	£20,982	205,504
1920	191,606	£66,701	431,636
1925	144,651	£49,249	441,510
1930	86,475	£36,177	385,447
1935	86,392	£38,111	501,157

* including parcels. # not available.

With the railway's arrival tourism took off, and was boosted by the rapid provision of the typical Victorian visitor-attractions near the seafront. By 1900 there were nearly 300 establishments offering holiday accommodation in Bridlington Quay, but only around 20 in the Old Town. With the inducement of reduced fares day-trippers also swarmed in (see Table 6.1 and Plate 6.1), and soon around a quarter of the working population was employed in catering and holiday accommodation. The expansion of the town and tourism required the NER to provide additional facilities to deal with the growing numbers of commuters and holidaymakers as explained in the next section.

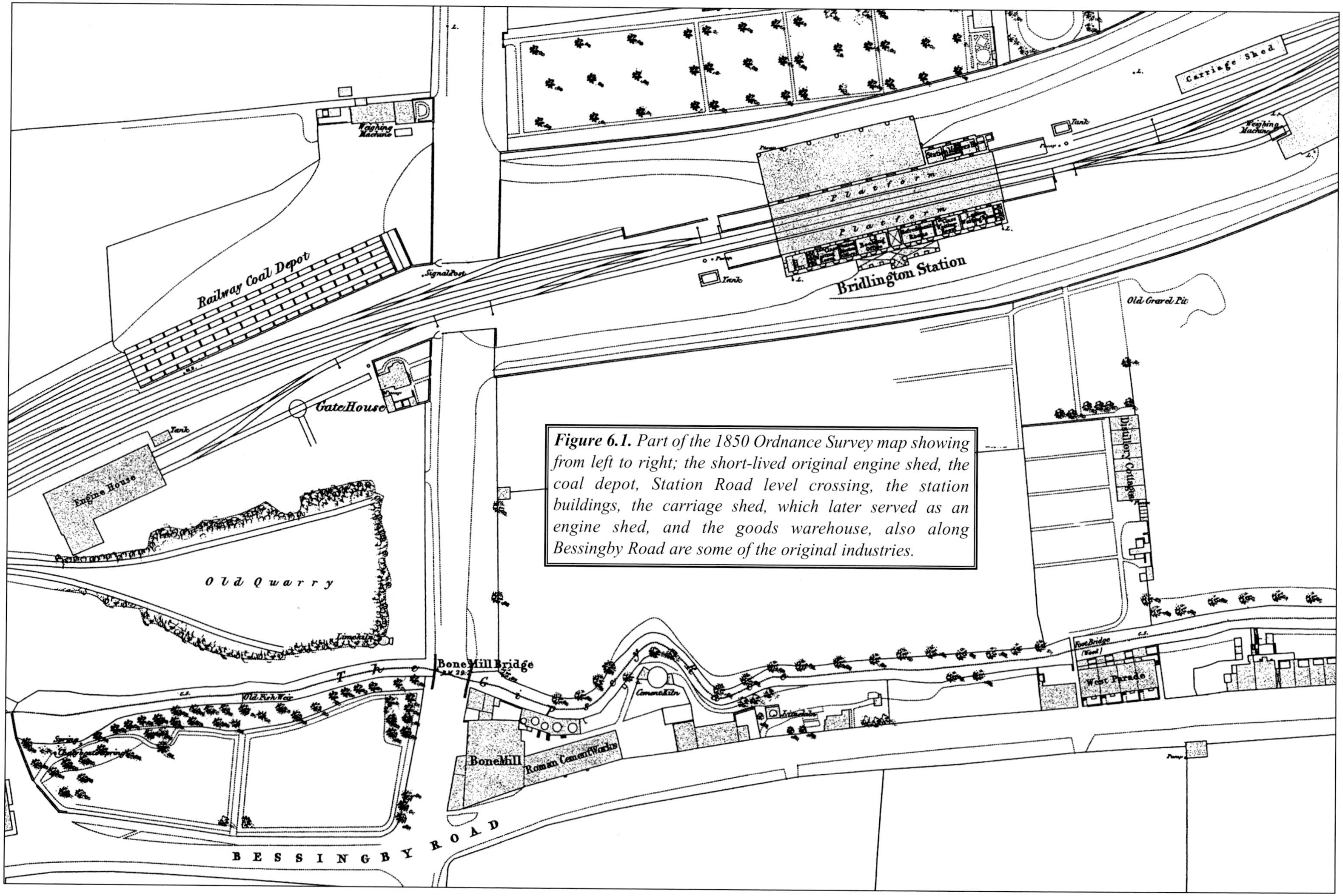

Figure 6.1. *Part of the 1850 Ordnance Survey map showing from left to right; the short-lived original engine shed, the coal depot, Station Road level crossing, the station buildings, the carriage shed, which later served as an engine shed, and the goods warehouse, also along Bessingby Road are some of the original industries.*

Bridlington Station (6)

Today's visitor to Bridlington encounters a stylish station of 1912, whose spacious concourse has an arched roof, rather like a miniature trainshed, leading through to an Up platform and bay covered by an elegant glass verandah. Cross the footbridge and one is in a different world, with a bare Down platform backed by the modest remnant of the 1846 entrance building. All this no more than hints at a complex building history, which saw the station expand in three phases: 1873, 1892 and 1912; only to be pruned back in two stages: 1961 and the 1980s.

The original station comprised a trainshed like those at Driffield and Filey fronted by a one-storey office range with a colonnaded portico, serving the Up platform. Behind the trainshed was a second, shorter span forming a cabstand for the Down platform and supported at its outer edge on a cast-iron arcade; the stationmaster's house was a slender range attached to the rear wall of the trainshed (see Figure 3.4).

The weekend holiday traffic outgrew these premises and in 1873-4 the platforms were lengthened by 50% at the west end, the trainshed being extended to match.(7) (Figure 6.2) The platforms were also widened, so that the Up one took in the site of the adjoining track and the Down one was moved over, continuing through the rear wall of the trainshed, which was opened up with arches, as at Driffield. To increase the office and waiting room accommodation, the refreshment rooms were moved into a new two-storey range at the west end, tactfully set back from the original frontage by Benjamin Burleigh, NER assistant architect, who included first-floor sitting and bedrooms and a wine and beer cellar. It took a further ten years to obtain a footbridge (1884) and five more to get rid of the stationmaster's house, which was an obstruction to the Down platform: in 1889 he was built a new one between the goods yard and Quay Road.(8)

The second enlargement was begun in July 1892, and involved further platform lengthening plus the provision of a bay on the Up side and a separate excursion station on a site some way to the south.(9) To accommodate the additional tracks, Station Road level crossing, at the west end, was replaced by an overbridge with ramped access down to the station frontage, where William Bell (NER Architect 1877-1914) replaced the elegant colonnade with a glazed verandah. His extension to the trainshed was roofed

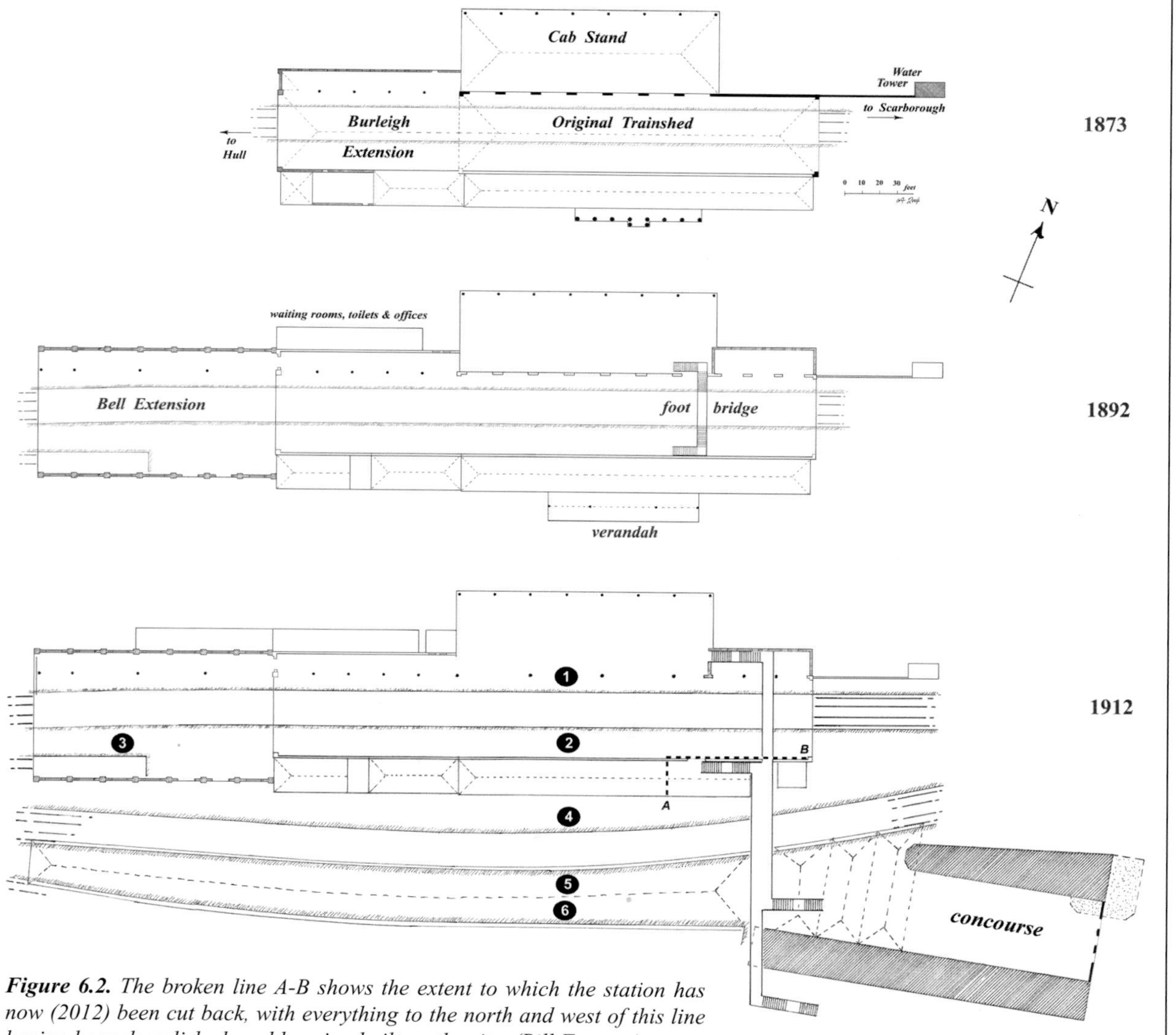

Figure 6.2. The broken line A-B shows the extent to which the station has now (2012) been cut back, with everything to the north and west of this line having been demolished, and housing built on the site. (Bill Fawcett)

with a higher and wider span than the original, ending in glazed gables and employing pairs of trussed rafters rather than the Euston truss of the earlier roof. The Down platform also received some long-overdue toilets and general and ladies' waiting rooms. Well into the work, Bell persuaded his directors to employ savings on some contracts to improve the Down platform circulation by substituting columns and girders for the original rear wall.

At the end of all this, the station still had just two through platforms and a short bay, far from sufficient to cope adequately with all the trains being handled at summer weekends. The NER Act of 1890 had also included powers to replace the level crossing of Bessingby Road by a bridge, and in 1901 the company's officers recommended that this work proceed along with the purchase of additional land as a possible site for a new goods station.(10) Their view

Plate 6.2. *Bridlington station frontage in an 1880s photograph. On the left is the two-storey range added to accompany the first extension to the trainshed in 1873. To the right is the original one-storey frontage, with its prominent portico which would be removed in 1892. (Ken Hoole Study Centre Collection)*

Plate 6.3. *This provides an illuminating contrast with Plate 6.2, showing the same area before 1961 from a viewpoint about thirty feet further back. On the left is the final 1892 extension to the trainshed, with holidaymakers waiting to board the southbound train, headed by B1 No 61084. It is drawing into Platform 4, which was built in front of the original station facade in 1912. At the same time, Platforms 5 and 6 were added, graced by the elegant glass roof seen on the right. (Ken Hoole Study Centre Collection)*

was that the existing goods yard would be absorbed by further extensions to the passenger station; they no doubt realised also that some of the yard would be required if an overbridge were ever to be provided in place of the busy Quay Road level crossing. Bessingby Road bridge was built but nothing was done about the station, provoking the Mayor of Bridlington, CG Southcott, to hold a public meeting on 5 March 1909, which passed a resolution urging the NER to provide better and safer station accommodation for the burgeoning traffic.(11)

Under the combined urging of their own officers and the local citizenry the NER directors finally gave way and carried out the very thorough enlargement of 1911-12, which doubled the platform accommodation.(12) In an ingenious scheme, which avoided encroaching on the goods yard, the new platforms were placed in front of the existing station, even though this entailed destroying the arched ramp down from the twenty-year-old bridge, a task done in a spectacular manner (13) (Plates 6.4, 6.5 and 6.6). This gave the station four through platforms and a bay, ranging in length between about four and five hundred feet, plus the short bay of 1892.

The new concourse is on a much larger scale than the old offices and is built in smooth red brick with faience details in a finish closely replicating sandstone but easy to keep clean; a fine example of this is the array of booking windows. For a decade the refreshment rooms remained in the earlier building but in 1919 plans were made to move them to the concourse. The first scheme was drawn up by Arthur Pollard, Bell's long-term deputy and successor as Architect. This provided for a single general refreshment room adjoining the station entrance but the directors changed their minds and decided to have a

Plate 6.4. *Work has begun in 1911 for the doubling of the platform accommodation. To the right can be seen the curving edge of what would become Platform 6. To the left, the windows of the Bell extension of 1892 have been boarded up. In between, what remains of the arched ramp is being prepared for demolition by explosives. (Ken Hoole Study Centre Collection)*

Plate 6.5. *BANG! (John M Richardson Collection)*

distinct First Class room as well. The scheme was therefore reworked by Pollard's successor, Stephen Wilkinson, and carried out in 1922-3.(14) The class distinctions have long vanished but the premises retain their original features: the smaller First Class room has some particularly attractive woodwork.

Little changed in the following four decades, but in 1961 British Railways decided to unroof the trainshed and install cantilevered steel awnings of the type seen at Driffield. This was more expensive than carrying out the repairs then required, but it was seen as yielding big economies in long-term maintenance and, somewhat fatuously, as helping to project a 'modern' image. In the event, this was money wasted. The sixties brought a decline in the railway's holiday business, due not just to road competition but also the beginnings of cheap air travel to overseas resorts. Holiday and excursion trains faded out during the seventies, meaning that all Bridlington's traffic could be handled at the 1912 platforms. The remainder were abandoned in March 1983, their site lying empty for some years before being developed for housing. All that remains of the Victorian station today is the eastern part of the 1846 frontage, chopped through by the 1912 footbridge and forming a screen wall to a waiting hall at the bottom of its steps.

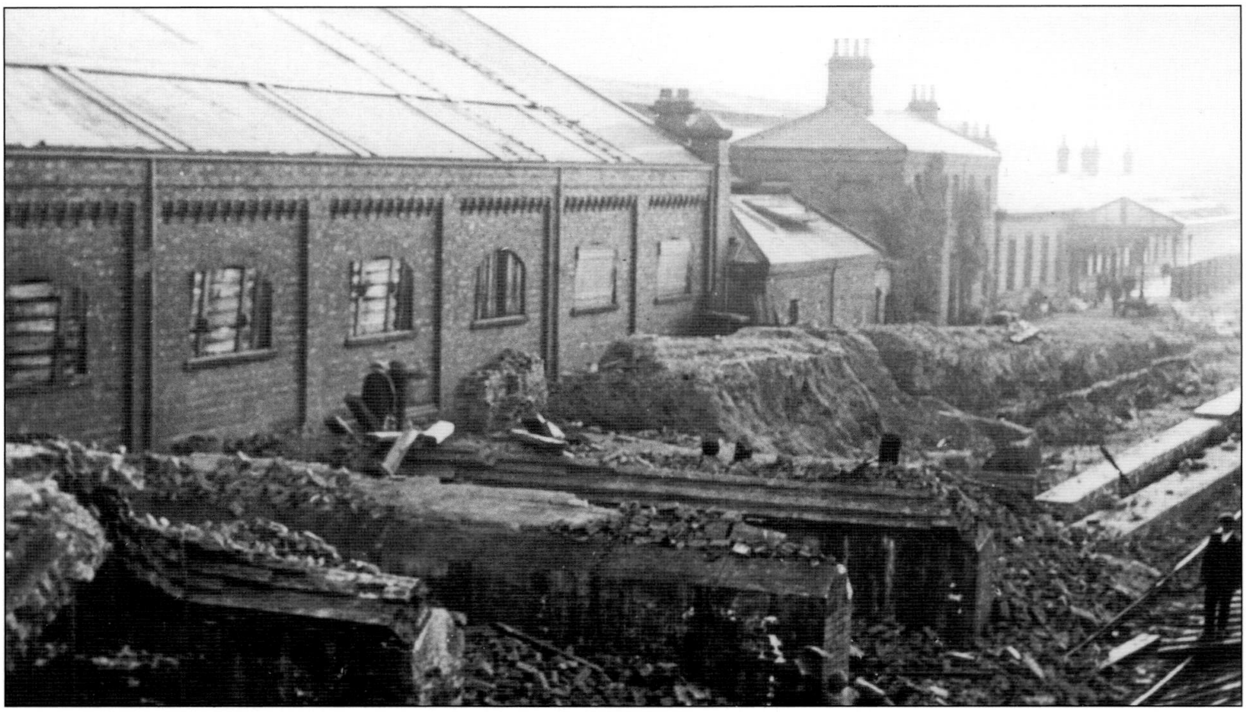

Plate 6.6. *The aftermath. (Ken Hoole Study Centre Collection)*

Plate 6.7. *Progress being made with glazing the 1912 roof over Platforms 5 and 6. As soon as the glass has been installed, the NER's distinctive cast-iron gutter and valancing will be added to the eaves, as seen on the right. Because of its broader span, the 1892 phase of the trainshed roof bulks larger at left than the remainder of that structure. At far right we glimpse the gable of the 1912 concourse. (Ken Hoole Study Centre Collection)*

Plate 6.8. *The 1912 frontage of the station with the 1922 refreshment room to the right. For an interior view of the 1912 concourse, see Colour Plate 5 (page 28). (Bill Fawcett)*

Plate 6.9. *John Mallon took this atmospheric view, looking north through the station, no later than 1960. From William Bell's 1892 trainshed, with its Polonceau trusses, we see into the original station as lengthened in 1873; the front car of the DMU lies partly within this extension. To the left, a brick pier marks the end of the 1873 work, beyond which is the line of columns which replaced the rear wall in about 1893. The wall had previously been opened up with arches to permit platform widening and an associated slewing over of the tracks. Platform 2's line of gas lamps is strongly evocative of the British Railways era, but they would soon be going, along with the trainshed itself. (John F Mallon / Joint NERA - Ken Hoole Study Centre JF Mallon Collection)*

Plate 6.10. *From Station Road bridge (circa 1960) we see the original cabstand and lengthened trainshed, with the broader and higher 1892 roof bulking large to the right. (John F Mallon / Joint NERA - Ken Hoole Study Centre JF Mallon Collection)*

Plate 6.11. *May 1961 and Tom Rounthwaite captures the dismal process of demolition. The original trainshed has already been unroofed; the 1892 one has been completely stripped, and the cabstand has lost its slates. The Platform 2 offices and 1892 trainshed wall will be retained, and soon the new cantilevered steel platform awnings will take shape alongside, while gas lamps, like that in the foreground, will give way to neat fluorescent tubes. No replacement was deemed necessary for the cabstand. (Tom Rounthwaite)*

Figure 6.3 (below). *The siding diagram for Bridlington showing the facilities available in 1926. Siding No 66 is on the alignment of the start of the Harbour Branch (LNER / NERA Collection)*

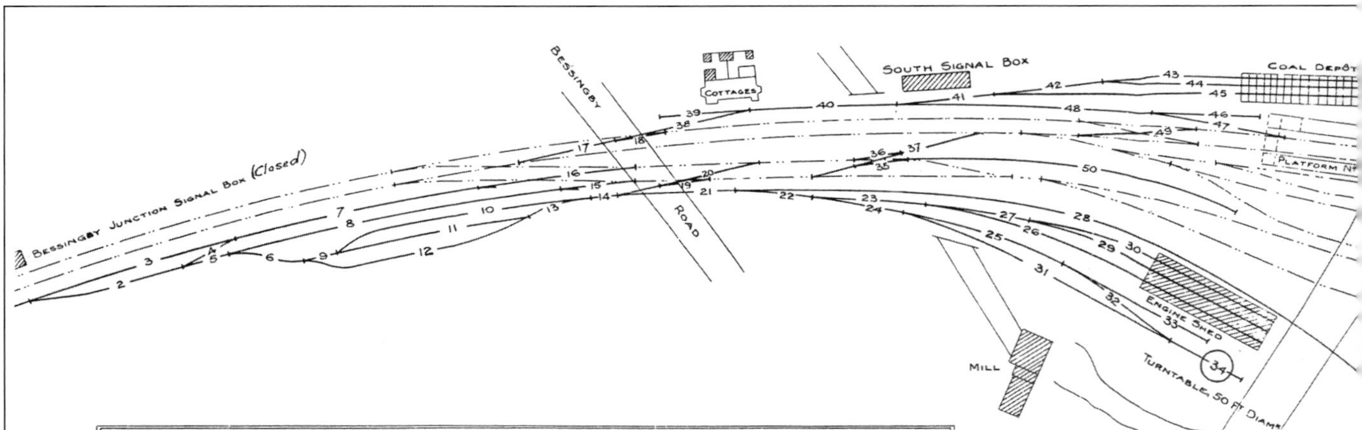

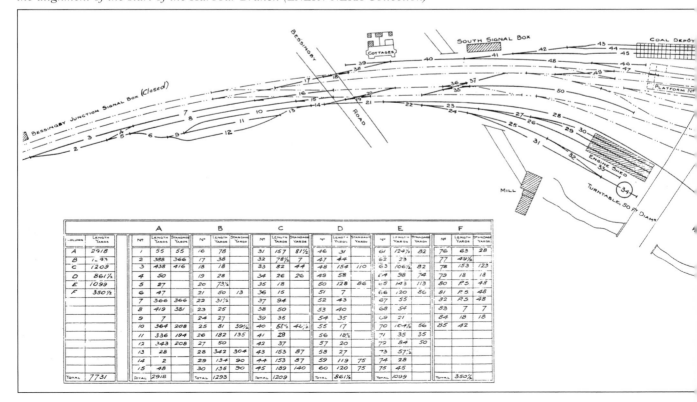

		A			B			C			D			E			F		
Column	Length Yards	Nº	Length Yards	Standage Yards	Nº	Length Yards	Standage Yards	Nº	Length Yards	Standage Yards	Nº	Length Yards	Standage Yards	Nº	Length Yards	Standage Yards	Nº	Length Yards	Standage Yards
A	2918	1	55	55	16	78		31	157	81½	46	31		61	124½	82	76	63	28
B	1293	2	388	366	17	38		32	78½	7	47	44		62	23		77	49½	
C	1209	3	438	416	18	18		33	82	44	48	154	110	63	106½	82	78	153	123
D	861½	4	50		19	28		34	26	26	49	58		64	98	74	79	18	18
E	1099	5	27		20	73½		35	18		50	128	86	65	143	113	80	P.S.	48
F	350½	6	47		21	50	13	36	15		51	7		66	120	86	81	P.S.	48
		7	366	366	22	31½		37	94		52	43		67	55		82	P.S.	48
		8	419	381	23	25		38	50		53	40		68	54		83	7	7
		9	7		24	27		39	35		54	35		69	21		84	18	18
		10	364	208	25	81	39½	40	52½	42½	55	17		70	104½	56	85	42	
		11	336	194	26	182	135	41	28		56	18½		71	35	35			
		12	343	208	27	50		42	37		57	20		72	84	50			
		13	28		28	342	304	43	153	87	58	27		73	57½				
		14	2		29	134	90	44	153	87	59	119	75	74	28				
		15	48		30	135	90	45	189	140	60	120	75	75	45				
Total	7731	Total	2918		Total	1293		Total	1209		Total	861½		Total	1099		Total	350½	

Goods Traffic

When the railway opened, in addition to the agricultural trade, there were several mills, a cement works, a bone mill for the manufacture of fertilizer, breweries, foundries, agricultural implement makers, gravel pits, quarries and a gasworks. The gasworks was re-sited from midway between the two towns to be next to the railway, and was served by sidings with their own coal cells until it closed in 1968. The railway provided a large goods shed to the design of GT Andrews, 19 coal cells (each served by three tracks), a loading dock and some sidings – two to serve the almost defunct chalk quarry. The industries that existed before the railway have all disappeared, but new ones were introduced after the Second World War on industrial estates, and provide limited employment.

In 1845 a branch, about three-eighths of a mile long, was authorized from the station to the harbour; it was completed in 1851, but, with the decline in use of the harbour, it totally failed to live up to expectations.(15) It was disused by 1866, but remained in situ until 1917. A scheme to revive and extend it on to the pier was proposed to the NER directors, on 6 June 1879, by the Bridlington Quay North Sea Fishing Company. The NER engineer reviewed the scheme and concluded that the cost of re-opening the branch would be nearly £3,800, and that a locomotive would have to be stationed in Bridlington to work the traffic on the 1 in 33 gradients (suggesting that there was no shunting locomotive based there at that time). Wisely, the directors did not think 'that the business to be carried out by the Fishing Company would be materially affected by the fact of their being obliged to cart their fish from the Harbour to the Station, as this has to be done in many other important fishing places', and refused the application.(16)

Plate 6.12. *At 11-05 am on 11 July 1940, German bombers made a daylight raid on the town causing damage to the timber end of the goods warehouse, and setting fire to some ammunition wagons in the goods yard. Three railwaymen received George Medals for their bravery following the incident. The damaged end of the warehouse, shown in this newspaper cutting, was never rebuilt even though it had been modified as recently as 1938 to provide two extra bays for lorries.*

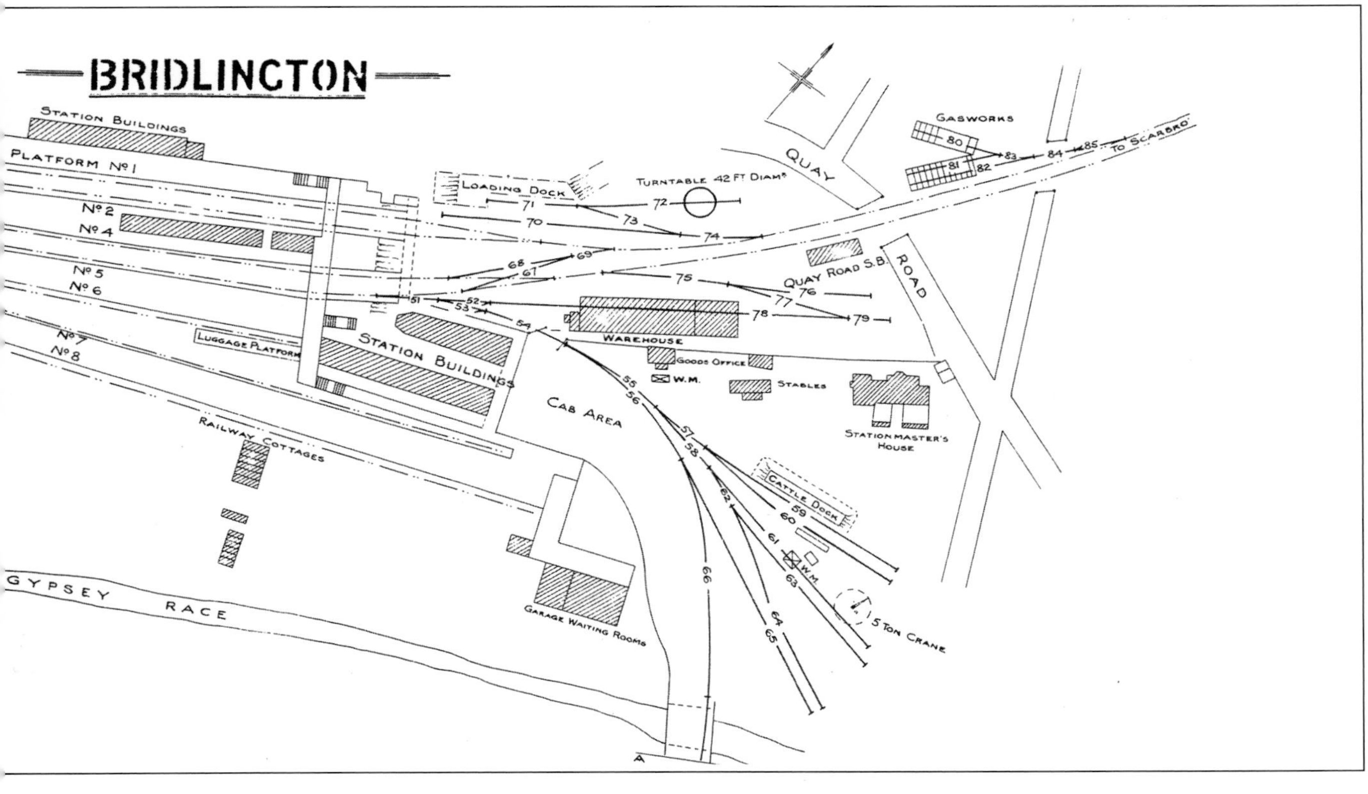

Plate 6.13. *The route of the former Bridlington Harbour Branch on 8 August 1962. (Ken Hoole / Ken Hoole Study Centre Collection)*

The following figures (Table 6.2) show that the fish traffic was not significant, particularly when compared with Scarborough which forwarded around 7,000 tons and Hull over 100,000. The total of forwarded traffic was never very large: for example, in 1913 it only came to 12,000 tons whereas inward goods, almost a half coal, were nearly 70,000 tons. All the coal was distributed by coal merchants until 1912 when the stationmaster entered the business, in a small way, earning him an average annual profit of £29. In 1923 it was by-products from the gasworks that made up a third of the total outward goods traffic. Livestock in NER days averaged about 11,000 heads per annum with twice as many being received as forwarded. After 1930 goods traffic started its terminal decline; December 1976 saw the coal siding 'out of use pending removal',(17) but while the goods shed had been dispensed with, public facilities for other goods still lingered until the mid-1980s.

Table 6.2: the LNER's comparison of goods traffic forwarded.(18)

Bridlington	**1913**	**1923**	**1924**
Grain	2,928	2,380	2,873
Gas Water [ammonia]	1,040	1,074	1,218
Timber, Round	898	106	#
Scrap, iron and steel	367	552	172
Creosote, Tar and Pitch	331	2760	219
Fish	310	477	432
Manure	284	605	1,499
Timber	204	#	#
Ale & Ale Empties	139	105	129
Gravel & Sand	136	130	#
Livestock, wagon loads	251	326	335
Iron Ore	#	#	250

less than 100 tons.

Locomotive Facilities

Figure 6.1 shows the original two-road engine shed, 15-feet diameter turntable and water tanks, which were almost certainly provided for the line's opening in 1846, when Bridlington was a terminus. After the line was completed through to Scarborough, in the following year, it appears that the engine shed had little use since the 1891 Ordnance Survey shows all its tracks removed and the building described as a warehouse; see Figure 6.4.(19) A Locomotive Committee minute for 17 June 1875 states that the NER accepted a tender of £522 for 'a new engine shed', but minutes are often misleading.(20) There was no new engine shed at this time, and the minute probably refers to the conversion of the original carriage shed, at the Scarborough end of the station, into a building to house one locomotive. This was accessible only by a 42-feet diameter turntable that had been provided by I'Anson & Company in 1871 for £375; see Figure 6.3, siding No 72. With the rapid growth of normal and excursion traffic this small shed became totally inadequate, and, to meet current and future requirements, a contract was let in June 1892 at a price of £3,439 for a three-road shed to house nine locomotives; alongside was installed a 50-feet diameter turntable (extended to 55 feet in 1929), provided by Cowans Sheldon for £385.(21) (See Colour Plate 7 on page 29.) The shed lay east of the original one, which was demolished to accommodate the approach tracks. The old shed had been tenanted as warehousing by Medforth & Hutchinson (corn and feed merchants), so the NER provided them with new, rail-served premises east of Station Road. These were built in 1892 at a cost of £1,161 and the firm continued in business until 1969.(22)

Water for the locomotives was initially pumped from the Gypsey Race to three tanks: one by the shed and one at each end of the station, the latter pair holding 4,500 gallons each (see Figure 3.7 on page 26). The 1873 station enlargement meant the west-end tank had to be re-erected adjacent to Station Road. Twenty years on, its ironwork was re-used to double the height of the east-end one when the new engine shed was accompanied by a 25,000 gallons tank; by this time the water was supplied by Bridlington Corporation. Three water columns were situated in the station, and one in the shed yard.(23)

Bridlington never had a locomotive coaling stage, and engines based there needed to replenish at Hull, Scarborough or other destinations. The Sentinel steam-shunters had to get their supplies direct from wagons, and locomotives on excursions were expected to have enough in their tenders to get them back home or go to Scarborough to top up. The 1912 improvements included provision of carriage sidings on the Hull side of Bessingby Road Bridge, but as weekend excursions increased these were only capable of accommodating half the trains, the remainder were stabled as far afield as Driffield and, on Sundays after the Second World War, at Filey Holiday Camp.

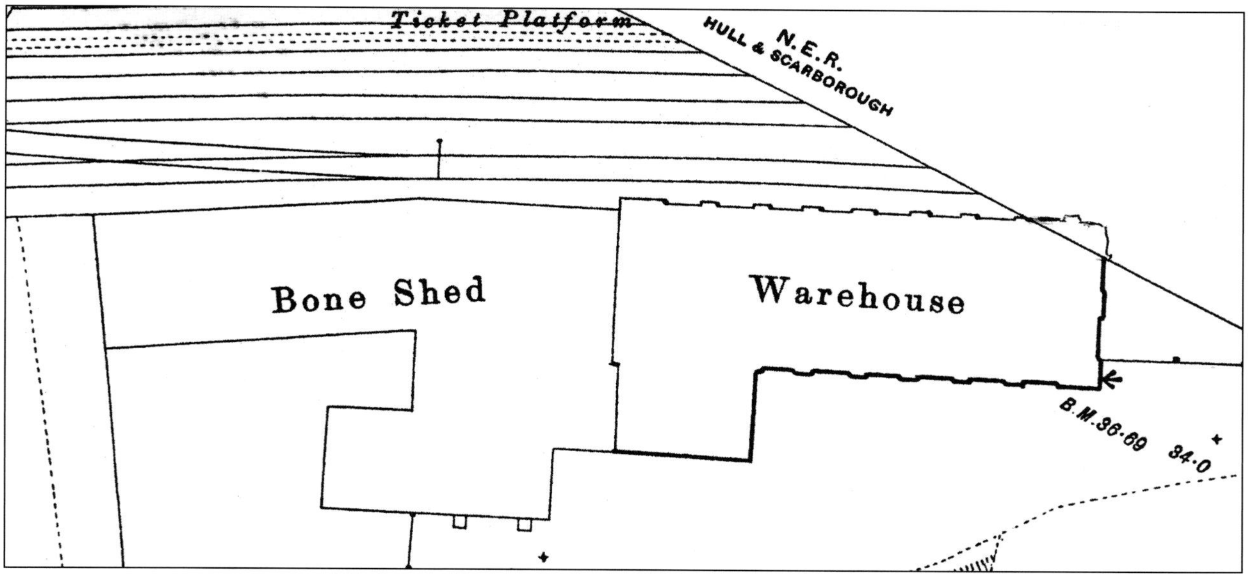

Figure 6.4. *A vignette from the 1891 Ordnance Survey map showing the original shed extended and used as warehousing without rail connections. Part of the ticket platform can be seen at the top.*

Plate 6.14. *A postcard view of the almost brand new engine shed showing the typical motive power used on the branch around 1900; 2-4-0s for the passenger traffic (No 1101, 40 Class, and No 274, Class G1) and on the right the first of the 59 Class 0-6-0s for the freight. To the left of the locomotives is the brick wall of the coal cells, and in front of that is the end of the wooden platform used for collecting tickets before Bridlington became a 'closed' station. (E Pouteau / Ken Hoole Study Centre Collection)*

Plate 6.15. *A view taken from the top of a signal showing a typical line up of weekend motive power on a summer afternoon in the 1950s. Classes represented are: B1, B16, D49, K3 and ex LMS Black Fives. (Ken Hoole Study Centre Collection)*

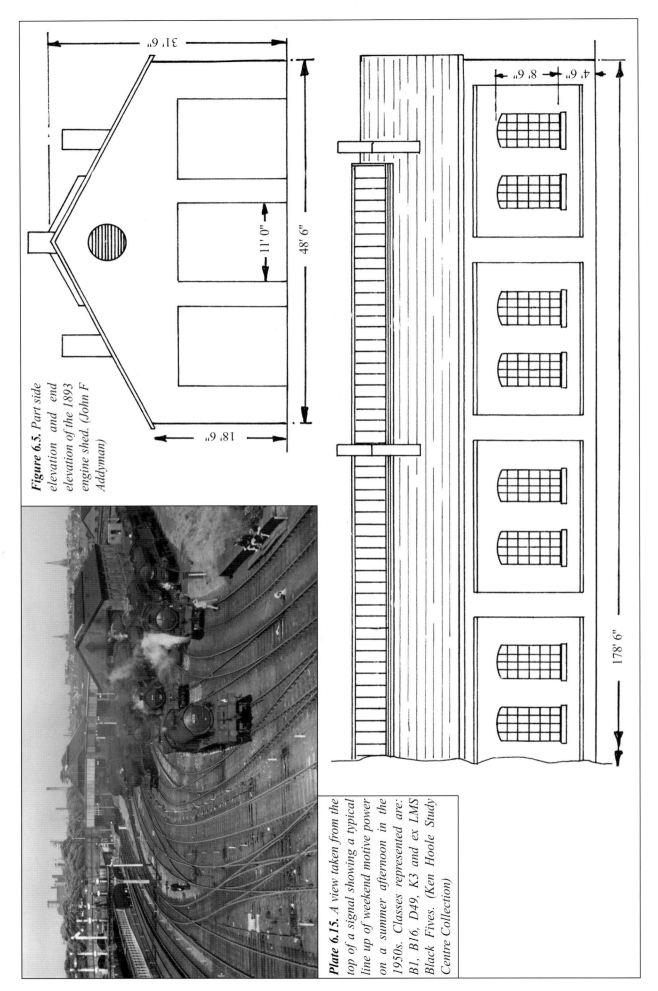

Figure 6.5. *Part side elevation and end elevation of the 1893 engine shed. (John F Addyman)*

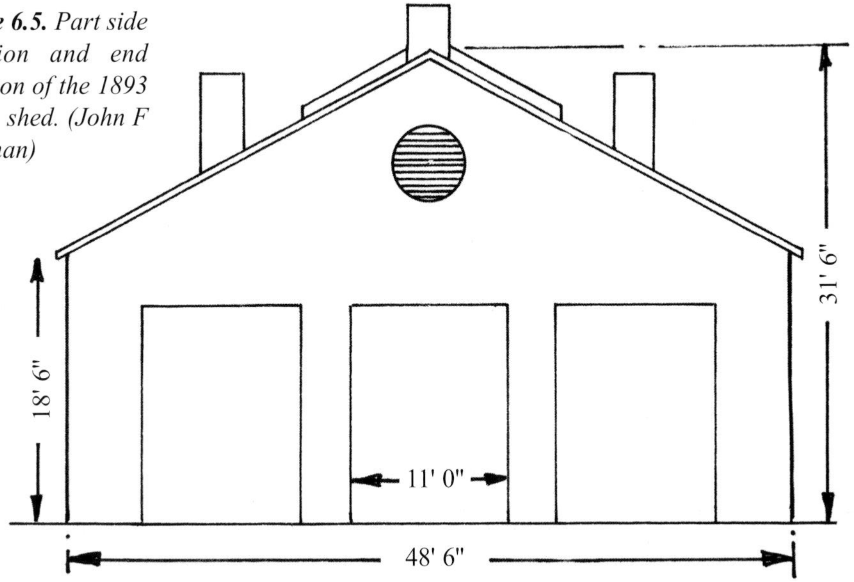

Plate 6.16. *In May 1959 the Institution of Water Engineers visited some new treatment works near Driffield and their secretary, railway enthusiast and author WO Skeat, thought it would be appropriate if part of the rail journey could be behind one of the few remaining Class B12s. No 61577 was chosen, but finished its journey with a hot box. Here we see a fireman transferring coal from its tender to its replacement, Class B1 No 61377, at Bridlington shed on 14 May 1959. (Ken Hoole / Ken Hoole Study Centre Collection)*

Locomotive Allocations

As a young man the railway historian Ken Hoole (1916-1988) lived in Bridlington, and the comprehensive description of the duties worked by its shed in his *North Eastern Locomotive Sheds* (1972) is reproduced here, with some updating and the permission of the publishers.

The duties of the shed were almost wholly passenger workings to Hull, Scarborough and Leeds, and on these turns, before World War 1, Class 901 and Class 1265 2-4-0s were used. From 1914 Class G 4-4-0s took over and these were replaced by seven (later eight) of the larger Class F (LNER D22) until 1925 when they were, in turn, replaced by a similar number of Class M (LNER D17/1) 4-4-0s. The following year the Smith three-cylinder compound, No 1619, went to Bridlington, and it worked from there until withdrawn in October 1930 – still in LNER green livery.

The D17/1 engines spent some nine years at Bridlington, and in that time they put in some really good work and were popular with their crews, handling trains of four to six coaches in the winter months and up to ten on summer Saturdays. They also put up some speedy running, perhaps not to be wondered at after their exploits in the 1895 races to Aberdeen, when only a couple of years old. One turn involved running the 8-05 am Bridlington to Hull train over the $30^3/_4$ miles in 37 minutes. Speeds of 70mph were regularly obtained between Driffield and Beverley, and the journey was often accomplished in 34 or 35 minutes, provided a clear run into Hull Paragon station was obtained. Another interesting turn was that involving two trips to Leeds and back, commencing with the 7-52 am from Bridlington and ending with the 4-52 pm from Leeds. The intermediate trips at 10-40 am Leeds to Bridlington, and 2-12 pm Bridlington to Leeds ran during the summer months only. Prior to World War 1 Bridlington men worked the express service to Sheffield with Class J 'singles'.

Bridlington shed used about ten sets of men daily, most engines being double-shifted, with one engine on boiler wash-out and one spare each day. The Sentinel six-cylinder steam railcar, No 2245 *Criterion,* was allocated to Bridlington from February 1931 until April 1941. In 1932 the ten duties were reduced to nine and spit into links of three and six turns; the three sets of men worked both on locomotives and the railcar, whilst the other six were employed solely on locomotives. By this time there were also two Sentinel steam shunters at Bridlington; No 174 for shunting the local goods yard, and No 100 for shunting Driffield each day. As two men were required on the footplate, when 100 was running to Driffield, a shunter was trained to ride with the driver, and they also shunted the yards of the intermediate stations. In August 1934 Bridlington received two new Class D49/2 engines from Darlington Works, No 230 *The Brocklesby* and No 238 *The Burton*: the only two engines known to have gone new to the shed! However, Hull soon got its covetous eyes on this pair, and in 1935 they were exchanged for older D49/3 engines No 318 *Cambridgeshire* and No 335 *Bedfordshire*; the former was renowned in the area for its extremely bad riding.

In 1939 the great redistribution of motive power in the North Eastern Area brought the transfer of six Class C6 4-4-2s to Bridlington in June and July (Nos 700, 742, 784, 1776, 1792 and 1794). What a comedown for these Atlantics, once the pride of the ECML between York and Edinburgh. Bridlington men certainly did not like them and did not want them; they were too big and clumsy after the engines they had been used to, and, with no drop grate and only limited facilities at the small depot, the fire took much more throwing out at the end of the day. In addition Class D20 4-4-0 Nos 1234 and 2016 joined the Atlantics.

After 18 months at Bridlington, increased wartime traffic meant that the Atlantics could be much better used on the main line again; four left for Heaton and two for Gateshead in November and December 1940. At this time the services worked by Bridlington shed were severely curtailed, and in place of the six Atlantics only two Class D20 Nos 2024 and 2101 were sent. D20 No 1234 was withdrawn in May 1943, and 1078 eventually arrived from Gateshead as a replacement. 1947 saw the same four D20s, by now renumbered 2345/53/60/83, but between 1947 and 1951 there were frequent exchanges of D20s between Bridlington and other sheds; Nos 62355/62/65/75/87/97 all spent a period there. In 1949 D49 engines returned in the shape of 62701 and 62707, followed in 1950 by 62703, 62750 and 62766, and the class worked the passenger trains until displaced by diesel multiple units (DMUs) in September 1957.

The run-down of the Sentinel shunters in the 1950s led to two new classes being allocated to Bridlington when the last Sentinel No 68148 (formerly 174) left in December 1953 after almost 25 years. It was replaced by Class N8 0-6-2T No 69378. Later two Class G5 0-4-4T (Nos 67280 and 67341) appeared, and these were the last steam locomotives to be stationed there; they departed on 8 June 1958, and the shed closed on 1 December. With the departure of steam, there were initially four DMUs stabled overnight, but by the early 1990s, as Bridlington drivers retired, these had disappeared, resulting in later and earlier timings for the first and last trains of the day. For a few years the shed also provided turning, watering and daytime stabling for engines working summer trains. The former shed then went into commercial use and was destroyed by a fire on 21 February 1986 when used for storing furniture.

In 1914 the locomotive foreman in charge of the shed was James Dunn, who received £143 per annum; he retired in 1923, and was followed by William Taylor who died in November 1931. A shed chargeman, Ned Ford, then became responsible for running the shed for the last 12 months of his 50 years of service, and in December 1932, a foreman fitter was appointed. At this time the shed was under the direct control of the Hull district locomotive superintendent – for many years a well-known ex NER man, OP Hutchinson, formerly of Tyne

Plate 6.17. *Almost a full house at Bridlington on 25 August 1956, with Class D49/2 No 62745 'The Hurworth' departing from Platform 4. A Class J39 and two Class B1s can also be seen. (Ken Hoole / Ken Hoole Study Centre Collection)*

Dock, and finally district locomotive superintendent at Darlington. In an effort to obtain efficiency and economy the LNER combined the posts of stationmaster and locomotive shedmaster, and Bridlington was one of the first depots to come under this new arrangement. There was still a man in charge of the shed, but he was responsible to the stationmaster for the clerical and operating side of the work, and to the district motive power superintendent for the technical and stores side. This meant that if an engine was late off the shed the stationmaster could take the matter up directly with the man in charge. Previously protocol had demanded that he write to the district operating superintendent, who would write to the district locomotive superintendent, who in turn would have to write to the man at the shed; the reply would have to go back the same way.

Staff (24)

Now with most country stations unmanned, and others only attended for limited hours, it is well to remember that even the smallest station would have at least one member of staff on duty to issue tickets and meet each train. By 1880 Bridlington had a staff of over 30, excluding the permanent way men, and, over the next 30 years, the number was further increased to match the demands of an annual influx that was rising to over 400,000 passengers. The official staff registers no longer exist so it is only possible to get a glimpse of the personnel involved at a station like Bridlington from the NER/LNER magazines; these were issued every month from 1911 and gave details of appointments, retirements and deaths in every grade.

Thomas Henry Shipman, who retired at the end of March 1913, was by far the longest-serving stationmaster at Bridlington, having been appointed in September 1885. During his tenure he had witnessed the number of trains increase from 10 per day to a maximum of around 60, and the enlargement of the station and locomotive facilities to accommodate them.(25) He was followed by E Lumbard until 1922, and then by John Martin who retired in 1936.(26) Between Mr Martin's retirement and the end of the Second World War Messrs Allen, Purnell, Johnson, Woods and Handley filled the post of stationmaster; their salary was around £400 per annum. The last had been an assistant stationmaster at Liverpool Street, until November 1944, and must have been relieved to get away from the indiscriminate rain of German rockets on the capital.

Prior to the 1912 extensions an assistant stationmaster was provided, and there were chief clerks controlling the staff dealing with passenger and goods traffic. Some clerical staff retained individual titles such as; passenger, goods, telegraph, booking and parcels clerk. Most porters came under the control of the station inspector, but a few worked for the goods traffic foreman. Other occupations mentioned in the staff magazines include; signalmen, guards, ticket collectors, refreshment room staff, ladies waiting room attendants, carriage cleaners, police constables, depot agent, checkers, loaders, leading carter, carters and vanmen. The transition from horse to motorized deliveries, around the time of the First World War, removed traditional occupations connected with the railway's stables and introduced new ones to handle their replacements.

A permanent way inspector was based at Bridlington, and had several gangs of platelayers to maintain the track towards Burton Agnes and Speeton where his district met with those of the inspectors at Driffield and Filey, respectively. On the motive power side there was a shed foreman/chargeman, several sets of drivers and firemen, boiler washers, labourers and engine cleaners. Tragically, no less than five engine and carriage cleaners, from Bridlington on active service, were killed and another two were taken prisoners of war by the Germans in 1917. A shed labourer, GH Howes, was awarded the Military Medal for heaving an unexploded bomb out of his trench.

The staffing at Beverley and Driffield would be similar, but with a little more emphasis on goods handling.

***Plate 6.18.** The use of cast-iron girders in railway bridges had been condemned after the Tay Bridge disaster in 1879, but here we see one, cast by Crosskills in 1846 to cross the Gypsey Race, being removed from Bridlington as late as March 1974 – almost a century later! (John M Richardson Collection)*

Train Departures from BRIDLINGTON

Saturday, 21st July, 1956

Time	Platform	To
6.25 am	6	Driffield, Beverley, Cottingham, Hull *(from Bridlington)*
6.35 am	1	Bempton, Hunmanby, Filey, Seamer, Scarborough (Central) *(from Hull)*
7.10 am	1	Carnaby, Burton Agnes, Lowthorpe, Nafferton, Driffield, Hutton Cranswick, Lockington, Arram, Beverley, Cottingham, Hull *(from Bridlington)*
7.35 am	6	Driffield, Market Weighton, Selby *(from Bridlington)*
8.00 am	5	Driffield, Beverley, Cottingham, Hull *(from Bridlington)*
8.18 am	5	Lowthorpe, Nafferton, Driffield, Hutton Cranswick, Lockington, Beverley, Cottingham, Hull *(from Scarbro)*
8.43 am	4	Brighouse (for Rastrick), Elland, Greetland, Halifax Town *(additional train – timetabled in Special Traffic Notice)*
8.51 am	1	Flamborough, Bempton, Speeton, Hunmanby, Filey, Seamer, Scarborough (Central) *(from Hull)*
8.53 am	5	Driffield, Hull *(from Scarborough (Central))*
9.12 am	5	Carnaby, Burton Agnes, Lowthorpe, Nafferton, Driffield, Hutton Cranswick, Arram, Beverley, Cottingham, Hull *(from Scarborough (Central))*
9.25 am	5	Northallerton, Eaglescliffe, Stockton, West Hartlepool, Seaham, Sunderland, Newcastle *(from Filey Holiday Camp)*
9.40 am	1	Filey *(from Leeds)*
9.48 am	5	Chesterfield (Midland), Belper, Duffield, Derby (Midland), Burton-on-Trent, Tamworth (High Level), Birmingham (New Street), King's Norton *(from Filey Holiday Camp)*
9.51 am	1	Filey, Scarborough (Central) *(from Hull)*
9.58 am	4	York *(from Filey Holiday Camp)*
10.08 am	5	Rotherham (Central), Sheffield (Victoria) *(from F.H.C.)*
10.25 am	1	Filey, Scarborough (Central) *(from Sheffield (Midland))*
10.28 am	4	Micklefield, Garforth, Cross Gates, Leeds (City) *(from Filey Holiday Camp)*
10.40 am	1	Filey, Scarborough (Central)
10.46 am	5	Pontefract (Baghill), Wath (Central), Wombwell (Central), Stairfoot (for Ardsley), Barnsley (Court House), Summer Lane, Dodworth, Penistone, Guide Bridge, Manchester (London Road) *(from Scarborough (L. Road))*
10.55 am	6	Driffield, Beverley, Cottingham, Hull *(from Bridlington)*
11.01 am	1	Flamborough, Bempton, Hunmanby, Filey, Seamer, Scarborough (Central) *(from Hull)*
11.06 am	4	York, Cross Gates, Leeds (City) *(from Filey)*
11.18 am	5	Rotherham (Masboro'), Sheffield (Midland), Chesterfield (Midland), Ambergate, Belper, Duffield, Derby (Midland) *(from Filey)*
11.23 am	1	Filey Holiday Camp *(from Leeds)*
11.23 am	4	Huddersfield, Stalybridge, Manchester (Victoria) *(from Filey Holiday Camp)*
11.41 am	1	Filey, Scarborough (Central) *(from Hull)*
11.49 am	2	Filey, Scarborough (L. Road) *(from Chesterfield (Midland))*
11.50 am	5	Doncaster, Grantham, Peterborough (North), London (Kings Cross) *(conveys Restaurant Car) (from Filey Holiday Camp)*
11.56 am	7	Rotherham (Central), Sheffield (Victoria) *(from Brid.)*
11.57 am	1	Filey, Scarborough (L. Road) *(from Stalybridge)*
12.04 pm	5	Driffield, Beverley, Hull *(from Scarborough (Central))*
12.05 pm	2	Filey Holiday Camp *(from York)*
12.13 pm	4	Thornhill (for Dewsbury), Mirfield, Brighouse (for Rastrick), Sowerby Bridge, Hebden Bridge, Todmorden, Littleborough, Rochdale, Bury (Knowsley Street), Bolton (Trinity Street), Wigan (Wallgate), Liverpool (Exchange) *(from Scarborough (Londesborough Road))*
12.20 pm	1	Filey, Scarborough (Central) *(from Blackburn – not advertised; departure point could vary)*
12.23 pm	8	Selby, South Milford, Micklefield, Garforth, Cross Gates, Leeds (City) *(additional train from Bridlington – timetabled in Special Traffic Notice)*
12.29 pm	5	Burton Agnes, Lowthorpe, Nafferton, Driffield, Hutton Cranswick, Lockington, Arram, Beverley, Cottingham, Hull *(from Scarborough (Central))*
12.30 pm	1	Filey Holiday Camp *(from Manchester (Exchange))*
12.38 pm	2	Filey, Scarborough (L. Road) *(from Leicester (Central))*
12.45 pm	4	Kirkby Bentinck, Hucknall (Central), Bullwell Common, Nottingham (Victoria), Arkwright Street, Loughborough (Central), Leicester (Central) *(from Scarborough (Londesborough Road))*
12.47 pm	1	Filey, Scarborough (L. Road) *(from Sowerby Bridge)*
1.07 pm	1	Filey Holiday Camp *(from Sheffield (Victoria))*
1.10 pm	4	Normanton, Wakefield (Kirkgate), Horbury & Ossett, Thornhill (for Dewsbury), Heckmondwike (Central), Liversedge (Central), Cleckheaton (Central), Lightcliffe, Halifax Town, Sowerby Bridge, Todmorden, Walsden, Heywood, Broadfield *(from Scarborough (Londesborough Road); extended from Sowerby Bridge to Broadfield in Special Traffic Notice)*
1.23 pm	1	Filey, Scarborough (L. Road) *(from Basford (North))*
1.25 pm	7	Stainforth & Hatfield, Doncaster, Conisbrough, Mexborough, Kilnhurst (Central), Rotherham (Central) *(from Bridlington)*
1.33 pm	2	Filey Holiday Camp (conveys Refreshment Car) *(from London (Kings Cross))*
1.35 pm	8	Pontefract (Baghill), Moorthorpe & South Kirkby, Bolton-on-Dearne, Swinton (Central), Sheffield (Victoria) *(from Bridlington)*
1.39 pm	1	Flamborough, Bempton, Filey, Scarborough (Central) *(from Hull)*
1.42 pm	5	Carnaby, Lowthorpe, Nafferton, Driffield, Hutton Cranswick, Lockington, Arram, Beverley, Cottingham, Hull *(from Scarborough (Central))*
1.52 pm	2	Filey, Scarborough (L. Road) *(from Liverpool (Exchange))*
2.00 pm	7	Leeds (City) *(from Bridlington)*
2.02 pm	1	Filey, Scarborough (L. Road) *(from Manchester (London Rd))*
2.17 pm	1	Filey Holiday Camp *(from Newcastle)*
2.20 pm	8	Castleford (Central), Stanley, Ardsley, Morley (Top), Bradford (Exchange) *(from Bridlington)*
2.30 pm	5	Mirfield, Brighouse (for Rastrick), Elland, Greetland, Halifax Town *(additional train – timetabled in Special Traffic Notice)*
2.40 pm	4	Elland, Greetland, Sowerby Bridge, Luddendenfoot, Mytholmroyd, Hebden Bridge, Blackburn, Darwen, Spring Vale, Horwich *(from Scarborough (Central) – not advertised; destination nominally Blackburn but could vary)*
2.46 pm	1	Filey, Scarborough (L. Road) *(additional train – timetabled in Special Traffic Notice)*
2.50 pm	6	Driffield, Beverley, Hull *(from Bridlington)*
3.06 pm	1	Bempton, Hunmanby, Filey, Seamer, Scarborough (Central) *(from Hull)*
3.23 pm	4	Doncaster, Retford, Ollerton, Edwinstowe, Mansfield (Central), Sutton-in-Ashfield (Central), Kirkby-in-Ashfield (Central), Hucknall (Central), Bulwell Common, Basford (North) *(from Scarbro (L. Rd.))*
3.36 pm	5	Burton Agnes, Lowthorpe, Nafferton, Driffield, Hutton Cranswick, Lockington, Arram, Beverley, Cottingham, Hull *(from Scarborough (Central))*
4.08 pm	1	Filey Holiday Camp *(from Gloucester (Eastgate))*
4.34 pm	1	Flamborough, Bempton, Hunmanby, Filey, Scarborough (Central) *(from Hull)*
4.45 pm	1	Filey Holiday Camp *(from York)*
4.50 pm	5	Driffield, Beverley, Hull *(from Bridlington)*
5.23 pm	5	Carnaby, Burton Agnes, Lowthorpe, Nafferton. Driffield, Hutton Cranswick, Lockington, Arram, Beverley, Cottingham, Hull *(from Scarborough (Central))*
6.25 pm	5	Carnaby, Burton Agnes, Lowthorpe, Nafferton, Driffield, Hutton Cranswick, Arram, Beverley, Cottingham, Hull *(from Bridlington)*
6.50 pm	5	Driffield, Beverley, Cottingham, Hull *(from Scarborough (Central))*
7.01 pm	1	Flamborough, Bempton, Hunmanby, Filey, Seamer, Scarborough (Central) *(from Hull)*
7.03 pm	4	Driffield, Market Weighton, Pocklington, York *(from Filey)*
7.14 pm	5	Carnaby, Burton Agnes, Nafferton, Driffield, Beverley, Cottingham, Hull *(from Scarborough (Central))*
7.50 pm	7	Driffield, Market Weighton, Selby, South Milford, Micklefield, Garforth, Cross Gates, Leeds (City) *(from Bridlington)*
8.20 pm	1	Driffield, Beverley, Cottingham, Hull *(from Bridlington)*
9.20 pm	5	Lowthorpe, Driffield, Hutton Cranswick, Lockington, Arram, Beverley, Cottingham, Hull *(from Scarborough (Central))*
11.05 pm	5	Carnaby, Lowthorpe, Nafferton, Driffield, Hutton Cranswick, Beverley, Cottingham, Hull *(from Bridlington)*

Figure 6.6. *Train departures from Bridlington, Saturday, 21 July 1956.*

Endnotes:

1. VCH *Yorkshire East Riding, Volume 2,* (1954) pages 51-4.
2. *Ibid.* pages 30-5.
3. Thompson J, *Historic Sketches of Bridlington,* (1821) page 151.
4. Copy of a document held in Bridlington Library.
5. TNA RAIL 527/2141.
6. This section written by Bill Fawcett.
7. TNA (The National Archives) RAIL 527/30 NER Locomotive Committee 19 September 1873 Min (Minute) 13310 approved the plans and let the work to WG Barritt at £2,617-13-5.
8. TNA RAIL 527/37 NER Way & Works Committee 20 December 1883 Min 1010 approved the footbridge at £278; 527/644 Contracts Summary Book records SM house begun 18 March 1889.
9. The NER Act of 1890 gave powers for the road diversion and new overbridge. TNA RAIL 527/40 NER Way & Works Committee 16 June 1892 Min 7137 let three works to TP Barry of York: the station enlargement at £3,477, the excursion station at £3,412, and a new engine shed at £3,439. The new road bridge had already been let to John Nelson of York on 21 January. 3 January 1895 Min 9034 approved Bell's scheme to substitute columns for the rear wall – the savings which paid for this included about £360 from the excursion station.
10. TNA RAIL 527/75 NER Traffic Committee 19 September 1891 Min 121243 recommended to the Board the General Manager's proposal for the bridge, additional land, a new signal cabin at the west end of the station, two new excursion lines, new lines to the engine shed and an extension to the coal depot lines.
11. Original poster in Bridlington Library.
12. TNA RAIL 527/50 NER Way & Works Committee 15 June 1911 Min 19102 let the new footbridge and alterations to Station Road bridge to Samuel Butler of Stanningley at £2,099-15-5; 21 September Min 19202 let the station improvements to Quibell Son & Greenwood at £8,687-4-0. RAIL 527/649 NER Contracts Summary Book reveals the supplier of the faience as Alfred Whitehead of Leeds.
13. *NER Magazine Volume 1,* 1911, pages 278-80 described the demolition, on 3 August.
14. TNA RAIL 527/52 NER Way & Works Committee 16 November 1922 let the contract to HE Turner & Son of York. The price of £3,182-19-1 is vastly higher pro rata than that of the 1911 work, indicating the scale of wartime inflation. Plans for both Pollard and Wilkinson schemes survive.
15. TNA RAIL 770/5 YNM Board 18 October 1850 Min 797 asked Cabry to proceed forthwith with the construction of the branch.
16. TNA RAIL 527/15.
17. Traffic Notice No 49/1976.
18. *Section B; Stations – traffics forwarded from*, LNER 1925.
19. 10 feet to the mile OS of 1850 and 1890.
20. TNA RAIL 527/23 Min 15559.
21. TNA RAIL 527/50 Way and Works 16 June 1892 Min 7137.
22. *Ibid.* 21 July 1892 Min 7150.
23. *Servicing the North Eastern Railway's Locomotives,* edited by JG Teasdale (2007).
24. This section is based on research by Ann and Peter Los.
25. *NER Magazine Volume 3*, 1913 page 118.
26. TNA RAIL 527/1912 and 1913.

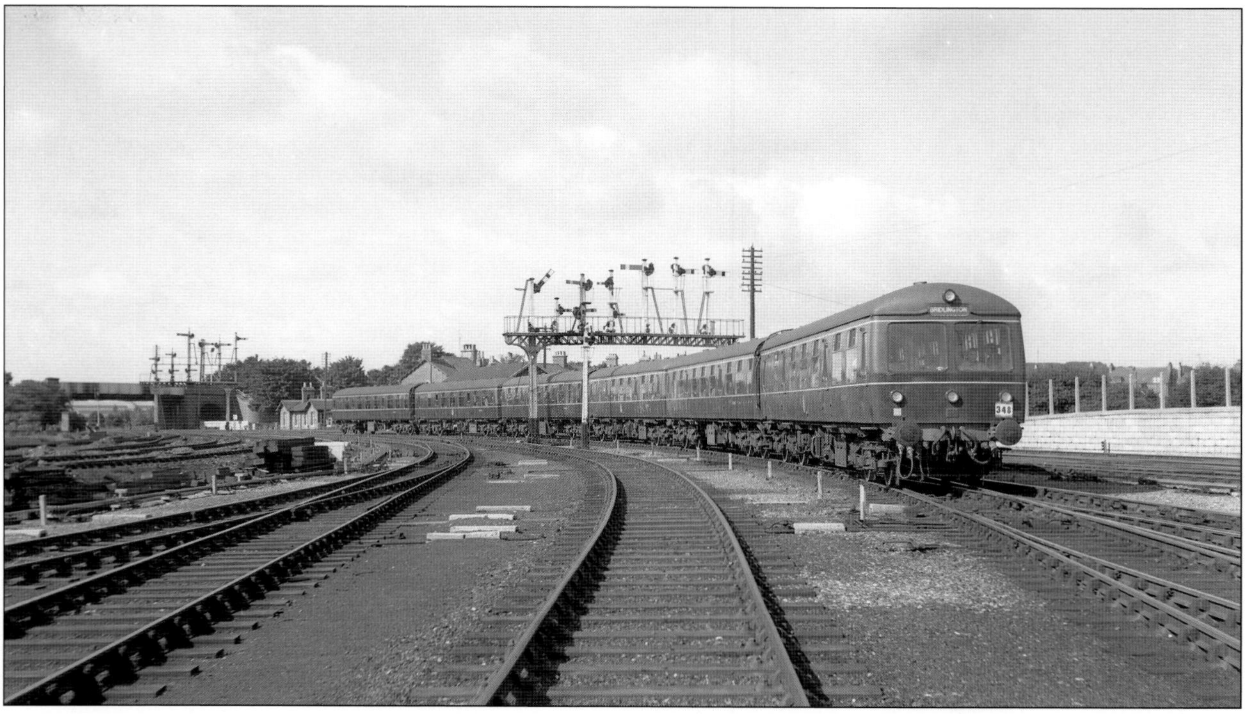

Plate 6.19. *This Cravens' DMU was only a few months old when it entered Bridlington with an excursion from Selby in 1956. (Neville Stead)*

Chapter 7 : Filey

John Farline and Bill Fawcett

Introduction

Although Filey is widely known as a seaside resort, it is the smallest of the towns served by the line, with a population in 2001 of 6,468: half that of Driffield. At the dawn of the Nineteenth Century the figure was just 501, and Filey was merely one of many small villages on the Yorkshire coast that were entirely reliant on the fishing industry. By then Scarborough was already a long-established and fashionable resort, and Filey was beginning to attract interest as a more secluded bathing place. Its physical advantages were a broad beach sheltered by the rocky promontory of Filey Brigg to the north and grassy slopes rising steeply to the west. At one stage Filey men fished as far out as the Dogger Bank, but the lack of a harbour meant that the industry eventually concentrated on in-shore fishing, using the traditional cobles, which can be dragged up and down the beach.

Plate 7.1. *Filey soon after the arrival of the railway, with the Brigg in the distance and development well advanced in the Crescent (left).*

The first guide to Filey, as a resort, appeared in 1828, but the key to its prompt and orderly development was the action of John Wilkes Unett (1770-1856), a solicitor born in Stafford and practising in Birmingham. In 1835-6 he purchased large tracts of land overlooking the sea and got the Birmingham architect Charles Edge to devise a street layout. The land was developed in the usual way by selling or leasing plots, many taken up by Scarborough architects and builders, and the railway was critical to the success of this venture, which gave us the dignified stucco terraces of The Crescent, largely completed by the eighteen-sixties.(1)

Public services on the railway from Seamer began on 6 October 1846, with a formal opening the previous day.(2) The initiative to celebrate this was taken by Henry Bentley, a brewery owner from Woodlesford near Leeds, whose seaside home was *Ravine Villa* at Filey. A local committee organised a procession through the streets, led by Bentley's works band, and entertainment for the general populace included a fireworks display by a celebrated Leeds 'pyrotechnist'.

George Hudson was the guest of honour at *Ravine Villa*, where the indoor banquet was accompanied by an outdoor spread for a further seventy guests and, amid the usual speeches, Sir Thomas Legard, of Ganton, made the celebrated remark:

'Railways and railway shares were dark as night,
Men said that Hudson ruled, and all was right.'

Afterwards, the party made their way back to the station, where the men who built the line had been enjoying a feast of beef, bread and ale also provided by Mr Bentley.

Despite the impetus given by the railway, Filey's growth was slow and steady: from a population of 1,231 in 1841, on a par with Hunmanby, to 1,881 twenty years later and only 3,003 by 1901. For a long time the town remained a resort for members of the middle and upper classes, and, while a majority of summer visitors came from the north of England, surveys made in 1857, 1870 and 1890 reveal that as many as 17% were from London and 12% from the Home Counties and the south-east.

As well as visitors staying in the town, Filey attracted large numbers of day trippers travelling at excursion rates which made the seaside accessible to less affluent members of the community. A further development was the opening in 1945 of Billy Butlin's Filey Holiday Camp. Situated two miles south of the town, above Hunmanby Sands, most visitors in the early years arrived by train, using Filey station and a linking East Yorkshire bus service until the camp's own branch line and station were fully completed in 1947.

The Railway Goods Premises and Traffic

Approaching Filey by train from the south, we skirt the gardens of Mr Bentley's *Ravine Villa*, now a public park whose cafe occupies the site of his elegant mansion. At this point the sea is just a quarter mile away, but we then swing north-west, heading inland to the station, which was built in open fields and backed onto open country until well into the Twentieth Century. As at the other towns, the goods and coal yards occupied distinctly separate sites. The coal yard was situated on the right-hand side of the line, on the approach to the station, and had a line of fourteen cells served by two tracks. The town had no public gas supply until 1852, when a gasworks was built alongside.

Continuing through the station, the former stationmaster's house is seen on the left just before we cross the main road, coming to the site of the goods yard on the right. Filey goods shed was the customary GT Andrews structure. The enclosed brick portion was longer than its counterpart at Driffield (104 feet compared with 83) and was designed with four entrances on the road frontage as against Driffield's three. The middle pair extended down to ground level, evidently to serve a pair of cart docks, though one of these was bricked up for most, if not all, of its life; the outer pair finished at platform level, as at Driffield. The roof over the loading area at the north end had been lost by 1900 and another change was the rebuilding of the rail entrance at the south end with a flat lintel, to provide more headroom. The yard layout and proximity of the level crossing meant that road traffic could be held up for ten minutes or more while shunting took place.

Freight was never an important part of the Filey picture, and the NER had no difficulty finding space alongside the goods yard for the extra cottages for block signalmen which were built in 1875 along with a house for the permanent-way inspector.(3) Fish traffic was surprisingly slight, with just 164 tons being forwarded in 1913; this compares with 7,791 at Scarborough. Not only would the catch have been relatively modest; a large proportion probably made its way to the tables of holidaymakers. Nonetheless, fish traffic had its own siding and loading stage across the line from the goods yard, and it would have developed further had an 1878 scheme gone ahead to provide a harbour for the fishing fleet. A prominent figure in this Filey Harbour & Pier Company venture was Lord Claud Hamilton, a director and later chairman of the Great Eastern Railway, who approached the NER for support.(4) The company, wisely, refused to subscribe. (See Colour Plate 6 on page 28.)

The main inward traffic was coal. From 3,309 tons in 1881, coal traffic had risen to 8,833 by 1927 and still averaged about 8,500 tons in the early nineteen-fifties, at which period the depot was leased out to a local coal merchant, Midgeley's, who took responsibility for all public weighing, although other merchants still had their own coal cells there as well.(5) In addition, the Filey Laundry bought in supplies directly from collieries to the coalyard, as would the gasworks, which had no siding of its own. A by-product of gas-making was tar, despatched monthly by rail, the wagon being stood on the coal cells and filled via a standpipe. Income from his own coal sales brought a healthy boost to the stationmaster's salary. The latter was £240 in the early Twentieth Century at a time when his Beverley counterpart was earning £400, however annual coal revenue of up to £158 did a lot to make life sweeter.

In NER days, the goods figures were such as you might expect for a town with no industrial base in the days when nearly all commodities were brought in by rail: a high ratio of inward to outward traffic. Thus the decade 1905-9 saw an average of 958 tons forwarded each year with 5,083 being received. The First World War brought a drop in the received average to 3,691 tons for 1915-19, reflecting a dearth of holidaymakers, but it recovered to pre-war levels in 1920-4 and shot up to an average of 10,349 for 1925-9.(6) However, the rot was setting in from 1929 and the figure sank below 3,000 throughout 1931-3. By contrast, the modest forwarded average, despite ups and downs, had increased to almost 2,000 tons in 1930-4.

During the nineteen-fifties, it remained 'business as usual' for the goods department. There was still fish traffic, and every weekday morning the stationmaster had to check the amounts landed by the local fleet.

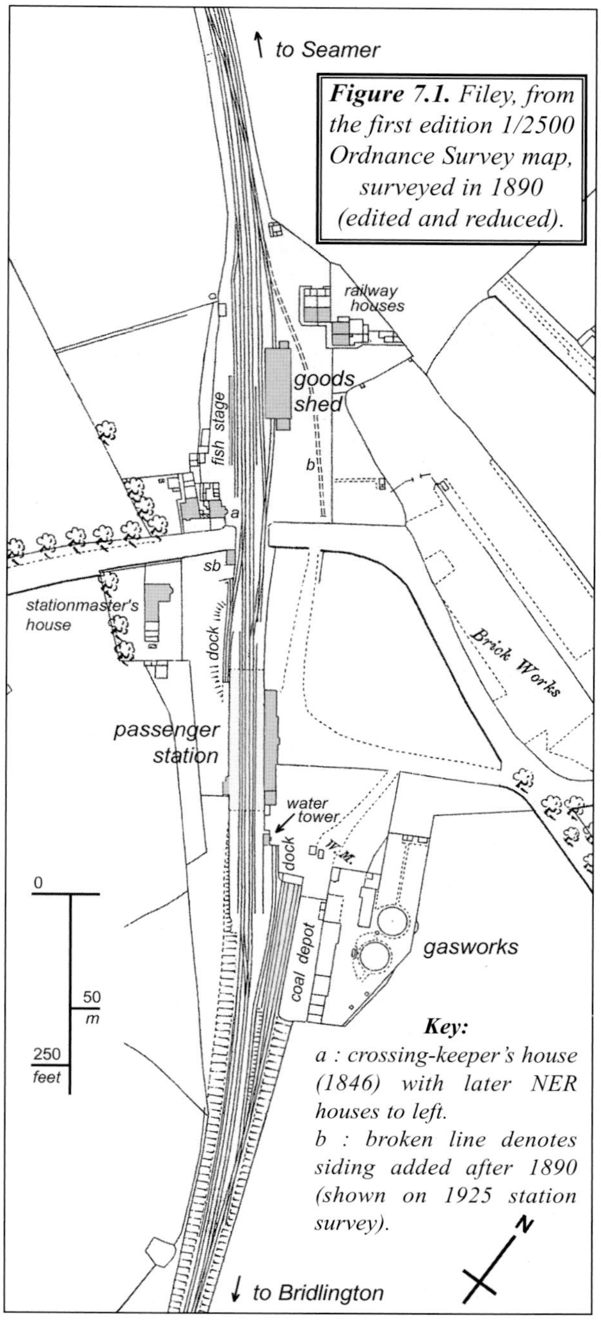

Figure 7.1. *Filey, from the first edition 1/2500 Ordnance Survey map, surveyed in 1890 (edited and reduced).*

Key:
a : crossing-keeper's house (1846) with later NER houses to left.
b : broken line denotes siding added after 1890 (shown on 1925 station survey).

Packed into wooden boxes, the fish were generally despatched in special vans three or four times a week, including one van for King's Cross. Fish boxes were also carried in the guards' vans of passenger trains, and travellers in the adjacent compartment would soon become aware of their presence! Bait for the fishing industry was brought by train, on a regular basis, from Boston in Lincolnshire.

However, the 1955 BR Modernisation Plan envisaged the town's goods sundries being handled by road from a railhead at Scarborough's Gallows Close goods station, although the coal depot was expected to continue. Filey goods station eventually closed on 10 August 1964, when goods facilities were withdrawn from all the intermediate stations between Seamer and Bridlington. The goods shed was demolished in 1969, along with the 1875 NER housing, and the site has been redeveloped as the *Silver Birches* residential care home. The coal yard is now occupied by business premises.

Plate 7.2. *View north from the station in 1944 with what appears to be a Class B16 locomotive heading past the goods shed, to the right of which are the houses built by the NER in 1875. The siding heading off in front of the signalbox ended behind the trainshed. (Ken Hoole Collection)*

Plate 7.3. *An unidentified BR Standard Ivatt 4MT 2-6-0 shunting the return pick-up goods in September 1962. (Filey Town Archives Collection)*

Plate 7.4. *A similar view to Plate 7.2, taken in the late 1950s. The level crossing timbers are being replaced by a tarmac surface and the opportunity is being taken to remove the siding seen on the left of the earlier picture. The carriage on the far side of the road is an old six-wheeler parked at the end of the fish-dock siding and used as a mess by the men working on the crossing. To the right of the characteristic Andrews goods shed are the yard crane and the revolving board signal used to control the exit from the yard. (John Farline Collection)*

Passenger Facilities and Traffic

Some idea of the extent of Filey's holiday traffic under the NER can be gleaned from an Edwardian snapshot. 1906 saw 240,318 tickets being collected at Filey, as against 55,783 issued there. The returns for Bridlington are, unfortunately, incomplete but its outward bookings that year were almost 130,000. Bridlington, however, boasted an expanded station which by 1912 would run to five platforms, plus a distinct excursion station. Filey made do with its original two passenger platforms, although these were much lengthened over the years. This reflects the fact that Bridlington served as terminus and stabling point for many holiday trains. The only significant stabling available at Filey was the goods yard loop, sandwiched between the running lines and goods shed, with 108 yards of standage.

Plate 7.5. *The north end of Filey station in 1894 with Class F No 1532 leaving for Scarborough. The locomotive was built in 1890 to handle main-line express services but the class was soon displaced to secondary routes by the introduction of new express designs in 1892-4. The trainshed is seen with the deep timber valancing added in 1872. In the foreground is the headshunt for the goods run-round loop, later replaced by a trap point as shown in British Railway Journal volume 25. (HS Sheldon, courtesy VCK Allen)*

Plate 7.6. *Whit Sunday 1905, with a special train from Scarborough bringing visitors to watch motor racing on Filey Sands. It is headed by No 675 of Class G1. Introduced in 1887 as a 2-4-0 design for use on important secondary routes, they soon found employment on the Hull - Scarborough line and continued to work there until the early 1920s. All were altered from 2-4-0 to 4-4-0, No 675 being dealt with in May 1904. To the left we can see the narrow wooden ticket platform, with just fields beyond. (F Fisher)*

Filey station building is one of the best surviving examples of its era, a status reflected in its exceptional Grade II* listing. The basic design adopted by Andrews at Filey and Driffield has already been outlined in Chapter 3, so we can focus here on the way in which Filey has developed. Approaching the entrance, one's eye is caught by the cantilevered glass verandah which the NER added to the front in 1910.(7) Filey was the last town on the line to receive this feature, the work being carried out by the local firm of Arthur Haxby, who built one at the Down platform exit through the trainshed rear wall at the same time. Designed in the office of William Bell, NER Architect, and fabricated from steel strip and angle, the entrance verandah is much simpler than the richly-detailed cast-iron affairs traditionally used by the railway, as at Driffield.

The station evidently began life with a water tower at each end, as at the other town stations, but the north one was removed to make way for a siding and dock at the back of the Down platform. The south one survives, minus its tank, as the best remaining example of this particular design. The platforms quickly outgrew the trainshed but, in contrast to Bridlington, no additional roofing has ever been provided. The North Eastern's main improvements to the shed were to provide glazed end screens and a footbridge. The latter was first considered at the end of 1883, when Filey was one of several places earmarked to receive the company's new standard cast-iron bridge.(8) This was not urgent, and passengers had to wait until 1889 for one supplied by the well-known ironfounders Butlers of Stanningley.(9) It was too long to fit entirely within the trainshed, so the Down platform landing and stairs were sited outside the rear wall and neatly covered in. The end screens were installed in 1872, accompanied by deep timber valancing which hid from view Andrews' elegant bowstring girders; much of this survived into 1949, but disappeared soon after.(10)

The station offices underwent little significant change during their first half century; see Figures 7.2 and 7.3. On the right of the entrance was a refreshment room, tenanted in 1854 by Bryan Hebden, who had been the first stationmaster.(11) It enjoyed limited success, vanishing from some timetables and then re-emerging, but finally closed in 1883 and was made into a general waiting room, catering for Second and Third Class passengers.(12) At an early stage the men's toilets were also re-planned. Originally these comprised a w/c adjoining the First Class waiting room and facilities within the water towers; the better provision required by growing holiday traffic was found by extending the left-hand (south-eastern) wing of the office range in a style matching the arcaded original. No waiting rooms were provided at first on the Down platform, the trainshed being considered sufficient shelter, but in 1894 the NER relented and built a small room onto the rear wall of the shed.(13)

A desire for a covered cabstand was expressed by Filey Local Board, meeting NER directors back in 1878, and eventually bore modest fruit as the 1910 front and rear entrance verandahs.(14) These accompanied work designed to increase the space for the booking office, left luggage and parcels business; fitting round the traffic, this was only completed in 1913. Visible traces of this on the station frontage are a widening of the lower part of the original entrance and the creation of a second one alongside; both lead into a booking hall created by removing the partition between the original entrance hall and booking lobby.

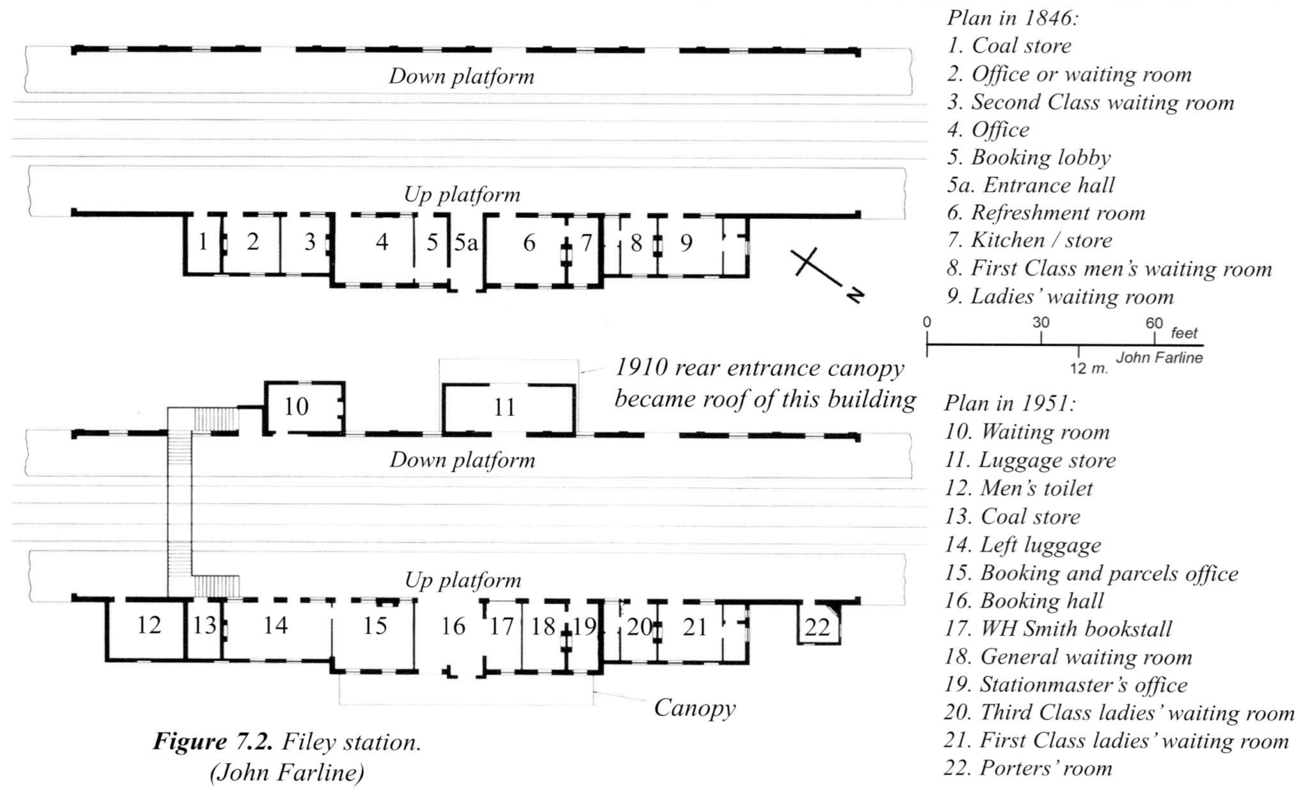

Figure 7.2. *Filey station. (John Farline)*

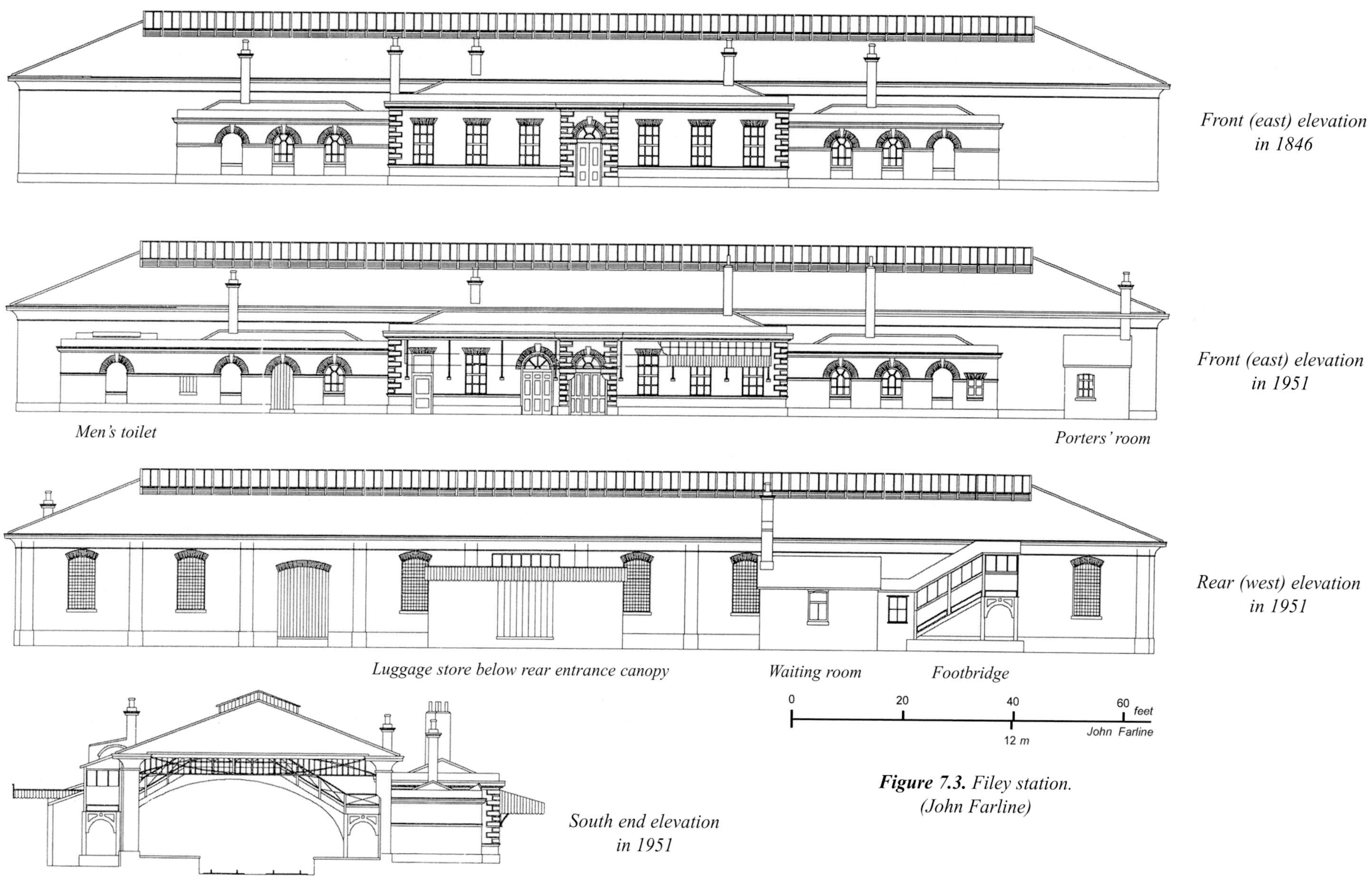

***Figure* 7.3.** Filey station.
(John Farline)

A bookstall was later created for WH Smith by opening up the right-hand wall of this hall and abstracting part of the main waiting room. Thus the balance between office space and waiting rooms had changed drastically by the end of the NER's existence. The extent of the parcels business can be gauged by returning to the 1906 figures, which show 6,724 outward parcels and 17,072 received; by 1913 the latter figure was almost 28,000.

The opening of Butlin's Holiday Camp in 1945 brought more traffic on summer Saturdays. To cope with this, the footbridge was given an extra set of Up-platform steps leading towards a secondary exit, next to the water tower, which was adapted as a ticket collector's booth.

Plate 7.7. *The Up platform water tower together with the exit gate installed for early Butlin's traffic. (Bill Fawcett, 1972)*

Plate 7.8. *A modern view of Filey station showing the restored trainshed. (Bill Fawcett, 2009)*

Plate 7.9. *The station frontage; both chimneys seen here have been remodelled, losing their original elegant stone copings. (Bill Fawcett, 2009)*

Plate 7.10. *A Nineteenth-century view north from a vantage point near the bottom of the present footbridge steps. On the left is the board crossing which was the sole access prior to the bridge being built in 1889. Above the unidentified station staff we see gas lanterns on the elegant cast-iron brackets which were a feature of all Andrews trainsheds. Between these is the original arched entrance, which disappeared in the later NER alterations. The view appears to predate the 1883 adaptation of the refreshment room. (F Fisher)*

Plate 7.11. *Looking south through the trainshed and footbridge in 1972. The change in fencing and materials indicate the final extension made to the far end of the Up platform. (Bill Fawcett)*

The Camp having acquired its own station by 1947, the steps were removed a few years later, but clear evidence remains: the shaving back of the south-eastern pier of the trainshed to make space for the stairs, and the handsome cast-iron NER exit gates salvaged from another station. Another relic is the brick room built under the rear exit verandah to store passengers' luggage, then routinely consigned in advance.

Ticket platforms were introduced in 1862, as at Driffield, but the only one which has been identified lay to the south of the station, dealing with northbound trains. Only needed at busy times, it probably fell out of use during the eighteen-nineties, though it was still there in 1905. It was removed prior to platform extensions the following year, which brought the lengths to 390 feet (Up) and 405 (Down); an 1888 lengthening had already made them 364 and 383. Thus by 1906 the station could just about handle an eight coach train of modern bogie stock, though six-wheelers still dominated the scene

Traffic trends after the First World War echo those we have seen elsewhere. Bookings from Filey recovered to 77,649 in 1920 but soon began to fall in the face of bus competition, slumping below 20,000 in 1932. Collected tickets reached 141,210 in 1918 but fell dramatically, to 66,279, in 1926. Stationmaster James Taylor (in post 1908-27) blamed the fall in inward traffic on the prolonged Miners' Strike, which impoverished many families in the north-east coalfield. Having subsequently dropped below 46,000 the figure was back to 61,067 in 1935. Ironically, on retiring Mr Taylor became a partner in a nearby garage.

The Second World War brought fresh traffic, with a Free French base being established on the outskirts of town and a much larger RAF training base taking over Butlin's Holiday Camp: 'RAF Hunmanby Moor' had a full complement of about five thousand. Afterwards, the station saw a growth in holiday business, and by the late nineteen-forties was employing more than twice as many people as the NER had back in 1884. Then, stationmaster Richard Harrison (in post from at least 1879 to 1893) had charge of seven passenger department staff plus two goods staff. The post-war crew comprised a regular staff of three clerks, three porters and a relief porter, two signalmen and a relief signalman, a road van driver, two goods clerks, a warehouseman and a coal porter. For the summer period these were supplemented by a ticket collector, three clerks, a porter and another van and driver.

Since then, the run down in holiday traffic and abandonment of parcels business mean that Filey station is now unstaffed, with the booking office and adjacent rooms occupied by a local taxi firm. Signalling staff disappeared from the scene with the modernisation of signalling and level crossings, which led to the closure of Filey box at the end of the day's traffic on Sunday 25 June 2000. The signalbox was later demolished but the station survives in fine condition and still offers the luxury of a waiting room and toilets, while the premises are well cared for by a peripatetic cleaning team.

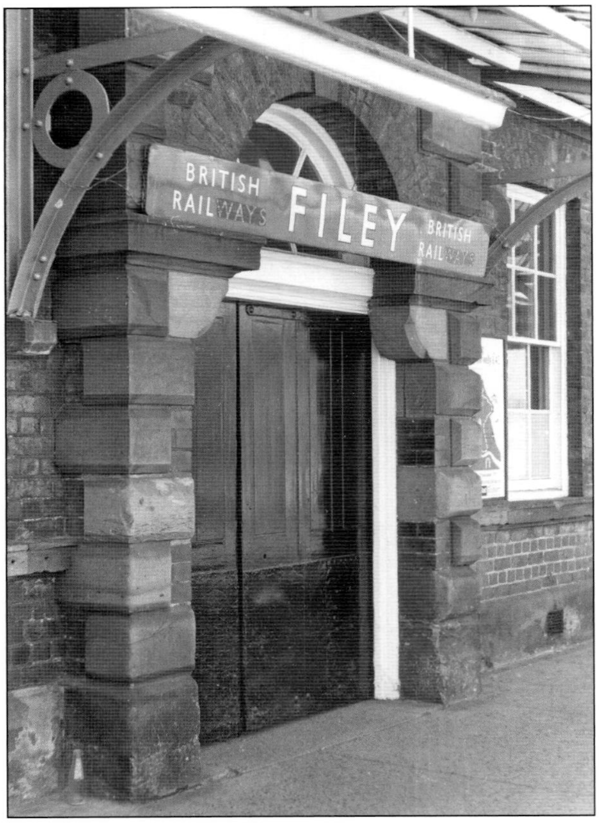

Plate 7.12. *The station entrance in 1972, showing how the doorway was widened but then corbelled in to support the original impost moulding and arch. The North Eastern Region nameboard has been brought into line with the BR corporate image by painting over the 'ways' of British Railways. (Bill Fawcett)*

At one stage this happy outcome seemed unlikely. During the Second World War the glass had been stripped from the trainshed ridge skylight as an air-raid precaution. Though it was reinstated afterwards, maintenance arrears led to the whole ridge ventilator being removed in the late nineteen-sixties. At the time British Rail contemplated dismantling the entire shed roof and replacing it by low-level awnings as had already happened at Driffield and Bridlington. The areas most liable to corrosion in the days of steam were the hipped ends and, for the time being, BR was content to dismantle the one at the north end. The other followed within a decade, giving the station a rather forlorn appearance, while the open ridge made the remaining structure highly vulnerable to the weather.

By 1988 it was clear that the roof could not remain indefinitely in this limbo, and BR applied for listed building consent to remove it and substitute individual platform canopies. By then, Filey's significance was widely recognised and had been heightened by the recent unroofing of Malton station, so Scarborough Council refused consent. An appeal, handled by written representations, brought objections from a variety of local and national bodies including the Victorian Society and North Eastern Railway Association. English Heritage firmly opposed the idea and the appeal was dismissed on 6 April 1989, although certain works were allowed, such as a reduction of the office chimneys.(15)

To qualify for grant aid towards the costly repairs needed, BR was required to reinstate the lost elements of the roof using appropriate materials; its response was an exemplary piece of restoration, carried out by the railway's own workforce. Grants came from English Heritage, the recently-formed Railway Heritage Trust, Filey Town Council and Scarborough Borough Council.(16) Work began in 1990 and entailed stripping the roof back to its ironwork and sorting this out; the major problem was localised wasting of the bars which serve as king and queen rods (the vertical members) and tie rods. This was tackled by a technique of building up the wasted section in a way which reinstates its original integrity.

Plate 7.13. *In contrast to, yet contemporary with Plate 7.6, we see one of two petrol-electric autocars put into service in 1904, with an 85 horsepower engine driving a 550 volt generator supplying a pair of DC motors. From August 1904 until the end of June 1908, one at least was engaged on a summer shuttle service between Scarborough and Filey and is seen here at the Down platform. (John Farline Collection)*

Plate 7.14. *The last class of 4-4-0 locomotive to become a regular feature of the line was the LNER D49. Here we see No 62751, 'The Albrighton', built in July 1934, with the 2-55 pm departure to Hull in May 1949. (P Ward)*

Plate 7.15. *'The Albrighton' waiting to leave the north end of the station with a summer Saturday special in the late 1950s. We see the dock face on this side of the platform, formerly served by the siding seen in Plate 7.2. (S Fawcett)*

Filey Holiday Camp

Sir Billy Butlin (1899-1980) did not invent the holiday camp but carried it to a new level, determined to give families, in particular, a blend of privacy and community which the traditional guest house could not provide, backed up by an extensive entertainment programme. His first camp was Skegness, opened at Easter 1936, and Filey was under construction from May-June 1939. War intervened and Butlin came to an arrangement with the War Ministry whereby they would finance completion of the camp, which would then be used to house service personnel in training; similar arrangements were made at Ayr and Pwllheli. Thus Filey Camp spent the war as RAF Hunmanby Moor.

Within weeks of hostilities ending in Europe, Butlin reclaimed half of Filey Camp, which welcomed its first visitors in July 1945. The LNER helped with advertising and agreed to provide a 'siding' to the site, two miles south of the town centre. The Ministry of War Transport issued an order in July 1945 authorising construction of this well-built $^3/_4$ mile long branch. A few trains worked the branch in 1946, the camp's first full season, including a Pullman special on 21 October which brought 400 notables from London to a performance of Puccini's *La Bohème* on the 50th anniversary of its première, a publicity gambit marking the start of a week of opera by the San Carlo company of Naples. However, the railway's formal opening only took place on 10 May 1947.

The branch comprised a pair of double-track curves, leaving the main line at Royal Oak North and South Junctions and converging on the terminus to form a triangle, which was used for turning train engines. The station was very simple, with four tracks serving two island platforms, 900 feet long and built up from reinforced concrete panels. It lay on the opposite side of the A165 road from the Camp, a link eventually being provided by a subway through which passengers and their luggage were conveyed by trolley trains. Alongside the platform lines were three engine release roads, enabling arriving locomotives to pull forward,

Plate 7.16. *Filey Camp Branch: building the bridge over Raikes Lane. Its abutments are almost complete but the embankments for the two curves to the main line (seen in the background) have some way to go. (Ken Hoole Collection)*

Plate 7.17. *The Camp branch nearing completion, with Raikes Lane bridge in the middle distance. (Ken Hoole Collection)*

reverse past their trains, turn on the triangle, which entailed running the wrong way on the Up main line, and then return to one of the servicing sidings.(17)

The Camp trains ran on Saturdays in the season, augmented by some Wednesday excursions; at other times the main-line signals controlled by the junction boxes were left 'off'. Staff from Hull manned the station on Saturdays but any Wednesday work was looked after by the Filey stationmaster, seconding some of his own staff to the Camp. The signalling was operated by relief signalmen living in the locality. In addition to passenger trains, the pick-up goods would occasionally be diverted into the Camp with supplies.

Plate 7.18. *The formal opening on 10 May 1947. Lord Middleton (far left), Lord Lieutenant of the East Riding, has just unveiled this nameboard; next to him stands Billy Butlin and then LNER director Geoffrey Kitson. (Ken Hoole Collection)*

Plate 7.19. *The scene a few minutes later. The locomotive is Class B1 No 1018 'Gnu'. (John Farline Collection)*

Figure 7.4. *Filey Holiday Camp.*
Sketch based on an LNER plan dated March 1946.
(Richard Pulleyn)

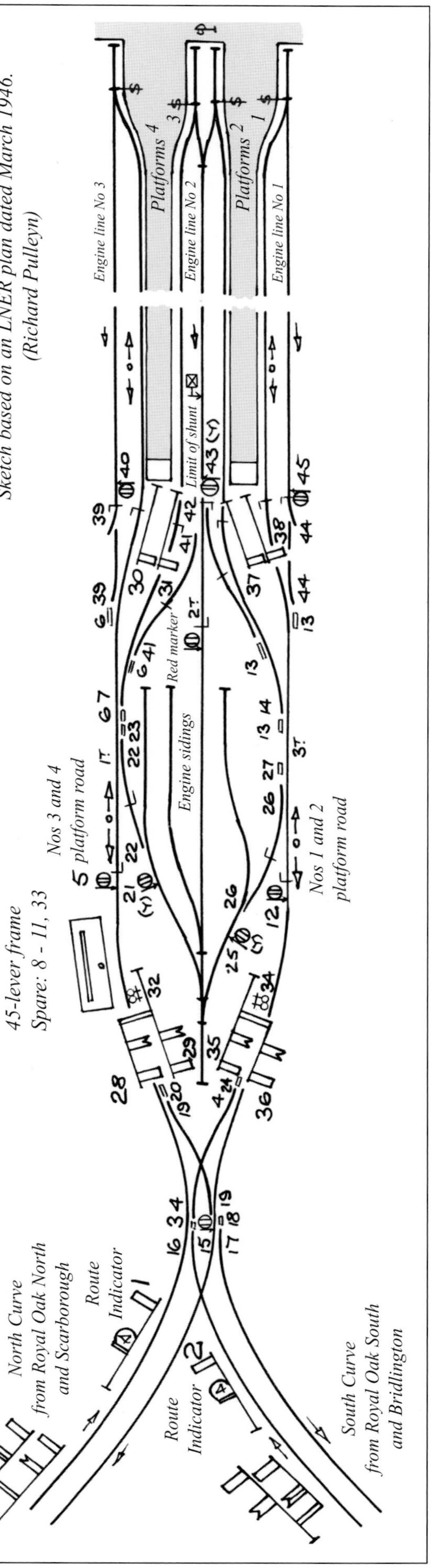

Table 7.1. Summer Saturday traffic dealt with at Royal Oak South signalbox on the morning and afternoon of 23 August 1947. (Kindly supplied by Neville Stead.)

Up Trains:

Paasing times and tablet numbers			Engine	Class
07-59	2485	07-25 Scarborough – Hull	2992	C7
08-35	2489	08-15 Scarborough – Hull	2723	D49
08-39	2671	08-35 Filey Camp – Newcastle upon Tyne EP	1424	B16
09-14	199	09-10 Filey Camp – Birmingham New Street EP	1455	B16
09-20	2493	08-53 Scarborough – Hull	2707	D49
09-52	774	Scarborough – Ashton under Lyne ADDL	2775	D49
09-57	3043	09-55 Filey Camp – York EP	1945	K3
10-25	129	09-55 Scarborough – King's Cross EP	1407	B16
10-28	129	10-25 Filey Camp – King's Cross(1)	1932	K3
10-54	201	10-50 Filey Camp – Sheffield Victoria EP	1393	B7
11-14	777	Scarborough – Castleton ADDL	1435	B16
11-32	2675	11-10 Scarborough – Hull	1071	B1
11-55	2499	11-18 Scarborough – Hull	1899	K3
12-07	203	11-55 Scarborough LR – Leicester Central EP	1449	B16
12-38	787	12-10 Scarborough – Liverpool Exchange EP	1457	B16
12-44	776	12-40 Filey Camp – Manchester Exchange EP	1065	B1
12-59	2679	12-55 Filey Camp – York EP	1407	B16
13-05	778	Scarborough – Rochdale ADDL	1819	K3
13-23	2696	12-55 Scarborough – Sheffield Midland EP	1467	B16
13-33	2503	13-03 Scarborough – Hull	2757	D49
13-45	205	13-20 Scarborough LR – Sheffield Victoria EP	1447	B16
14-10	2513	13-45 Scarborough LR – Manchester Central EP	1183	B1
14-23	2689	13-55 Scarborough – Hull	1923	K3
14-39		light engine	2885	C1
14-55	2517	14-25 Scarborough – Hull	2954	C7
15-11	788	14-45 Scarborough – Manchester Victoria EP	1809	K3
15-16	3120	empty stock from Filey Camp	982	V2
15-28	211	15-00 Scarborough LR – Nottingham Victoria EP	1120	B1
15-36		light engine	1458	B16
16-18	2685	15-54 Scarborough – Hull	*not recorded*	
16-26		light engine	2720	D49
16-46	2525	16-23 Scarborough – Hull	2353	D20
17-28		light engine	1438	B16
17-46	80	empty stock from Filey Camp	1932	K3

Notes: Scarborough LR is Londesborough Road Excursion Station.

1. Scarborough and Filey Camp portions combined at Bridlington and No 1932 took the train forward from there as far as Doncaster, returning on the Camp portion of the Down King's Cross train, which passed Royal Oak at 17-24. No 1407 returned light engine from Bridlington to the Camp, passing at 11-15.

Down Trains:

Paasing times and tablet numbers			Engine	Class
07-40	199	empty stock to Filey Camp	2720	D49
08-51	129	empty stock to Filey Camp	1932	K3
09-35	2468	07-50 Hull – Scarborough OP	1071	B1
09-55	2672	08-40 Hull – Scarborough EP	1899	K3
10-15	2472	09-00 Hull Scarborough	2757	D49
11-15		light engine to Filey Camp	1407	B16
11-29	2676	10-05 Hull – Scarborough	1923	K3
11-46	190	08-40 Sheffield Victoria – Scarborough LR EP	1183	B1
12-06	351	Silkstone – Scarborough ADDL	1167	B1
12-18	2678	10-20 York – Filey Camp EP	982	V2
12-40	2476	10-50 Hull – Scarborough	2992	C7
13-12	134	07-45 Leicester Central – Scarborough LR EP	1120	B1
13-29	761	08-55 Manchester Victoria – Scarborough EP	1461	B16
13-51	140	10-50 Sheffield Victoria – Filey Camp EP	2885	C1
13-59	2686	12-25 Hull – Scarborough	2353(1)	D20
14-22	2488	12-50 Hull – Scarborough	2703	D49
14-42	3120	08-20 King's Norton (Worcs) – Filey Camp EP	1458	B16
14-54	026	09-50 Bulwell Common (Notts) – Scarbro' LR EP	1438	B16
15-04	760	09-03 Liverpool Exchange – Scarborough EP	1872	K3
15-13	1085	10-15 Newcastle – Filey Camp EP	940	V2
15-25	2492	13-20 Hull – Scarborough	2707	D49
16-00	2496	14-30 Hull – Scarborough	2988(2)	C7
16-10	772	11-40 Manchester Exchange – Filey Camp EP	1917	K3
16-17	138	10-30 Manchester Central – Scarborough LR EP	1397	B7
16-27	2638	14-30 York – Filey Camp EP	1817	K3
17-15	2502	15-45 Hull – Scarborough	2355	D20
17-24	80	11-10 ex King's Cross: Filey Camp portion	1932	K3
17-30	80	11-10 ex King's Cross: Scarborough portion	1871(3)	K3

Notes:

1. No 2353 was pilot to a second locomotive, which returned on No 2685.
2. Class C7 was rapidly vanishing by then: No 2988 was withdrawn in July 1948, No 2992 in November and the last of the class in December.
3. Train divided at Bridlington, with Scarborough portion leaving there at 16-35.

An idea of the early days is given by Table 7.1, which lists trains passing Royal Oak South on Saturday 23 August 1947.(18) This only includes Camp trains working via Bridlington, but just a couple of others seem to have come in by the Scarborough route. The picture is impressive. Departing campers began with the 8-35 to Newcastle, followed by trains to Birmingham New Street and York. The 10-25 for King's Cross was combined at Bridlington with a portion from Scarborough, shortly followed by a train to Sheffield Victoria. The Camp outward traffic finished with departures to Manchester Exchange and York at 12-40 and 12-55. By then the inward traffic had begun, with the passage of the first train from York at 12-18. This was followed by Camp trains from Sheffield, King's Norton (Birmingham), Newcastle, Manchester and York, again, ending up with the King's Cross train at 5-24 pm. A couple of venerable express classes were to be seen among the locomotives: a Great Northern 'Large Atlantic' (LNER Class C1) working one of the Sheffield trains and North Eastern Class Z (C7) Atlantics ending their lives on the locals.

The King's Cross train was the heaviest to work to the Camp and the only one to provide restaurant and buffet facilities, features which would surely have been welcome on the Glasgow train which began in 1957. Nicknamed the 'Gorbals Express', this worked via Scarborough and York, entailing two reversals, which called for ingenious planning in the days of steam. In the 1959 timetable it left Filey Camp at 7-53 am, arriving in the gloomy surroundings of Queen Street Low Level station just after 4 pm. With the demise of steam, Camp trains were commonly formed by diesel multiple-units, at least eight-car sets, although diesel locomotives were also to be seen. This made the service much easier to operate, and was a factor, along with declining passenger numbers, in the pruning carried out at the terminus in April 1972, which included the abandonment of Platforms 3 and 4.

The Camp was a great success, and in 1955 welcomed about 75,000 holidaymakers, of whom 40,000 came directly by train.(19) However, car ownership was rising and of the 104,000 visitors catered for in 1960, just 26,000 travelled to the Camp station with a further 8,000 coming via Filey Town station. By 1975 visitor numbers were 166,000 but only 11,900 of these travelled in the Camp trains and 2,900 to Filey Town. The Camp branch was not covered by the Section 39 grant for the loss-making Hull - Scarborough passenger service, and British Rail contemplated closing it in 1972, at which point Butlins stepped in with a recurrent grant towards its costs.

However, the gap between costs and revenue continued to widen, and in 1976 BR formally proposed closure. At a hearing of the Transport Users Consultative Committee in March 1977, the chief objectors were Scarborough and Filey councils while Transport 2000 proposed the rather unrealistic alternative of a new station on the main line, near Primrose Valley. The branch was formally closed from 26 November 1977 but the last passenger train of the season would have left two months before. The Camp itself fell victim to changing holiday patterns, and closed at the end of the 1983 season. An attempt to revive it in other hands failed and the Camp buildings were demolished during 1989-91.

Plate 7.20. *The Camp station on 16 September 1950. Passengers have come on the trolley-train seen to the right and are heading for what is thought to be the 10-35 train to King's Cross, standing in Platform 1. Its neighbour will be the 11-37 departure to Leeds. A gas tank wagon standing in the loop at the left is likely to be fuelling a kitchen car on the London train. (P Ward)*

List of Stationmasters, Filey

Bryan Hebden [1846-]
Henry Darby [-1855-]
Charles Milner [-1867-1872-]
Richard R Harrison [-1879-1893-]
John B Steel [-1901-1905-]
James Taylor (1863-1932) [April 1906-retired 31 July 1927]
LW Binning [February 1928-retired 1 August 1935] previously relief clerk at York
RW Gordon [January 1942-1950]
Harold Fawcett [July 1950-retired 1965]

Endnotes:

1. David Neave & Nikolaus Pevsner, *The Buildings of England: Yorkshire: York and the East Riding,* Penguin, 1995. Unett retained his Birmingham ties and died in Leamington Spa.
2. *Yorkshire Gazette,* 10 October 1846.
3. TNA (National Archives, Kew) RAIL 527/31 NER Locomotive & Works Committee 28 January and 25 February 1875.
4. TNA RAIL 527/15 NER Board 7 June 1878 Min (Minute) 7851; 27 September 1878 Min 7897; 21 November 1879 Min 8035 document three successive attempts to interest the NER. The 1850s had seen a proposal for a Harbour of Refuge for the Royal Navy.
5. CA Midgeley was listed as 'coal agent' by Kelly in 1929.

Plate 7.21. *A postcard view of the Camp itself. (John Farline Collection)*

Plate 7.22. *On the morning of 25 August 1956 a train of empty stock was being worked from Bridlington to the Camp. Unfortunately, the vacuum hose between engine and coaches had not been connected, leaving the latter without any brakes, as the driver discovered when, having coasted down from Speeton summit, he tried unsuccessfully to slow down at Hunmanby. The engine was put into reverse while the fireman applied the handbrake and kept popping his whistle to indicate that the train was out of control. Royal Oak South box sent the message that the train was running away to the Camp box, where signalman Harry Metcalfe acted promptly to halt a train approaching from the north and give the runaway a straight run into the empty Platform 3. With handbrakes screwed down in the end coaches, speed was reduced from more than 40 mph at Royal Oak South to about 25 when it hit the buffers, the engine crew having jumped out shortly before. Class K3 No 61846 came to a fairly abrupt halt after displacing the concrete wall panel and riding up on the fill behind. The passengers waiting to travel to Derby on this train were bussed to Filey station and accommodated on the regular services instead, while the Hull Dairycoates breakdown train was called out and had the K3 back on the rails by 4-30 pm. (Ken Hoole Study Centre Collection)*

6. Goods and passenger traffic figures are taken mainly from TNA RAIL 527/2142: a volume of annual summary figures for stations in the York District, 1902-35.
7. Network Rail York drawings 82/279, 82/280, 82/305. TNA RAIL 527/656 William Bell Pocket Book lists this work at £164-19-10.
8. TNA RAIL 527/37 NER Way & Works Committee 11 October 1883 Min 760.
9. TNA RAIL 527/39 NER Way & Works Committee 8 August 1889 Min 5029. The cost was estimated at £340. The work would have been started after the end of the summer season.
10. TNA RAIL 527/30 NER Locomotive & Works Committee 12 January 1872 Min 11707 approved the design of Thomas Prosser, the NER Architect, for the screens; it was similar to one he'd recently done for Malton. 9 February 1872 Min 11792 let the contract to J Broadley for £58-6-11.
11. *Gillbanks Directory*, 1855. By then the stationmaster was Henry Darby.
12. TNA RAIL 527/37 NER Way & Works Committee 14 June 1883 Min 497. 1 November Min 882 approved a tender of £91 from TP Barry.
13. TNA RAIL 527/42 NER Way & Works Committee 4 January 1894 Min 8227; 8 February Min 8324 let this to F Haxby of Filey at £89-3-0.
14. TNA RAIL 527/33 NER Locomotive & Works Committee 3 January 1878 Min 18447; 17 January Min 18482; the directors agreed to consider the idea.
15. The inspector conducting the appeal was JM Steers, who visited the site on 23 January 1989 and made his report on the 25th. This is appended to the letter of 6 April 1989 from the Secretary of State for the Environment, refusing the appeal. He actually consented to the demolition of the water tower, which was unlisted but lay within the curtilage of the station, although its significance as part of the ensemble had been pointed out; however, BR chose to retain that and it has since been listed, Grade 2, in its own right.
16. Grants initially were: Railway Heritage Trust £100,000; English Heritage £73,600; Filey Town Council £15,000; Scarborough Borough Council £10,000. Some were later increased.
17. A full account of the branch appears in John Farline, 'The Filey Holiday Camp Branch' in *British Railway Journal No 42,* Summer 1992. For further details see John Farline, 'Filey Station' and 'Filey Holiday Camp Branch' in Martin Bairstow, *Railways in East Yorkshire : Volume 3.* Further drawings of Filey's railway buildings appear in John Farline, 'Filey Station' in *British Railway Journal No 25,* 1989, and *Railway Modeller,* October 2009/April 2010.
18. Drawn up by Neville Stead and based on the train register for Royal Oak South and working timetable.
19. TNA AN176/108 (with extra material in 109) File of BR documents relating to the Filey Camp branch closure.

Plate 7.23. *Stationmaster James Taylor retired at the end of July 1927 and is pictured here with his successor, Mr LW Binning (left), who had to implement modest staff reductions, losing a passenger clerk and lad porter two years later. (John Farline Collection)*

Plate 7.24. *Class B16 No 61446 heading a holiday train to Scarborough past Royal Oak South; the signalbox, with its splayed corners and concrete slab roof, was a classic example of late LNER design. (Neville Stead Collection)*

Chapter 8: Smaller Stations and their Traffic

John F Addyman

Introduction

The North Eastern Railway handed over 600 stations to the LNER in 1923, but only 100 of these survived to be privatized after the infamous Railways Act of 1993. The Hull - Scarborough is fortunate as half its original stations remain open for passengers, but all have lost their freight traffic. Before the railway came the transport needs of the area were met by a few scheduled coaches and numerous horse-drawn carriers' carts augmented at the southern end by navigations served from the River Hull. Surprisingly, besides servicing the outlying villages, some carriers were still maintaining a weekly, or even daily, service parallel to the railway after 1900, and some must have survived to become mechanized rivals. As seen in Chapter 12 the NER was the first to introduce buses and steam-lorries into the area from 1903, and others soon realized their advantages in handling livestock, goods and passengers from the railway's catchment area, very much to its detriment. In the 1920s the railways not only had to cope with losing much of their traffic to roads, but with inflation that had quadrupled their wages bill and other costs since the 1880s. For example, the salaries for the stationmasters at the smaller stations had risen from £50-52 per annum to £200-230 between 1880 and 1920 but fares and rates had not kept pace.

The NER was very keen on producing statistics, and many are still available to give a *partial* picture of traffic trends in the years when the railway was of greatest value to the communities that it served. The NER printed a book listing every station, the villages it served and their total population together with the number of passengers booked at each station for the years 1901 and 1910. For example, in 1901, Lowthorpe was considered to serve the whole population of Lowthorpe (189), Gembling (105), Harpham (193), Great Kelk (122), Little Kelk (60), Ruston Parva (84) and half of Beeford (324), Foston-on-the-Wolds (97) and Kilham (473), making a total 1,647. The number of tickets booked at Lowthorpe for the year was 9,795 giving a statistic of 5.95 journeys per head.

There is also a handwritten file (TNA RAIL527/2179) giving details, for every year from 1885 to 1914, of passenger, coal, livestock and goods traffic for each station together with revenue and staff costs. Another manuscript (TNA RAIL527/2142) gives a summary of the goods and passenger traffic and their receipts from 1900 to 1935. These are not as detailed as they might have been, but still give a valuable overview of each station's activities, and highlight the very significant loss of passengers and freight to road transport from 1920. The table 'Goods Traffic Forwarded' reproduced for each station in this chapter comes from an LNER booklet comparing the traffic of the best pre-war year (1913) with the mid-1920s before the roads took a real toll. The table does not cover many individual categories of goods as they fell below its cut-off of 100 tons, and we know little of the make-up of inward traffic. Farmers would need coal, seeds, animal feeds, fertilizer, disinfectants, building materials and agricultural implements; their livestock, in and out, would peak for the spring and autumn sales. Around 1900, 'The butcher, the baker and the candlestick maker' were amongst the 30, or more, trades to be found in each town or major village, and most would send or receive goods via the railway, some just using the parcels service; the factories, breweries and mills would require wagon-load traffic, but details are lost in the mists of time.

The siding diagrams (often wrongly referred to as 'white prints') have been reproduced for each station, and show the very limited accommodation for handling goods on this line. The sidings at Arram and Gristhorpe could hold less than ten wagons, and some of the others only 20. The autumn must have stretched the facilities to the limit with livestock and grain traffic being at their heaviest, and coal being brought in ready for the winter. Coal cells for the smaller stations were at Cottingham, Hutton Cranswick, Nafferton, Flamborough and Hunmanby; these could use bottom-door wagons, but the other stations would need to unload via side-doors, and the coal to be stacked in the open.

Cottingham

Grid Reference TA 051328; mileage from Hull 3 miles-77 chains; altitude of rails 19 feet.
Current status: unstaffed halt served by around 70 trains per day. Closed goods 5 January 1970.
Population: 1901 3,751; 2001 17,263.
Journeys originating: 1911 114,909; 2009-10 199,000.

Goods Traffic Forwarded	1913	1923	1924
Grain	393	423	473
Vegetables	123	932	1,065
Livestock	46	43	55
Roadstone	#	168	#

less than 100 tons. Livestock in wagon loads, remainder in tons.

Kelly's Directory for 1889 described Cottingham: 'From its proximity to Hull and the easy communication therewith by railway, this place is now the residence of many of the merchants and professional men of Hull'. Being just 4 miles from Hull it has high passenger numbers, and for 100 years from 1865 was served by the Hull - Scarborough and Hull - York trains. Now the Hull - Scarborough service is augmented by a frequent shuttle between Hull and Beverley, but, due to bus concessions, the passenger numbers have gone against the national trend and declined by 7% since 2006. In 1911 the NER calculated the station booked 23 journeys per head of population served; this was over four times the average for all the stations in the Hull district superintendent's area, and twice that for the whole of the NER system; the current figure is over 11 journeys per head but based on a much larger population. Passenger figures had risen from around 80,000 in the late 1880s to 142,000 in 1920 with receipts rising from £2,500 to £9,500. Local buses were then introduced, and journeys plummeted to 57,000 in 1924, but amazingly recovered to 104,000 by 1926, and remained around this figure for the next decade. The buses obviously fell well short of the trains for journey times, and were not helped by the delays at Hull's notorious level crossings.

Plate 8.1: Cottingham. *A 1960s view of the station looking north, with 1874 Station signal cabin in the foreground. (John F Mallon / Joint NERA - Ken Hoole Study Centre JF Mallon Collection)*

Unfortunately, with 'Goods Traffic Forwarded' only showing categories above 100 tons we do not know what the other 370 tons from Cottingham in 1913 was made up of, and we can only guess what the inward goods were as these were credited to their forwarding stations. One thing the LNER figures show is that by the mid-1920s Cottingham's market gardens were booming and able to supply their produce much further afield than their original destination of Hull.

Plate 8.2: Cottingham. *Class B16/1 No 1429 hauls a train of mainly ex-NER non-corridor stock past the goods warehouse circa 1948. The main lines have 95lbs/yd track, but the siding, beside the warehouse, has much older second-hand 82lbs/yd track. (Neville Stead)*

After 1885 the goods forwarded from Cottingham was normally in the 1,000 to 1,500 tons range, but why a sudden peak between 1907 and 1911 averaging 2,340 tons before declining to the lowest ever figure of 884 tons in 1913? The goods received peaked from the normal 4-6,000 tons to average 18,000 tons over the same years – was there a building boom? Other figures show that, over the three decades, the livestock handled averaged 1,500 heads, coal rose from around 6,000 tons to 8,000 tons per annum, and the station was very profitable as the receipts were often as much as ten times the staff costs.

The original station buildings survive on the Down platform, while in 1890 the NER provided Hull-bound passengers with a lengthy waiting shed sandwiched between a pair of waiting rooms/toilets. The latter were probably for ladies and First Class passengers. The standard NER cast-iron footbridge was erected in the late 1880s, possibly as a result of accidents to passengers crossing the tracks on the level.

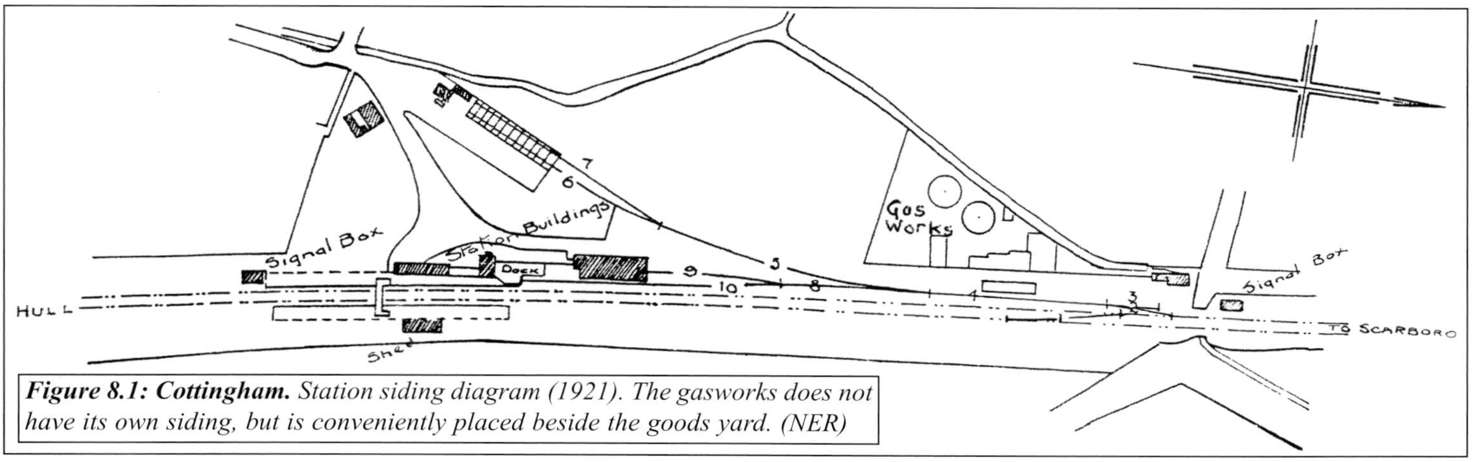

Figure 8.1: Cottingham. *Station siding diagram (1921). The gasworks does not have its own siding, but is conveniently placed beside the goods yard. (NER)*

Plate 8.3: Cottingham (left). *Well into the DMU era Class B1 No 61084 arrives at Cottingham with a train from York in August 1962. (Neville Stead)*

Plate 8.4: Arram (opposite page). *Looking towards Hull, showing the extensions added to original, single-storey gate house after it became a station. (HGE Wilson, 1977)*

Arram

Grid Reference TA 035442; mileage from Hull 11 miles-16 chains; altitude of rails 13 feet.
Current status: unstaffed halt served by 12 trains per day. Closed goods 4 May 1964.
Population: 1857 302; 1901 347; 2001 1990.
Journeys originating: 1911 4,804; 2009-10; 1759.

Goods Traffic Forwarded

	1913	1923	1924
Grain	351	476	383
Livestock	78	64	62

Livestock in wagon loads, grain in tons.

In 1846 a $10\frac{1}{2}$-mile branch from Arram to Hornsea had been authorized. The hamlet of Arram is situated around the station, but the larger village of Leconfield, which it serves, is about $1\frac{1}{2}$ miles to the west. Possibly when the scheme failed, after Hudson's downfall, the Y&NM did not consider Leconfield deserved its own station, having a small population and being only three miles from Beverley. However, approaches to the NER brought Arram into the timetables from September 1855. Initially the crossing-keeper's house must have served as the station premises, but modifications were authorized in 1862 to increase the facilities to the tune of £159, with further improvements in 1891, costing £221. In the mid-1880s it was handling around 6,000 passengers a year, 800 heads of livestock, 430 tons of coal and 1,000 tons of goods traffic. Until the First World War the receipts comfortably covered the wages of the three staff at the station. The station was considered for temporary closure along with Bempton and Carnaby, in January 1917, as a wartime economy that was not implemented.

The population of Leconfield was significantly increased by the opening of an RAF base in 1936, which served Fighter Command during and after the war; it is now an MoD driver training school, and an RAF Rescue helicopter base. During the war years the

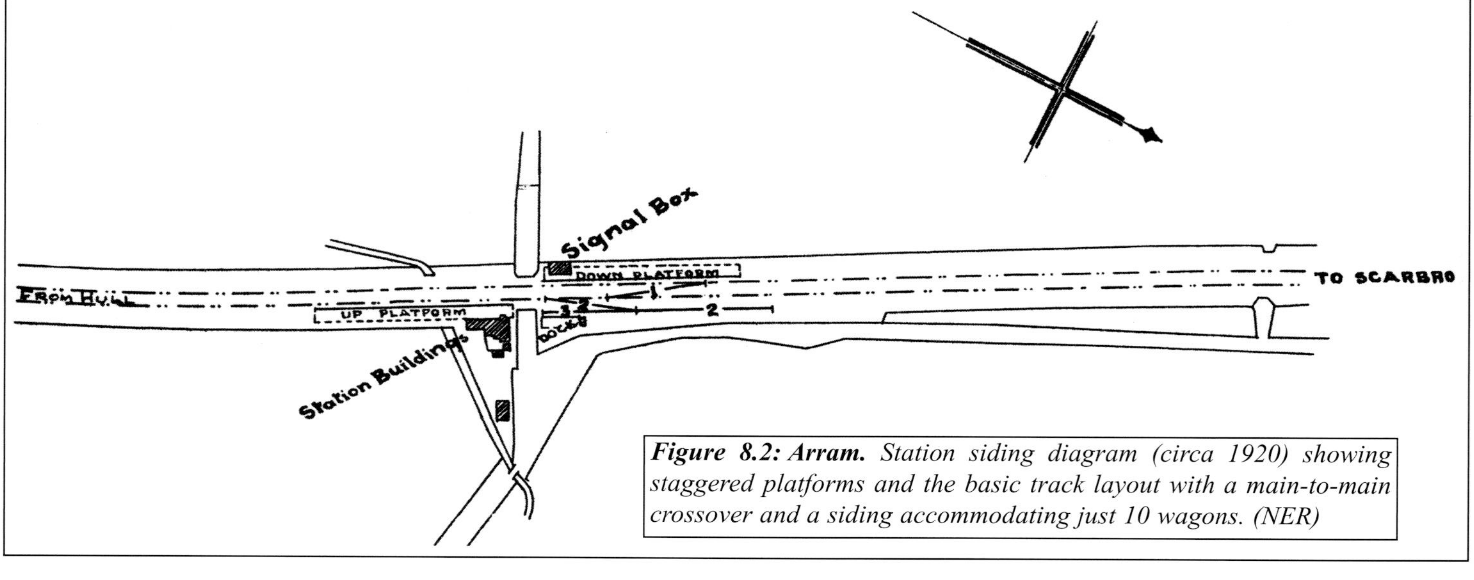

Figure 8.2: Arram. *Station siding diagram (circa 1920) showing staggered platforms and the basic track layout with a main-to-main crossover and a siding accommodating just 10 wagons. (NER)*

station must have seen a large, temporary increase in passenger and goods traffic to serve the airfield. In 1963 the Beeching Report considered its depleted passenger numbers justified closure, and a census in 1966 showed that only 20 people were using the station each day. However, when the line became grant-aided in 1969 the station was reprieved because Arram was not served by any bus services. Even though its passenger numbers have increased by 70% since 2005 it is now only averaging one passenger for every two trains that stop there.

Lockington (controlling Kilnwick Gates)

Grid Reference TA 026469: mileage from Hull 12 miles-76.5 chains: altitude of rails 15 feet.

Current status: closed to passengers and goods 13 June 1960.

Population served: 1901 943. Journeys originating: 1901 9,573.

Goods Traffic Forwarded	1913	1923	1924
Grain	694	912	699
Livestock	220	186	158
Timber, Round	#	#	145

less than 100 tons. Livestock in wagon loads, remainder in tons.

Lockington station was situated on Aike Road and the NER considered it served the villages of Lockington, Beswick, Kilnwick, Lund, Scorborough and one-third of the population of Watton. Although there has never been a road from Aike to Arram the NER thought it would use Arram rather than Lockington. Before the railway was built goods for the area were handled by a 'coal wharf' a few yards east of the station site. This was the head of the navigable stretch of the Aike Beck (also known as Coal Beck), running two miles south-east to the River Hull. It was soon superseded by the railway, and the turning basin and its immediate connection had been obliterated by 1890 although the remainder survived as a drain for almost a hundred years before being filled in; it should not be confused with the 'Coal Dyke' shown on modern OS maps adjacent to the Aike road.

In NER days the station had a staff of five to book between 9,000 and 10,000 passengers each year. Livestock handled rose from around 1,000 in the 1880s to 4,000 prior to the First World War. The coal traffic, of around 1,900 tons in the 1880s, had virtually halved in the same period, with Lockington being mainly supplied by coal merchants from Beverley. Goods received averaged 1250 tons and forwarded 1,900 per annum giving total receipts of twice the staff costs. In 1866 an old engine shed from Hull Drypool was re-erected at Lockington to form the goods warehouse at a cost of £79. Lockington controlled the siding at Kilnwick Gate, two-miles further north, and no doubt assisted the man that was employed there to handle up to 1,600 heads of livestock, 500 tons of coal and 2,000 tons of goods per annum. Kilnwick had a small warehouse, loading dock and a siding holding 10 wagons.

As part of the LNER economies carried out at many smaller stations, Lockington and Arram came under the

Figure 8.3: Lockington. *Siding diagram (1921) showing sidings for a maximum of 22 wagons. (NER)*

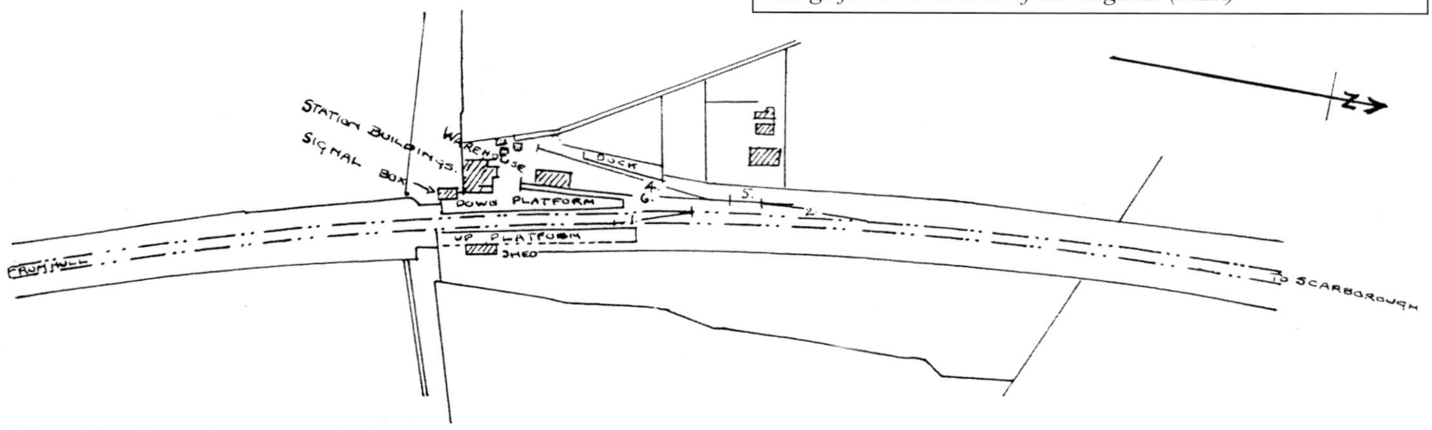

control of one stationmaster from 1929. Lockington station, being at least two miles from the nearest village, was badly hit by road transport with goods traffic under 1,000 tons and the tickets booked having fallen to below 2,500 by 1933; it was closed prior to the Beeching Report. Twenty-six years after closure it gained notoriety as the site of the second most tragic level crossing accident in Britain, see Chapter 11.

Plate 8.5: Kilnwick Gates. *Looking south towards Hull on 13 May 1960. For a view of the lever frame in Kilnwick signal box, see Plate 10.9. (John F Mallon / Joint NERA - Ken Hoole Study Centre JF Mallon Collection)*

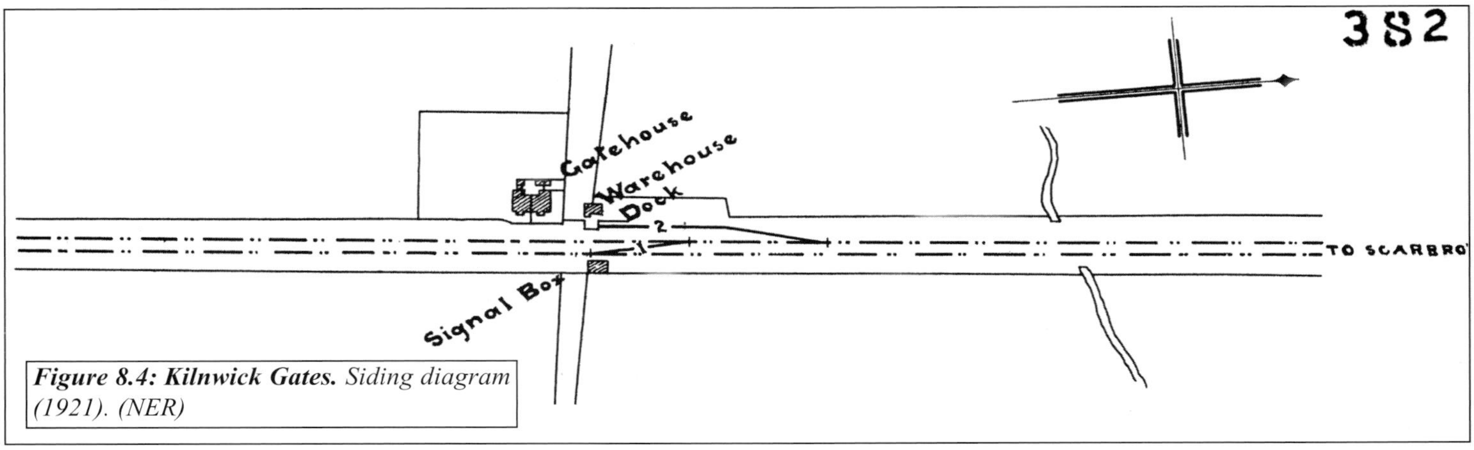

Figure 8.4: Kilnwick Gates. *Siding diagram (1921). (NER)*

Hutton Cranswick

Grid Reference TA 028522: mileage from Hull 16 miles-21 chains: altitude of rails 32 feet.
Current status: unstaffed halt served by 38 trains per day. Closed goods 10 August 1964.
Population: 1901 907; 2001 2,015.
Journeys originating: 1911 16,513; 2009-10 16,733.

Goods Traffic Forwarded	1913	1923	1924
Grain	1,200	1,875	1215
Hay, Clover, &c	263	160	584
Beans and Peas	#	109	111
Livestock	202	164	88

less than 100 tons. Livestock in wagon loads, remainder in tons.

Hutton Cranswick station is situated in Cranswick, about a mile from the neighbouring village of Hutton, and serves a rich agricultural area. George Hudson was a landowner in the vicinity, and arranged the station as a goods railhead, with coal cells and a substantial goods shed to the standard Andrews' pattern. The station did not generate the expected amount of traffic, and the villages being just off the main road and around three miles from Driffield may have influenced the goods and livestock figures.

Minor improvements by the NER typify what was done to update wayside stations. Thus a ladies' waiting room was added in 1887, accompanied by a short verandah roof which has long gone though its site is still obvious. The Up platform had a standard open-fronted timber waiting shed, whose comfort was improved in 1899 by enclosing the front and installing a stove. The last beneficiary was stationmaster, John Burniston, who was given a bathroom in 1912.

In NER days the station had a staff of four to handle a fairly constant 17,000 passenger bookings per annum and the goods traffic. The coal traffic averaged about 3,500 tons per annum, and, in accordance with normal NER policy, profits of the sales from the coal depôts supplemented the stationmaster's salary. Here, together with a local dealer, he acted as a coal agent for the immediate area (see table at the end of this chapter). Livestock averaged below 3,500 heads and the average annual tonnage of traffic forwarded prior to the First World War was 1,450 and received was 2,050; by 1934 the total in and out was below 1,500 tons. Road transport really hit, losing the railway 10,000 annual passenger journeys by 1935, but the station avoided the Beeching cuts. The former goods warehouse has been converted in exemplary fashion into a dwelling.

Plate 8.6: ***Hutton Cranswick.*** *Looking south towards the station showing the goods yard with neither a weed nor a wagon in sight! As with many stations on the line the platforms have been extended by a cribbage of old sleepers. (John F Mallon / Joint NERA - Ken Hoole Study Centre JF Mallon Collection) See Plates 3.10 and 3.11 for views of the station buildings.*

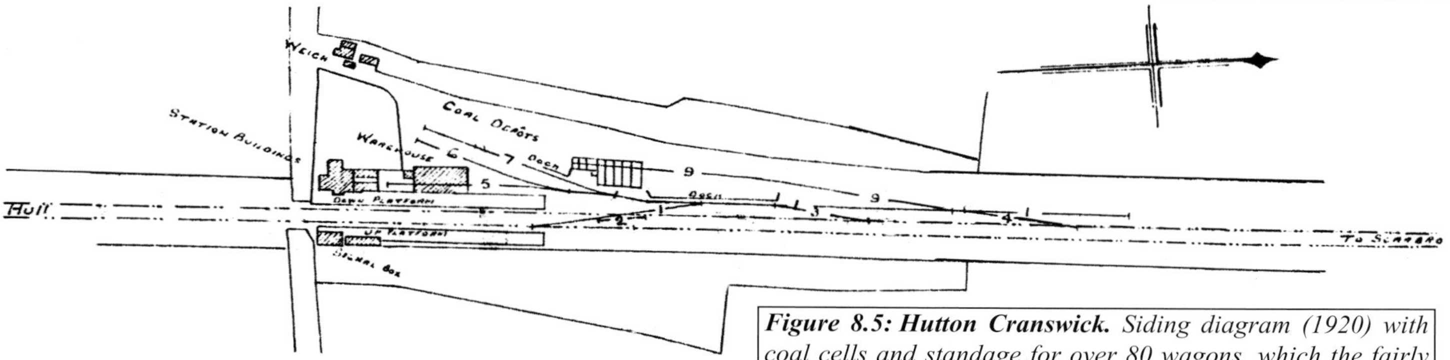

Figure 8.5: Hutton Cranswick. *Siding diagram (1920) with coal cells and standage for over 80 wagons, which the fairly limited traffic could never justify. (NER)*

Nafferton

Grid Reference TA 058584; mileage from Hull 21 miles-54 chains; altitude of tracks 33 feet.
Current status: unstaffed halt served by 38 trains per day. Closed goods 5 July 1976.
Population: 1901 1,232; 2001 2,184.
Journeys originating: 1911 20,177; 2009-10 13,950.

Goods Traffic Forwarded	1913	1923	1924
Flour, Bran, &c.	7,299	10,654	10,897
Grain	1,354	1,446	1,111
Livestock	184	87	56
Hay, Clover, &c	113	#	114
Vegetables in Bulk	#	101	#

less than 100 tons. Livestock in wagon loads, remainder in tons.

Nafferton was considered to serve Wansford one-mile away, Brigham four-miles away and North Frodingham five-miles distant, giving a total figure of 1,700 potential passengers. In 1901 they booked 22,000 tickets giving almost 13 journeys per head of population per annum, but the numbers had halved by 1935. A staff of four had to man the signal box and handle passengers, 2,000 heads of livestock, 2,400 tons of coal and lime and 7,850 tons of goods traffic; in 1901 the staff costs came to £319 with receipts of £2,487. From 1933 Nafferton controlled Lowthorpe.

This was one of the few wayside stations originally to receive a goods shed, and this is now the best surviving example of this Andrews' design. Across the line from it is the site of the Station Mill, served by its own private siding and built in 1878 by Matthias Nornabell, who had previously run his grain mill at Wansford, possibly in the premises of the former carpet factory. After his death his widow ran the business until TS Thirsk & Son took over in 1906, and extended the mill to greatly increase production; by 1924 they were forwarding nearly 11,000 tons of their products by rail, and the tonnages of goods remained high in the 1930s. The review for the Beeching Report, carried out in the autumn of 1962, showed that Nafferton was the only smaller station still to be handling more than 5,000 tons of freight per annum, and this explains its late closure to goods traffic. However, livestock ceased to be carried by BR in December 1964, when the last wagons of Irish cattle arrived at Nafferton via Holyhead.

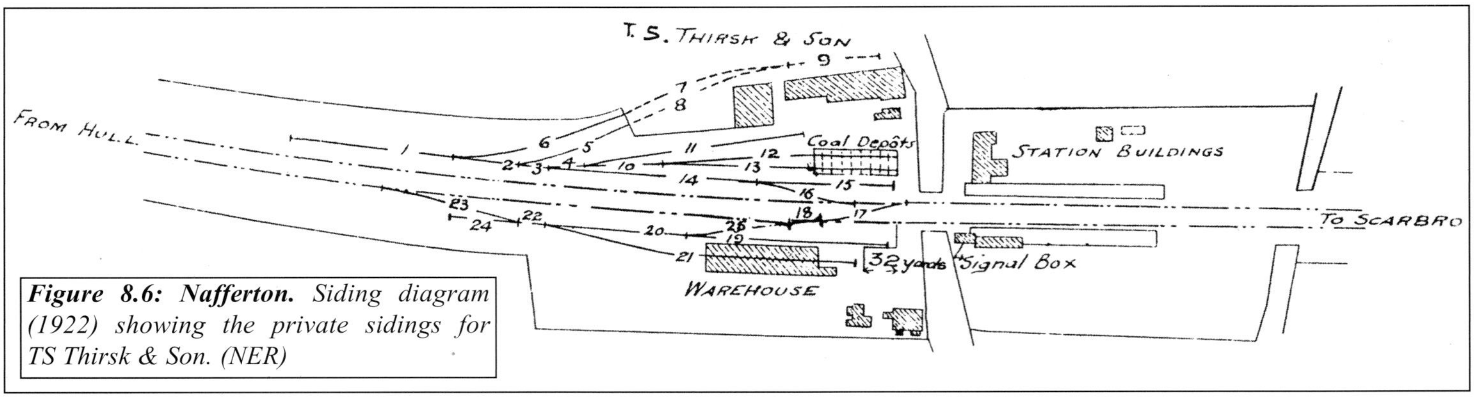

Figure 8.6: Nafferton. *Siding diagram (1922) showing the private sidings for TS Thirsk & Son. (NER)*

Plate 8.7: Nafferton. *The station prior to 1907 showing the original 1874 signal box, and a number of white-clad mill workers waiting for trains. A single coal wagon is on the depot, and a birdcage-roof guards van can be seen to the right of it. (NERA Collection)*

Plate 8.8: Nafferton. *Looking south in June 1965 with Thirsk's mill on the right, and the Andrews' goods shed to the left of the train. (Neville Stead)*

Lowthorpe

Grid reference TA 090601; mileage from Hull 23 miles-64 chains; altitude of rails 39 feet.

Current status: closed to passengers 5 January 1970. Closed goods 2 November 1964.

Population served: 1901 1,647. Journeys originating: 1901 9,795.

Goods Traffic Forwarded	1913	1923	1924
Grain	1,367	1,724	1,442
Livestock	297	171	110
Beans and Peas	#	108	#
Timber, Round	#	#	248
Vegetables in Bulk	#	#	135
Hay, Clover, &c.	#	#	439

less than 100 tons. Livestock in wagon loads, remainder in tons.

The NER considered this station served nine villages, the largest two being four and seven miles away; Harpham, Great and Little Kelk and Lowthorpe, all within two miles of the station, contributed less than one-third of the population served. The already diminishing passenger figures reflected this with the journeys booked per head of population having dropped from over seven in the 1880s to below six by 1901. However, the booming livestock, coal and goods traffic more than made up for the poor passenger numbers.

When the railway was built the expectations for goods traffic cannot have been high as only a short siding was provided on the down side, and the goods shed was not authorized until 1853. The farmers had to petition the NER about the serious delays to their livestock before a siding, 250yds long with a loading dock, appeared on the Up side in 1895. The annual livestock traffic grew from around 4,500 heads in the 1880s to 11,000 prior to the First World War. The coal traffic, which had to be handled without the aid of coal cells, rose from around 1,700 to over 2,200 tons in the same period. The average annual tonnages for goods in and out were 3,060 and 2,600 respectively, and the average revenue for all the freight traffic was £920 against £425 from the passenger fares. Compared with some of the other stations the staff of three had their work cut out to handle all the traffic, particularly prior to the additional siding being provided in 1895. The station house had to be rebuilt in 1872 to provide a second storey and a ground floor office extension; the cost was £323.

The 1920's LNER figures show the livestock traffic had become particularly vulnerable to road haulage, and by the 1930s, if we allow for inflation, the goods receipts were a quarter of the pre-1914 figure. Complete closure was inevitable after the Beeching review.

Plate 8.9: Lowthorpe. *A view looking northwards, as a southbound goods makes its way through the station. Note the platforms staggered each side of the level crossing – a very common arrangement on the North Eastern Railway. The single-storey signal box is on the Up side of the line, on the far side of the level crossing. Circa 1895, this box would be raised to two storeys, approximately concurrent with the laying of new sidings and the construction of a new loading dock. Indeed, this dock seems to be already in situ here, just to the right of the locomotive; it would appear that work on the signal box will soon commence. (Lens of Sutton Association)*

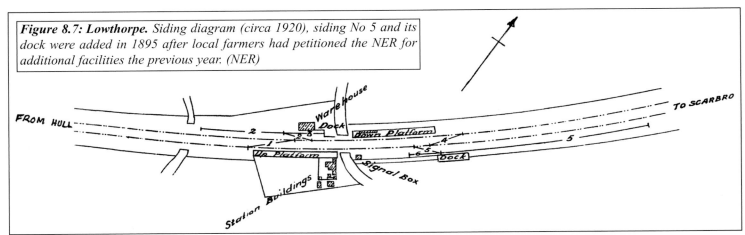

Figure 8.7: Lowthorpe. *Siding diagram (circa 1920), siding No 5 and its dock were added in 1895 after local farmers had petitioned the NER for additional facilities the previous year. (NER)*

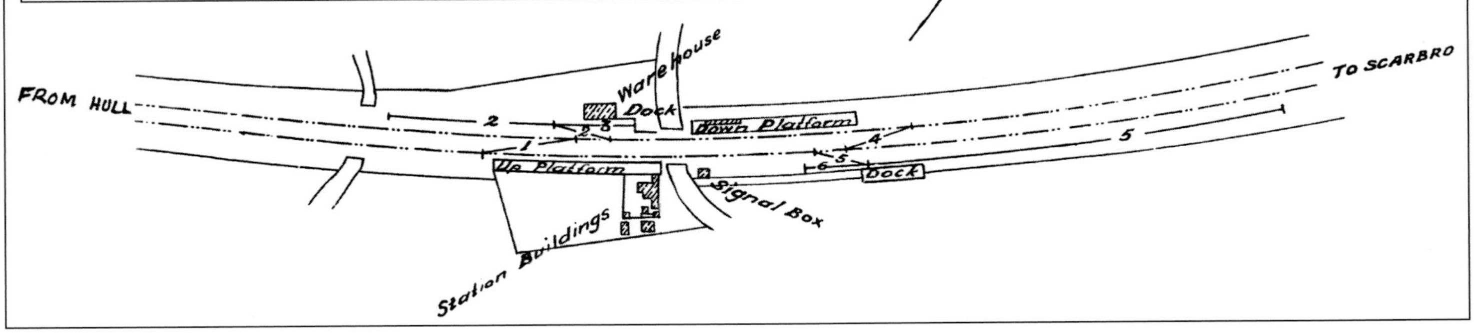

Plate 8.10: Lowthorpe. *A general view of Lowthorpe looking north on 3 May 1960. Note the NER lower-quadrant signal still in use. This may have been installed circa 1895 when the signalling was being modified to accommodate the new dock and siding. The signal would have been very much taller when new; as seen here, it has been cut down, a task undertaken on 24 May 1940. A task possibly undertaken subsequently was to 'godfather' the base; i.e. to strengthen it with old rails, which was a standard method of reinforcing rotten posts. (John F Mallon / Joint NERA - Ken Hoole Study Centre JF Mallon Collection)*

Burton Agnes

Grid Reference TA 108623; mileage from Hull 25 miles-45 chains; altitude of rails 46 feet.
Current status: closed to passengers 5 January 1970. Closed goods 2 November 1964.
Population served: 1901 1,480. Journeys originating: 1901 12,543.

Goods Traffic Forwarded	1913	1923	1924
Grain	4,815	4,893	4,094
Hay, Clover, &c.	109	#	233
Livestock	414	181	133
Beans and Peas	#	211	174

less than 100 tons. Livestock in wagon loads, remainder in tons.

Burton Agnes was another of those stations where most of the 'population served' came from some distance away with only 330 living near the station. The NER split the population of the more remote villages between two or three stations, for example, only 25% of the people in Barmston, five miles away, were considered to use Burton Agnes with the majority, probably those travelling to Bridlington and the North, using Carnaby. The passenger journeys rose from around 9,500 in the 1880s to over 11,000 during the First World War, but when the buses arrived the numbers fell to below 3,000 by 1926.

In 1854 Burton Agnes got a two-storey grain warehouse, in addition to the goods shed, and the significant tonnages of grain forwarded justified its provision. It was one of the few stations where, helped by the grain traffic, the average goods forwarded (5,150 tons) exceeded those received (3,575 tons) between 1885 and 1914. Heads of livestock peaked at 15,425 before 1900 and went into slight decline by 1914, but, as usual, started to disappear to road transport after the mid-1920s. Up to the First World War the takings for the station were six times the staff costs.

Figure 8.8: Burton Agnes. *Siding diagram (1908); siding No 7 (behind the station buildings) and the associated dock were added in 1903. (NER)*

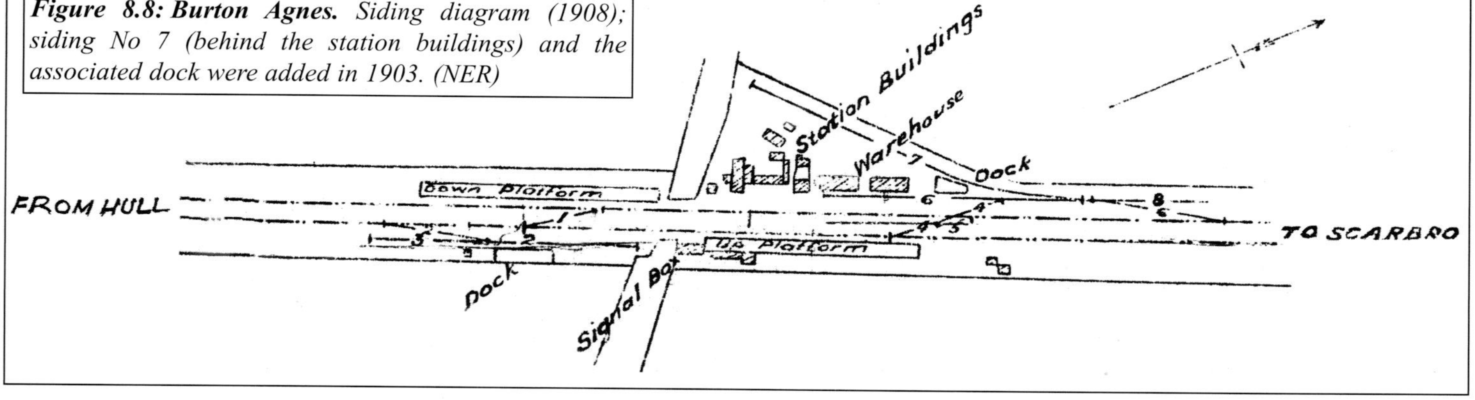

Alterations carried out in 1903 made room for a larger dock with a separate space for horses. This reminds us at that time many horses travelled by rail being part of the 'other passenger receipts' which included, parcels, carriages, dogs, etc. Valuable animals travelled in horse boxes attached to most passenger trains and others in cattle vans as livestock. A typical note in the 1901 public timetable reads: 'Horse boxes and carriage trucks are not conveyed to or from intermediate stations by these trains.' The trains referred to were 8-25 am, 10-28 am and 5-20 pm ex Scarborough but only the 5-40 am ex Hull. The shunting needed to attach or detach the vehicles on the other trains would be carried out as slickly as possible to reduce delays to the services.

Plate 8.11: Burton Agnes. *Looking north in 1972 showing from left to right; the 1874-1903 signal box, station building, 1875 cottages and grain warehouse. (John M Fleming)*

Carnaby

Grid Reference TA 148649; mileage from Hull 28 miles-56 chains; altitude of rails 33 feet.
Current status: closed to passengers 5 January 1970. Closed goods 4 May 1964.
Population: 1901 192. Journeys originating: 1901 6,100.

Goods Traffic Forwarded	1913	1923	1924
Grain	671	883	707
Livestock	162	81	66
Roadstone	#	137	#
Hay, Clover, &c.	#	#	179

less than 100 tons. Livestock in wagon loads, remainder in tons.

Carnaby, though only two-and-a-quarter miles from Bridlington station, served a total population of 600 from as far afield as Barmston, over four-miles away; this gave it between 10 and 11 journeys per person per annum in the early 1900s. The staff of three had an easy life dealing with less than 20 passengers a day as the station did not handle goods traffic until 1911, and for many years prior to that the passenger receipts barely equalled the wages bill. From 1912 an additional man was employed to help handle the 3,300 livestock, 700 tons of coal and 2,000 tons of goods, and the revenue started to exceed the wages by a small margin. This traffic, formerly handled in Bridlington, had to be dealt with in a single siding with a small loading dock. Being near to Bridlington its passenger traffic was hard hit by the buses; a one-day census in 1966 recorded no one using the station. Carnaby was the only station on the branch to get a camping coach, but it was available for just four years from 1935.

Around 1900 Carnaby could have become a junction station if the authorized Bridlington and North Frodingham Light Railway had been built, see Chapter 12.

Traffic was considerably boosted in 1943 when it was decided to construct three parallel runways nearly $1^3/_4$ miles long, and much wider than usual, to assist the landing of aircraft damaged by enemy action, or in difficulties because of mist or fog. These became operational in March 1944, and were used by 1,400 bombers over the next 14 months. A system of fog-dispersal, called FIDO, which burnt large quantities of petrol in channels on each side of the runways, was used to provide clear visibility for pilots in poor conditions. The construction and maintenance of the landing-strip, and the fuel used by FIDO, provided additional traffic for the railway and the meagre siding accommodation had to be extended. In the foggy December of 1944 nearly $1^3/_4$ million gallons of fuel had to be brought in by rail tankers, and nearly 100 bombers were guided in on *one* night just before Christmas. After the airfield closed the site was used as a Thor missile base, and became an industrial estate from 1972.

Figure 8.9: Carnaby. *Siding diagram (1912) showing the recently added siding and loading dock. (NER)*

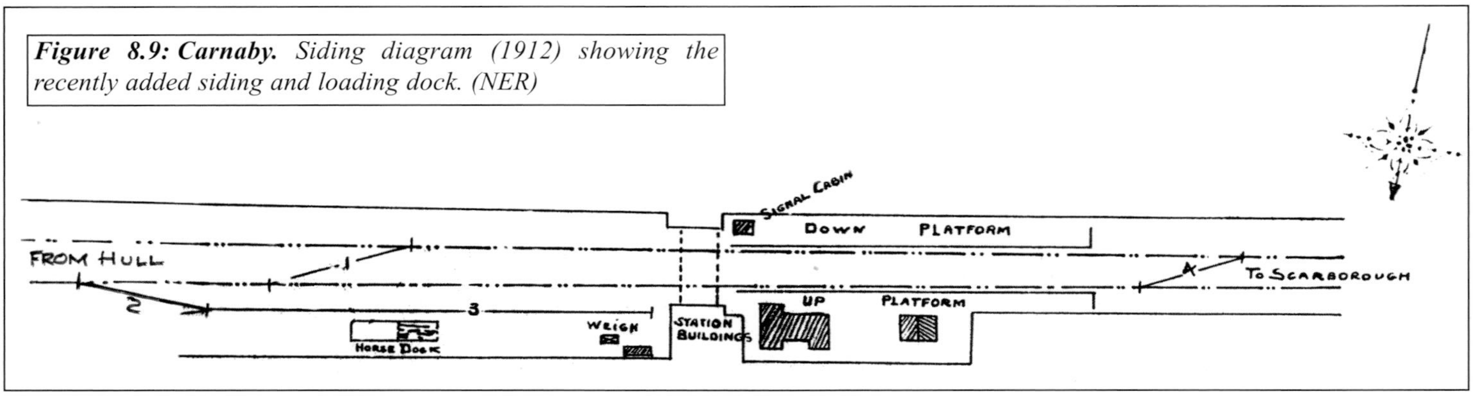

Plate 8.12: Carnaby. *A 1960s view looking towards Bridlington. The original station was just the one-storey twin gatehouse design, apparently also including a platelayer's house. In 1909 the stationmaster was given a new house, to a standard NER design of the period, which enabled both the platelayer and station offices to be granted more space (total cost £463). (John F Mallon / Joint NERA - Ken Hoole Study Centre JF Mallon Collection)*

Plate 8.13: Carnaby. *The original single-storey station buildings looking rather dilapidated in 1977. (HGE Wilson)*

Flamborough

Grid Reference TA 195700; mileage from Hull 33 miles-27 chains; altitude of rails 166 feet.
Current status: closed to passengers 5 January 1970. Closed goods 10 August 1964.
Population served: 1901 413. Journeys originating: 1901 12,350.

Goods Traffic Forwarded	1913	1923	1924
Fish	386	311	274
Grain	#	319	262
Gravel & Sand	143	#	#
Livestock	57	18	15

less than 100 tons. Livestock in wagon loads, remainder in tons.

Until July 1884 this station was called Marton after the hamlet just east of the railway, rather than after Flamborough two-miles away. Although the village was nearly five-miles from Bridlington the NER considered that 75% of its population of 1,300 would use that station rather than Flamborough's. The number of tickets booked seems to disprove this assumption, and the journeys per head were probably nearer 10 per annum for the whole population rather than the 29 for the 25% assumed by the NER. From the 1870s omnibuses from Flamborough village met the trains in the summer months, but tourists attracted to the area for the first time might have been horrified to find that it was then a further two miles walk to the picturesque Flamborough Head. However, if an 1887 proposal had gained support the journey from the station to the village and on to the North Landing would have been made on a steam tramway; see Chapter 12.

Fishing was the main industry in the village with the catches of cod, lobsters and crabs being landed from cobles on the tiny beaches of North and South Landings, on each side of Flamborough Head. In the 1880s, although the annual value of the catch was in excess of £6,000, being mainly crustaceans, it only provided around 150 to 200 tons of traffic for the railway to load via its dedicated fish dock in the goods yard. Flamborough got a suite of coal cells, and some of its 2,000 tons per annum was used to prepare lobsters and crabs for their markets. The agricultural traffic was light, with around 2,000 heads of livestock and small quantities of grain being handled each year. North of the station the railway entered a cutting, which had been enlarged in 1876 to provide a ballast quarry, and up to the First World War was served by sidings on both sides of the running lines. Although not one of the most profitable stations on the line its NER receipts came to between three and four times the wages costs of its staff of three; the passenger receipts had peaked at £3,124 in 1921, but had halved by the 1930s.

Plate 8.14: Flamborough. *A special hauled by Classes K4 No 3442 and K1 No 62005 passing Flamborough on 6 March 1965 to mark the closure of a number of East and North Riding branches from that day. (Neville Stead)*

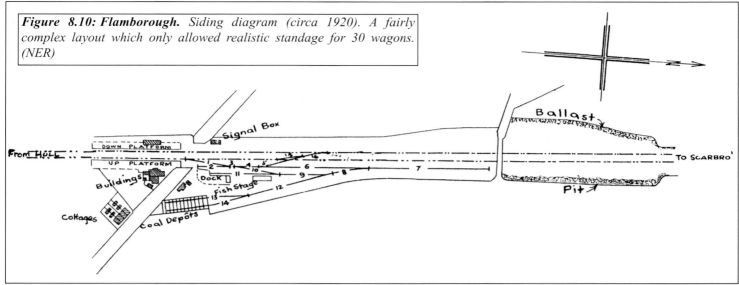

Figure 8.10: Flamborough. *Siding diagram (circa 1920). A fairly complex layout which only allowed realistic standage for 30 wagons. (NER)*

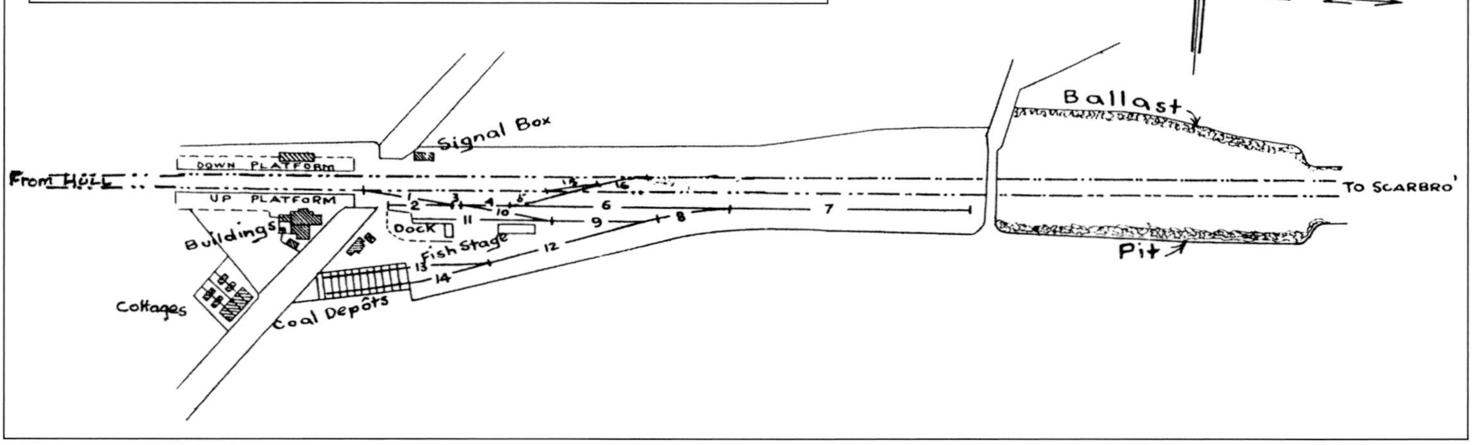

Plate 8.15: Flamborough. *A general 1960s view of the station yard looking towards Bridlington. (John F Mallon / Joint NERA - Ken Hoole Study Centre JF Mallon Collection) See also Figure 3.6 for drawings of the station house.*

Bempton

Grid Reference TA 189717; mileage from Hull 34 miles-43 chains; altitude of rails 231 feet.
Current status: unstaffed halt served by 18 trains per day. Closed goods 10 August 1964.
Population: 1901 442; 2001 1,050.
Journeys originating: 1901 7,503; 2009-10 4,921.

Goods Traffic Forwarded	1913	1923	1924
Grain	#	184	260
Livestock	70	32	29

less than 100 tons. Livestock in wagon loads, grain in tons.

Bempton and the adjoining village of Buckton were only on the railway because the line was forced to deviate from the direct route northwards to avoid very steep gradients or much heavier earthworks; the railway from Bridlington to Filey is actually $3^{1}/_{2}$ miles longer than the main road. The railway's management did not have great expectations for the traffic and only provided a staff of two to handle passengers and goods. The villagers were faithful to their station, each averaging up to 20 journeys per year. Considering that over half the land around the villages was pasture the livestock handled was relatively low, at 1,500 to 2,000 heads per annum. Coal usage rose from around 100 tons in the 1880s to over 600 by 1910, and the goods in and out, for the three decades prior to the First World War, averaged 550 and 280 tons per annum, respectively. In the early 1900s the average station receipts, of £450, were generally more than twice the staff costs. By 1930 Bempton was under the control of Flamborough's stationmaster, making an annual saving of £200.

Guide books and posters drawing attention to the thousands of sea-birds that nest on the spectacular chalk cliffs to the east of the village, and the station providing a good starting point for cliff-top walks, meant that the passenger numbers in 1935 (7,850) were in excess of 1901.

Plate 8.16: Bempton. *The station seen as approached from the village. The well maintained station house remains, but the signal box and waiting shed have been demolished. (Ian K Watson)*

Plate 8.17: Bempton. *Bempton looking towards Scarborough in the early 1900s. (Ken Hoole Study Centre)*

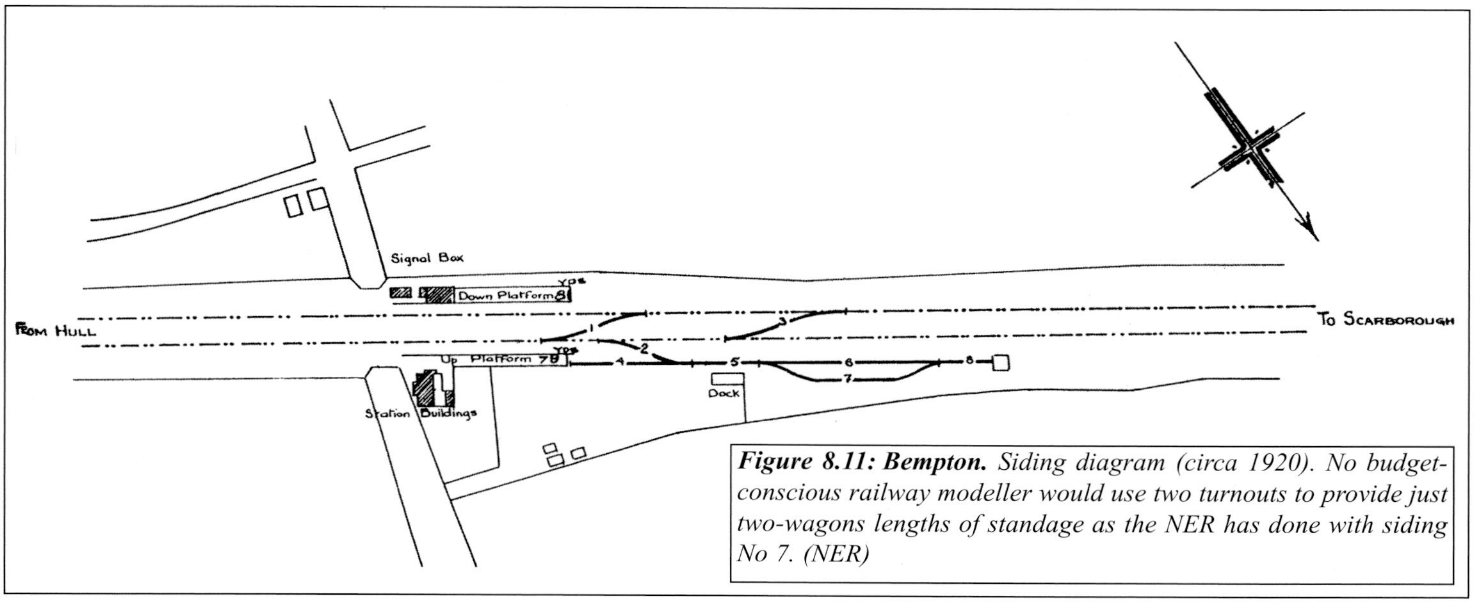

Figure 8.11: Bempton. *Siding diagram (circa 1920). No budget-conscious railway modeller would use two turnouts to provide just two-wagons lengths of standage as the NER has done with siding No 7. (NER)*

Speeton

Grid Reference TA 149738; mileage from Hull 37 miles-36 chains; altitude of rails 314 feet.
Current status: closed passengers 5 January 1970. Closed goods 4 May 1964.
Population served: 1901 411. Journeys originating: 1901 3,100.

Goods Traffic Forwarded	1913	1923	1924
Grain	370	868	763
Livestock	75	28	24

less than 100 tons. Livestock in wagon loads, grain in tons.

Speeton, the highest station on the line, was considered to serve Argham and some of the population of Grindale and Reighton. The summit of the line (345 feet AOD requiring a 310 feet climb from Bridlington) is about a mile east of Speeton station and coincides with the current county boundary of North and East Yorkshire. Here the railway swings due west to allow its winding descent to Filey, whereas the main road, following a direct line, still has to climb to its summit of over 400 feet near Reighton.

Although the passenger numbers were less than Bempton's the freight figures were a little better. Coal averaged 650 tons from 1890, and the heads of livestock were around 2,000 per annum. The goods in and out were each over 700 tons, and again the receipts were more than double the costs of the staff of two. When Bempton was considered for temporary closure to passengers during the First World War it is strange that Speeton, with half the passengers, was not. As usual 1920 was the peak year for passenger travel with 4,400 journeys starting at the station; by 1928 the number was down to 364 – one a day. Speeton came under the control of Hunmanby from 1925.

Both Speeton and Bempton were provided with coal cells when the line opened, but these had been removed by 1890. This seems very strange as it was an NER policy to provide coal cells to help its handling at almost every station.

Plate 8.18: Speeton. *The view on 1 September 1960 from the main-to-main crossover looking towards Scarborough. (John F Mallon / Joint NERA - Ken Hoole Study Centre JF Mallon Collection)*

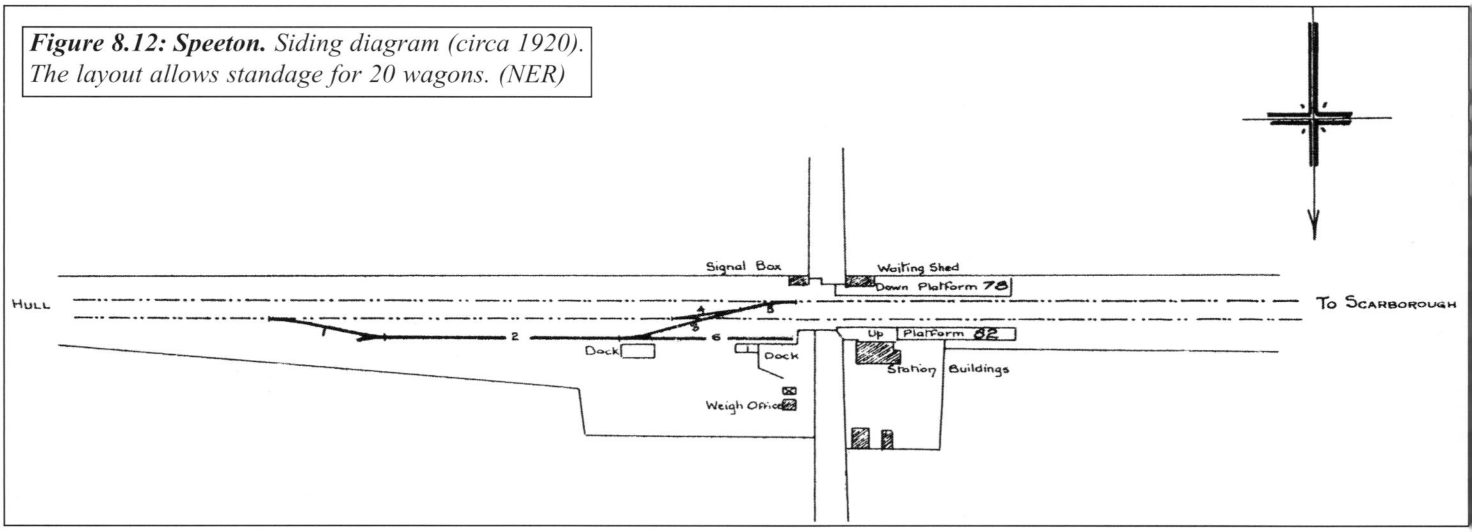

Figure 8.12: Speeton. *Siding diagram (circa 1920). The layout allows standage for 20 wagons. (NER)*

Hunmanby

Grid Reference TA101766; mileage from Hull 41 miles-54 chains; altitude of tracks 194 feet.

Current status: unstaffed halt served by 18 trains per day. Closed: goods 10 August 1964; parcels 1974.

Population: 1901 1,289; 2001; 3,279

Journeys originating: 1911 19,600; 2009-10 10,250

Goods Traffic Forwarded	1913	1923	1924
Grain	3,169	3,310	3,069
Bricks	5,655	1,529	2,799
Livestock	221	127	178
Hay, Clover, &c.	#	#	246

less than 100 tons. Livestock in wagon loads, remainder in tons.

Little had changed in Hunmanby for over 100 years until major housing developments started in the 1960s, with 50 acres of housing being completed between Bridlington Street and the railway plus another 30 to the north of the village. By the 1970s it was making the claim to be the 'largest village in England'.

Prior to the First World War, the station had a staff of five to handle all the goods and passenger traffic, which produced annual receipts of around £3,000 per annum. Passenger numbers plunged from 34,000 in 1918 to around 2,000 in the 1930s. Records show an average of 7,500 heads of livestock were forwarded or received each year. Bricks and tiles had been made here since the early eighteenth century, and the brickworks east of the station were established in the 1890s; they soon had an agreement with the NER for their own private siding. Whittaker's brickworks were the first on the scene, but sold part of the site to local entrepreneur FW Parker (1861-1934). Parker introduced brick kilns in 1919 and took over Whittaker's around 1930, but brick making ceased in 1940 when the quality of the clay deteriorated. Parker is described in a 1905 directory as 'engineer, agricultural implement, motor and cycle maker & brick maker'. He also ran a haulage business, first with traction engines and later with lorries, employing a total workforce of around 100. He had a well-equipped workshop and assembled cars before 1914, and immediately after the war opened a garage about 100 yards from the station. Reputedly he built the first garage in Filey, and many of the local garage proprietors had learned their trade from him – not a friend of the railway!

At the outset there was no goods shed, but in March 1853 the YNM completed building a rail-served warehouse which they let for £25 per annum to Messrs Dawson; in the same month they let a contract to Mr Hall to build a goods shed for their own use. The Dawson warehouse was subsequently leased to William Page, a York corn and seed merchant. Other small sources of traffic for the railway were a brewery, which closed circa 1890, and the Woodlands Dairy Company Limited which then opened. Gas was produced in the village from 1853, but the works seems to have closed around 1900. Hunmanby was provided with coal cells adjacent to Sands Road crossing, some 350 yards from the station. The total tonnage of coal, coke and lime handled there by David Wilcock, the coal merchant, varied between 3,000 and 4,000 tons per annum up to 1920.

Hunmanby Hall, originally home of the Osbaldestons, became a Methodist boarding school for girls in 1928 and remained so until 1991. An official ledger of the 'parcels' forwarded up to 1974 shows that the school used the railway for the girls' trunks and cycles at the beginning and end of the academic year. Other parcels traffic included mushrooms (as many as 50 boxes a day), racing pigeons, machinery spares and produce sent to agricultural shows. The total revenue from parcels in 1969 was £150 – around 1910 it had been twice that figure, *without* allowing for inflation.

Figure 8.13: Hunmanby. *Siding diagram (1922). Siding No 20 was a private one dating from the 1890s to serve the brickworks, and it is possible the NER extended its own siding accommodation at the same time. (NER)*

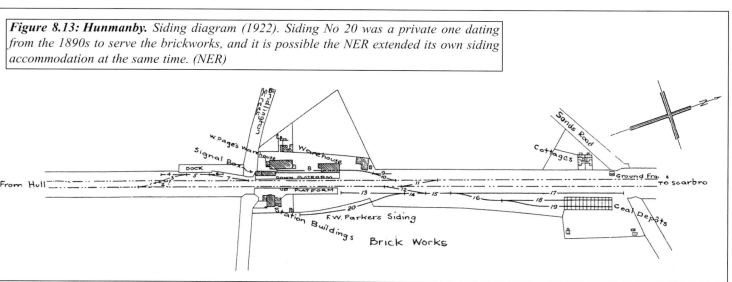

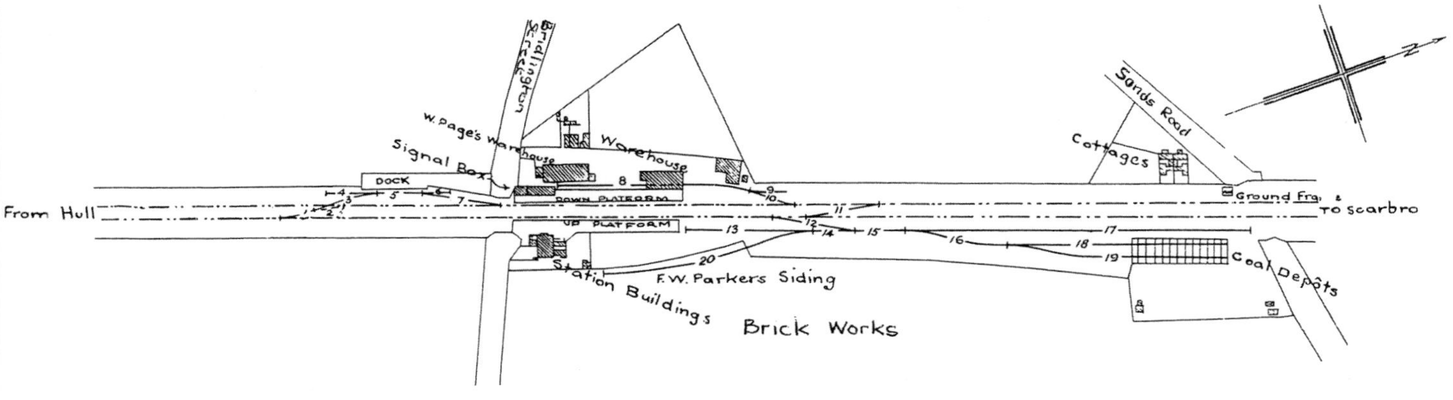

Plate 8.19: Hunmanby. *A postcard view of Hunmanby looking towards Scarborough, possibly taken around the time of the First World War. The shed, in front of the signal box, is not shown on the siding diagram, and was probably used for parcels. The tall chimneys of the brickworks can be seen. (NERA Collection)*

Plate 8.20: Hunmanby. *The station house in July 1991. (Bill Fawcett)*

Plate 8.21: Hunmanby. *A Scarborough-bound Pacer exchanges tablets at Hunmanby in July 1991. These units were not popular with drivers or passengers and were soon replaced by Sprinters. (Bill Fawcett)*

Gristhorpe

Grid Reference TA 082815; mileage from Hull 46 miles-41 chains; altitude of tracks 108 feet.
Current status: closed to passengers and goods 16 February 1959.
Population served: 1901 346. Journeys originating: 1901 5,770.

Goods Tonnage Forwarded	1913	1923	1924
Grain	112	119	117

Gristhorpe station also served Lebberston, but their small populations did not raise a lot of revenue. With the villages being only around $2^1/_2$ miles from Filey one wonders why the company even bothered to provide a single siding, holding seven wagons. In most years no livestock was handled, and the best year, 1901, only saw 45 heads. Coal traffic rose from around 200 tons in the 1880s to around 500 in 1910; forwarded goods averaged 150 tons per annum. Received goods jumped from an average of 160 tons prior to 1896 to 1,230 before the First World War. The NER receipts were more than double the staff costs, but the passenger numbers then fell from 7,570 in 1920 to below 1,500 by 1928. Surprisingly it survived to be closed just three years prior to the Beeching review. Gristhorpe was controlled by Filey from 1931.

In 1897 Gristhorpe got new station buildings at a cost of £506, and these were erected just to the west of the old house, which may have suffered from structural problems. At the time of writing, the level crossing gates at the station site are still manually operated on this 'no through road' from the village. The building to house the equipment for automatic half-barriers was erected several years ago, but has never been brought into use because of a dispute over land ownership, which means the taxpayer and rail-user has to foot the bill for manning the crossing.

Figure 8.14: Gristhorpe. Siding diagram (1926). The siding holds 10 wagons. (NER)

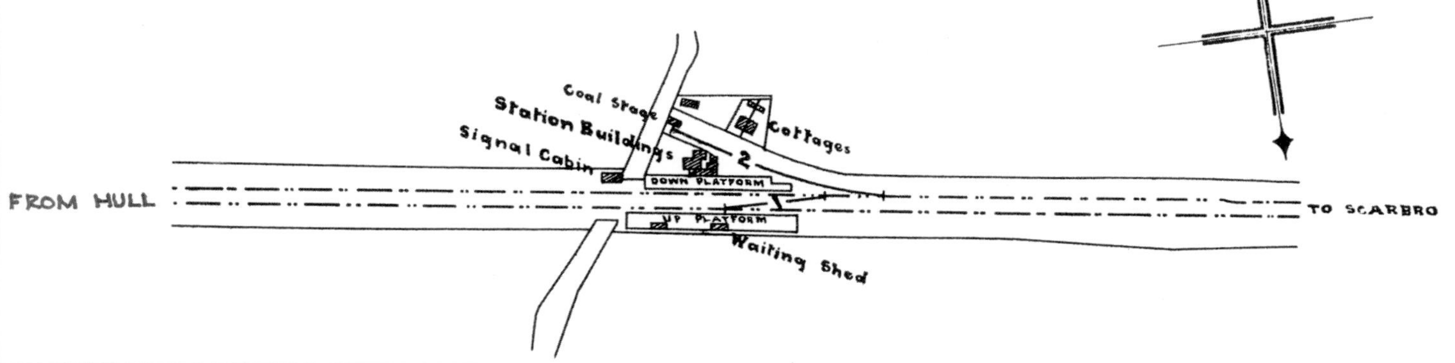

Plate 8.22: Gristhorpe. *A postcard view of the station, looking towards Scarborough, showing the 1897 station buildings on the left. (NERA Collection)*

Cayton

Grid Reference TA 058824; mileage from Hull 48 miles-17 chains; altitude of the rails 108 feet.
Current status: closed 5 May 1952. Closed temporarily from 20 September 1915 until 1 May 1921.
Population: 1901 300. Maximum number of tickets sold was 5,705 in 1914.

It was never considered worthwhile to provide sidings to handle goods traffic as the village was less than two-miles by road from Seamer station. Prior to the First World War, the station handled between eight and 16 passengers on an average day; it was not until 1903 that the receipts actually exceeded the staff costs. The average fare would have covered a return journey to Filey or Scarborough. In 1894 William Snowdon was promoted to be stationmaster at Cayton, and, being a very keen gardener, used his abundance of free time to beautify the station. When he retired in November 1913 he had gained no fewer than 12 first, one third and one special prize in the NER station gardens competition – possibly a record.

Cayton was the only station on the line to close during the First World War, and the first to close permanently, in 1952. After the temporary closure many passengers did not return, and only 1,800 tickets were booked for 1922. In 1929 the station averaged just one passenger a day, and it got worse - 1934 saw only 77 passengers paying a total of £14 in fares. When the LNER carried out a programme of closures of loss-making branch lines and stations, around 1930, one wonders why this and some of the other intermediate stations on the line survived. All the stations on the adjacent York and Scarborough line, which was joined just over two miles from Cayton, had been closed to passengers in 1930 with the exception of Malton and Seamer. One economy had been made in 1925 as Cayton lost its own stationmaster and came under Seamer's control; from the start of the Second World War the station only had a Saturday service of one train each way, and this remained the case until closure.

Stationmasters for Smaller Stations

Taken from Kelly, Post Office, Slater and White's Directories and NER/LNER Magazines. Where dates are separated by commas these refer to the dates that the names first and last appear in the available directories, but where dates are separated by hyphens these indicate that the starting and finishing years of the appointments are known. This information courtesy of Ann and Peter Los.

Cottingham

William Philips	1851, 1855.
Frederick Mountain	1867, 1879.
Charles D Naylor	1887, 1889.
Robert Smith	1893-1910.
Arthur J Sawden	1910-1921.
J Mowforth	1921-1932.
WH Farr	1932-1940.

Arram

Thomas Gordon	1882-1885.
Richard Newlove	1885-1913.
WE Dixon(1)	1913-1915.
W Young	1915-1917.
J Alexander	1917-1918.
WB Keefe	1919-1920.
Edward M Watson	1920-1921.
GH Shepherd	1921-1925.
W Habbershaw(1)	1925-1929.
WE Dickson	1929-1931.
J Ainslie	1931-?

Plate 8.23: Cayton. *A photograph showing Stationmaster William Snowdon, his daughter? and the other two staff in front of the magnificent gardens. This view was taken prior to a new timber signal box being provided in 1908. (Ken Hoole Study Centre Collection)*

Lockington	
William Dawson	1851, 1879.
Charles Hott	1887, 1893.
Thomas Wilkinson	1901, 1905.
Thomas Dowthwaite	1913, 1915.
WE Dixon(1)	1915-1933.
J Ainslie	1933-?
Hutton Cranswick	
William Taylor	1851.
Richard R Harrison	1872.
J Lee	1879.
William Gill	1887, 1901.
John Burniston	1905-1917.
AT Potter	1917-1920.
JW Sellers	1920-1930.
J Cherrington	1930-1942.
A Miller	1942-?
Nafferton	
Benjamin Robinson	1851.
John Thompson	1872.
William F Thompson	1879.
John M Nunns	1887, 1905.
Mark Savage	1913-1933.
JH Raney(2)	1933-1944.
Lowthorpe	
George Seller	1872.
Robert Marr	1879.
George Pearson	1887, 1893.
George Hott(2)	1901-1933.
Burton Agnes	
John Dobson	1846, 1851.
George Duke	1872, 1879.
William Overend	1887, 1893.
Arthur J Sawden	1901, 1905.
John Swales	1913-1922.
A Hill	1922-1931.
JF Dixon(3)	1931- ?
Carnaby	
Robert Thalwall	1872.
John Mason	1879, 1887.
Arthur Atkinson	1889, 1901.
Robert Hinchliffe	1905-1914.
Charles Longfield	1919-1927.
JF Dixon(3)	1931-1933.
HG Moor	1933-1935.
H Dodson	1935-1938.
TW Shaw	1938-1941.
Flamborough	
John Watson	1879.
Henry Hornby	1887, 1901.
Alfred D Woodward	1907-1929.
TW Martin	1929-1932.
JW Taylor(4)	1932-?
WA Hill	?-1942.
C Russell	1943-1946.
Bempton	
Robert Bartliff	1872.
Thomas Wilkinson	1887, 1901.
William Cowton	1901-1916.
E Temple	1916-1922.

Plate 8.24: Cayton. *Another view of the station gardens. Note too the chocolate bar vending machine conveniently located for passengers entering the station via the level crossing. (Ken Hoole Study Centre Collection)*

W Richardson	1922-1930.
TW Martin	?-1932.
JW Taylor(4)	1932-?
Speeton	
Ralph Gilbertson	1872.
William Cowburn	1879.
Robert Bartliff	1887.
John G Inness	1889.
George Ford	1893.
James Potter	1901.
EL Harland	?-1913.
J Warwick	1913-1914.
RH Tindall	1914-1917.
S Lund	1917-1922.
H Blackburn	1913-1925.
Hunmanby	
Francis Speck	1855.
William Martin	1872.
Frederick Vause	1879.
Jasper Robinson	1887.
Frederick Agar	1889.
Joseph Newsham	1893.
William C Scott	1901.
John Nicol	1905.
Leonard Render	1910-1917.
RH Tindall	1917-1923.
S Lund	1923-1941.
Gristhorpe	
John Wilkinson	1879.
John Hartas Lawson	1887, 1889.
John Smith	1893.
George Smith	1901.
James Marsden	1905, 1913.
E Temple	1919-1921.
HW Grant	1921-?
Cayton	
John Moss	1872, 1879.
William Wilkin	1889, 1893.
William Snowdon	1894-1913.

Notes:
1. Combined with SM Lockington during the First World War.
2. Combined with Lowthorpe.
3. Combined with Carnaby.
4. Combined with Bempton.

Some Station Statistics

Station	SM's salary 1920 £	Average annual coal profits £
Cottingham*	350	135
Arram	200	7
Lockington	230	34
Hutton Cranswick*	230	42
Nafferton*	260	88
Lowthorpe	230	78
Burton Agnes	230	103
Carnaby	200	31
Flamborough*	230	95
Bempton	200	14
Speeton	200	26
Hunmanby*	240	Nil
Gristhorpe	200	18
Cayton	160	No sidings

Notes:
* indicates that this station had coal cells. The salaries at the stations that retained their stationmasters remained constant into the 1940s. The coal profits are for the years 1906 to 1920 except for Carnaby which did not handle coal until 1912. The profits had to be shared with all the station staff that assisted in handling the coal. The stationmasters at Hunmanby chose to leave the coal trade totally to local merchants. Information courtesy of David J Williamson.

Plate 8.25: Cayton. *Even though the station had been closed for 12 years, when this photograph was taken, the platforms are still well maintained. There were no sidings at Cayton, and the signalman's only duty was to control the level crossing on the Cayton to Folkton road. Note the original 1846 waiting shed on the left (Down) platform. (Neville Stead)*

Plate 8.26. *Manchester-based Class B9, No 6105 of Great Central origin, is seen standing in the goods loop near Cherry Tree Crossing, Beverley when working a very long, mixed goods from York to Hull on 27 July 1932. (Ken Hoole Study Centre Collection)*

Plate 8.27. *Many locomotives of the southern constituent companies of the LNER worked on the Hull - Scarborough, mainly on excursions, but a number of ex-GNR 4-4-2Ts (LNER Class C12) were allocated to Hull in the mid-1930s. Here we see No 67394 hauling a Hull - Beverley service out of Cottingham, on 24 August 1948, immediately after its first BR overhaul at Doncaster Works. (DL Wilkinson / Ken Hoole Study Centre Collection)*

Chapter 9 : Train Services (1)

David R Smith

The Early Years

From its opening to Bridlington on 7 October 1846 the Hull - Scarborough line shared tracks with the Hull - Selby line for a short distance, first from Hull Kingston Street, and then from 8 May 1848 from Paragon station. At the Scarborough end it joined the York line at Seamer. Otherwise for the first 19 years of its existence the train service was self-contained. At first there were just three passenger trains in each direction on weekdays, but traffic built up steadily so that by January 1861 there were departures from Hull as follows:

Departure	Destination	Type of train	Arrival
6-30 am	Scarborough	passenger	9-10 am
9-0 am	Scarborough	goods and cattle	3-10 pm
9-30 am	Driffield	alternate Wednesdays, empty cattle wagons	
10-0 am	Driffield	passenger	10-50 am
10-10 am	Bridlington	goods	3-10 pm
12-30 pm	Scarborough	passenger	3-15 pm
2-0 pm	Beverley	passenger	2-20 pm
4-20 pm	Beverley	Tuesdays only, market train	4-40 pm
4-45 pm	Scarborough	passenger	7-30 pm
7-30 pm	Bridlington	passenger	9-0 pm

In the Up direction passenger trains left Scarborough for Hull at 6-30 am, 11-25 am and 4-35 pm with additional trains from Beverley to Hull at 8-50 am (Tuesdays only), and 2-30 pm, and others left at 11-10 am from Driffield and 4-0 pm from Bridlington. A non-stop cattle special ran from Driffield on alternate Wednesdays at 3-30 pm. There was a 2-0 pm daily goods and mineral from Bridlington and a 3-0 pm goods and cattle from Scarborough stopping at all the intermediate stations except Cayton. On Sundays there was one passenger train in each direction, leaving Hull at 7-0 am and Scarborough at 3-15 pm.

In 1865 the section of line between Beverley and Market Weighton opened, giving a through service from York to Hull, adding four or five trains between Beverley and Hull, and in 1890 the line from Market Weighton to Driffield opened to give a direct route from the West Riding to Bridlington.

1898 Services

The 1890s saw a build-up of commuter traffic from Bridlington, Beverley and Cottingham into Hull, resulting in a considerably expanded train service as seen in the October 1898 timetable. The section from Hull to Bridlington was open between 5-0 am and midnight, and the remainder to Seamer from 6-0 am until 9-30 pm. There were 25 northbound passenger departures from Hull on weekdays (three or four on Sundays); seven terminated at Beverley and another seven branched off for York leaving 11 trains (12 on Saturdays) between Beverley and Driffield. From Driffield to Bridlington the service was augmented by six trains from the Market Weighton branch, including two starting at Leeds. There have never been enough local passengers between Bridlington and Scarborough to justify a large number of trains, and seven trains each way (one on Sundays) fulfilled their year-round needs.

Stopping trains took between two-and-a-quarter and two-and-a-half hours for the full 53 miles, but the line's fastest, the 8-35 am from Scarborough, ran non-stop from Bridlington to Hull (ticket platform) in 40 minutes with a 56.25 mph pass to pass average between Driffield and Beverley. The fastest train between Bridlington and Leeds (63 miles), the 8-20 am ex Bridlington arrived Leeds at 10-8 am; in the reverse

Appendix A to the Rules and Regulations and to the Working Time Table...

From 1st January, 1898, and until further notice.

Maximum Loads of Goods Engines, &c.

	At a speed of 20 miles per hour		At a speed of 25 miles per hour	
	No of loaded goods wagons	Weight in tons	No of loaded goods wagons	Weight in tons
Between Hull and Bridlington	50	400	45	360
From Bridlington and Scarbro	26 to 30	210	25	200

Three empty goods, cattle, or mineral wagons to average as two loaded goods wagons. No train to exceed fifty wagons. The load to be reduced one-eighth during unfavourable weather.

When the train load consists entirely or almost entirely of pig iron the maximum loads shewn above must be reduced by one-third.

direction one train started from Milford Junction at 3-20 pm.

Ticket platforms were provided at Scarborough, Bridlington and Hull, but their usage was already declining; at Scarborough only two of the seven trains from Bridlington had their tickets collected there, the remainder were checked at Seamer.

An element of unreliability was admitted in the Working Time Table (WTT) regarding the 10-0 am York - Scarborough express, due into Seamer at 11-3 am to connect with the 11-15 am Scarborough - Hull. A note in the WTT stated:

> When the 10-0 am express from York is 30 minutes or upwards late in departure from Malton, the Hull train must be despatched from Seamer at the proper time and a special train run with passengers to Bridlington on arrival of the York train, returning empty immediately to Scarborough. Mr. Steel, Seamer to arrange.

The winter Sunday timetable featured one train each way at 7-0 am ex Hull and 5-0 pm from Scarborough. In summer 1898 this was supplemented by a 10-15 am from Hull and an 8-30 pm from Scarborough, aimed at day-trippers. There were also two all-the-year-round workings between Hull and Beverley, leaving Hull at 9-0 am and 9-15 pm A relief to the 5-0 pm from Scarborough ran between Driffield (depart 6-15 pm) and Hull between 1 April and 31 October; this train resurfaced in the 1930s and will be referred to later.

In the summer months there were already additional trains between Hull, Bridlington and Scarborough, also Leeds, Selby and Bridlington, and short workings between Bridlington and Filey and Filey and Scarborough. The line was becoming quite busy with excursions into all three resorts, some from a considerable distance away, particularly on Saturdays. There was now a timetabled train from Scarborough at 12-7 pm (SO) to Leicester calling at Filey, Bridlington, Driffield and Selby.

In 1898 the basic service out of Hull Goods comprised: 4-50 am (Tuesday only) York; 5-50 am York; 7-45 am Bridlington; 9-25 or 11-20 am Scarborough; 10-0 am Driffield (continued as 1-20 pm Driffield to Scarborough); 12-45 pm York; 1-35 pm Beverley goods pilot; 7-45 pm York express fish. There were corresponding Up workings into Hull although one working, the 10-0 am goods ex Scarborough, hauled by a York engine, diverted at Driffield to become the 2-10 pm 'Driffield coal' to York where it arrived at 5-15 pm. The timings varied; for example, the 9-25 am Scarborough goods ceased at the end of Scarborough's herring season and was replaced by the 11-20 am. Other trains had their timings adjusted on particular days to accommodate markets for which there were a series of additional cattle trains, particularly from Driffield which had an important cattle market serving a large area. This pattern of goods train working continued well into the 1930s, but there was further expansion of passenger services to come.

The Edwardian Era and the First World War

The expansion and prosperity of Hull – the population increased from 155,160 in 1881 to 275,552 in 1910 – coupled with the growth of seaside holidays brought increased traffic, including commuters, to Cottingham, Beverley, Bridlington and Scarborough. This was most apparent in the decade immediately prior to the war, when the number of trains increased accordingly. In the winter 1912-13 timetable there were 31 trains each way between Hull and Beverley (32 Saturdays, 5 Sundays). Ten terminated at Beverley, eight branched off for York whilst 13 continued to Driffield to be joined by seven from the Selby direction. Beyond Bridlington there were eight trains plus an extra from Filey, there was also a late train at 11-5 pm on Thursdays from Scarborough to Filey, which returned empty. The Sunday service beyond Beverley remained one train each way – not helpful to people who wished to travel on their only free day of the week. The fastest time had now become 39 minutes for the $30\frac{3}{4}$ miles non-stop from Bridlington to Hull (47.3 mph). There was also a 4-50 pm from Hull to Scarborough which ran non-stop to Filey in 59 minutes (45.13 mph). The morning business expresses from Bridlington to Leeds had been accelerated by seven minutes compared to 1898, but for some reason the return evening train required a change at Selby.

1913 and 1914 saw the climax of the pre-First World War services; in both summers there was a Bridlington - Sheffield business express, but the experiment ended with the war. Apart from the withdrawal of summer season trains and excursions passenger services were not initially affected by the war, but with the worsening situation in 1916 drastic reductions were made throughout the country from 1 January 1917, and it took several years to restore the frequency and speed of trains to pre-war standards.

Table 114.

HULL to BRIDLINGTON.

DOWN.	DISTANCE. M.	DISTANCE. C.		Class of Train. A (MINS.)	B (MINS.)	C (MINS.)
Hessle Road Jct. ...	–	–	pass	..	..	..
Beverley	7	61	arr.	18	21	25
Driffield	11	17	„	25	29	36
Bridlington	11	35	„	26	30	37

BRIDLINGTON to HULL.

UP.	M.	C.		A (MINS.)	B (MINS.)	C (MINS.)
Bridlington	–	–	dep.	–	–	–
Driffield	11	35	arr.	26	30	37
Beverley	11	17	„	25	29	36
Hessle Road Jct. ...	7	61	pass	19	22	26

Figure 9.1. *Point to point freight times, 1911. (NER)*

After 1920

The summer 1922 timetable, the last before the grouping of 1923, listed 29 trains departing Hull on weekdays (six Sundays). Eight of these terminated at Beverley (four Sundays), six served York, and 15 (two Sundays) went on to Bridlington or Scarborough. Pre-1914 the last train from Hull to Bridlington left at 10-57 pm, but now this ran as an extra on Thursdays and Saturdays only; on other days the last train to Bridlington left at 9-10 pm. Beyond Bridlington there were nine trains (10 Saturdays, 3 Sundays), supplemented by a service of five local trains (four Sundays) between Filey and Scarborough. In 1922 the fastest timings were 40 minutes for the 8-0 am and 8-52 am Bridlington - Hull trains, and the best Scarborough - Hull was 82 minutes.

The NER, and later the LNER, actively encouraged holidaymakers in Scarborough to visit the nearby resorts, and the Scarborough - Filey summer autocar workings were one such example; in later years most of this short-distance traffic transferred to buses.

The next major development came in 1928 when Sir Ralph Wedgwood, the LNER's chief general manager, proposed wholesale revisions of the local services out of Hull, based on the regular interval principle, in order to combat competition from the local buses. This was introduced on Monday 8 April 1929, and the Hull - Beverley service was the main beneficiary with a half-hourly service at 15 and 45 minutes past the hour provided throughout the day. This was supplemented by the Scarborough and York trains, some of which were retimed to fit in with the

> ***Appendix to the General Rules and Regulations and to the Working Time Table...***
> *Volume 1*, From 1st March, 1922, and until further notice.
> Position of Brake Vans on Excursion Trains [part]
> General Rules 165 and 170
> On the following sections of line excursion trains run without a van in the rear, the van as a rule being attached next the engine:-
> Hull to Scarborough.
> Scarborough to Hull.
> When only one guard is with the train he must ride in the van, and when there are two guards one must travel in the van and the other in the last compartment. (O.9891)

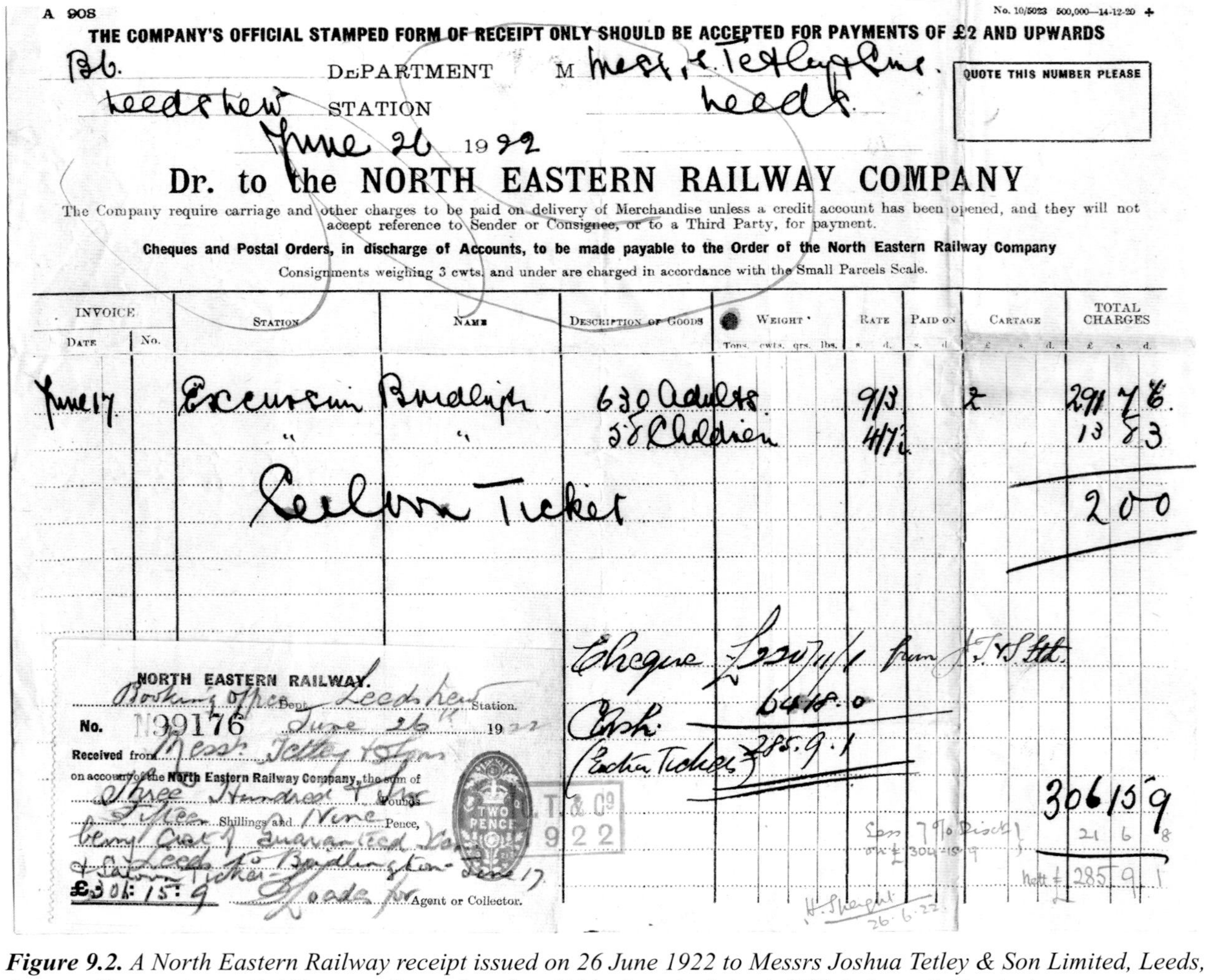
A 908 No. 10/5023 500,000—14-12-20

THE COMPANY'S OFFICIAL STAMPED FORM OF RECEIPT ONLY SHOULD BE ACCEPTED FOR PAYMENTS OF £2 AND UPWARDS

Bb. DEPARTMENT M Messrs. J. Tetley & Sons. QUOTE THIS NUMBER PLEASE

Leeds New STATION Leeds.

June 26 1922

Dr. to the NORTH EASTERN RAILWAY COMPANY

The Company require carriage and other charges to be paid on delivery of Merchandise unless a credit account has been opened, and they will not accept reference to Sender or Consignee, or to a Third Party, for payment.

Cheques and Postal Orders, in discharge of Accounts, to be made payable to the Order of the North Eastern Railway Company

Consignments weighing 3 cwts. and under are charged in accordance with the Small Parcels Scale.

Invoice Date	No.	Station	Name	Description of Goods	Weight	Rate	Paid on	Cartage	Total Charges
June 17		Excursion	Bridlington	630 Adults		9/3			291 7 6
		"	"	58 Children		4/7½			13 8 3
		Leeds Return Ticket							2 0 0

Cheque £220/14/- from J.T.&S. Ltd.
Cash 64/18/0
(Extra Ticket) 285.9.1

306/15/9

NORTH EASTERN RAILWAY.
Booking Office Dept. Leeds New Station.
No. 99176 June 26th 1922
Received from Messrs. Tetley & Sons
on account of the North Eastern Railway Company, the sum of Three Hundred & Six Pounds, Fifteen Shillings and Nine Pence, being cost of guaranteed Excursion Leeds to Bridlington - June 17
£306: 15: 9 Agent or Collector.

Figure 9.2. A North Eastern Railway receipt issued on 26 June 1922 to Messrs Joshua Tetley & Son Limited, Leeds, for a staff excursion to Bridlington. (Reproduced at 63% of original size.) (WF Astbury Collection)

regular interval pattern. The Sunday service was basically hourly throughout the day. Sentinel steam railcars had been introduced at Hull in 1927, and the use of these was an integral feature of the new timetable, working 16 (seven Sundays) of the new services.

However, the interval timetable failed to improve revenue sufficiently; Beverley's tickets booked were 169,541 in 1927 and had fallen to 88,937 by 1932 with a reduction in revenue from £24,660 to £15,859. During July and August 1931 Bridlington was handling 185,245 passengers, but there was a 3% fall in the next season to 179,701. From 22 September 1930 some of the lightly loaded trains were withdrawn. The service then settled into a pattern of which the winter timetable of 1935-6 was typical. Beverley was now served by a minimum of 43 trains each weekday (44 Wednesday, 45 Saturday, seven Sundays). Beyond Beverley there were nine trains to and eight from York, and 14 (three Sundays) serving Driffield. Here they were joined by five weekday trains from Selby or Leeds, plus one from Malton, giving a total of 20 weekday trains between Driffield and Bridlington; beyond Bridlington there were nine trains – incidentally the same number as in 2012. The extension of the Malton - Driffield train to form the 8-5 am to Bridlington was to cater for children attending school there. Mention was made earlier of a Sunday evening relief train from Driffield to Hull. This re-surfaced around 1930, and is understood to have been provided for fishermen who were attracted to the trout streams close to the line. The last two examples show the lengths that the railway was prepared to go to provide a service.

The fastest trains were now the 8-25 am from Scarborough and the 8-5 am from Bridlington, both of which ran the last $30^{3}/_{4}$ miles non-stop with averages of 50 mph. The Leeds business trains, the 7-56 am from Bridlington and 4-52 pm from Leeds now covered the 63 miles with three stops in 88 minutes.

There were less prominent but interesting workings; the first and last trains of the day between Hull and Bridlington were worked by Sentinel railcars. A Hull car worked the 5-28 am non-stop arriving Bridlington at 6-20 am and returned as the 6-30 am calling at Driffield, Beverley and Cottingham, reaching Hull at 7-25 am. A Bridlington car, which worked two return trips to Selby, formed the 8-45 pm Wednesday and Saturday only all stations to Hull arriving 9-51 pm. It returned at 10-50 pm calling at Cottingham, Beverley and Driffield, finally arriving at Bridlington at 11-57 pm having covered 230 miles in the day. Other railcar workings included the 3-25 pm Hull - York and the 4-48 return, usually worked by one of the three Armstrong Whitworth diesel-electric units, running the 42-miles non-stop in 52 minutes. There was even a train starting at Arram; the 8-15 am Hull to Beverley continued as empty stock to Arram returning as an advertised service at 8-46 am to Hull. The purpose of this move appears to have been to avoid shunting moves at Beverley, which would conflict with other trains between 8-30 and 8-40 am.

Plate 9.1. *Class D17/2 (NER Class Q) No 1909 near Cottingham on 13 May 1936 at the head of an express. (NERA T Smeaton Collection)*

1938-9 : A High Water Mark?

1938 was the year that the Holidays With Pay Act was passed, and was something of a watershed for the services on the Hull-Scarborough line. Previously not all workers had been paid during their holidays, and it increased the opportunity for holidays in places like Bridlington, Filey and Scarborough. The outbreak of war on 3 September 1939 put paid to seaside holidays for the duration, and caused significant changes to railway service patterns afterwards. The public timetables for the last two months of peace are shown on the next pages, but at the busiest times the WTT indicated that up to three additional 'relief trains' could be run each day.

Between Hull and Beverley the local service was virtually the same as 1935. On Saturdays three trains traversed the Hessle Road - Cottingham South line to reach Bridlington; see Chapter 12. There was also an unadvertised Thursday evening excursion from Hull (6-10 pm) to Bridlington (return 10-43 pm). On Sundays the carriages and locomotive of the 4-7 pm York - Bridlington formed the 6-0 pm Bridlington - Hull, and returned to York at 7-55 pm via Beverley and Market Weighton. The morning York-Bridlington train continued to Filey at 2-30 pm, returning from there at 8-0 pm giving York passengers a chance to spend part of the day at both places. Taking into account 'Q' reliefs (the letter for 'run as required' in WTT), and excursions, Bridlington saw 30 trains arriving and departing on most summer Sundays.

Table 105 — **HULL, BRIDLINGTON, FILEY AND SCARBOROUGH.**

MONDAYS TO FRIDAYS INCLUSIVE

Station	am	am	am	am	C am	am	am	am	am	F am	am	am	pm	pm
					From Heeley (L.M.S.)				York dep 10-15 am		Leeds dep 10-15 am			
HULL (A) dep	5 38	5 50		8 0		8 53	9 45			10 40		11 5	12 45	1 15
Cottingham (A)		5 58		8 8		9 6	9 53			10 48		11 13	12 53	1 23
Beverley (A) arr		6 5		8 15		9 13	10 1			10 58		11 20	1 0	1 30
Beverley (A) dep		6 10		8 17		9 15	10 3			11 0		11 22	1 1	1 32
Arram				8 23								11 31		1 39
Lockington		6 19		8 28										1 44
Hutton Cranswick		6 25		8 34								11 40		1 51
Driffield arr	6 4	6 31		8 40		9 29	10 18					11 46	1 15	1 57
Selby (Table 106) dep								9 13			10 46			
Driffield dep	6 6	6 35	8 3	8 43		9 31	10 20	10 26			11 29	11 49	1 16	2 1
Nafferton		6 40	8 8	8 48				10 31				11 54		2 6
Lowthorpe		6 45	8 13	8 53								11 59		2 11
Burton Agnes		6 49	8 17	8 57								12 3		2 16
Carnaby		6 55	8 23	9 3								12 9		2 22
Bridlington arr	6 21	6 59	8 27	9 7	9 23	9 46	10 35	10 44	11 12	11 25	11 44	12 13	1 30	2 26
Bridlington dep		7 2		9 10	9 30	9 49	10 38			11 29		12 18	1 33	2 31
Flamborough		7 8		9 16								12 25		2 42
Bempton		7 13		9 21								12 30		2 47
Speeton		7 21										12 38		2 55
Hunmanby		7 28		9 34								12 45		3 3
Filey arr		7 33		9 39	9 55	10 9	10 58			11 49		12 50	1 53	3 8
Filey dep		7 35		9 43	9 57	10 12	11 1			11 53		12 54	1 55	3 10
Gristhorpe				9 48										3 15
Cayton				9 52										3 19
Seamer (B)				10 0								1 4		3 24
SCARBOROUGH (Cen.) (B) arr		7 51		10 6	10 15	E 10 25	11 15			12 8		1 10	2 10	3 30
York (Table 109) arr		9 5				11h30	1 L 5					2k7	3 20	4 39

Station	X pm	L pm	pm	pm	pm	pm	pm	pm	pm	pm	pm	X pm	pm	pm
		Leeds dep 1-37 pm							Leeds dep 4-52 pm	Through Train—King's Cross (dep 1-40 pm) to Scarboro' Restaurant Car to Doncaster				
HULL (A) dep			2 35	3 13		4 30	5 8	5 30			6 5		7 0	7 50
Cottingham (A)			2 43	3 21		4 38					6 13		7 8	
Beverley (A) arr			2 50	3 28		4 45	5 20				6 20		7 15	8 2
Beverley (A) dep			2 51	3 29		4 46	5 21				6 21		7 16	8 4
Arram						4 52							7 22	
Lockington						4 57							7 27	
Hutton Cranswick						5 4					6 33		7 33	
Driffield arr			3 6	3 43		5 10		5 56			6 39		7 39	8 18
Selby (Table 106) dep	1 24	2 6			4 8				5 22	5 32		5 50		
Driffield dep	2 39	2 50	3 7	3 45	5 3	5 12		5 57	6 5	6 15	6 40	7 1	7 41	8 19
Nafferton						5 17							7 46	
Lowthorpe						5 22							7 51	
Burton Agnes						5 26							7 55	
Carnaby						5 32							8 1	
Bridlington arr	2 57	3 5	3 21	4 0	5 18	5 36	5 48	6 12	6 20	6 30	6 55	7 23	8 5	8 33
Bridlington dep				4 2			5 50			6 33	6 57			8 37
Flamborough				4 9							7 3			8 43
Bempton				4 14							7 8			8 48
Speeton											7 16			
Hunmanby				4 27							7 23			9 0
Filey arr				4 32			6 12			6 55	7 28			9 5
Filey dep				4 34			6 13			6 57	7 29			9 7
Gristhorpe														9 12
Cayton														
Seamer (B)				4 45							7 39			
SCARBOROUGH (Cen.) (B) arr				4 51			6 26			7 10	7 45			9 23
York (Table 109) arr				5k49			8 b0				9 3			10d55

MONS. TO FRIDAYS INC.—con.

Station	pm	D pm	WO pm
HULL (A) dep	9 15		11 23
Cottingham (A)	9 23		11 31
Beverley (A) arr	9 30		11 38
Beverley (A) dep	9 32		11 39
Arram	9 38		
Lockington	9 43		
Hutton Cranswick	TT		
Driffield arr	9 52		11 58
Selby (Table 106) dep			
Driffield dep	9 54		11 59
Nafferton	9 59		
Lowthorpe	10 4		
Burton Agnes			
Carnaby			
Bridlington arr	1015		12 19
Bridlington dep		10 20	
Flamborough			
Bempton		10 29	
Speeton			
Hunmanby			
Filey arr		10 43	
Filey dep		10 44	
Gristhorpe			
Cayton			
Seamer (B)			
SCARBOROUGH (Cen.) (B) arr		11 0	
York (Table 109) arr			

FOR SERVICE ON SATURDAYS SEE PAGE 79a

SUNDAYS

Station	am	am	Y am	am	am	am	Y am	pm	pm	¶ pm	Y pm	pm	pm	¶ pm	pm	pm
			York dep 9-35 am			Leeds dep 10-30 am		Deepcar dep 10-4 am					York dep 4-7 pm			
HULL (A) dep	7 0	9 30		1020	1030		1130		1230	1 30		2 30		5 30	6 0	9 0
Cottingham (A)	7 8	9 38			1038		1138		1238			2 38		5 38	6 8	9 8
Beverley (A) arr	7 15	9 45		1032	1045		1145		1245	1 42		2 45		5 45	6 15	9 15
Beverley (A) dep	7 18	9 46		1034	1046		1146		1247	1 44		2 47		5 48	6 16	9 16
Arram	7 24				1052											
Lockington	7 29															
Hutton Cranswick	7 36								1258			2 58				
Driffield arr	7 42				11 6		12 1		1 5	1 59		3 5		6 6	6 31	9 31
Selby (Table 106) dep						11 4										
Driffield dep	7 45				11 9		12 2		1 7	2 0		3 7	4 50	6 8	6 32	9 32
Nafferton	7 50								1 12			3 12				
Lowthorpe	7 55															
Burton Agnes	8 0															
Carnaby	8 6															
Bridlington arr	8 11	1015	1049	11 1	1124	12 4	1217	1253	1 26	2 15		3 26	5 5	6 27	6 47	9 46
Bridlington dep	8 15	1018		11 4	1129				1 30		2 30	3 30			6 50	
Flamborough	8 23				1136										6 57	
Bempton	8 28															
Speeton	8 36															
Hunmanby	8 45															
Filey arr	8 50	1040		1126	1153				1 52		2 52	3 52			7 14	
Filey dep	8 53	1042		1128	1155				1 54			3 54			7 16	
Gristhorpe	8 58															
Cayton																
Seamer (B)	9 9															
SCARBOROUGH (Cen.) (B) arr	9 14	1055		1142	12 8				2 7			4 7			7 30	
York (Table 109) arr		12 4			2 32				3 50			5 45			8 40	

A For complete service between Hull and Beverley see Table 97.
B For other trains between Seamer and Scarborough see Tables 109, 112.
C Mondays only and not after 28th August (7th August excepted).
D Wednesdays only and not after 6th September
E Calls or Mondays to set down only.
F Not after 15th September.
L Not after 8th September.
TT Calls 9-49 pm when required to set down only.
WO Wednesdays only.
X One class only.
Y Not after 10th September.
b Runs 24th July to 8th Sept. inclusive.
d Not after 15th September.
h Commencing 12th Sept. arrives 11-55 am.
k Connection at Seamer.
¶ Excursion; passengers holding tickets other than Excursion tickets may travel by this train.

Figure 9.3A. *Passenger timetables from 3 July to 24 September 1939 (not showing the local trains between Hull and Beverley). In addition there would have been excursions arriving at Bridlington virtually every day in August, so it would be catering for upwards of 35-40 trains each weekday, and more still on Saturdays.*

The trains marked 'X' at the top of the columns were worked by Sentinel railcars, but note that none operated beyond Beverley on Saturdays. Also note the gaps of around three hours between trains serving the smaller stations. (LNER)

Table 105—*continued.* — **SCARBOROUGH, FILEY, BRIDLINGTON AND HULL.**

MONDAYS TO FRIDAYS INCLUSIVE

Station	am	am	am	am	am	am	X am	am	am	am	am	am	X am	am	am
				Leeds arr. 9-22 am										Through Train—Scarborough to King's Cross Restaurant Car from Hull (arr. 3-47 pm)	
York (Table 109) dep								4 59				9k 0			10k0
SCARBOROUGH (Cen.) (B) dep								7 40		8 25		9 55		10b25	11 5
Seamer (B)								7 46				10 1			1112
Cayton								7 52							1118
Gristhorpe								7 56							1122
Filey arr								8 1		8 38		1010			1127
Filey dep								8 3		8 39		1012		10b39	1128
Hunmanby								8 9							1134
Speeton								8 17							1142
Bempton								8 23							1148
Flamborough								8 26							1151
Bridlington arr								8 30		8 59		1032			1155
Bridlington dep	6 35	6 45	7 20	7 56	8 5	8 15			8 35	9 1	9 10	1035	1043	11 0	1158
Carnaby			7 25						8 40						12 3
Burton Agnes			7 31								9 19				12 9
Lowthorpe		DD	7 35								9 23				1213
Nafferton		FF	7 40								9 28				1218
Driffield arr	6 50	7 5	7 45	8 10		8 30			8 53		9 33	1050	11 3		1223
Selby (Table 106) arr		8 14		8 54									1215		
Driffield dep	6 51		7 46			8 32					9 34	1052			1225
Hutton Cranswick			7 53								9 40				1231
Lockington			8 1												1237
Arram			8 8				8 46				9 49				1242
Beverley (A) arr	7 5		8 14			8 46	8 52				9 55	11 6			1248
Beverley (A) dep	7 6		8 15			8 47	8 55				9 56	11 7			1252
Cottingham (A)	7 13		8 23				9 3				10 3	1114			1259
HULL (A) arr	7 21		8 31		8 42	8 59	9 11			9 38	1011	1122		11 35	1 7

FOR SERVICE ON SATURDAYS SEE PAGE 80a

Station	WO pm	WX pm	L pm	pm	X pm	pm	pm	pm	F pm	pm	pm	pm	C pm	H pm	pm
			Leeds arr. 3-41 pm							York arr 7-55 pm		Leeds arr 9-0 pm	Heeley (LMS) arr 10-48 pm		
York (Table 109) dep				12k50		2 40	3L30		5d 5		5 15		6 5		6 5
SCARBOROUGH (Cen.) (B) dep	12c55			2 20		4 25	5 15		6 13		6 30		7 10		7 37
Seamer (B)				2 27		M	5 21				6 36				
Cayton				2 33			5 27								
Gristhorpe				2 37			5 31				6 43				
Filey arr	1c 9			2 42		4 38	5 36		6 27		6 48		7 24		7 51
Filey dep	1c11			2 43		4 41	5 38		6 30		6 49		7 26		7 53
Hunmanby				2 50			5 44								
Speeton				2 59			5 52								
Bempton	1c27			3 5			5 58								
Flamborough				3 9			6 1				7 9				
Bridlington arr	1c33			3 13		5 1	6 5		6 49		7 13		7 48		8 13
Bridlington dep	1 37	1 37	2 15	3 15	3 35	5 4	6 9	6 30	6 52	7 0	7 16	7 30	7 53	8 8	8 18
Carnaby				3 20			6 14								
Burton Agnes				3 26		5 13	6 20								
Lowthorpe	1 48	1 48		3 31		5 17	6 24				JJ				
Nafferton	1 53	1 53		3 36		5 22	6 29				JJ				
Driffield arr	1 58	1 58	2 29	3 41	3 55	5 27	6 34	6 44	7 7		7 32	7 44		8 23	8 34
Selby (Table 106) arr			3 10		5 4			7 47				8 29			
Driffield dep	1 59	1 59		3 43		5 29	6 36		7 9		7 34			8 26	8 37
Hutton Cranswick				3 50			6 42								
Lockington				3 57			6 48								
Arram				4 2			6 53								
Beverley (A) arr	2 13	2 13		4 8		5 43	6 59		7 24		7 48			8 42	8 52
Beverley (A) dep	2 15	2 15		4 10		5 45	7 1		7 26		7 50			8 45	8 55
Cottingham (A)	2 22	2 22		4 17		5 52	7 8		7 34		7 57			8 53	9 2
HULL (A) arr	2 30	2 30		4 25		6 0	7 16		7 42		8 5			9 19	9 10

MONS. TO FRIS. INC.—con.

Station	X WO pm	pm	L pm	pm
York (Table 109) dep		6 55		8F15
SCARBOROUGH (Cen.) (B) dep		8 30	9 15	9 55
Seamer (B)		8 36		
Cayton				
Gristhorpe				
Filey arr		8 45	9 29	10 9
Filey dep		8 46	9 30	1010
Hunmanby		8 52		
Speeton				
Bempton		9 4		
Flamborough				
Bridlington arr		9 12	9 50	1030
Bridlington dep	8 25	9 15	9 55	1034
Carnaby	8 30			
Burton Agnes	8 36			
Lowthorpe	8 40			
Nafferton	8 45	G		
Driffield arr	8 50	9 30	1010	1049
Selby (Table 106) arr				
Driffield dep	8 51	9 31	1013	1051
Hutton Cranswick	8 57			
Lockington	9 3			
Arram	9 8			
Beverley (A) arr	9 14	9 45	1028	11 5
Beverley (A) dep	9 15	9 46	1029	11 7
Cottingham (A)	9 23	9 53		1114
HULL (A) arr	9 31	10 1	1044	1122

SUNDAYS

Station	am	am	am	pm	pm	pm	pm	pm	pm	Y pm	pm	pm	pm	pm	¶ pm	Y pm	¶ pm
										York arr. 9-40 pm		Deepcar arr 11-57 pm	Leeds arr. 10-54 pm				
York (Table 109) dep		9 15	1020		1 10	3f35		4 12			6 0						
SCARBOROUGH (Cen.) (B) dep		1040	1125		2 20	4 40		5 22			8 10			8 40			
Seamer (B)								5 28									
Cayton																	
Gristhorpe								5 38									
Filey arr		1053	1138		2 33	4 53		5 43			8 23			8 53			
Filey dep		1055	1140		2 35	4 55		5 44		8 0	8 24			8 54			
Hunmanby								5 51									
Speeton								6 1									
Bempton								6 7									
Flamborough			12 0					6 12									
Bridlington arr		1115	12 4		2 55	5 15		6 16		8 20	8 46			9 16			
Bridlington dep	8 45	1118		2 0		5 20	6 0	6 21	7 45	8 23	8 50	8 58	9 12	9 20	9 35	9 45	1043
Carnaby								6 26									
Burton Agnes								6 32									
Lowthorpe								6 36									
Nafferton	8 56							6 41	7 58							9 58	
Driffield arr	9 2	1133		2 15		5 35	6 15	6 46	8 3		9 6			9 36	9 50	10 3	11 2
Selby (Table 106) arr													1017				
Driffield dep	9 3	1134		2 16		5 37	6 16	6 49	8 5		9 8			9 37	9 51	10 4	11 6
Hutton Cranswick	9 10					5 44		6 56	8 12							1011	
Lockington	9 17					5 51		7 3									
Arram	9 22							7 8									
Beverley (A) arr	9 28	1149		2 31		5 56	6 31	7 14	8 25		9 23			9 52	10 6	1022	1123
Beverley (A) dep	9 30	1151		2 32		5 58	6 32	7 16	8 27		9 26			9 55	10 8	1023	1126
Cottingham (A)	9 37	1158		2 39		6 5		7 23	8 35		9 34			10 2		1030	1135
HULL (A) arr	9 45	12 6		2 47		6 13	6 44	7 31	8 43		9 42			1011	1020	1038	1143

A For complete service between Beverley and Hull see Table 97.
B For other trains between Scarboro' and Seamer see Tables 109, 112.
C Mondays only and not after 28th August (7th August excepted).
DD Calls when required to take up.
F Not after 15th September.
FF Calls at 7-0 am when required to take up for beyond Driffield.
G Calls at 9-25 pm when required.
H Runs 17th July to 8th September inclusive.
JJ Calls at Lowthorpe 7-20 and Nafferton 7-25 pm when required to set down
L Not after 8th September.
M On Mondays calls at 4-31 pm when required to take up only.
WO Weds only. WX Weds excepted.
X One class only. Y Not after 10th Sept
b Conveys passengers for beyond Bridlington only.
c Not after 6th September.
d Fridays only; also runs on Mondays until 28th August inclusive.
f Not after 3rd September. On 10th September leaves 3-0 pm.
k Connection at Seamer.
¶ Excursion; passengers holding tickets other than Excursion tickets may travel by this train.

Figure 9.3B.

Table 105—continued — HULL, BRIDLINGTON, FILEY AND SCARBOROUGH.

SATURDAYS ONLY

Station	am	am	am	F am (Deepcar dep 5-45 am)	am	am	am	am	am (Leeds dep 9-20 am)	K am (Low Moor (LMS) dep 7-59 am)	N am (Chesterfield (LMS) dep 7-25 am)	am (York dep 10.15 am)	R am	H am (Derby (LMS) dep 8-23 am)	L am (Sheffield (Vic.) dep 9-15 am)
HULL (A) dep	5 38	5 50			8 0	8 58		9 45					1040		
Cottingham "		5 58			8 8	9 6		9 53					1048		
Beverley arr		6 5			8 15	9 13		10 1					1058		
Beverley dep		6 10			8 17	9 15		10 3					11 0		
Arram "					8 23										
Lockington "		6 19			8 28										
Hutton Cranswick "		6 25			8 34										
Driffield arr	6 4	6 31			8 40	9 29		1018							
Selby (Table 106) dep				7 30			8 50								
Driffield dep	6 6	6 35	8 3		8 43	9 31	10 1	1020							
Nafferton "		6 40	8 8		8 48		10 6								
Lowthorpe "		6 45	8 13		8 53										
Burton Agnes "		6 49	8 17		8 57		1013								
Carnaby "		6 55	8 23		9 3										
Bridlington arr	6 21	6 59	8 27	8 33	9 7	9 46	1021	1035	1044	1055	11 6	1112	1125	1134	1141
Bridlington dep		7 2		8 38	9 10	9 49		1038		11F0	1111		1129	1140	
Flamborough "		7 8			9 16										
Bempton "		7 13			9 21										
Speeton "		7 21													
Hunmanby "		7 28			9 34										
Filey arr		7 33		9 3	9 39	10 9		1058		11F24	1136		1149	12 5	
Filey dep		7 35		9 5	9 43	10 12		11 1		11F26	1138		1153	12 6	
Gristhorpe "					9 48										
Cayton "					9 52										
Seamer "					10 0										
SCARBORO' (C) Londesbro' Rd. (B) arr				9 22						11F40	1156			1227	
SCARBORO' (C) Central "		7 51			10 6	10 25		1115					12 8		
York (Table 109) arr		9 5			11j10	11 30		1 5					1r32		

Station	am (Leeds dep 10-15 am)	am	N am (Leeds dep 10-45 am)	N pm (Leicester (Central) dep 8-25 am)	E pm (Bradford (Exchange) dep 10-18 am)	G pm (Nottingham (Vic.) dep 9-40 am)	N pm (Liverpool (Cen.) dep 8-35 am)	K pm (Leicester (LMS) dep 8-25 am)	pm	pm	F pm (Blackburn (LMS) dep 10-0 am)	pm		pm
HULL (A) dep		1118							1233	1250		1 15		
Cottingham "		1126							1241			1 23		
Beverley arr		1133							1248	1 3		1 30		
Beverley dep		1135							1250	1 4		1 32		
Arram "												1 39		
Lockington "												1 44		
Hutton Cranswick "												1 51		
Driffield arr		1149								1 19		1 57		
Selby (Table 106) dep	1046		1114											1 24
Driffield dep	1132	1151								1 21		2 1		2 39
Nafferton "		1156										2 6		
Lowthorpe "												2 11		
Burton Agnes "												2 16		
Carnaby "												2 22		
Bridlington arr	1147	12 8	1216	1228	1235	1244	1251	1 6	1 23	1 37	1 45	2 26		2 57
Bridlington dep				1235		1252		1 12		1 42	1 50			
Flamborough "										1 50				
Bempton "														
Speeton "														
Hunmanby "														
Filey arr				1 2		1 16		1 36		2 8	2 16			
Filey dep				1 4		1 18		1 38		2 11	2 18			
Gristhorpe "														
Cayton "														
Seamer "														
SCARBORO' (C) Londesbro' Rd. (B) arr				1 20		1 40		1 53			2 40			
SCARBORO' (C) Central "										2 25				
York (Table 109) arr										3c43	4 5			

SATURDAYS ONLY—continued

Station	pm (Leeds dep 1-37 pm)	pm	Through Train—King's Cross (dep 11-25 am) to Bridlington. Restaurant Car to Selby.	H pm	N pm	pm	pm (York dep 3-25 pm)	pm	pm	pm	pm (Leeds dep 4-52 pm)
HULL (A) dep		2 35			3 3	3 13			4 30	5 8	
Cottingham "		2 43			3 11	3 21			4 38		
Beverley arr		2 50			3 18	3 28			4 45	5 20	
Beverley dep		2 51			3 19	3 29			4 46	5 21	
Arram "									4 52		
Lockington "									4 57		
Hutton Cranswick "									5 4		
Driffield arr		3 6				3 43			5 10	5 35	
Selby (Table 106) dep	2 11							4 8			5 22
Driffield dep	2 55	3 7				3 45		5 3	5 12	5 36	6 5
Nafferton "									5 17		
Lowthorpe "									5 22		
Burton Agnes "									5 26		
Carnaby "									5 32		
Bridlington arr	3 10	3 21		3 25	3 47	4 0	4 20	5 18	5 36	5 48	6 20
Bridlington dep					3 51	4 2				5 50	
Flamborough "						4 9					
Bempton "						4 14					
Speeton "											
Hunmanby "						4 27					
Filey arr					4 11	4 32				6 12	
Filey dep					4 14	4 34				6 13	
Gristhorpe "											
Cayton "											
Seamer "					4 26	4 45					
SCARBORO' (C) Londesbro' Rd. (B) arr											
SCARBORO' (C) Central "					4 32	4 51				6 26	
York (Table 109) arr						5k49				8N0	

Station	Restaurant Car (until 9th September inclusive)—King's Cross (dep 1-40 pm) to Scarborough. On 16th and 23rd September Through Train King's Cross to Scarborough. Restaurant Car to Doncaster.	pm	pm	pm	pm	pm	D pm (Leeds dep 7-40 pm)	pm	pm
HULL (A) dep			6 5		7 0	7 50		9 15	1123
Cottingham "			6 13		7 8			9 23	1131
Beverley arr			6 20		7 15	8 2		9 30	1138
Beverley dep			6 21		7 16	8 4		9 32	1139
Arram "					7 22			9 38	
Lockington "					7 27			9 43	
Hutton Cranswick "			6 33		7 33			9 49	
Driffield arr			6 39		7 39	8 18		9 55	1158
Selby (Table 106) dep		5 32		5 52					
Driffield dep		6 15	6 40	7 3	7 41	8 19		9 57	1159
Nafferton "					7 46			10 2	
Lowthorpe "					7 51			10 7	
Burton Agnes "					7 55			10 11	
Carnaby "					8 1			10 17	
Bridlington arr		6 30	6 55	7 25	8 5	8 33	9 4	10 21	1219
Bridlington dep		6 33	6 57			8 37		10N24	
Flamborough "			7 3			8 43			
Bempton "			7 8			8 48		10N33	
Speeton "			7 16						
Hunmanby "			7 23			9 0			
Filey arr		6 55	7 28			9 5		10N47	
Filey dep		6 57	7 29			9 7		10N48	
Gristhorpe "						9 12			
Cayton "									
Seamer "			7 39						
SCARBORO' (C) Londesbro' Rd. (B) arr									
SCARBORO' (C) Central "		7 10	7 45			9 23		11N 4	
York (Table 109) arr			8q50			1055			

A For complete service between Hull and Beverley see Table 97.
B For other trains between Seamer & Scarboro' see Tables 109, 112.
C 600 yards between Central and Londesborough Road Stations.
D Runs 22nd July to 2nd September inclusive.
E Runs 22nd July to 26th August inclusive.
F Not after 19th August.
G Runs 22nd July to 26th August inclusive.
H Not after 26th August.
K Not after 2nd September.
L Runs 15th July to 9th Sept. inclusive
N Not after 9th September.
R Not after 16th September.
c On 16th and 23rd September arrives York 4-39 pm.
j Runs 15th July to 9th Sept. inclusive
k Connection at Seamer.
q On 16th and 23rd September arrives 9-3 pm.
r On 16th September arrives York 2-7 pm.

FOR SERVICE MONDAYS TO FRIDAYS AND SUNDAYS SEE PAGE 79

Figure 9.3C.

Table 105—continued — SCARBOROUGH, FILEY, BRIDLINGTON AND HULL.

SATURDAYS ONLY

FOR SERVICE MONDAYS TO FRIDAYS AND SUNDAYS SEE PAGE 80

Station	am	am	am	am (Leeds arr 9-22 am)	am	am	am	am	am	am	am (York arr 10-55 am)	am	am
York (Table 109) dep							4 59					9k 0	
SCARBRO' (C) Central dep							7 40		8 25			9 55	
SCARBRO' (C) Lon'bro'Rd (B) "													
Seamer "							7 46					10 1	
Cayton "							7 52						
Gristhorpe "							7 56						
Filey arr							8 1		8 38			1010	
Filey dep							8 3		8 39			1012	
Hunmanby "							8 9						
Speeton "							8 17						
Bempton "							8 23						
Flamborough "							8 26						
Bridlington arr							8 30		8 59			1032	
Bridlington dep	6 35	6 45	7 20	7 56	8 5	8 15		8 35	9 1	9 10	10 0	1035	1043
Carnaby "			7 25										
Burton Agnes "			7 31							9 19			
Lowthorpe "		DD	7 35							9 23			
Nafferton "		FF	7 40							9 28			
Driffield arr	6 50	7 5	7 45	8 10		8 30		8 53		9 33		1050	11 3
Selby (Table 106) arr		8 14		8 54									1215
Driffield dep	6 51		7 46			8 32				9 34		1052	
Hutton Cranswick "			7 53							9 40			
Lockington "			8 1										
Arram "			8 8							9 49			
Beverley (A) arr	7 5		8 14			8 46				9 55		11 6	
Beverley dep	7 6		8 15			8 47				9 56		11 7	
Cottingham "	7 13		8 23							10 3		1114	
HULL arr	7 21		8 31		842	8 59			9 38	1011		1122	

Station	Through Train—Scarborough to King's Cross (arr 3-47 pm) Restaurant Car from Hull	am	am	N am (Leicester (Cen.) arr 4-9 pm)	L pm (Sheffield (Vic.) arr 3-22 pm)	pm (York arr 2-12 pm)	pm	G pm (Sheffield (Vic) arr 3-54 pm)	E pm (Bradford (Exchange) arr 4-25 pm)
York (Table 109) dep			10k 0						
SCARBRO' (C) Central dep		10b25	11 5						
SCARBRO' (C) Lon'bro'Rd (B) "				1145					
Seamer "			11 12						
Cayton "			11 18						
Gristhorpe "			11 22						
Filey arr			11 27	1159					
Filey dep		10b39	11 28	12 2					
Hunmanby "			11 34						
Speeton "			11 42						
Bempton "			11 48						
Flamborough "			11 51						
Bridlington arr			11 55	1223					
Bridlington dep		11 0	11 58	1228	1 5	1 15	1 25	1 40	1 55
Carnaby "			12 3						
Burton Agnes "			12 9						
Lowthorpe "			12 13				1 35		
Nafferton "			12 18				1 40		
Driffield arr			12 23				1 45		
Selby (Table 106) arr									
Driffield dep			12 25				1 46		
Hutton Cranswick "			12 31						
Lockington "			12 37						
Arram "			12 42						
Beverley (A) arr			12 48				1 59		
Beverley dep			12 52				2 0		
Cottingham "			12 59				2 7		
HULL arr		11 35	1 7				2 15		

Station	N pm (Through Carriage (until 2nd Sept. inclus.) to Manchester (London Rd.); Liverpool (Central) arr 6-35 pm)	M pm	pm (Leeds arr 3-41 pm)	Z pm (Leeds arr 3-50 pm)	N pm	N pm (Heeley (L.M.S.) arr 6-0 pm)	pm (Leeds arr 4-50 pm)	pm	pm
York (Table 109) dep					1225			12k50	
SCARBRO' (C) Central dep					1 50			2 20	
SCARBRO' (C) Lon'bro'Rd (B) "						2 8			
Seamer "								2 27	
Cayton "								2 33	
Gristhorpe "								2 37	
Filey arr					2 8	2 23		2 42	
Filey dep					2 11	2 24		2 43	
Hunmanby "					2 17			2 50	
Speeton "								2 59	
Bempton "					2 29			3 5	
Flamborough "					2 34			3 9	
Bridlington arr					2 39	2 47		3 13	
Bridlington dep	2 5	2 10	2 15	2 25	2 42	2 52	3 10	3 15	3 35
Carnaby "								3 20	
Burton Agnes "								3 26	
Lowthorpe "								3 31	
Nafferton "					2 56			3 36	
Driffield arr		2 24	2 29	2 39	3 1			3 41	3 55
Selby (Table 106) arr			3 10	3 20			4 14		5 4
Driffield dep		2 25			3 4			3 43	
Hutton Cranswick "								3 50	
Lockington "								3 57	
Arram "								4 2	
Beverley (A) arr		2 43			3 22			4 8	
Beverley dep		2 45			3 26			4 10	
Cottingham "		2 53			3 34			4 17	
HULL arr		3 1			3 43			4 25	

SATURDAYS ONLY—continued

Station	K pm (Leicester (L.M.S.) arr 9-10 pm)	K pm (Low Moor (L.M.S.) arr 7-39 pm)	F pm (Blackburn (L.M.S.) arr 8-50 pm)	H pm	pm	N pm (Leeds arr 6-59 pm)	H pm (Derby (L.M.S.) arr 9-20 pm)	pm	pm	R pm
York (Table 109) dep	1 55				3d20			4f12		5 5
SCARBRO' (C) Central dep					4 25			5 15		6 13
SCARBRO' (C) Lon'bro'Rd (B) "	3 20		4 7				4 55			
Seamer "								5 21		
Cayton "								5 27		
Gristhorpe "								5 31		
Filey arr	3 35		4 22		4 38		5 10	5 36		6 27
Filey dep	3 36		4 24		4 41		5 12	5 38		6 30
Hunmanby "								5 44		
Speeton "								5 52		
Bempton "								5 58		
Flamborough "								6 1		
Bridlington arr	4 1		4 47		5 1		5 36	6 5		6 49
Bridlington dep	4 6	4 35	4 51	4 57	5 4	5 25	5 41	6 9	6 30	6 52
Carnaby "								6 14		
Burton Agnes "					5 13			6 20		
Lowthorpe "					5 17			6 24		
Nafferton "					5 22			6 29		
Driffield arr				5 14	5 27			6 34	6 44	7 7
Selby (Table 106) arr						6 18			7 47	
Driffield dep				5 16	5 29			6 36		7 9
Hutton Cranswick "								6 42		
Lockington "								6 48		
Arram "								6 53		
Beverley (A) arr				5 33	5 43			6 59		7 24
Beverley dep				5 35	5 45			7 1		7 26
Cottingham "				5 42	5 52			7 8		7 34
HULL arr				5 50	6 0			7 16		7 42

Station	pm (York arr 7-55 pm)	pm	pm (Leeds arr 9-0 pm)	F pm (Deepcar arr 10-36 pm)	P pm	pm	pm	N pm	pm	N pm		
York (Table 109) dep		5 15				6 5	6 55		8 15	9 30		
SCARBRO' (C) Central dep		6 30				7 37	8 30	9 15	9 55	1045		
SCARBRO' (C) Lon'bro'Rd (B) "				7 10								
Seamer "		6 36					8 36			1051		
Cayton "												
Gristhorpe "		6 43								1058		
Filey arr		6 48		7 24		7 51	8 45	9 29	10 9	11 3		
Filey dep		6 49		7 26		7 53	8 46	9 30	1010	11 4		
Hunmanby "							8 52					
Speeton "												
Bempton "							9 4					
Flamborough "		7 9					9 10					
Bridlington arr		7 13		7 48		8 13	9 14	9 50	1030	1125		
Bridlington dep	7 0	7 16	7 30	7 53	8 8	8 18	9 17	9 55	1034			
Carnaby "							9 22					
Burton Agnes "							9 28					
Lowthorpe "		JJ					9 32					
Nafferton "		JJ					9 37		1044			
Driffield arr		7 32	7 44		8 23	8 34	9 42	1010	1049			
Selby (Table 106) arr			8 29									
Driffield dep		7 34			8 26	8 37	9 44	1013	1051			
Hutton Cranswick "							9 50					
Lockington "							9 56					
Arram "							10 1					
Beverley (A) arr		7 48			8 42	8 52	10 7	1028	11 5			
Beverley dep		7 50			8 45	8 55	10 9	1029	11 7			
Cottingham "		7 57			8 53	9 2	1016		1114			
HULL arr		8 5			9 1	9 10	1024	1044	1122			

A For complete service between Beverley and Hull see Table 97.
B For other trains between Scarbro' and Seamer see Tables 109, 112.
C 600 yards between Londesboro' Road and Central Stations.
DD Calls at Lowthorpe when required to take up only.
E Runs 22nd July to 26th August inclus
F Not after 19th August.
FF Calls at 7-0 am when required to take up for beyond Driffield.
G Runs 29th July to 26th August. inclusive.
H Not after 26th August.
JJ Calls at Lowthorpe 7-20 and Nafferton 7-25 pm when required to set down.
K Not after 2nd September.
L Runs 15th July to 9th Sept inclusive
M Runs 29th July to 2nd Sept inclusive
N Not after 9th September.
P Runs 22nd July to 9th Sept inclus
R Not after 16th September
Z Runs 22nd July to 2nd Sept inclusive.
b Conveys passengers for beyond Bridlington only.
d Commencing 9th Sept leaves York 2-40 pm
f On 16th and 23rd Sept dep 3-50 pm.
k Connection at Seamer.

Figure 9.3D.

Goods and Minerals

The trains scheduled to run between 4 July 1938 and 25 September 1938 are listed in the table reproduced below. There are several points of interest: (a) There are no booked cattle trains as this traffic was switching to road, and rail movement was now by special trains, run as required, or in wagons attached to scheduled goods trains. (b) Down goods trains now run earlier than in previous years. (c) During the late 1920s and early 1930s the LNER purchased a number of Sentinel steam shunting locomotives, which were dispersed around the system. One left Scarborough at 7-15 am shunting Seamer, Filey and Hunmanby, and Filey again on the return journey. One of the two Bridlington Sentinels worked at Driffield all day calling at the intermediate stations on its way home, and Beverley used a Sentinel for seven hours for shunting and making up trains. (d) The afternoon pilot from Hull to Cottingham only ran beyond Hull Radiator Sidings (near the 2 milepost) when required; observations indicate that this rarely happened.

Down Goods Workings

Description	Depart	From - To	Arrive
	3-5 am	MO Hull Goods - Bridlington	6-15 am
No 2 Express	3-40 am	SO Hull Goods - Scarborough Gallows Close	6-45 am
	3-50 am	SO Hull Goods - Bridlington	6-5 am
No 2 Express	4-5 am	SX Hull Goods - Scarborough Gallows Close	6-48 am
	4-25 am	SX Hull Goods - Bridlington	6-41 am
Class D	7-0 am	Hull Goods - York	?
Pilot	8-0 am	Hull Goods - Radiator Sidings - Cottingham	?
Class D	9-0 am	SX Hull Goods - Scarborough Gallows Close	11-55 am
Sentinel shunter	10-15 am	Dairycoates Shed - Beverley	?
Sentinel shunter	11-15 am	SX Hunmanby - Scarborough Shed	1-40 pm
Sentinel shunter	2-6 pm	SX Driffield - Bridlington	3-40 pm
Engine + van	2-10 pm	SX Hessle Road Junction - Radiator Sidings	?
	4-0 pm	SX Hull - York	6-40 pm
Pilot	4-10 pm	SX Hull goods - Radiator Siding or Cottingham	?
No 1 Express	6-15 pm	SX Hull Goods - York	7-45 pm
No 1 Express Fish	7-15 pm	SX Hull Goods - Edinburgh	2-30 am

Up Goods Workings

Description	Depart	From - To	Arrive
Sentinel shunter	7-15 am	SX Scarborough shed - Hunmanby	?
Sentinel shunter	7-30 am	SX Bridlington - Driffield	8-0 am
No 2 Express	7-30 am	Scarborough Gallows Close - Hessle Road Junction	10-40SX 11-16 SO
Pilot	9-45 am	Cottingham - Hull Goods	10-55
Class A	7-10 am	York - Hessle Road Junction	10-47 am
Class D	8-0 am	York - Hessle Road Junction	?
Class D*	9-0 am	SX Scarborough Gallows Close - Hessle Road Junct	?
No 2 Express	11-55 am	SX York - Hessle Road Junction	1-54 pm
Class D	3-45 pm	SX Bridlington - Hull Goods	?
Pilot	5-10 pm	SX Cottingham - Radiator Sidings - Hull Goods	?
Sentinel shunter	6-2 pm	Beverley - Dairycoates Shed	?
No 2 Express	7-10 pm	Thurs Excepted York - Hull Goods	8-37 pm Tu, W, FO; 8-55 pm M, SO
Class A	7-10 pm	Thurs Only York - Hull Goods	10-55

* Class B from Driffield

The Wartime Years

The emergency timetables, introduced on 11 September 1939, had been planned well in advance, but quickly proved to be too restrictive; train frequencies had been roughly halved and within days additional trains were introduced. During the succeeding two months frequent changes were made, but on 4 December a new timetable came in which, with exceptions mentioned later, lasted more or less as the basic service until post-war enhancements were introduced in October 1946.

Basically there were 37 (39 Saturdays) departures and arrivals at Hull; 19 (21 Saturdays) terminated at Beverley, and of the remainder seven reached Scarborough, four terminated at Bridlington and seven served York. On Sundays there were initially two trains each way between Hull and Scarborough, with four more locals between Hull and Beverley. Bridlington-Selby was served by three stopping trains plus, for a short time, the Leeds business train – one of the first casualties, and never reinstated.

The invasion scare of the summer of 1940 saw restrictions on entry to the area, and for a few months a 10-00 pm curfew was imposed along the coast, at least as far north as Scarborough. The 9-15 pm Hull - Bridlington train was curtailed at Driffield, making the 7-15 pm the last train beyond Driffield. During the heavy air raids in May 1941, an unexploded bomb fell on the Hull - Selby line near Anlaby Road, closing that line for approximately two weeks. This meant that trains to and from Doncaster and Leeds had to use the Scarborough line between Paragon and Cottingham Junction, where they reversed and made for Hessle Road Junction and beyond. As several of these trains had identical timings to the Scarborough line trains severe reductions had to be made to the latter services to accommodate the main-line trains until the normal route was re-opened.

During the summer of 1944 drastic reductions were made to all services throughout Britain to accommodate military traffic in connection with the D-Day landings and to conserve fuel. These lasted from 22 May 1944 until the introduction of the October timetable. On the Hull - Scarborough line practically every train was withdrawn between 9-0 am and 4-0 pm, Monday to Friday; the exceptions being one train each to Beverley and Bridlington. On Saturdays there were fewer cancellations and, in response to public pressure, two additional trains were introduced between Hull and Scarborough over the August Bank Holiday weekend. Restoration of a later evening train to Bridlington came in stages; in October 1941, the 9-30 pm Hull - Driffield train continued empty on Saturdays to Bridlington, returning as the 11-0 pm advertised service to Hull. Its main morale-boosting purpose was to transport the RAF dance band, which performed at the Spa in Bridlington, back to Arram for Leconfield air base. By May 1943 the outward journey was advertised to

Table 105 — HULL, BRIDLINGTON, FILEY, and SCARBOROUGH

Miles	Station	Week Days																											Sundays			
		mrn	mrn	mrn		mrn	mrn	mrn (Dep. Selby 9 30 mrn (Table 106))	mrn	mrn		aft E	aft S	aft	aft S	aft	aft (Dep. Selby 2 36 aft (Table 106))	aft		aft E		aft	aft (Dep. Selby 5 50 aft (Table 106))	aft		aft			mrn	aft	aft	aft
—	Hull dep	5 37	5 50	..	..	8 0	9 5	..	..	1130	..	..	1250	1 20	..	2 45	..	4 30	..	5 20	..	5 30	..	7 15	..	9 30	..	..	7 0	4 45	..	7 0
4	Cottingham	..	5 59	..	..	8 8	9 13	..	..	1139	..	..	..	1 29	..	2 54	..	4 39	..	..	..	5 39	..	7 24	..	9 39	..	..	7 8	4 54	..	7 9
8½	Beverley	..	6 11	..	..	8 17	9 22	..	..	1150	..	..	1 4	1 39	..	3 3	..	4 48	..	5 34	..	5 48	..	7 35	..	9 48	..	..	7 21	5 3	..	7 18
11½	Arram	..	..	..	..	8 25	..	..	..	1157	..	..	..	1 46	..	..	..	4 54	..	..	..	5 54	..	7 41	..	9 55	..	..	7 27	..	..	..
13	Lockington	..	6 20	..	..	8 30	..	..	..	..	..	..	..	1 51	..	..	..	4 59	..	..	..	5 59	..	7 46	..	10 0	..	..	7 32	..	..	..
16½	Hutton Cranswick	..	6 26	..	..	8 36	..	..	..	12 6	..	..	..	1 58	..	..	..	5 7	..	..	..	6 5	..	7 53	..	10 7	..	..	7 40	..	..	..
19½	Driffield arr	6 5	6 32	..	..	8 42	9 37	1043	..	1212	..	..	1 20	2 4	..	3 20	3 49	5 15	..	5 49	..	6 11	7 5	7 58	..	1013	..	..	7 46	5 21	..	7 36
	Driffield dep	6 8	6 37	7 55	..	8 46	9 39	1046	..	1216	..	..	1 21	2 9	..	3 22	3 53	5 18	..	5 50	..	6 15	7 6	8 1	..	..	..	..	7 50	5 24	..	7 38
21½	Nafferton	..	6 42	8 0	..	8 52	..	1052	..	1221	..	..	..	2 15	..	..	..	5 23	..	..	..	6 20	..	8 7	..	..	..	..	7 55	..	..	..
23¾	Lowthorpe	..	6 47	8 5	..	8 57	..	.	..	1227	..	..	..	2 20	..	..	..	5 28	..	..	..	6 25	..	8 12	..	..	..	..	8 0	..	..	..
25¾	Burton Agnes	..	6 51	8 9	..	9 1	..	1058	..	Aa	..	..	..	2 25	..	..	..	5 32	..	..	..	6 30	Hh	8 17	..	..	..	..	8 5	..	..	..
28¾	Carnaby	..	6 57	8 15	..	9 7	..	..	..	Aa	..	..	..	2 31	..	..	..	5 38	..	..	..	6 36	..	8 23	..	..	..	..	8 11	..	..	..
30¾	Bridlington arr	3 22	7 1	8 19	..	9 11	9 55	11 6	..	1240	..	..	1 38	2 36	..	3 38	4 10	5 43	..	6 6	..	6 40	7 28	8 27	..	..	..	..	8 16	5 41	..	7 54
	Bridlington dep	..	7 4	..	..	..	9 57		1155	..	..	1 43	1 43	..	2 40	3 42		..	..	6 10	..	6 45		..	..	..	..	..	8 20	..	7 0	..
33½	Flamborough	..	7 10	..	..	..	..		12 1	..	..	1 51	1 51	..	2 48	3 48		..	..	..	..	6 51		..	..	..	..	..	8 26	..	7 7	..
34½	Bempton	..	7 15	..	..	..	..		12 6	..	..	..	..	..	..	3 53		..	..	..	..	6 56		..	..	..	..	..	8 31	..	7 12	..
37½	Speeton	..	7 23	..	..	..	..		1214	..	..	..	..	..	..	4 2		..	..	..	..	7 4		..	..	..	..	..	8 39	..	7 20	..
41½	Hunmanby	..	7 30	..	..	..	..		1221	..	..	..	..	..	..	4 9		..	..	..	..	7 10		..	..	..	..	..	8 48	..	7 27	..
44½	Filey arr	..	7 35	..	..	..	1019		1226	..	..	2 10	2 10	..	3 7	4 14		..	..	6 32	..	7 15		..	..	..	..	..	8 53	..	7 32	..
	Filey dep	..	7 40	..	..	..	1020		1230	..	..	2 14	2 14	..	3 10	4 17		..	..	6 34	..	7 19		..	..	..	..	..	8 57	..	7 34	..
46½	Gristhorpe	..	7 45	..	..	..	..		..	..	..	Vv	..	..	Vv	4 22		..	..	..	..	..		..	..	..	..	..	9 2	..	..	..
48½	Cayton	..	Ss	..	..	..	..		..	..	..	..	..	..	..	..		..	..	..	..	..		..	..	..	..	..	..	..	..	..
50½	Seamer	..	Nn	..	..	..	1031		1242	..	..	..	..	..	3 21	4 33		..	..	..	..	7 31		..	..	..	..	..	9 13	..	7 44	..
53¾	Scarborough (Central) arr	..	8 0	..	..	..	1037		1248	..	..	2 28	2 33	..	3 27	4 39		..	..	6 48	..	7 37		..	..	..	..	..	9 19	..	7 50	..
95¾	109 York arr	..	9 9	..	..	11Y50			1Y58	..	..	..	..	..	4Y37	5Y38		..	..	..	..	9Y7		..	..	..	..	..	1152	..	8Y52	..

Miles	Station	Week Days																											Sundays			
		mrn		mrn (Arr. Selby 8 36 mrn (Table 106))		mrn	mrn		mrn	mrn		mrn	mrn		mrn		aft E	aft S	aft E	aft S	aft (Arr. Selby 5 3 aft (Table 106))	aft	aft	aft (Arr. Selby 8 11 aft (Table 106))		aft	aft		mrn		aft	aft
	109 York dep	..	..		..	..	..	..	4 35	..	..	..	..	..	10Y15	..	..	..	..	1 20		3Y10	..		..	5Y10	..	..	4 35	..	..	5Y0
—	Scarborough (Central) dep	..	..		..	..	..	..	7 30	..	..	8 16	..	..	11 18	..	1 10	1 10	2 10	2 25		4 20	..		..	6 20	..	..	10 0	..	..	6 0
3	Seamer	..	..		..	..	..	..	7 36	..	..	..	..	..	11 25	..	1 16	1 16	2 17	2 32		4 27	..		..	6 26	..	..	10 7	..	..	6 7
5½	Cayton	..	..		..	..	..	..	..	..	..	..	..	..	Ss	..	..	..	..	..		..	..		..	..	..	..	..	..	..	..
7½	Gristhorpe	..	..		..	..	..	..	7 46	..	..	..	..	..	Ss	..	..	..	..	2 40		..	..		..	6 34	..	..	1015	..	..	6 15
9½	Filey arr	..	..		..	..	..	..	7 51	..	..	8 30	..	..	11 39	..	1 26	1 26	2 29	2 45		4 37	..		..	6 39	..	..	1020	..	..	6 20
	Filey dep	..	..		..	..	..	..	7 53	..	..	8 31	..	..	11 42	..	1 27	1 27	2 32	2 47		4 42	..		..	6 41	..	..	1022	..	..	6 22
12½	Hunmanby	..	..		..	..	..	..	7 59	..	..	..	..	..	11 48	..	..	..	2 38	2 53		..	..		..	6 46	..	..	1028	..	..	6 29
16½	Speeton	..	..		..	..	..	..	8 7	..	..	..	..	..	11 56	..	..	..	2 47	3 2		..	..		..	6 55	..	..	1036	..	..	6 38
19½	Bempton	..	..		..	..	..	..	8 13	..	..	..	..	..	12 2	..	..	..	2 53	3 8		4 59	..		..	7 1	..	..	1042	..	..	6 44
20½	Flamborough	..	..		..	..	..	..	8 16	..	..	..	..	..	12 5	..	..	..	2 57	3 12		..	..		..	7 8	..	..	1045	..	..	6 48
23	Bridlington arr	..	..		..	..	..	..	8 20	..	..	8 52	..	..	12 9	..	1 49	1 49	3 1	3 16		5 6	..		..	7 12	..	..	1050	..	..	6 52
	Bridlington dep	6 30	..	7 0	..	7 20	8 0	..	8 25	8 32	..	8 54	10 0	..	12 14	..	..	1 53	3 10	3 18	3 35	5 11	6 25	6 50	..	7 20	..	..	1055	..	2 50	7 2
25½	Carnaby	..	..	..	..	7 25	..	..	..	..	..	..	10 5	..	12 19	..	..	..	3 15	3 23	..	..	6 30	..	..	..	..	..	11 0	..	..	7 7
28½	Burton Agnes	..	..	..	..	7 31	..	..	..	..	..	..	1011	..	12 25	..	..	..	3 21	3 29	..	5 19	6 36	..	..	..	..	..	11 6	..	..	7 13
30	Lowthorpe	..	..	Yy	..	7 35	..	..	..	8 43	..	..	1015	..	12 29	..	..	2 2	3 26	3 34	..	5 23	6 40	..	..	..	..	..	1110	..	..	7 17
32½	Nafferton	..	..	7 16	..	7 40	..	..	..	8 48	..	..	1020	..	12 34	..	..	2 7	3 31	3 39	..	5 28	6 45	..	..	..	..	..	1115	..	..	7 22
34½	Driffield arr	6 45	..	7 20	..	7 45	8 14	..	8 41	8 53	..	9 9	1025	..	12 39	..	..	2 12	3 36	3 44	3 51	5 33	6 50	7 4	..	7 37	..	..	1120	..	3 5	7 27
	Driffield dep	6 47	..	7 23	..	7 46	8 16	..	8 43	..	..	9 10	1028	..	12 41	..	..	2 14	3 39	3 46	3 53	5 35	6 53	7 7	..	7 40	1033	..	1122	..	3 7	7 30
37½	Hutton Cranswick	..	..	..	..	7 53	..	..	..	..	..	..	1034	..	12 47	..	..	..	3 46	3 53	..	5 42	6 59	..	..	..	1040	..	1129	..	..	7 37
40¾	Lockington	..	..	..	..	8 1	..	..	..	..	..	..	..	..	12 53	..	..	..	3 53	4 0	..	..	7 6	..	..	..	..	..	1137	..	..	7 44
42½	Arram	..	..	..	..	8 8	..	..	..	..	..	..	1042	..	12 58	..	..	..	3 59	4 5	..	5 51	7 11	..	..	..	..	..	1145	..	..	7 49
45½	Beverley	7 3	..	..	..	8 15	8 33	..	9 1	..	..	9 26	1051	..	1 8	..	..	2 32	4 8	4 13	..	5 59	7 21	..	..	7 58	1054	..	1153	..	3 24	7 58
49½	Cottingham	7 10	..	..	..	8 23	..	..	9 8	..	..	..	1058	..	1 15	..	..	2 39	4 15	4 20	..	6 6	7 29	..	..	8 5	11 2	..	12 1	..	3 31	8 5
53¾	Hull arr	7 18	..	..	..	8 31	8 45	..	9 16	..	..	9 38	11 7	..	1 23	..	..	2 48	4 23	4 28	..	6 15	7 38	..	..	8 13	1111	..	1210	..	3 40	8 14

Aa Calls on Wednesdays and Saturdays. **E** or **E** Except Saturdays **Hh** Calls to set down except on Saturdays.
Nn Calls on Mondays only. **S** or **S** Saturdays only **Ss** Calls on Saturdays only. **Vv** Calls when required. **Y** Connection at Seamer.
Yy Calls when required to take up only.
For **LOCAL TRAINS** between Hull and Beverley see Table 97 For **OTHER TRAINS** between Seamer and Scarborough, Tables 109 & 112

Figure 9.4. *A typical wartime timetable, this one commences on 5 October 1942 and as usual is in force 'until further notice'. (LNER)*

Bridlington on Saturdays, but restoration on other days had to wait until the war ended. About the same time an additional return working between Bridlington and Hull came into operation on Sunday afternoons. Early in the war an unadvertised, Sunday workman's train was introduced leaving Hull for Beverley at 6-0 am and returning at 6-30 am; this train continued for several years after the war.

Decelerations added minutes to the schedule of most trains, but there were exceptions as two trains still covered the $11^1/_4$ miles from Bridlington to Driffield, start to stop, in 14 minutes (48.2 mph). The 8-16 am business train from Scarborough was decelerated by nine minutes, but called additionally at Driffield and Beverley, making its overall time 82 minutes for the $53^1/_4$ miles, giving a very creditable 39 mph average.

Basic goods services were largely unchanged from the pre-war pattern, but, in addition to troop trains, the proliferation of aerodromes in the East Riding demanded numerous trains of fuel oil and munitions. A consequence of the war conditions was very late running, keeping signalmen on duty beyond the time the line normally closed. For example, the section between Beverley North and Hull should have closed at midnight, but the evening goods from York, on some occasions, did not reach Beverley before the early turn signalmen took up duty at 4-0 am!

Post-War Recovery

The years between the introduction of an improved timetable on 7 October 1946 and the refusal of British Rail's application to close the line in 1969 was a period of mixed fortunes. Soon trainloads of holiday makers descended on Bridlington and Scarborough, and a new source of traffic was Butlin's Holiday Camp, near Filey, for which a new branch and station were officially opened on 10 May 1947 (see Chapter 7). The holiday traffic and day excursions peaked in 1960-1 at almost pre-war levels. Short distance travel, particularly between Hull and Beverley, was affected by the lower fares of competing buses, and First Class business travel from Scarborough and Bridlington into Hull had virtually disappeared by 1969. Goods traffic continued its pre-war decline, and ultimately ceased with the withdrawal of the Hull - Bridlington pick-up goods in 1976.

The 1946 timetable saw two additional trains between Hull and Scarborough, bringing the total to nine; the Hull-Bridlington timetable was unbalanced – 15 Down (13 Saturdays), 13 Up (14 Saturdays). Main features were a restoration of 5-30 pm SX Hull - Bridlington fast, and a later train at 8-30 pm from Scarborough to Hull. The 8-15 am from Scarborough now reached Hull 9-33 am, covering the $19^1/_2$ miles from Driffield in 25 minutes (46.8 mph). A morning train between Bridlington and Hull and back was reintroduced on Sundays. Hull to York gained an extra train each way, including the short-lived Hull - Glasgow express. Between Hull and Beverley there were now 40 trains each weekday, and nine on Sundays. This pattern continued for several years, although by 1953 the 8-30 pm from Scarborough did not run in the winter months. In the same year the Hull - Beverley service was down to 31 trains on weekdays (7 on Sundays), reflecting road competition.

There was no attempt to restore the Bridlington - Leeds business train, but in 1949 there was a 7-45 am from Bridlington to Market Weighton which gave a York connection (arrive 8-58 am) and, by the following year, a return service at 5-53 pm SX from Market Weighton arriving Bridlington at 6-32 pm This facility was still available after the Selby - Bridlington stopping trains, now down to two each way, were withdrawn in the same year.

In the winter of 1956 there were still 15 trains each way between Hull and Bridlington, eight of which continued to Scarborough, but between Hull and Beverley the service was down to 26/27 trains on weekdays, although on Sundays there were now eight; an unadvertised and an empty coaching stock working had become advertised trains. Bridlington - Selby was down to one morning train each way timed to give York connections at Market Weighton. Return was afforded by the 5-47 pm SX Selby - Bridlington, which included a through carriage from Leeds. 1956 was the last year that all the services were steam-operated as January 1957 saw the introduction of diesel multiple units (DMUs).

Meanwhile the pattern of summer Saturday holiday trains and excursions quickly approached pre-war levels. By 1950 there were 44 trains into Bridlington from the South, 26 of which continued to either Filey Holiday Camp or Scarborough; this level of traffic remained constant through the 1950s. In 1961 the respective figures were 42 and 25, the slight decline reflecting the withdrawal of the Selby stopping trains. The booked service was supplemented by 'specials' from towns that did not have a weekly service, *e.g.* Bolton for its holiday week. Destinations ranged from Worcester, King's Cross, Liverpool and Derby to York, Leeds and Tyneside.

Excursion traffic also built up, particularly on Sundays. On 28 July 1957 a handwritten departure board at Bridlington station listed 23 trains leaving between 6-00 pm and 10-5 pm, all heading south. They included two first class private excursions to Knottingley, and three to closed lines or stations. The first train was the 6-0 pm for Little Weighton, North Cave, Wallingfen, North Eastrington and South Howden. Later departures served the Garforth-Castleford line and the closed stations between Market Weighton and Selby. Earlier that afternoon the carriage sidings to the south of the station were packed with coaching stock, and there were more than 30 locomotives on shed including; 4F 44054, 5MTs 44824 and 45447, together with B16s, B1s and others.

Sunday scenic excursions to Whitby and Scarborough were revived in the late 1940s, leaving Hull between 9-0 and 10-0 am They travelled outwards via Driffield and Malton, which required reversals at each end, and arrived in Whitby between 12 noon and 1-0 pm for a three hour stay. The train then continued to Scarborough for a similar break before finishing with a run to Hull to arrive between 9-0 and 10-0 pm.

Table 105 — HULL, BRIDLINGTON, FILEY, and SCARBOROUGH

Week Days

Miles	Station		mrn	mrn	mrn	mrn	mrn G	mrn	mrn	mrn G	mrn A	mrn J	mrn	mrn F	mrn	mrn D	aft H	aft G	aft A	aft S	aft A	aft S	aft E	aft A
—	Hull	dep	5 30	5 55	..	8 0	TC from Leeds dep 7 55 mrn (Table 106)	9 0	9 15	TC from Leeds dep 8 50 mrn (Table 106)	TC from Rotherham & Masboro' dep. 7 45 mrn (Tables 67 and 98)	10 0	..	TC from Sheff'd (V) dep 8 40 mrn (Table 67)	10 40	1115	TC from Bradford (Ex) dep. 9 38 mrn (Tables 90 and 87)	TC from M'chester (V), dep. 8 55 mrn (Table 98)	TC from Leices'r (LMS) dep 8 25 mrn (Table 114)	1225	TC from Sheffield (V.), dep 10 30 mrn (Table 67)	1250	..	TC from Leicester (C.), dep. 8 55 mrn (Table 2)
4	Cottingham		..	..	..	8 8		9 9	9 24			10 9	..		10 49	..				1234		..	..	
8¾	Beverley		..	..	..	8 17		9 19	9 33			1018	..		10 59	1131				1243		1 4	..	
11¼	Arram		5 49	..	..	8 25		..	..			..	..		11 6	..				..		..	..	
13	Lockington		..	6 15	..	8 30		..	..			..	..		..	..				..		..	..	
16¼	Hutton Cranswick		..	6 21	..	8 36		..	..			..	..		11 15	..				..		..	..	
19½	Driffield	arr	6 1	6 27	..	8 42		9 34	9 50			1035	1043		11 21	1148				1259		1 20	..	
		dep	6 6	6 33	7 50	8 46		9 36	9 52			1037	1046		11 24	1150				1 0		1 21	..	
21½	Nafferton		6 11	..	7 55	8 52		..	..			..	1052		11 29	..				..		..	..	
23¾	Lowthorpe		6 16	..	8 0	8 57		..	..			..	..		11 35	..				..		..	..	
25½	Burton Agnes		6 20	..	8 4	9 1		..	..			..	1058		11 39	..				..		..	..	
28¾	Carnaby		6 26	..	8 10	9 7		..	..			..	..		11 45	..				..		..	..	
31	Bridlington	arr	6 31	6 48	8 14	9 11	9 42	9 52	10 8	1034	1046	1054	11 6	1113	11 50	1210	1225	1245	1257	1 16	1 23	1 38	..	1 48
		dep	6 42	..	..	9 15	..	9 55	10 11	..		1058		1119	11 55	..		1250	1 2	1 18	1 28	1 43	1 43	1 53
33¼	Flamborough		6 49	..	..	9 22	..	..	..	..		..	Dep. Selby 9 30 mrn (Table 106)	..	12 1	..		..	..	..	..	1 51	1 51	..
34½	Bempton		6 55	..	..	9 28	..	..	..	..		..		..	12 6	..		..	..	..	..	1 56	1 56	..
37½	Speeton		7 4	..	..	9 37	..	..	..	..		..		..	12 14	..		..	..	..	..	..	..	..
41¾	Hunmanby		7 12	..	..	9 45	..	..	..	..		..		..	12 21	..		..	..	..	..	..	..	..
44½	Filey	arr	7 17	..	..	9 50	..	10 18	10 34	..		1121		1141	12 26	..		1 17	1 27	1 38	1 50	2 13	2 13	2 23
		dep	7 22	..	..	9 55	..	10 21	10 37	..		1124		1146	12 30	..		1 20	1 30	1 41	1 55	2 17	2 17	2 27
46½	Gristhorpe		7 27	..	..	10 0	..	..	..	..		..		..	..	..		..	..	..	..	..	Vv	..
48½	Cayton		Ss	..	..	..	..	..	..	..		..		..	..	..		..	..	..	..	..	..	..
51	Seamer		Nn	..	..	..	..	10 33	..	..		1137		..	12 42	..		..	..	..	..	..	2 28	..
53¾	Scarborough (Central)	arr	7 42	..	..	10 12	..	10 39	10 52	..		1143		12L2	12 48	..		1 35	1 45	1 56	2L10	2 31	2 34	2L41
95¾	109 York	arr	9 9	..	..	11S25	..	11Y50	12C35	..		1 10		..	1Y54	..	..	..	..	3A8	..	..	..	..

Station		Week Days—continued																Sundays							
		aft G	aft	aft S	aft A	aft	aft		aft	aft	aft E	aft E	aft	aft	aft	aft		mrn	mrn		aft	aft	aft		
Hull	dep	TC from Liverp'l (Ex.) dep. 9 3 mrn (Table 98)	1 20	..	TC from Man'r (C) dep. 10 30 mrn (Tables 67 &98)	2 30	..	..	3 25	4 30	5 10	5 30	5 35	..	7 20	9 30	..	6 30	9 0	..	4 45	..	7 0	..	..
Cottingham			1 29	..		2 39	..	..	3 34	4 39	..	..	5 44	..	7 29	9 39	..	6 39	..	..	4 54	..	7 9	..	..
Beverley			1 39	..		2 48	..	..	3 45	4 48	5 24	..	5 50	..	7 40	9 48	..	6U51	9 15	..	5 3	..	7 18	..	..
Arram			1 46	..		..	..	..	..	4 54	..	..	5 59	..	7 46	9 55	..	6 57	..	..	..	..	..	..	..
Lockington			1 51	..		..	..	..	..	4 59	..	..	6 4	..	7 51	10 0	..	7 2	..	..	..	..	..	..	..
Hutton Cranswick			1 58	..		..	..	..	..	5 7	..	..	6 10	..	7 58	10 7	..	7 10	..	..	..	..	..	..	..
Driffield	arr		2 4	..		3 4	3 53	..	4 1	5 15	5 39	5 56	6 16	7 23	8 3	1013	..	7 16	9 32	..	5 21	..	7 36	..	..
	dep		2 9	..		3 6	3 57	..	4 3	5 18	5 40	5 57	6 19	7 24	8 6	1017	..	7 20	9 34	..	5 24	..	7 38	..	..
Nafferton			2 15	..		..	..	..	..	5 23	..	..	6 24	..	8 12	1023	..	7 25	..	..	..	..	..	..	..
Lowthorpe			2 20	..		..	..	..	..	5 28	..	..	6 29	..	8 17	1029	..	7 30	..	..	..	..	..	..	..
Burton Agnes			2 25	..		..	..	..	..	5 32	..	..	6 34	Hh	8 22	1034	..	7 35	..	..	..	..	..	..	..
Carnaby			2 31	..		..	..	..	..	5 38	..	..	6 40	..	8 28	1040	..	7 41	..	..	..	..	..	..	..
Bridlington	arr	1 58	2 36	..	3 3	3 22	4 14	..	4 20	5 43	5 56	6 13	6 44	7 46	8 32	1044	..	7 46	9 50	..	5 41	..	7 54	..	..
	dep	2 3	..	2 40	3 15	3 26	Dep. Selby 2 40 aft (Table 106)	..	4S25	..	6 0	..	6 48	Dep. Selby 6 8 aft (Table 106)	..	..	..	7 50	..	..	..	6 45	..	..	..
Flamborough		..	..	2 48	..	3 32		..	..	..	..	..	6 54		..	..	..	7 56	..	..	..	6 52	..	..	..
Bempton		..	..	..	..	3 38		..	..	..	..	..	6 59		..	..	..	8 1	..	..	..	6 57	..	..	..
Speeton		..	..	..	..	3 45		..	..	..	..	..	7 7		..	..	..	8 9	..	..	..	7 5	..	..	..
Hunmanby		..	..	..	..	3 53		..	..	..	..	..	7 13		..	..	..	8 18	..	..	..	7 12	..	..	..
Filey	arr	2 33	..	3 7	3 40	3 58		..	4S48	..	6 22	..	7 18		..	..	..	8 23	..	..	..	7 17	..	..	..
	dep	2 36	..	3 10	3 45	4 2		..	4S51	..	6 25	..	7 21		..	..	..	8 27	..	..	..	7 19	..	..	..
Gristhorpe		..	..	Vv	..	4 7		..	..	..	..	..	..		..	..	..	8 32	..	..	..	..	..	..	..
Cayton		..	..	..	..	..		..	..	..	..	..	..		..	..	..	..	..	..	..	..	..	..	..
Seamer		..	..	3 21	..	4 18		..	..	..	..	..	7 33		..	..	..	8 43	..	..	..	7 29	..	..	..
Scarborough (Central)	arr	2 51	..	3 27	4L 8	4 24		..	5S7	..	6 39	..	7 39		..	..	..	8 49	..	..	..	7 35	..	..	..
109 York	arr	..	..	4Y37	..	5Y25		..	..	..	8 40	..	9Y6		..	..	..	9Y47	..	..	..	8Y55	..	..	..

For **LOCAL TRAINS** between Hull and Beverley, see Table 97

For **OTHER TRAINS** between Seamer and Scarborough, see Tables 109 and 112

NOTES

- **A** or A Sats only. Runs 8th June to 28th September inclusive
- **D** Saturdays only. Runs 29th June to 14th September inclusive
- **E** or E Except Saturdays
- **F** Saturdays only. Runs 13th July to 28th September inclusive
- **G** or C Sats only. Runs 1st June to 14th September inclusive
- **H** Saturdays only. Runs 13th July to 14th September inclusive
- **Hh** Calls to set down except on Saturdays
- **J** Saturdays only. Runs 29th June to 31st August inclusive
- **L** Londesborough Road Station. 600 yards from Central Sta.
- **Nn** Calls on Mondays only
- **S** or S Saturdays only
- **Ss** Calls on Saturdays only
- **TC** Through Carriages
- **U** Arr 6 46 mrn
- **Vv** Stops when required
- **Y** Connection at Seamer

Table 105—*continued* — SCARBOROUGH, FILEY, BRIDLINGTON, and HULL

Week Days

Miles	Station		mrn		mrn	mrn	mrn	mrn	mrn	mrn	mrn	mrn G	mrn S	mrn	mrn K		aft A	aft A	aft E	aft S	aft G	aft F	aft H	aft A
	109 York	dep	..	..	Arr. Selby 8 36 mrn (Table 106)	..	..	4 30	..	..	..	..	..	10Y15	1050	..		..	..	..	..	..	..	..
—	Scarborough (Central)	dep	..	..		..	..	7 25	..	8 15	8 53	..	1110	11 18	1216	..	TC to Rotherham and Masboro', arr. 3 48 aft (Tables 98 and 67)	1255	1 3	1 3	..	1L20	..	1L45
2¼	Seamer		..	..		..	..	7 31	..	..	9 0	..	..	11 28	..	..		..	1 9	1 9	..	..	..	..
5¼	Cayton		..	..		..	..	..	..	..	..	..	..	Ss	..	..		..	..	..	..	..	..	..
7¼	Gristhorpe		..	..		..	..	7 41	..	..	..	..	..	Ss	..	..		..	1 17	1 17	..	..	..	..
9½	Filey	arr	..	..		..	..	7 46	..	8 29	9 10	..	1126	11 42	1234	..		1 10	1 22	1 22	..	1 37	..	2 1
		dep	..	..		..	..	7 50	..	8 30	9 13	..	1129	11 45	1237	..		1 15	1 24	1 24	..	1 42	..	2 7
12¼	Hunmanby		..	..		..	..	7 56	..	..	9 19	..	..	11 51	..	..		..	1 30	1 30	..	..	..	..
16¼	Speeton		..	..		..	..	8 4	..	..	9 27	..	..	11 59	..	..		..	1 38	1 38	..	..	..	..
19¼	Bempton		..	..		..	..	8 10	..	..	9 33	..	..	12 5	..	..		..	1 44	1 44	..	..	..	..
20¼	Flamborough		..	..		..	..	8 13	..	..	9 36	..	..	12 8	..	..		..	1 47	1 47	..	..	..	..
22¼	Bridlington	arr	..	..		..	..	8 17	..	8 51	9 40	..	1153	12 12	1 1	..		1 37	1 51	1 51	..	2 6	..	2 32
		dep	6 30	..	7 0	7 20	8 0	8 25	8 30	8 53	9 45	11 5	1156	12 17	1 6	..	1 15	1 42	..	1 55	2 5	2 12	2 30	2 38
25¼	Carnaby		..	..	..	7 25	..	..	..	..	9 50	TC to Leeds, arr. 12 53 aft (Table 106)	..	12 22	TC to Liverpool (Ex.), arr. 5 39 aft (Table 98)	..		TC to Sheff'd (LMS) arr 4 10 aft (Table 114)	..	..	TC to Leeds, arr. 4 3 aft (Table 106)	TC to Sheff'd (V.), arr. 5 0 aft (Table 67)	TC to Bradf'd (Ex.), arr 5 25 aft (Tables 87 and 90)	TC to Manc'r (C.), arr. 6 55 aft (Tables 98 & 67)
28¼	Burton Agnes		..	..	7 9	7 31	..	..	..	..	9 56		..	12 28		..			..	..				
30	Lowthorpe		..	..	7 13	7 35	..	..	..	..	10 0		..	12 32		..			..	2 6				
32¼	Nafferton		..	..	7 18	7 40	..	..	8 46	..	10 5		..	12 39		..			..	2 11				
34¼	Driffield	arr	6 45	..	7 22	7 45	8 14	8 41	8 51	9 7	1010		1212	12 44		..			..	2 16				
		dep	6 47	..	7 25	7 46	8 16	8 43	..	9 8	1013		1214	12 46		..			..	2 18				
37½	Hutton Cranswick		..	..	..	7 53	..	8 50	..	..	1019		..	12 52		..			..	..				
40¾	Lockington		..	..	..	8 1	..	..	..	..	..		..	12 58		..			..	..				
42½	Arram		..	..	..	8 8	..	..	..	..	1028		..	1 3		..			..	..				
45½	Beverley		7 3	..	..	8 15	8 33	9 4	..	..	1036		1232	1 13		..			..	2 37				
49¾	Cottingham		7 10	..	..	8 23	..	9 11	..	..	1043		..	1 20		..			..	2 45				
53¾	Hull	arr	7 18	..	..	8 31	8 45	9 19	..	9 33	1052		1245	1 28		..			..	2 54				

Station		Week Days—continued																Sundays						
		non D	aft	aft G	aft	aft A	aft G	aft	aft	aft	aft	aft	aft E	aft	aft S			mrn	mrn		aft	aft	aft	
109 York	dep	12 0	1Y20	..	Arr. Selby 5 24 aft (Table 106)	..	..	3 0	..	..	Arr. Selby 8 34 aft (Table 106)	5 8	..	6 45	..	..	..	..	8Y45	..	..	..	5Y0	..
Scarborough (Central)	dep	1 55	2 25	2 45		3L42	3 54	4 20	..	6 0		6 23	..	8 30	..	..	..	..	9 45	..	..	..	6 0	..
Seamer		..	2 32	..		..	..	..	..	..		..	..	..	..	..	..	..	9 52	..	..	..	6 7	..
Cayton		..	..	..		..	..	..	..	..		..	..	..	..	..	..	..	..	..	..	..	..	..
Gristhorpe		..	..	..		..	..	..	..	..		6 34	..	..	..	..	..	..	10 0	..	..	..	6 15	..
Filey	arr	2 16	2 42	3 2		3 58	4 10	4 35	..	6 16		6 39	..	8 46	..	..	..	..	10 5	..	..	..	6 20	..
	dep	2 19	2 47	3 5		4 1	4 14	4 40	..	6 19		6 41	..	8 49	..	..	..	..	10 7	..	..	..	6 22	..
Hunmanby		..	2 53	..		..	..	4 46	..	..		6 46	..	..	..	..	..	..	10 13	..	..	..	6 29	..
Speeton		..	..	..		..	..	..	..	..		6 55	..	..	..	..	..	..	10 21	..	..	..	6 38	..
Bempton		..	3 6	..		..	..	5 0	..	..		7 1	..	..	..	..	..	..	10 27	..	..	..	6 44	..
Flamborough		..	..	..		..	..	..	..	..		7 8	..	..	..	..	..	..	10 30	..	..	..	6 49	..
Bridlington	arr	2 44	3 13	3 30		4 25	4 38	5 7	..	6 44		7 12	..	9 12	..	..	..	..	10 35	..	..	..	6 53	..
	dep	2 50	3 18	3 35	3 45	4 30	4 44	5 12	6 25	6 50	7 0	7 20	8 20	9 17	11 5	..	..	1030	10 40	..	2 35	6 50	7 2	..
Carnaby		..	3 23	TC to Manchester (V.) arr 7 25 aft (Table 98)	..	TC to Leices'r (C.), arr 9 34 aft (Table 2)	..	5 17	6 30	..	..	..	..	..	1110	..	..	..	10 45	..	..	..	7 7	..
Burton Agnes		..	3 29		..		..	5 23	6 36	..	..	..	..	..	1116	..	..	..	10 51	..	..	..	7 13	..
Lowthorpe		..	3 34		..		..	5 27	6 40	..	..	..	..	..	1120	..	..	..	10 55	..	..	..	7 17	..
Nafferton		..	3 39		..		..	5 32	6 45	..	..	..	..	..	1125	..	..	..	11 0	..	..	..	7 22	..
Driffield	arr	3 7	3 44		4 1		5 1	5 37	6 50	7 7	7 14	7 37	8 37	9 34	1130	..	..	1046	11 5	..	2 50	7 5	7 27	..
	dep	3 10	3 47		4 3		5 4	5 40	6 53	7 10	7 17	7 40	8 40	9 36	1133	..	..	1048	11 7	..	2 52	7 7	7 30	..
Hutton Cranswick		..	3 55		..		..	5 47	6 59	..	..	..	..	..	1140	..	..	..	11 14	..	..	..	7 37	..
Lockington		..	4 3		..		..	5 54	7 6	..	..	..	..	..	..	..	..	..	11 22	..	..	..	7 44	..
Arram		..	4 9		..		..	6 1	7 11	..	..	..	..	..	1149	..	..	..	11 30	..	..	..	7 49	..
Beverley		3 30	4 19		..		5 24	6 9	7 21	7 30	..	7 58	8 58	9 55	1157	..	..	11 7	11 38	..	3 9	7 24	7 58	..
Cottingham		..	4 26		..		..	6 16	7 29	..	..	8 5	9 5	10 2	12 6	..	..	..	11 46	..	3 16	7 31	8 5	..
Hull	arr	3 44	4 34		..		5 39	6 25	7 38	7 44	..	8 13	9 13	1010	1215	..	..	1120	11 55	..	3 25	7 40	8 14	..

For **LOCAL TRAINS** between Beverley and Hull, see Table 97

For **OTHER TRAINS** between Scarborough and Seamer, see Tables 109 and 112

NOTES

- **A** Saturdays only. Runs 8th June to 28th September inclusive
- **D** Saturdays only. Runs 29th June to 31st August inclusive
- **E** or E Except Saturdays
- **F** Saturdays only. Runs 13th July to 28th September inclusive
- **G** Saturdays only. Runs 1st June to 14th September inclusive
- **H** Saturdays only. Runs 13th July to 14th September inclusive
- **K** Saturdays only. Runs 8th June to 21st September inclusive
- **L** Londesborough Road Station 600 yards from Central Station
- **S** or S Saturdays only
- **Ss** Calls on Saturdays only
- **TC** Through Carriage
- **Y** Connection at Seamer

Figures 9.5A and 9.5B. *Summer 1946 public timetable. (LNER)*

With the complete closure of the Malton and Driffield in October 1958 they continued for a few more years travelling outwards via Selby and York.

The introduction of DMUs began in January 1957 with the Hull-Beverley workings, and the winter of 1961-2 saw the full timetable using diesels. There was a general speeding up; the 8-15 am from Scarborough now reached Hull in 75 minutes, and between Hull and Bridlington the standard time for trains calling at Cottingham, Beverley and Driffield was 42-3 minutes. There were 16 trains between Hull and Bridlington, with eight continuing to Scarborough, and the Hull-Beverley frequency was now up to 31 trains. Conversely in 1958 all the Sunday trains were withdrawn in the winter months, a facility not restored until 1991. In summer there were eight trains on Sundays from Hull to Beverley, five continuing to Bridlington, three of which went on to Scarborough. In 1965 the Hull-Bridlington service was reduced by three trains, and with the York and Selby lines being closed completely other frequencies suffered.

The closure of five stations on 5 January 1970, after the line became grant-aided, allowed the service to be speeded up by a few minutes, with the standard time for an 'all stations' Hull - Bridlington train becoming 45 minutes. On summer Sundays there was a non-stop Hull - Bridlington train taking 33 minutes (56 mph) – the fastest ever over the line.

More Recent Years

Between 1969 and 1989 there were alterations, from time to time, which gradually boosted the number of weekday trains so that Hull - Beverley was back to 30-32 trains, Hull - Bridlington 15-17, and Bridlington - Scarborough 9-11. In the same period the Saturday holiday trains steadily diminished, and Filey Holiday Camp station closed at the end of the 1977 holiday season (last train ran on 17 September 1977), so by 1985 there were only four Saturday dated trains to and from Bridlington, supplemented by a Scarborough - Leicester via Bridlington train. Since the closure of the Cottingham South - Hessle Road Junction Branch, and the Selby - Driffield line in 1965 all these trains were routed by the new Cricket Ground Curve between Anlaby Road and Walton Street. Since the last of these, the Scarborough - Leicester train, was withdrawn in 1987 the Curve has seen no regular booked workings, although it continues to be used by occasional excursions, rail tours and Hull freights.

The Current Position (2013)

The withdrawal of holiday trains coincided with a reappraisal of the service as a whole. Any semblance of the 1929 regular interval pattern had long since disappeared, although the principle was being applied to other lines. In 1989 a completely new timetable was introduced between Hull and Bridlington, giving a half-hourly service throughout the day with a total of 27 trains; this was supplemented by 11 trains between Hull and Beverley. Subsequently, a slight reduction in the number of Beverley trains and one extra to Bridlington makes the current weekly totals 35 and 28 respectively. To facilitate this timetable the service between Bridlington and Scarborough has been reduced from 11-13 weekday trains to nine, providing a 90 minute frequency. For some years there was a 7-0 am from Filey to Scarborough, but this disappeared when the Regional Railways North East franchise was split to form separate TransPennine Express and Northern franchises.

There had been no Sunday trains in winter since 1958, but in 1991 they were reinstated between Hull and Bridlington providing between four and seven trains plus two extras between Hull and Beverley. In summer there was an enhanced service over the whole line, usually five trains between Hull and Scarborough, plus seven more as far as Bridlington. 4 March 2001 saw the last signal box closed (Hunmanby) between Bridlington and Seamer, and this made a winter Sunday service a more economic proposition, and in December 2009 the summer Sunday service became all year round. Currently this provides six trains between Hull and Scarborough, a further seven between Hull and Bridlington and one extra between Hull and Beverley.

A further development was the merging of the Sheffield - Doncaster - Hull and Leeds - Hull timetables with that for the Scarborough line, giving Scarborough, Filey and Bridlington a service of through trains to West and South Yorkshire destinations at regular intervals. The through trains to Doncaster and Sheffield continue to the present day, but through workings to Leeds and beyond ceased when the TransPennine franchise was created.

Club Saloons

From January 1903 until the Second World War, First Class season ticket holders, between Bridlington and Hull, were able to travel in their own coach, a club saloon, for, initially, an additional total sum of £30 per annum. A committee of six had gained an agreement with the NER, and formulated their own rules for the payment and use of the saloon. In February they were inviting other First Class passengers to join them on the 8-18 am train from Bridlington and 5-30 pm from Hull (12-50 pm Saturdays). The 20 passengers were each to pay 2*s*-6*d* ($12^1/_2$p) per month. The saloon continued to run throughout the war, and was so successful that a second started running from October 1919. The rate for the new saloon was £60 per annum, and from January 1920 the passengers in the original saloon were required to pay the same rate. August 1922 saw another group of 25 regular passengers wanting their own saloon, but initially the NER only offered a six-wheel vehicle, which they rejected; next year the LNER offered them a bogie coach for £100 per annum, which they accepted. The three saloons continued, with one of them extended to run through from Scarborough, until early 1930s, when the depression started to bite, and only one remained in 1939 to be discontinued at the beginning of the new conflict.

Post Office Sorting Carriage

From 1 May until 31 October 1901 a Royal Mail sorting carriage ran from Hull to Bridlington attached to the first passenger train on each weekday; it then ran each summer and from 1913 it started from Leeds. The service was suspended from 30 October 1916 until 17 June 1919, and ceased running altogether on

31 October 1926. Initially the carriage was 23-feet long vehicle No 292, but from March 1904 a 32-feet vehicle, No 334, was used until withdrawal in 1922. It was usual to store the vehicle at Hull during the winter months.

Weather Disruptions

Reference was made earlier to disruptions to the public timetables during the Second World War, but mention should also be made of the effects of adverse weather. The line between Bridlington and Filey is particularly vulnerable to snow, and services have been dislocated on several occasions since the line opened; February 1958 was one such occasion. Very heavy snow fell over the East Riding on Monday and Tuesday 24 and 25 February. On 25th a snowplough left Hull at 4-0 am to clear the line to Bridlington, but despite a 130 yard long drift at Arram, and having to remove a fallen tree and telegraph pole, it reached there in time for a Hull train to leave at 7-30 am. Later that morning the 10-35 am Hull - Scarborough and 11-30 am Scarborough - Hull ran into deep drifts in the cutting near Speeton. According to the *Hull Daily Mail*, for 26 February, after the trains had been stuck for several hours it appeared that the northbound train had the best chance of returning to Hull, and passengers from Filey and Scarborough were asked to climb down on to the line and transfer to it. Unfortunately the strong wind was causing further drifting and the train quickly became trapped again. A relief train containing 20 workmen was sent from Hull, and the Hull train was reached with some difficulty, but eventually they managed to dig it out. It reached Bridlington shortly before 3-0 am on 26th, where the station buffet was open and manned by the Women's Voluntary Service. Passengers from Scarborough and Filey had to find accommodation for the night, but the remainder, who had left Hull at 10-35 the previous day eventually returned to the city at 3-40 am. As the blockages were not cleared until later that day passengers wanting to get back to Scarborough had to travel via York.

Endnotes:

1. Based on personal observations by the author and public and working timetables 1850 to 2012.
2. *North Eastern Express* February 1986 pages 3-4, and RAIL527/1613.
3. Ward R and Sedgewick WA, *The Postal History of Bridlington, Filey and Hunmanby*, 1985, Chapter 7.

Plate 9.2. *NER First Class Saloon No 1029 was built to Diagram 41 in 1892 with seating for 16 passengers. In March 1911 it was altered for use as the dedicated Hull & Bridlington Club Saloon; Diagram 184. The seating was modified to comprise 17 individual seats in a large open saloon and 5 individual seats in a small compartment. Between saloon and compartment was a vestibule containing a lavatory. The carriage was steam heated and was lit by gas. (NER / NERA EW Smith Collection)*

Chapter 10 : Signalling

Nicholas P Fleetwood

The signalling of the line on opening is shrouded in mist; however, some documents from the 1850s still survive and from these it is apparent that the line was worked in a rather haphazard way, typical of railways of the time. On 6 August 1859 a report (1) was prepared for the Locomotive Committee on the signalling arrangements of the Hull to Scarborough line. From this it can be deduced that the line was provided with rotating disc board signals provided with red lights at each station and was worked on the Time Interval System. It is apparent that this basic form of signalling had been supplemented in the early 1850s by some semaphore 'Far' or 'Back' signals as advance warning signals. These signals are later described as 'Distance' signals but they should not be confused with the more modern commonly understood 'Distant' signal; they were a stop signal but one which the rules allowed the driver to pass at 'Stop' and, once he had brought his train to a stand, proceed slowly at caution as far as it was safe to do so. The stationmaster would operate the station signal and safety was helped by the gatemen who were employed to control the level crossing gates which were common on the line. Many of these crossings had been provided with 'Far' signals which were worked by wire operated by a small windlass. There are a number of telling comments about the attitude to safety at this time that were typified by the comment on Beverley.

> The station signal by day is a disc on the south end of the Down platform. Red on both sides it stands always ON; the reason assigned for this, is, that all trains stop there, it is of no use – indicating to the Gateman the state of the line in the Station; by night it is an ordinary lamp, shewing Red both ways which cannot be turned off, and therefore it is necessary when an engine has to pass without stopping to put the light out altogether.

The report makes recommendations for the provision of semaphore and 'Far' signals but a letter (2) from Thomas Cabry, NER Southern Division Engineer, states that with only seven trains a day he did not regard the matter as pressing.

By 1869 the Board of Trade was pressing the Company to introduce the Block System on its lines

Plate 10.1. *Flamborough signal box as photographed in 1977. This box dates from the introduction of block signalling on the line in 1874 and was originally a single-storey ground cabin in the S1s style. During 1899 it was raised to a two-storey cabin, which was apparently done by jacking up the original structure and building a new base. This work started on 9 February 1899 and was completed on 15 February 1899 during which time hand-signalling was in force. A similar operation had been undertaken at Lowthorpe in 1895. (HGE Wilson)*

and, with some reluctance, the costs of this together with an audit of safety arrangements were being established. At that time it was stated that 22 Block Section cabins were required of which seven already existed, five of these were in Hull or Scarborough and the two existing intermediate cabins were at Seamer Junction and Beverley Junction. At these locations signal cabins were provided but there was no interlocking. It would seem from a contemporary accident report (3) that the principal stations were connected by telegraph but that Time Interval working was still in force, certainly between Bridlington and Scarborough. The installation of locking frames and signal cabins was agreed in 1872 but as the whole of the NER had to be tackled, this was done in stages, and it was not until September 1874 that consideration was given to the Hull to Seamer Junction section. By this time additional temporary cabins had appeared at Cottingham Junction, Flemingate, Grove Hill, Driffield Junction, Driffield West, Wansford Road, Bessenby (sic) Road, and Bridlington Quay. On 22 October 1874 the proposed works were ordered to be carried out (4) and in addition 32 houses had to be constructed for the signalmen. In February 1875, J Broadley's tender of £6402 1*s* 0*d* for the construction of 34 cottages was accepted.

It would seem therefore that the block signalling requirements for the line, as set out in 1872, were completed by 1875, and that these plans proved remarkably resilient for the next 100 years. The only changes made were to accommodate increased traffic and, over the years, many of the signal cabins were enlarged, rebuilt or replaced, but mainly on the same sites.

In the later years of the Nineteenth Century considerable changes took place in the development of the railways of the East Riding. The York to Beverley was doubled from 1881, the Selby to Market Weighton line of 1848 was doubled in 1889-90, and the line from Market Weighton to Driffield was completed in 1890. All these alterations improved traffic levels and it was necessary to redouble the original line from Cottingham Junction to Hessle Road in 1899 (see Chapter 12).

The first developments after 1875 were in 1881, at Seamer station, which was provided with three additional houses to accommodate signalmen and porters,(5) whilst on 23 February 1882 it was proposed to lay in an independent siding capable of holding 40 wagons connected at both ends to the Down line at an estimated cost of £763.(6)

Bridlington

The next most significant change took place at Bridlington where, in 1893, three new platforms were provided together with locomotive facilities and sidings, all controlled from a new signal box.(7) This replaced the old station signal box, which was nearer the station platforms and which controlled the station crossing, itself bridged in 1893. The old signal box at Bessingby Road Crossing became a gate box. By 1898 the accommodation had again become inadequate and further additional sidings were provided worked from the 1893 signal box.(8) This was not the end of developments as the General Manager reported in 1901 that additional facilities were required to work traffic and these included the bridging of Bessingby Road. The cost of this would be £16,118.(9) This work took two years to complete but allowed the quadrupling of

Plate 10.2. *Carnaby signal box in August 1977; this is a box dating from the introduction of block signalling in 1874. A large window was later installed to improve visibility of the crossing. The box was extended at the platform end in 1911, for the introduction of the new siding, but in the original style, even down to the ornamental brickwork on the end. Note the remains of the original valancing. (HGE Wilson)*

the line across Bessingby Road and the provision of duplicate running lines into the station. The signal cabin of 1893 was increased in length by two-thirds and a new seasonal signal cabin was provided at Bessingby Junction between Carnaby and Bridlington. These enhanced facilities were available for use for the summer of 1903 but soon proved inadequate as by the end of 1910, a further £25,645 was committed for enlargement of the station and associated signalling improvements. These included the provision of two further through platforms and another bay platform,(10) whilst Bridlington South signal box was again extended; see Colour Plate 8, page 30. These works, completed in 1912, doubled its original length and at the same time Bridlington Quay box was extended and re-equipped. These proved to be the last extensions made and lasted virtually unchanged until rationalization commenced in the mid 1960s. This has continued progressively until the facilities have now been reduced nearly to the 1870s level. For example: in October 1968, the Engine Shed sidings were put out of use; followed on 25 November 1974 by the Carriage Sidings Nos 1 and 2 (the old excursion lines). The Down sidings went on 6 December 1976 and Platforms 1 and 2 on 20 March 1983.(11)

Other Locations

In the early Twentieth Century improvements and modernizations were taking place elsewhere: signal boxes were renewed at Cottingham, Beverley, Lockington, Hutton Cranswick, Driffield North, Nafferton, Burton Agnes, Speeton (see Colour Plate 9, page 31), Filey, Cayton and Seamer Junction. The line had originally been equipped almost exclusively with McKenzie Clunes & Holland 6-inch-centre pattern lever frames and as they became too small to control the layout, these were replaced by the same manufacturer's later pattern frames. Most of these changes consisted of additional sidings or crossovers, but at Beverley running independent lines were provided in 1911 and the arrangements between Seamer Junction and Seamer station, where a new down platform was provided in 1912, were expanded to accommodate traffic. From about 1906 the increasing provision of outer home signals enabled some of the smaller block section splitting boxes to be closed. Seamer Carr and Hutton Grange (Hutton Bank) were amongst the victims.

Telegraph communications had been available between the principal stations from Hull to Bridlington in 1847 (12) and by the mid 1850s was being used to advise of train movements, even though the line was being worked on the Time Interval System. The introduction of signal cabins and the Absolute Block System in 1875 rendered the *station* telegraphs largely unnecessary for signalling purposes, but they were still required for the transmission of goods and passenger advices so the system was gradually extended with even the minor signal boxes such as Watton being connected by 1903. After the First World War, the telegraph installations were gradually superseded by telephones.

Some track circuits started to be installed on the line from about 1918 but they only came into general use post 1945, and by the 1990s considerable sections of the remaining line were so fitted, enabling track circuit block to be introduced on some sections between Hull

Plate 10.3. *Lockington signal box in May 1977. This box is based on S4 style signal box dating from 1912, but with the locking room windows dating from an earlier style, and the steps at the rear of the building. It replaced, on the same site, an earlier box dating from 1874, and was closed and demolished in 1985. (HGE Wilson)*

and Bridlington. In 2011 the line is controlled by signal boxes at Hull Paragon, Hessle Road, Beverley, Driffield, Bridlington, and Seamer, which now controls what remains of the lines into Scarborough.

The First World War had a significant effect on the railways with incessant demands being made on them for men and materials, and it also produced significant changes in traffic patterns. The North Eastern along with other railways was required by the Railway Executive Committee to provide track, rolling stock and men for service in France. This led to a decision to single the line between Flamborough and Bempton and Speeton to Hunmanby which was carried out in 1917. These new sections of single line were worked on the Electric Token Tablet Block (ETTB) system from 16 March 1917.(13) Around this time steps were also being made to compensate for the lack of suitable men by using female crossing keepers and signal-women. To aid the reduction in signalmen, King Levers were installed at Watton, Kilnwick, Lockington, Lowthorpe, and probably elsewhere, to allow the signal boxes to be used just as gate boxes with crossing keepers.

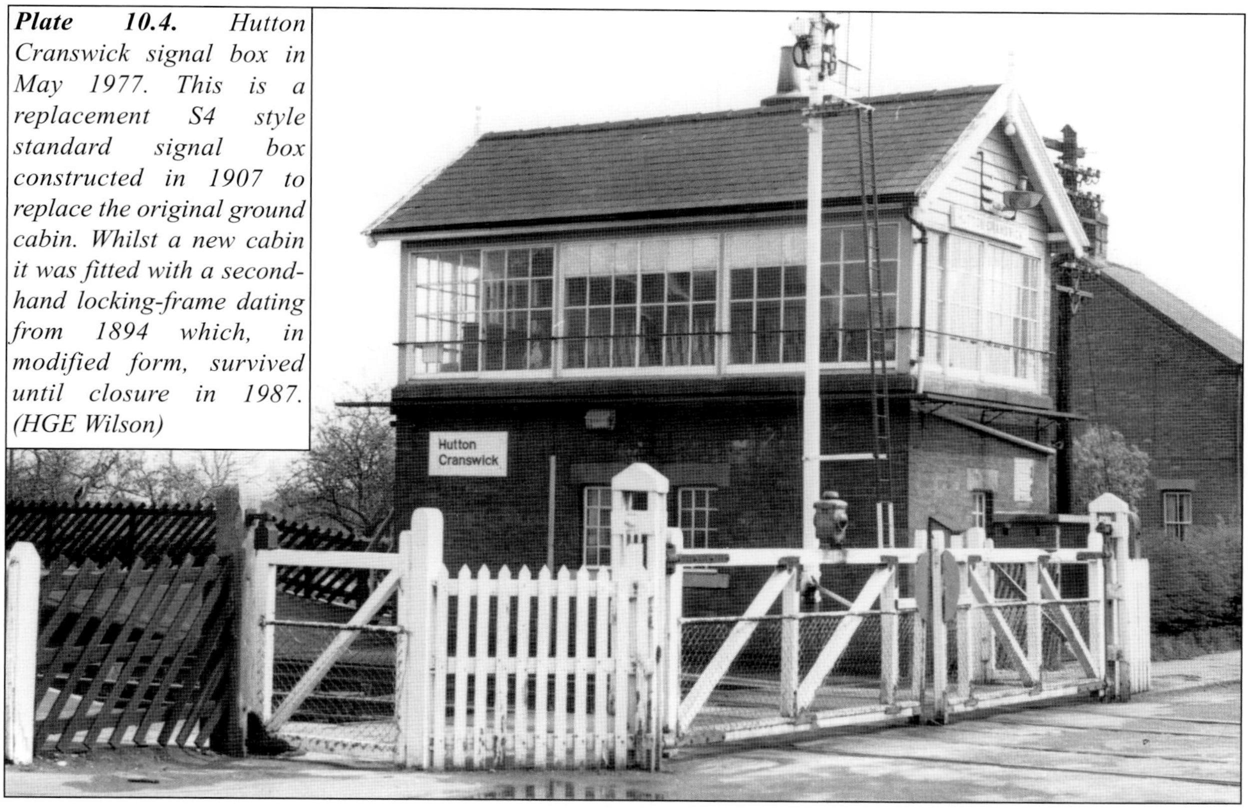

Plate 10.4. *Hutton Cranswick signal box in May 1977. This is a replacement S4 style standard signal box constructed in 1907 to replace the original ground cabin. Whilst a new cabin it was fitted with a second-hand locking-frame dating from 1894 which, in modified form, survived until closure in 1987. (HGE Wilson)*

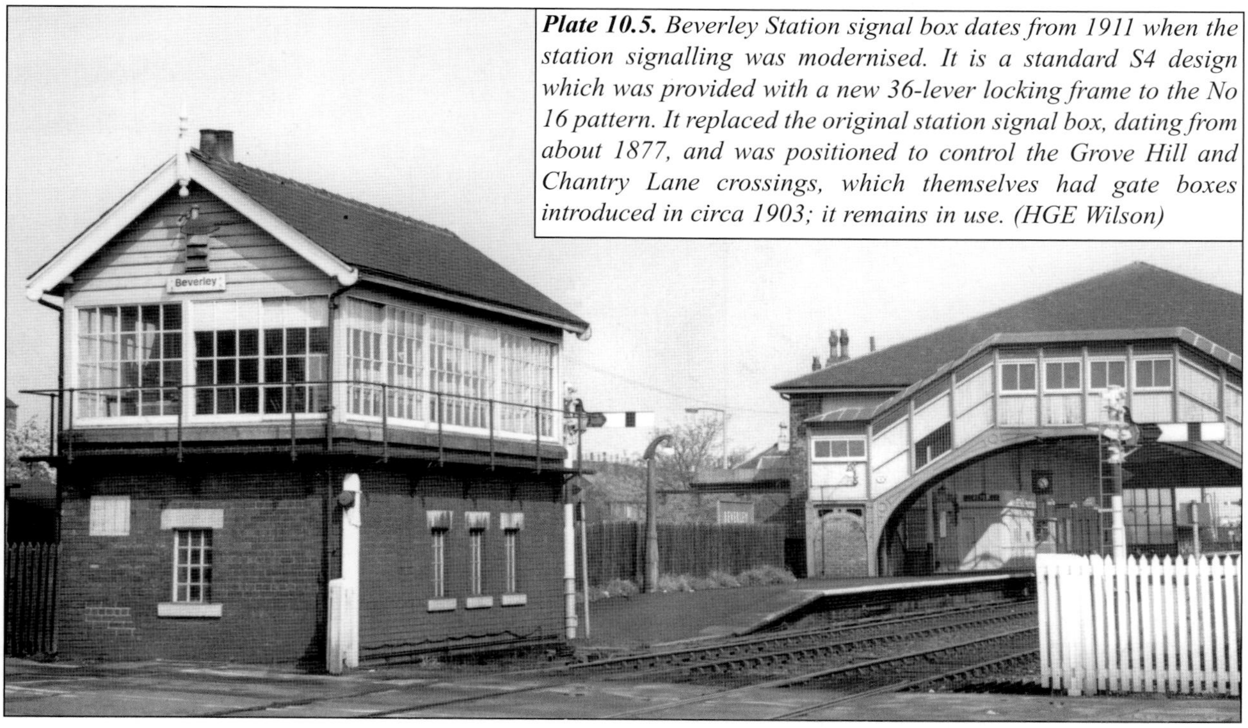

Plate 10.5. *Beverley Station signal box dates from 1911 when the station signalling was modernised. It is a standard S4 design which was provided with a new 36-lever locking frame to the No 16 pattern. It replaced the original station signal box, dating from about 1877, and was positioned to control the Grove Hill and Chantry Lane crossings, which themselves had gate boxes introduced in circa 1903; it remains in use. (HGE Wilson)*

Clearly the singling of the line had raised operational difficulties as by September 1919 works had been put in hand to reinstate Bempton as a passing place (14) and a block post, and to convert Speeton back into a passing place.(15) On 23 February 1922 the NER Traffic Committee decided that the line should be redoubled between Flamborough and Bempton and Speeton to Hunmanby at a total cost of £30,677.(16) The redoubled line was inspected by Major Hall on 17 October 1923.(17) After the resolution of disputes between the NER and the Government over payment,(18) the LNER went on to authorise the redoubling of the section from Bempton to Speeton at a cost of £11,449 (19) and this amount was charged to the Military Suspense Account. This final section was inspected by the Ministry of Transport on 8 July 1924.(20)

Filey Holiday Camp

The next major development was the provision of the Filey Holiday Camp Branch. The holiday camp had been first proposed by Billy Butlin in early 1939 and a planning application had been made for the camp in April 1939 which had been granted subject to holidaymakers being transported to the site by train.(21) The outbreak of the Second World War prevented completion of the camp as a holiday camp but it was finished under the auspices of Ministry of War and then used as an RAF camp. The site reverted to Billy Butlin in 1945, and permission was granted for the branch railway to be constructed. By 1946 the branch was sufficiently complete to enable the occasional train to run to the camp, however, the junctions were controlled by ground frames and hand points and the working controlled by an inspector.

Plate 10.6. *Burton Agnes signal box was opened in 1903 to replace the original ground cabin of 1874 which was sited on the opposite side of the line and remained, out of use, until recent times. The box illustrated is of the S1a type and must be amongst the last of that type constructed; it was closed in 1990. (Colin Ryder Collection)*

Plate 10.7. *Bridlington South signal box was the largest on the line with 125 levers. This structure dates from 1893 and was extended in 1903 and 1912. Originally in the S1a style it replaced the original Bridlington Station signal box and the Bessingby Crossing signal box. The glazed operating-floor windows were probably installed with the 1903 extension in the S2 style just coming into use and created a unique hybrid structure. It remains in use with a shortened No 16 pattern frame. (Colin Ryder Collection)*

There were a number of changes to the signalling on the main line to accommodate the station but the most notable was the provision of approach lit colour light distant signals. These only illuminated as the train approached them, which was a practical solution to the problem of limited battery life and were the subject of special authority.

The signal boxes, built to the current LNER style, controlling the junctions at Royal Oak South and North were opened on 9 May 1947, replacing the temporary ground frames, but the signal box at Filey Camp was not completed in time for the 1947 season and did not open until 3 May 1948; so for the 1947 season working of the station was again in the hands of ground staff and an inspector. The signal cabins were opened with relief signalmen as required. These arrangements continued until the branch was formally closed from 26 November 1977. The signal cabins remained intact until the end of the next summer season in order to allow the turning on the branch triangle of locomotives working steam-hauled excursions to Scarborough. Royal Oak North and Filey Holiday Camp then remained until 3 September 1978 and Royal Oak South until 1 October to allow track recovery trains to operate, after which date the signalling arrangements were restored to what they had been before the opening of the branch.

The Second World War

The Second World War brought about significant military traffic, with the establishment of various military camps and airfields in the East Riding. In 1943 new facing connections were installed at Hutton Cranswick (see Colour Plate 10, page 31) and Carnaby, which involved major alterations to the signalling arrangements. In both cases the arrangements were removed after the war ended and the pre-war facilities restored. At Arram the close proximity to Leconfield's runways caused special arrangements to be made to protect the railway from overshooting aircraft. These were first proposed in 1944 and instituted in July 1945 and consisted of emergency colour light signals, which were only illuminated in the case of emergency, activated by trip wires. Train crews were instructed to observe these signal aspects regardless of any contradictory indications from the nearby semaphore signals; similar arrangements were installed at other aerodromes throughout the Britain, and formed the pattern for the future. At Arram they were removed when the aerodrome ceased to be used for flying regular fixed-wing aircraft, and had gone by 1963.

Post War Restructuring

The withdrawal of local goods traffic following the publishing of the Beeching Report on 27 March 1963 led to the closure of all the wayside goods facilities. In May 1964 goods facilities were withdrawn at Arram, Carnaby and Speeton, followed in August by Bempton, Filey, Flamborough, Hunmanby and Hutton Cranswick; Cottingham and Nafferton followed in 1970 and 1976 respectively, with the goods facilities at Beverley, Driffield and Bridlington being the last to go. In each case the removal of goods yard connections led to signalling simplification, although at the principal stations this was a more drawn out affair, the first casualties being the connections to horse docks.

The closure of the Driffield to Malton Railway on 20 October 1958, Driffield to Market Weighton on 2 August 1965 and Beverley to York lines on 27 November 1965 paved the way for rationalisation of the signalling arrangements in both these places. Many signal boxes were reduced to gate boxes (see Appendix I : Signalling Table for dates) and the first tentative steps were taken to rationalising the numerous level crossings.

Plate 10.8. *Bridlington Quay signal box, also known as Quay Crossing, is another hybrid box being a much rebuilt and lengthened S1a cabin, which was provided with a new rear wall and S4 style operating floor in 1912. The original box on this site probably dated from about 1874 but did not control the crossing until 1902. The 1912 box had a 59-lever frame but this was progressively reduced before closure in 1998. (Colin Ryder Collection)*

The first major step to modernization was the singling of the line between Bridlington Quay and Hunmanby on 1 January 1973, although this was worked by traditional single ETTB (Electric Train Tablet Block) instruments. For the Bempton to Hunmanby section this was the second time that the line had been singled and worked under this system.

By the 1980s the railway had assumed its present format although the signalling had yet to be modernised. Since then colour light signals have been introduced as renewals have become necessary. Progressively, the level crossings were converted to Automatic Open Crossings (AOCR for remotely monitored or AOCL for locally monitored) but this programme was brought to an abrupt halt by the Lockington Accident on 26 July 1986 in which serious loss of life occurred not only to a road user but also to the rail passengers (see Chapter 11). The original Hull to Scarborough line had numerous crossings and, although steps had been taken to reduce these, some 200 still remained in 1925. Most of these were field or footpath crossings and those over public roads were controlled by proper gates under the supervision of a signalman or by a gateman. Over the years there had been a number of accidents but invariably the loss of life had been to the road users, largely due to the superior bulk of the steam engine. Lockington brought into focus a national problem and led to an investigation by Professor Stott into the safety of level crossings. His report was published on 17 July 1987 and this enabled the Department of Transport report on Lockington (22) to be published on 15 September 1987. The upshot of this accident was a change in national policy and that most of the AOCR crossings were converted to Automatic Half Barriers (AHB). Unfortunately, accidents still occur periodically as motorists ignore the barriers and road signals.

On 8 February 1998 the working of the single line from Bridlington to Hunmanby was changed to Track Circuit Block (TCB) and this was introduced from Seamer to Filey on 10 April 2000, and extended through to Hunmanby when Filey box closed. Hunmanby closed on 4 March 2001 after which the whole of the section Bridlington to Seamer was worked on TCB. Hull to Beverley is worked on TCB, but the sections Beverley to Driffield and Driffield to Bridlington are still worked on the Absolute Block system introduced in 1875.

Endnotes:

1. TNA (The National Archives, Kew) Rail 527/1117/4.
2. TNA Rail 527/1117/8.
3. Board of Trade Accident report into an Accident at Filey 24 November 1869.
4. TNA Rail 527/31 Loco Ways & Works Committee Min (Minute) 146556.
5. TNA Rail 527/68 Traffic Committee Min 12733.
6. TNA Rail 527/68 Traffic Committee Min 13077.
7. TNA MT6/649/3 Board of Trade Railway Inspector's report.
8. TNA MT6: 846/9 Board of Trade Railway Inspector's report.
9. TNA Rail 527/75 Traffic Committee Min 21243.
10. TNA Rail 527/49 Ways & Works Committee Min 18879.
11. Various Weekly Operating Notices.
12. Hull to Bridlington is shown as equipped with the telegraph on the OS map of 1852; 1847 is quoted in Steven Roberts' Report on the Electric Telegraph Company.
13. NER circulars O.1223 and 4 dated 1917; NERA Collection No 537.
14. Ministry of Transport file: PR 1327/19 – Inspection report; TNA MT29 or MT30.
15. Ministry of Transport file: PR 4404/19 – Inspection report; TNA MT29 or MT30.
16. TNA Rail 527/81 Traffic Committee Min 25058.
17. TNA MT 29/81 Ministry of Transport Inspector's Report.
18. TNA Rail 390/1570 Board Papers.
19. TNA Rail 390/56 LNER Traffic Committee Min 191.
20. TNA MT29/82 Ministry of Transport Inspector's Report.
21. John Farline: his comprehensive article was published in 1992 in *British Railways Journal* No 42.
22. HMSO 1987 ISBN 0 11 550832 5: Department of Transport Accident Report.

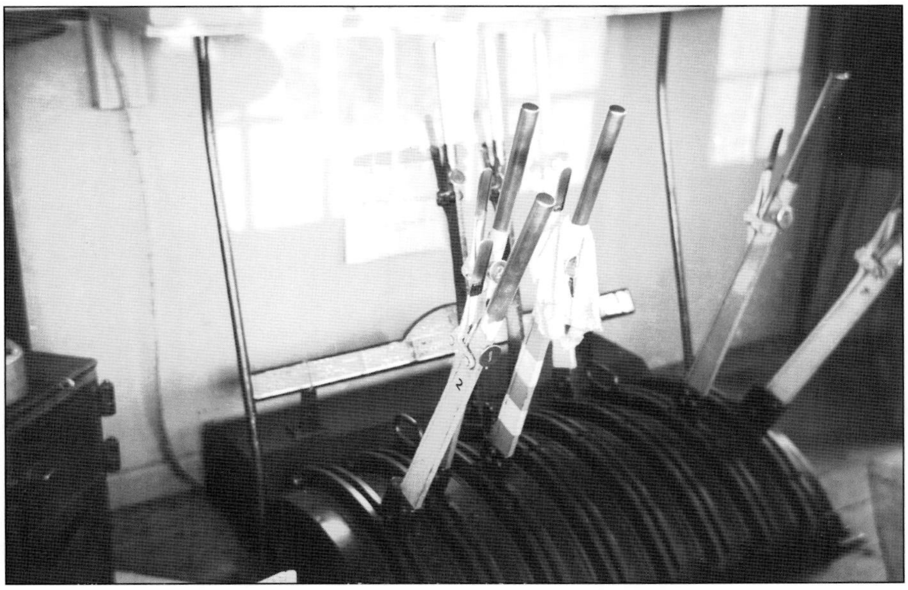

Plate 10.9. *A view of the 8-lever McKenzie, Clunes & Holland frame at Kilnwick, photographed on 13 May 1960; it would be replaced in November 1977 at the grand old age of 103. (John F Mallon / Joint NERA - Ken Hoole Study Centre JF Mallon Collection)*

Chapter 11 : Level Crossings

John F Addyman

During the Nineteenth Century, when the majority of our railways were built, there was a reluctance to provide bridges where railways crossed roads unless the topography dictated it; the cost of a bridge and its approaches varied between £500 for a farm track to around £3,000 for a major road. An Act, which gained the Royal Assent on 8 May 1845 (three days after the Bridlington Branch Select Committee hearing), allowed railway promoters to negotiate with the local Justices of the Peace about the provision of level crossings, but this usually failed to get bridges provided even at main road crossings.(1) This left a legacy, in the 1950s, of over 4,500 *public road* crossings on British Railways, which were time-wasting, expensive to man and, as shown below, potentially very dangerous.

Before building the Hull to Bridlington line there was agreement as the public did not want bridges and the railway could save at least £50,000 by not providing them. At the Hull & Selby, Bridlington Branch, Select Committee hearing on 5 May 1845, a Mr C Angus spoke for all the farmers on the line: 'Level crossings were undoubtedly the best adapted for the traffic, and he had great reason to complain of being compelled to carry his goods up steep bridges, instead of having them drawn at a comparatively easy rate on a level country.'

The whole Select Committee, and Robert Stephenson, as engineer for the promoters, were in favour of the level crossings, but one witness, a surveyor named Appleton, 'was of the opinion that level crossings were very dangerous'.(2) Mr Appleton was so right; the level crossings on the Hull & Scarborough line have had a very poor safety record including two of the worst crossing accidents ever.

Accident at Burton Agnes Level Crossing(3)

At 6-42 on the morning of 17 September 1947, a Bedford three-ton army lorry was making its third run needed to transport 50 German prisoners and their baggage from a nearby prisoner-of-war camp to catch the 7-09 am train to Hull from Burton Agnes. On its final trip the lorry contained two British NCOs and 26 Germans. The driver, a British staff-sergeant who was neither authorized nor qualified to drive the lorry, appears to have hit the accelerator pedal instead of the brakes as he approached the closed level crossing gates. The lorry smashed through the gates into the path of the 5-55 am train from Hull to Bridlington. The train, made up of a Class D49/2 locomotive (No 2772 *The Sinnington*), a four-wheeled van and five coaches, was travelling at about 55 mph when it struck the lorry; the two British NCOs and 10 Germans died as a result. No one on the train was hurt even though the leading van buffer-locked and one pair of its wheels was derailed. Fortunately the van re-railed itself about

Plate 11.1. *Over the years there were numerous accidents involving pedestrians, vehicles, machinery and livestock at footpath, farm and minor road crossings. Harpham Crossing, on a minor road 35 chains (700 metres) south-west of Burton Agnes, was controlled from a gatehouse equipped with instruments and bells to indicate the presence of trains. The board signal shown in the photograph was rotated to the danger position when the line was clear and the gates were opened to road traffic. In November 1935 the gates had been opened by farm labourers, leading cattle, without the gatekeeper's knowledge, resulting in several animals being killed. Locks were then fitted but, a year later due to vandalism, one was damaged resulting in a motorist, who was unfamiliar with the area, driving on to the crossing in front of a train. The car was a total wreck and the driver and his passenger died; the D49 locomotive 'The Atherston' suffered very minor damage. (John M Fleming, 1972)*

90 yards further on at an obtuse crossing leading into the sidings, and only minor damage was sustained by the 117 ton locomotive and its train. Even though the death toll was larger than Lockington, being an accident only involving military personnel who were not passengers, it got very limited publicity.

Accident at Lockington Level Crossing(4)

Nearly forty years later, on the morning of 26 July 1986, the 9-33 stopping-train from Bridlington to Hull was a diesel multiple unit (DMU) made up of four carriages carrying about 120 passengers. Simultaneously with the train reaching the level crossing, at the site of the former Lockington station, a Ford Escort van was driven directly into its path. The leading pair of wheels of the train was derailed when it struck the van, and the derailment became progressive.(5) The leading coach jack-knifed and ended up on its side at the bottom of the low embankment facing in the wrong direction. The three remaining coaches stayed upright, but the second coach ended up straddling both tracks almost 200 yards beyond the crossing. Both drivers, though seriously injured, survived, but eight in the train and a passenger in the van died; 10 passengers were detained in hospital.

The road from Lockington village to the railway, two miles away, becomes a minor 'no through road' after crossing the A164; it serves a number of farms and the hamlet of Aike to the east of the main road. Prior to December 1985 Lockington level crossing had full barriers controlled by the adjacent signal box, but in the previous July BR had applied for an Order, under Section 1 of the Level Crossings Act 1983, to convert the site to an Automatic Open Crossing Remotely monitored (AOCR). The installation was inspected and approved by the Ministry on 5 February 1986.

At Lockington the control was activated when the train occupied a track circuit and operated a treadle about three-quarters of a mile from the level crossing. The sequence for warning road traffic, prior to the train reaching the crossing, was a 10 second delay, and three seconds of steady yellow followed by at least 24 seconds of alternate flashing red lights; an audible warning, 'yodel alarm', started with the yellow lights and turned off when the red lights ceased flashing after the passage of the train. Motorists were warned in advance by the standard level crossing sign with a supplementary plate saying 'Automatic Control (No Barriers) STOP when lights show.' The crossing equipment was continuously monitored in Beverley signal box, and audible and visual alarms were activated there in the case of any malfunction.(6)

Much of the 22 page Ministry of Transport accident report by Major AGB King, which was not published until a year after the accident, was concerned with conflicting evidence about the safe operation of the lights controlling the road traffic. The crucial question was; were the lights operating at the time of the accident? A lorry driver and a postman could testify that they were working on the Aike side of the crossing as the doomed train approached, and there was no failure alarm in Beverley signal box. After the accident a number of people came forward to say that on previous occasions the lights had been giving very limited, or no warning, but none had picked up the crossing phone to inform Beverley signal box or reported it to the police at the time. BR admitted that, prior to the accident, there had been 'safe-side' failures where the lights had flashed for more than four minutes with no trains approaching the crossing. These had been detected in Beverley box and explained or rectified by signalling staff. BR had no evidence of any 'danger-side' failure although, in May 1986, a BR lorry-driver had used the crossing phone to say he thought the lights were not working when a car had crossed about 8 seconds before a train arrived, but the inspector concluded that by the time he had got out of his vehicle and walked to a position to see the lights the train had cleared the crossing and turned them off. Following standard procedure, after this alert, the trains were cautioned until the lights were checked and found to be working correctly.

After the accident, when the crossing was restored to remote from manual control, every function was fully recorded, and there was found to be no anomalies. During this period, when a motorist claimed that the lights had only shown red for 10 seconds, it could be proved that they had worked for the correct time. Major King concluded:

> The analysis and design of the signalling circuits, the results of the use of the recorder, the tests conducted after the accident, and the evidence, leave me in no doubt that the red traffic-light signals were flashing as the train approached and were operating correctly at the time of each of the alleged danger side failures.

Although the Ford van was cut into five pieces the driver survived, and was found sitting beside the railway after the accident. He claims to have no memory of the accident, but it was established that he had turned left out of an access just beyond the former station house, about 25 yards from the level crossing, and the van was in second gear permitting a speed between 10 and 24 mph. Anyone approaching the crossing from the junction with the A164 would see the red lights for at least 24 seconds, whereas the driver of the van, if he was looking, would only have been able to see them for two or three seconds. The specified height of the flashing lights was such that they would be cut off from view by the van roof as he approached the stop line. The most likely explanation, given by Major King, was that he 'was in some way distracted and did not look at the road traffic-light signals'. He would not have been able to miss seeing a barrier.

The taking of statements by Major King was delayed, initially for 10 weeks, at the request of Humberside Police who were considering prosecuting the van driver. However the Director of Public Prosecutions then gave permission to go ahead, although the decision, not to prosecute, was not made until after the inquest. On 27 February 1987, the inquest jury found that neither BR nor the van driver was to blame for the crash, and recorded verdicts of 'death by misadventure' – a decision that Major King totally agreed with. If neither was to blame then the sanctioning of the use the AOCR type of crossings at locations like Lockington must lead to serious questioning. Publication of the accident report was further delayed pending the outcome of a national review of the safety of automatic open level crossings conducted by Professor PF Stott. Discussions with the professor led Major King to the inevitable conclusion 'that the most effective way to reinforce the message to motorists that they must stop when the lights flash is to provide some form of barrier'.

A study of Continental practices in the late 1950s led to the first type of public-road, train-operated, crossings to use traffic-lights without barriers to be introduced from 1963. These were the Automatic Open Crossing, Locally monitored (AOCL); they were permitted on little-used railways with speeds below 35 mph, later 55 mph, to cross roads with low traffic volumes. After a collision, in January 1968, at an Automatic Half Barrier (AHB) crossing, between a train and a road transporter carrying a transformer, when 11 people were killed, recommendations were made that seriously increased the installation costs of AHB crossings. Despite a poor safety record with AOCL crossings, the remotely monitored version (AOCR) was introduced in 1983 to be used on higher-speed railways (70 mph at Lockington) to provide a cheaper alternative to AHBs, and by 1986 there were 44 AOCRs in use. After Lockington, the Stott report and public protests most AOCRs were soon converted to AHBs, and since 1994 only one remains (Lockington became an AHB on 23 October 1988). The AOCLs peaked in 1988 at 211 installations, but their number had been gradually reduced to 114 in 2010, mainly by conversions to AHBs.(7)

The gradual decrease in the total number of public road crossings to 1,400, further safety features being introduced, and a campaign to increase public awareness of the dangers has seen some reduction in incidents, but there was still an average of 10 vehicle collisions each year between 2000 and 2009 on Network Rail lines; fortunately only a small number resulted in fatalities. Statistics for that decade reveal 53 collisions at AOCLs, of which there was an average of 120 in use, whereas at roughly 450 AHBs there were 39.(7)

Two busy level crossings in Hull and two in Bridlington were replaced by bridges between 1871 and 1903, but to replace all the crossings with overbridges would be impractical and obscenely expensive, and would still not provide total safety. In 2001 ten people were killed and 76 injured, when a vehicle plunged from the M62 motorway on to the ECML at Great Heck, and in 2010 five passengers were injured when a concrete-mixer lorry fell off a bridge at Oxshott.

Endnotes:

1. 8 Victoria *cap* 20 page 370.
2. *Railway Chronicle,* 10 May 1845, page 544.
3. Report by Lt-Col E Woodhouse, dated 29 October 1947.
4. Report by Major AGB King, dated 21 August 1987.
5. A fatal accident in June 1976, at Kilnwick crossing, about one-mile from Lockington, when an Audi had been struck by a 7-car DMU and pushed for 700 yards did not result in a derailment, because the car had not disintegrated. The front wheel of the DMU, at Lockington, had been derailed by mounting the wrecked van's rear axle, and Major King thought the severity of the accident had been increased by the railway being on a low embankment at this point.
6. Report page 21, paragraph 124. Although it had no bearing on the accident, the remote monitoring, in the case of a danger-side failure, was a farce. The signalman was only alerted after a train had entered the level crossing's control area and the lights had failed to respond. He had no way of either cautioning the train or warning road users.
7. Rail Accident Investigation Board, report of an *Investigation into the safety of automatic level crossings on Network Rail's managed infrastructure,* Crown Copyright July 2011. The highest total of *reported* incidents at any AOCL, between 1998 and 2010, is 135 at Garve, where the Kyle of Lochalsh line crosses the A835 Ullapool road. As the trains (eight a day) must stop and proceed at no more than 10mph, there have been no collisions. Incredibly, this level crossing was allowed to *replace an overbridge* in the 1980s. As at other locations, there is now CCTV monitoring of motorists' behaviour. The introduction of mobile cameras at level crossings in the south-east resulted in 2,400 prosecutions for transgressions in 18 months from January 2011. In 2011 almost 50 pedestrians were killed by trespassing on Network Rail lines.

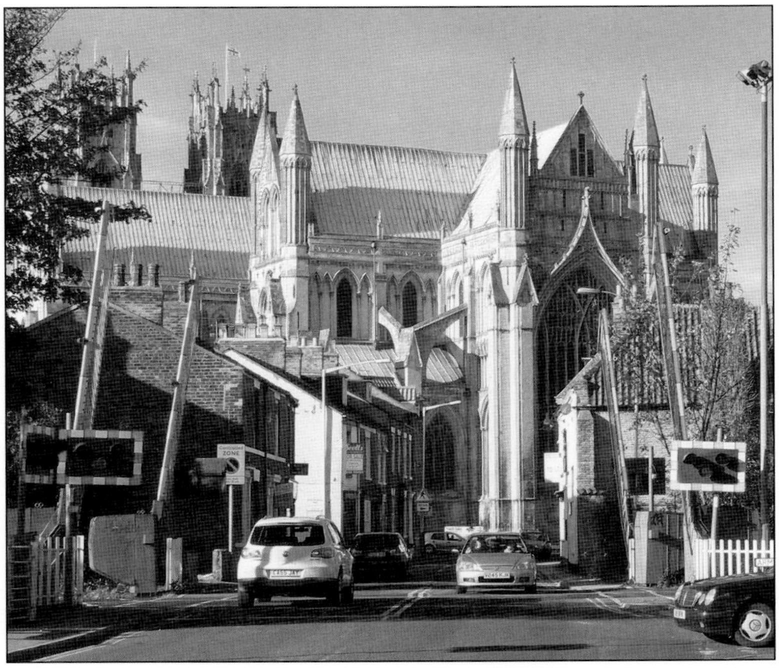

Plate 11.2. *Flemingate level crossing in Beverley, with full barriers, showing the impossibility of replacing it by a bridge on its present alignment. (John F Addyman, 2011)*

Chapter 12 : Other Railways to Be or Not to Be

John F Addyman

The Railway Mania and the East Riding

The years 1845 to 1847 saw the height of the 'railway mania' with a total of over 8,500 miles of railway *authorized* for construction in Great Britain, and many more projected; prior to this there were just 2,200 miles of railway open.(1) 1845 saw the East Riding joining in the act with the full length of Hull & Scarborough authorized, and plans deposited for six connecting lines from: a) York to Beverley, b) Selby to Market Weighton, c) Market Weighton to Hutton Cranswick, d) Arram to Hornsea, e) the Hull & Scarborough between Newington and Cottingham, via Sculcoates and Drypool, to the intended Victoria or East Dock, and f) and an extension from (e) at Drypool to stop at Patrington, four miles short of Withernsea. The engineers for these Y&NM proposals were Robert Stephenson and John Cass Birkinshaw.(2) Parliament authorized a), b) and d) in 1846, but only the first two were completed by the Y&NM/NER, however all the proposals were covered in some form during the next 45 years. For example, Hornsea was reached by the independent Hull & Hornsea Railway, using a totally different route; it opened in 1864 and was taken over by the NER just two years later.

Crossing the Wolds

The Hull & Selby had managed to maintain its virtually straight and level course all the way into Hull by coming extremely close to the Humber east of Ferriby to avoid crossing the southern outliers of the Yorkshire Wolds.(3) However, any railway between it and the York - Scarborough could not avoid crossing the Wolds at some point as exemplified by the long climbs needed between Bridlington and Filey.

The first proposal for a railway to cross the Wolds was in 1834 as mentioned in Chapter 1; it would have reached a height of about 350 feet between Warter and North Dalton on its way from Pocklington to Driffield. However, the first railway to penetrate the Wolds was the 20-miles long, steeply graded one from Malton to Driffield, which, in spite of a mile-long summit tunnel, climbed to over 400 feet above sea level. It was first proposed in 1845 and opened in 1853 just in time to become part of the nascent NER. Like other rural lines it never carried the volume of through traffic from distant industrial areas that its promoters had hoped for. Quarries at North Grimston and Burdale supplemented the agricultural traffic, but it closed to passengers in 1950 and to goods in 1958.(4)

The easiest crossing of the Wolds, with a summit of 184 feet, was east of Market Weighton on the direct line from York to Hull. This railway should have reached Beverley by 1850, but, like many others, its completion was delayed because of the financial problems resulting from George Hudson's fall from grace in 1849. Local agitation and a guarantee of financial support achieved its opening by the NER as a single-line in 1865; it was doubled in stages between 1881 and 1890. It served the community well for 100 years, but unfortunately Beeching recommended it for closure before planned, significant, working economies could be introduced.(5) Prior to closure, on 29 November 1965, its case was not helped by BR using the tactic of allowing through passengers to change at Selby for a Hull train as an alternative to the direct line on as many as half the weekday services; all the Sunday services were via Selby. For example, you could leave York on a weekday at 10-0 am, change at Selby and be in Hull by 11-0 am, or catch the direct train at 10-10 am and be in Hull by 11-7. Thus the closure brought little hardship to through passengers between York and Hull, but left Stamford Bridge, Pocklington, and Market Weighton and their surrounding areas almost as badly off for public transport as they had been 100 years earlier; it also endangered the Hull - Scarborough by reducing its passenger numbers between Beverley and Hull. Since 2000 there have been attempts to gain interest in re-opening the line, and studies of the problems and costs have been carried out, but being in Yorkshire rather than London or Scotland means its chances of getting government finance are very poor! The section between Market Weighton and Beverley is a pleasant cycle track, initially known as Hudson's Way but now renamed Wilberforce Way.(6)

The line from Selby to Market Weighton was opened on 1 August 1848, but it remained a rural, single-line backwater for the first 42 years of its life as its planned extension to join the Hull & Scarborough was not pursued by the Y&NMR after the Hudson debacle. However, the opening of the independently promoted Market Weighton to Driffield branch gave it a new lease of life, and it was doubled in 1890 in readiness for the through trains between the West Riding and Bridlington and Filey. The new line came about as a result of an 1883 proposal to extend the Scarborough - Whitby Railway, then under construction, from Seamer Junction via Burton Fleming, Driffield and Market Weighton to link up with the Hull & Barnsley (H&B), also under construction, near Howden.(7) The NER originally opposed the scheme, but then agreed to support it and work the traffic if it did not extend south of Market Weighton to join the rival H&B. The curtailed line was authorized on 6 August 1885 as the Scarborough, Bridlington and West Riding Junction Railway, but was only completed from Driffield to Market Weighton.(8) It opened to passengers on 1 May 1890, and was worked by the NER until formally vested in it from 1 July 1914. A climb of three-and-a-half miles from Market Weighton, with gradients between 1 in 95 and 1 in 100, was needed to surmount the Wolds at Enthorpe (280 feet AOD). The local usage was small leading to the intermediate stations of Enthorpe, Middleton-on-the-Wolds, Bainton and Southburn all being closed to passengers on 20 September 1954, along with those between Selby and Market Weighton, though both lines survived for goods and through passenger trains until

27 January 1964; see Plate 12.2. Several half-mile lengths of the track had been renewed only a decade before closure with 98lbs/yd. flat-bottom rails, which may still be in use in the Republic of Ireland as they were purchased, virtually un-worn, by Córas Iompair Éireann in 1965.

There were two schemes in the 1860s for lines from the Bridlington area following the Gypsey Race and the 'Great Wold Valley' *i.e.* the valley running via Rudston and Burton Fleming then parallel to and about four miles to the south of the York - Scarborough branch through Weaverthorpe and the Luttons. 1864 saw a line projected from Hornsea through the valley to Malton, but even when it was curtailed to a 10-mile long branch from Lowthorpe to Wold Newton it still could not get the necessary support. The second came about in 1865 as part of an ambitious package to link railways in Lincolnshire, Yorkshire and County Durham, which was to include a massive viaduct over the Humber near the site of the present suspension bridge; again it failed.(9)

Light Railway and Tramway Proposals

The Light Railways Act of 1896 made it much easier to gain authorization for lines in areas where their limited transport needs could not justify the high construction and running costs of normal railways. The facts that the motor vehicle was only just making its appearance, and most rural roads had very poor surfaces made the idea attractive to those whose livelihoods were disadvantaged by being some distance from the nearest railhead. The lightly-populated triangle of North Holderness between the Hull & Scarborough, north of Beverley, and the coast tapers from a width of 12 miles near Hornsea and meets the sea at Bridlington. The area is crossed by the present A1035 and A165 main roads whose alignments could have been largely followed by two independent light railways authorised in 1898 under the new Act.

Earlier, in 1889, plans had been deposited for a standard-gauge railway in the area from Beverley to serve North Frodingham and Beeford under the title of Beverley & East Riding Railway. Even though the initial proposal had little chance of success plans were submitted, in the following year, to include Railway No 2 extending it southwards to join the H&B at Little Weighton and Railway No 3 northwards to Bridlington. The NER must have refused running powers from Carnaby into Bridlington and through Beverley, leading to the most expensive and impractical parts of the project. In Beverley it was to cross the NER, on the level, just south of the station and cut through several properties to just miss the south-east corner of Beverley Minster before setting off towards Little Weighton (Figure 12.1). At the Bridlington end it intended to cross the NER north of Carnaby (grid reference TA 164655), and Quay Road near the Old Town (TA 176674) before curving east to terminate on the coast at TA 188673 – no wonder it was stillborn!(10)

This area's first under the 1896 Act, the Bridlington & North Frodingham Light Railway, was granted its order on 14 July 1898 to run $9\frac{1}{2}$ miles from Carnaby to Beeford serving Fraisthorpe, Barmston and Lisset (Figure 12.2). The second, the North Holderness Light Railway, was approved on 27 September to run from Beverley via Routh, Tickton, Leven and Brandesburton to North Frodingham, a distance of $12\frac{1}{2}$ miles. Both were to be standard gauge. The first served a population of less than 1,500, but as the second had slightly better potential the NER immediately started negotiations to take it over; the NER Act to transfer the North Holderness' powers was granted on 9 August 1899. The cost of the light railway had originally been estimated at £32,300, but by 1901 the NER engineer thought the cost would be 'not less than £74,000', which, though half that of a normal railway, the general manager considered too high for a line to serve a population of less than 2,500. A revised scheme for a 2 ft 0 in gauge steam tramway costing £38,000 was not received with any enthusiasm, and on 31 July 1902 it was suggested

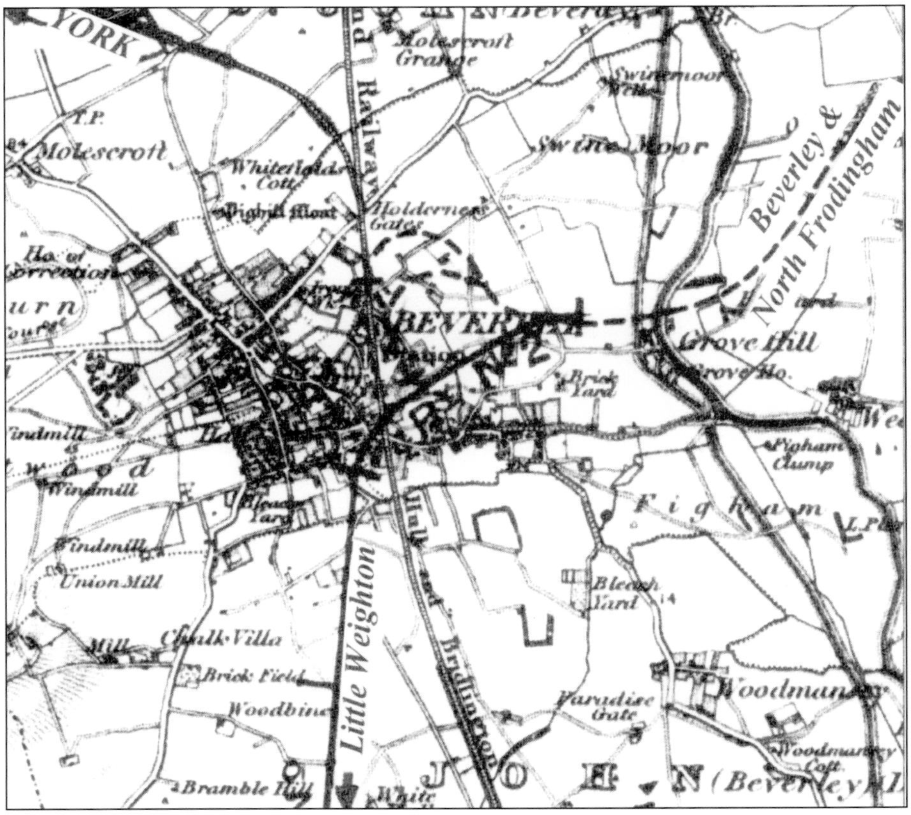

Figure 12.1. *Map showing the proposed route of the Beverley & East Riding Railway of 1890 through Beverley towards Little Weighton.*

to the NER traffic committee that a bus service could be an option. Although land was being purchased and contract drawings had been prepared (Figure 12.3) it was not until 29 January 1903 that the committee decided to establish the bus service in place of the light railway and extend it to serve Beeford. Three petrol buses, each seating 14 passengers, were purchased from Stirling Motor Carriages Limited, Edinburgh, for £900 each, allowing the service to commence on 7 September 1903 (Plate 12.1).

The four daily services, in each direction, were allowed 1 hour 50 minutes for the 14 miles from Beverley to Beeford, giving an average speed of just over $7^{1}/_{2}$ mph. With fares of around one penny per mile the buses were popular initially, and an additional, Thursdays only, service from Driffield to Beeford was introduced on 1 December 1903. Dürkopp and Saurer petrol buses were purchased for the service by the NER between 1904-6, and three five-ton steam lorries were authorized on 4 August 1904 to handle the goods traffic

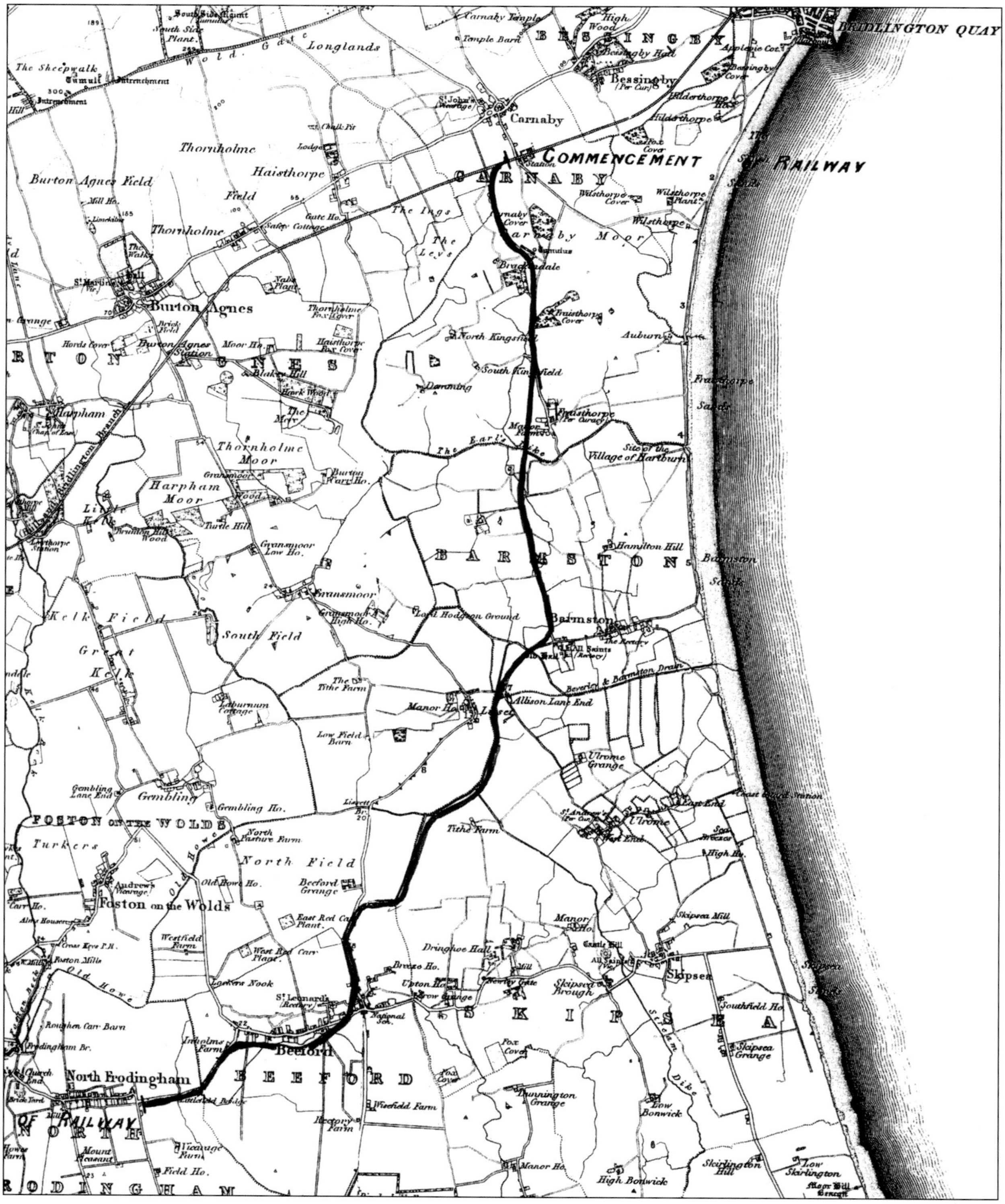

Figure 12.2. The abortive Bridlington & North Frodingham Light Railway of 1898, largely following existing roads, is shown by the thick black line.

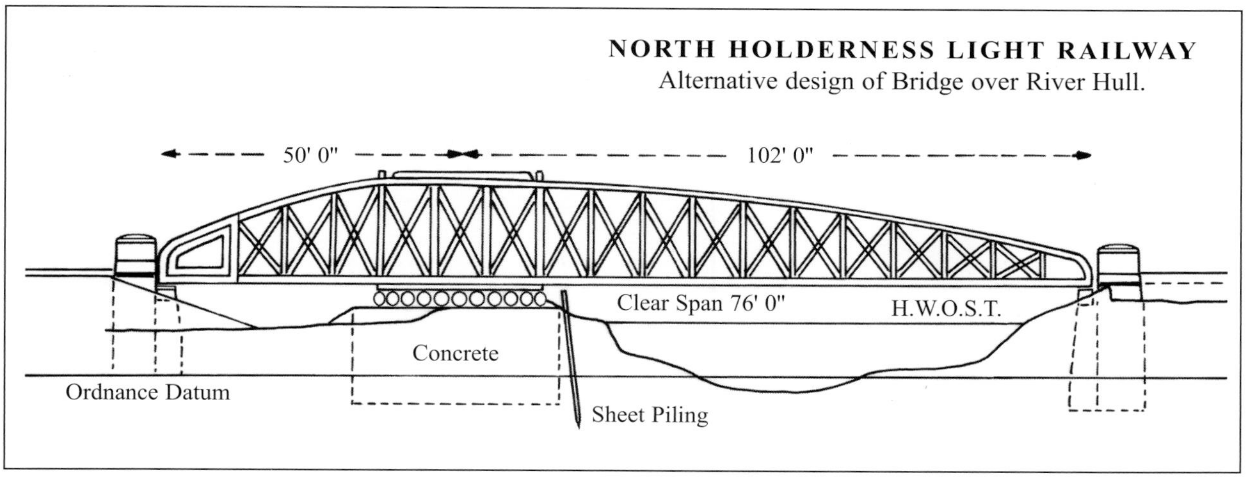

Figure 12.3. *The most expensive feature on the North Holderness would have been the swing bridge over the River Hull, which was to carry road and rail traffic. The other design was for a plate-girder bridge of similar profile. (Traced from an original drawing in the David J Williamson Collection)*

in the area. A short-lived Beeford to Hornsea service was introduced in May 1904, but frequent breakdowns caused by the poor state of the un-surfaced roads were to reduce public confidence in all the services. The summer of 1906 was to see the services virtually halved, and by 1913 the limited timetable was as shown at the bottom of the page.

By 1916 the exigencies of war saw the bus service cut back to just Beverley to Brandesburton, and the service to Beeford was never reinstated. In the first six-months of 1925 the buses made a total loss of £311, so the LNER decided to withdraw the services from 1 October 1925, selling out to the rival Newington Motor & Engineering Company. Obviously an expenditure of over £6,000 per mile on a light railway could never have been justified – the genius who suggested the buses saved the railway an awful lot of money.(11)

Another scheme that came to nothing was the three-feet gauge Flamborough Head Steam Tramways for which plans, by the London-based civil engineers Fairbank & Son, were first deposited in 1887. The project started from Flamborough station and for the first half-mile went in a northerly direction before turning due east by means of a very sharp curve. It crossed Danes Dyke by a viaduct and cutting at grid reference TA 214705 before joining the alignment of the B1255 from Flamborough village (at TA 224705) to North Landing; the total length would have been three-and-a-half miles (Figure 12.4).(12) At North Landing it was proposed to install a steam lift to connect the beach with the tramway for the fish traffic, which was expected to increase dramatically with this improved transport. The initial project was abandoned in 1891, but eventually a Flamborough & Bridlington Light Railway Order was granted on 21 March 1898 for a more ambitious, possibly electrically-operated, standard-gauge tramway. The alterations needed in Bridlington would have been complex, and as work had not started by

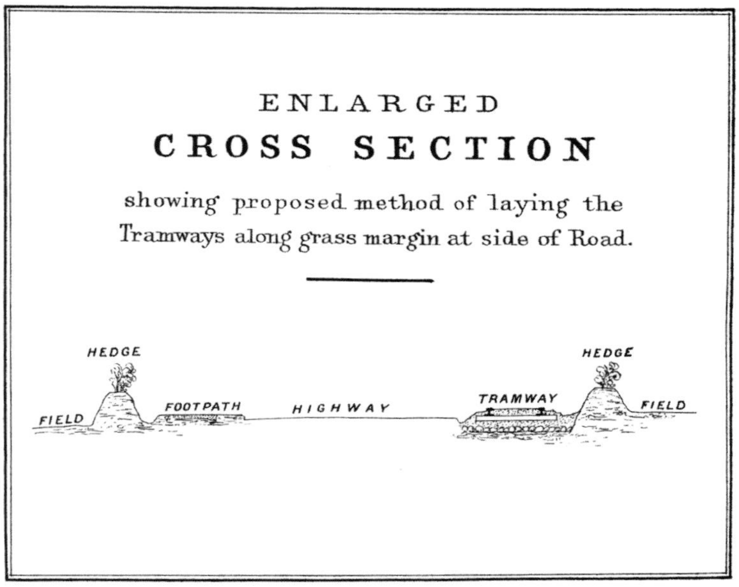

Figure 12.4. *This method of laying the Flamborough tramway adjacent to the road to North Landing was to be followed in the other light-railway proposals.(12)*

NER Beverley - Beeford Bus Service, 1913 Timetable:

Beverley to Brandesburton: depart 10-30 am (a); 1-40 pm; 4-35 pm (b); 6-15 pm.
Brandesburton to Beverley: depart 8-41 am; noon (c); 4-10 pm; 5-35 pm (b) 7-00 pm (d).
Brandesburton to Beeford: depart 11-25 am (d); 7-08 pm.
Beeford to Brandesburton: depart 8-00 am; 6-10 pm (d).
Driffield to Beeford: depart 5-10 pm (d).
Beeford to Driffield: depart 11-55 am (d).
Notes: *(a) runs 15 minutes earlier on alternate Wednesdays (Leven Court days); (b) Saturdays only when required; (c) Thursdays excepted; (d) Thursdays only.*

1902 the Board of Trade refused an extension of time when it was applied for. In 1898 the NER had shown a flicker of interest in the tramway, but prior to the First World War had then decided to serve Flamborough Head with buses, in the summer months, from Filey and Bridlington.(13)

Around 1900 a contractor's railway, using a steam locomotive, ran south along the seafront at Bridlington to supply the material for the new sea wall, and at the same time a proposal was mooted for a 1900-feet long pier extending into deeper water for passenger liners. This pier was to be served by a new railway, more than a mile long, running from its head to join the Hull - Scarborough near Bessingby.(14)

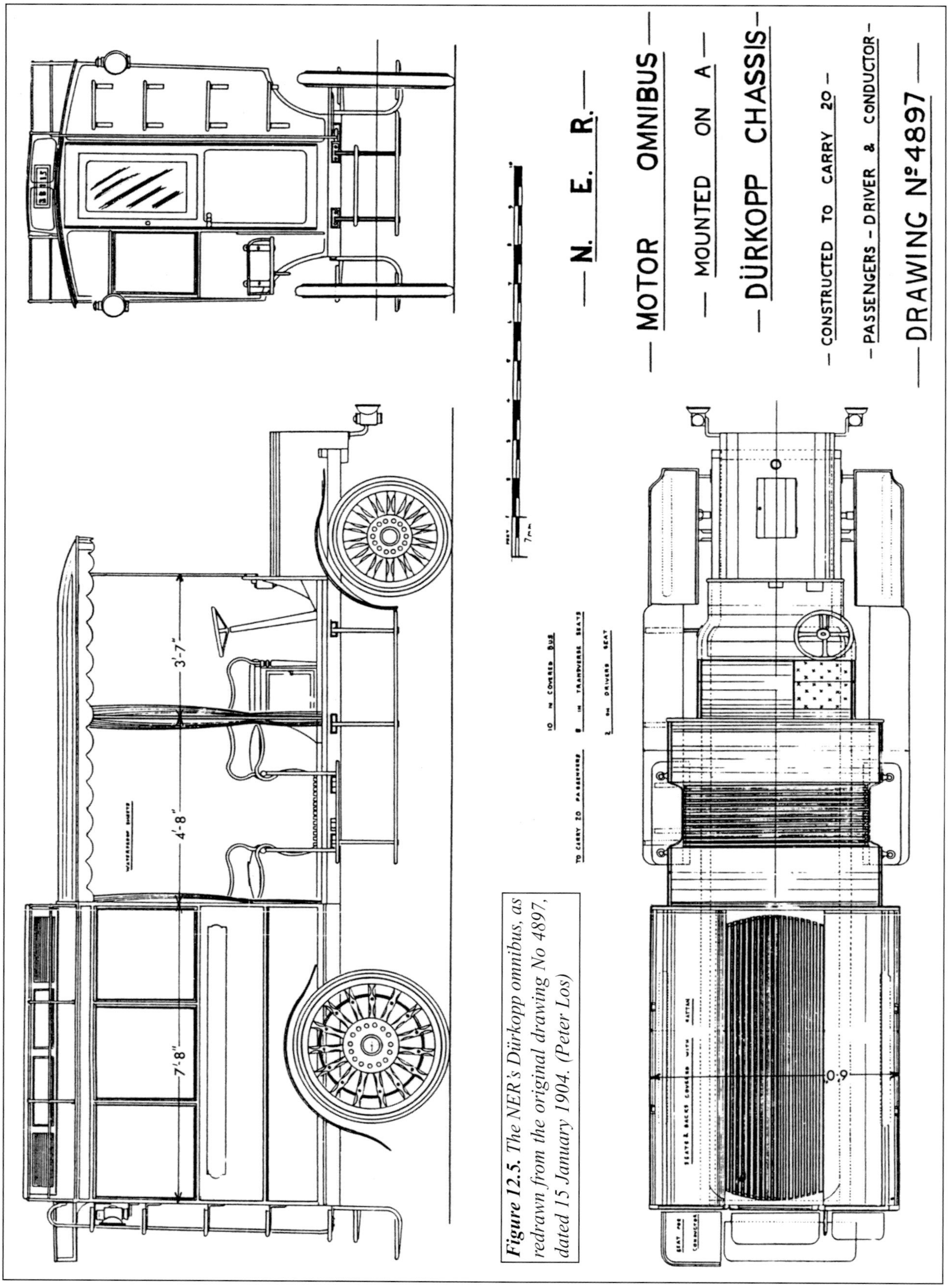

Figure 12.5. *The NER's Dürkopp omnibus, as redrawn from the original drawing No 4897, dated 15 January 1904. (Peter Los)*

Plate 12.1. *A postcard view of two of the original Stirling buses seen at Brandesburton in 1903. The buses were painted in the standard NER coaching stock livery of crimson lake.*

Plate 12.2. *Class 5MT No 44932 leaves the Market Weighton - Driffield branch at Driffield Junction with an excursion from Sharlston to Bridlington on 12 July 1959. Just beyond the rear of the train was the junction with the Malton - Driffield branch, which had closed the previous year. Engineer's rail motors were allowed to run between Cottingham and Seamer and between Selby and Driffield; in this view we see three of their garages, two on the left and one beside the third coach of the train. The space in the right foreground was originally occupied by a 45 feet diameter turntable. (Neville Stead)*

The Cottingham Branch (15)

With the diversion of all passenger trains into the new Paragon station in 1848 the section of the Hull & Scarborough between the original Hull & Selby terminus and Cottingham South Junction (referred to as the Cottingham or Newington Branch) became a single-line goods branch, whose function, in the early years, was to serve the Scarborough branch goods and Springhead Waterworks, and for a short time in the 1880s to bring in materials for the construction of the Hull & Barnsley Railway.

By the 1890s the NER had already begun the quadrupling of the main line from Selby to Hull to cater for the expanding goods and mineral traffic, and attention turned to increasing the usefulness of the Cottingham Branch. General manager, (Sir) George Gibb, reported to the NER traffic committee, on 6 April 1899, that to relieve congestion between Hull and Staddlethorpe and to enable a greater number of trains to be run between Hull and Selby via Cottingham and Market Weighton, it was desirable that the single-line be doubled and platforms provided on south side of Anlaby Road. The cost of the whole work estimated at £4,446 was approved with £500 of this expenditure relating to the provision of platforms for the Yorkshire Agricultural Show to be held at Hull in July 1900. The meeting authorized further expenditure of £1,170 to purchase land and build a special loading dock for livestock and agricultural implements arriving at the Show. The station became known as Newington Excursion Station, and was open for a few days each year to cater for the large crowds visiting the annual fair held on the city's fairground in Walton Street. The station appears to have closed during the First World War never to re-open.(16)

From 1899 the branch saw increasing use by dated holiday trains from the Goole/Doncaster direction as well as excursions to the coast (see Chapter 9) (Plate 12.3). The decrease in rail travel in the 1960s made the line a victim of the Beeching axe and become the only part of the original Hull - Scarborough to disappear; it was closed in May 1965 and the track was immediately lifted.

Between 1899 and 1930 there were endless discussions between the NER/LNER and Hull Corporation about the acute problems caused by the level crossings in the city. One scheme involving the Cottingham Branch was shown on a drawing dated, 23 March 1904, intriguingly headed 'Proposed Cottingham - Withernsea Branch', which presented a plan to remove all the remaining level crossings in Hull (two had already been bridged). Between a point south of Hessle Road and Newington Crossing the Cottingham Branch would be raised and a new line would branch off eastwards to cross over Spring Bank West, follow the course of the later Spring Bank North-Walton Street connection, and so on to West Parade Junction and Paragon station. From Spring Bank West another high-level line would be built to join up with the (raised) Victoria Dock Branch near Stepney.(17) No record has been found of the proposal getting as far as an NER committee or the Board.

Endnotes:

1. Lewin HG, *Railway Mania and its Aftermath,* (1936) page 473.
2. Hull History Centre C CQP/17, deposited plans.
3. The railway's proximity to the river has left it vulnerable to erosion.
4. Burton W, *The Malton & Driffield Junction Railway,* (1997) gives an exhaustive account of the line.
5. Some publications have stated that the closure was sanctioned by Barbara Castle, but she did not become Minister of Transport until four weeks *after* the trains had ceased to run.
6. Chapman S, *Hudson's Way*, (1986) gives an account of the line.
7. East Riding Archives (EYA) deposited plan QDP/191.
8. Tomlinson WW, *North Eastern Railway; its rise and development*, (1914, reprinted 1967) page 696. The section that, wisely, was not built was to run to the west of the Hull & Scarborough between Seamer and Nafferton.
9. *Ibid. pp.* 615, 622-3.
10. EYA deposited plans QDP/196, 200, 201. The solicitors were Addyman & Kaye of Leeds.
11. Hoole K, *North Eastern Railway Buses, Lorries & Autocars,* (1969) pages 9-13, 16-18 and 30, also TNA RAIL527/699.
12. Deposited plans in a private collection.
13. Hoole K, *A Regional History of the Railways of Great Britain, Volume 4,* page 61.
14. Photographs and documents in Bridlington Library.
15. This section is based largely on information provided by David R Smith.
16. Hoole K, *Railway Stations of the North East,* (1985) page 138.
17. TNA RAIL 527/666.

Plate 12.3. *The 8-20 am, Saturdays Only, King's Cross to Filey Holiday Camp is seen in July 1963 coming off the Cottingham Branch hauled by an unidentified Class 37. The crew had been changed at Hessle Road, and the train was due to pass Cottingham South at 12-24 before stopping at Bridlington from 1-2 to 1-9 and reaching Filey at 1-30 pm. The sidings on the left, with the continental ferry vans, served the National Radiator Company and its successors from 1906 (they were extended in 1918). During the 1960s the then owner bought tons of cast-iron chairs from redundant BR sidings in the locality for recycling into its products. (Ian K Watson)*

Chapter 13: Proposed Closure

John F Addyman

With British Railways' finances reduced from breaking even in 1955 to £100 million in the red by 1962 it was felt that something had to be done(1), and the Conservative government introduced the 1962 Transport Act to simplify the process for closing the parts of the system that were making the greatest losses. The Beeching Report of 1963, which based its findings on a survey of the amount of passenger and freight traffic handled by every station and branch on British Railways, identified the worst performers. The East Riding was listed to lose lines to York, Selby, Hornsea and Withernsea, and there must have been a sigh of relief in the area when the figures for the Hull - Bridlington - Scarborough line suggested it should be a 'Passenger Service to be Modified' rather than one to be closed.(2)

The Report showed that Beverley and Bridlington each had passenger receipts in excess of £25,000 per annum, with the line handling between 50,000 and 100,000 passengers each week between Hull and Bridlington. The freight traffic from Hull to Driffield came into 5,000 to 10,000 tons per week category, but north of Driffield it fell below 5,000 tons. Three of its stations, Beverley, Driffield and Bridlington, handled over 25,000 tons of freight per annum – the highest band considered in the Report.(2)

The branch closures, immediately following Beeching's Report, may have saved money but they also made railways inaccessible to many in rural areas. This produced a knock-on effect by reducing takings on the lines that remained, and inevitably led to further closures being mooted at regular intervals. In September 1966 the Hull - Scarborough was targeted for closure when it was found that the average passenger figures had dropped below 50,000 per week after the connecting lines from Beverley and Driffield to York and the West Riding had been axed in the previous year.(3)

As usual the notice of the proposed closure created an outcry from the public, trades unions, local councils and members of parliament, but having avoided being in the first group of Beeching closures was to the line's advantage. There was a growing political resistance as many Tory MPs in rural areas were finding it very difficult to defend the closures of the railways in their own constituency. The unnecessary haste in implementing the first round of closures (as little as eight weeks' notice in some cases) was not to be allowed to continue, as seen by the prolonged fight to save some branches.

A tired Conservative administration had eked out the final days of its 13-year rule by October 1964, but Labour did nothing in its early months to fulfil its remit to stem the flow of Tory railway closures. It was not until its second minister of transport, Barbara Castle (1910-2002), was appointed in December 1965 that the future of the nation's railways took a turn for the better. It was becoming obvious to many that the social and economic wellbeing of rural areas was being seriously affected by the closure of railways, and the Bill to allow government subsidies for loss-making passenger services was introduced by this dynamic minister. The fight to keep the Hull & Scarborough open was to extend for exactly three years so that her new Act was in place to ensure its salvation.

A change in the organization of British Railways with the merger of the Eastern and North Eastern Regions on 1 January 1967 may have had a profound effect on the branch's future. Some very senior railway managers would, if left to their own devices, have gone even further than Dr Beeching with line closures; the last general manager of the North Eastern Region, Arthur Dean (1903-1968), was one of them. Fortunately, Gerald Fiennes (1906-1985), the new general manager of the combined Region, firmly believed that railways had a future, and initiated immediate plans to seek economies to save the Hull to Scarborough service. Within two months of taking office he had organized an inspection of the line accompanied by senior railway officers, members of parliament and representatives of the local authorities; the date was 24 February 1967. He explained that the annual passenger income from the line was around £200,000, but the expense of running it was £150,000 more than its revenue. Economies could be made by: a) singling the line from Beverley to Seamer, b) installing automatic barriers or colour-lights at 26 of the 38 level crossings, c) making the stations unstaffed and introducing pay-trains (he had already done this in East Anglia) and, d) more effective use of rolling stock. He proposed that Bridlington alone should retain staff throughout the year, but Filey and Butlin's Holiday Camp stations could be manned in the summer months. He thought that the credits from the removal of most of one line north of Beverley and the redundant sidings would go a long way towards offsetting the capital costs of the barrier-crossing installations; a wages saving of around £2,000 per annum was expected to accrue at each automated crossing.(4)

The MPs and council representatives were impressed by Mr Fiennes' sincerity, and were prepared to consider favourably his stringent proposals. Having got the locals on his side the response from Barbara Castle's ministry, on 2 March 1967, did not look too encouraging. She had made a preliminary decision 'that she would not be justified in asking the [BR] Board to withhold publication of the formal notice of closure.' However, before making her final decision 'she would, of course also consider all the wider social and economic aspects'.(5) Her Bill, which was to become law as the 1968 Transport Act, would allow the government, under Section 39, to subsidize loss-making railways 'for social and economic reasons'. It was now up to BR and other interested parties to put up a convincing case to retain their railway.

The case for the Hull to Scarborough had to be

carefully argued to combat the financial situation which appeared a lot worse when the nationally agreed formula for subsidies was used to calculate the costs. The figure of £150,000, quoted by Mr Fiennes, had quadrupled by the time the first subsidy was agreed in 1969, and with freight rapidly disappearing the passenger services had to bear the whole cost of the maintenance of the line.

Many valid reasons could be given for saving the branch. As about 50% of Filey and Bridlington's visitors came from the West Riding, the Economic Planning Council for the Yorkshire and Humberside Region, based in Leeds, stated in October 1966 that it attached:

> ... great importance to the special value of the East-Coast holiday resorts to those that live and work in the heavily populated parts of the region, and to the need for adequate communications to enable them to maintain and develop these links.(6)

The Yorkshire resorts of Hornsea, Withernsea and Whitby had become inaccessible by rail from the West Riding in October 1964 and March 1965. If the Hull - Scarborough proposals were implemented only Scarborough would remain rail served, whereas all the Lancashire resorts retained rail connections to the West Riding – not what a Yorkshireman would consider fair!

The government's ploy that the former rail passengers could be carried by augmenting the bus services was ludicrous. The buses would have more than doubled the commuting times for regular passengers, and certainly have discouraged holiday users. The futility of the substitute bus was seen between York and Whitby on a Saturday morning in August 1965 when only one passenger alighted in Whitby – in the previous year scores of holidaymakers would have arrived at the same time by train.(7)

Table 13.1: Comparison of journey times by train and bus.

Journey	Train	Bus
Cottingham - Hull	7 mins	20 mins
Beverley - Hull	13 mins	31 mins
Driffield - Hull	30 mins	1 hr 6 mins
Bridlington - Hull	44 mins	1 hr 38 mins
Filey - Hull	1 hr 6 mins	2 hrs 20 mins
Scarborough - Hull	1 hr 19 mins	2 hrs 46 mins

It was argued that the roads out of Hull were poor and congested, making the buses unacceptably slow. Table 13.1 gives a comparison of the times, and shows, for example, a commuter from Bridlington to Hull would have his or her return journey increased by over $1^{3}/_{4}$ hours.(8) This would be unacceptable to many, and the options of using a car, moving house, changing jobs or even becoming unemployed would need serious consideration. A 1966 census showed Bridlington handled over 800 passengers a day – how many of these would transfer to the buses?

Unemployment in Bridlington and Filey was already running at more than twice the national average, and closure of the railway, particularly with its effect on holiday trade, would make it significantly worse. The local authorities were aware that savings by one government department could result in increasing the costs of another, and calculated that after the closure of the railway the unemployment benefits to be paid in the area could rise to as much as £300,000 per annum.(9)

The objections by the local authorities and individuals, totalling 1,174, were sent to the Area Transport Users Consultative Committee (TUCC). The TUCC was privy to BR's figures for revenue and running costs, which were confidential, and it alone could assess the complete picture. Its recommendation to the minister on the degree of 'hardship' that would result from the closure generally determined the fate of a line.

The passage of Barbara Castle's Transport Bill through parliament meant that there was a moratorium on line closures, and from autumn 1967 BR regional staffs were working out the true cost of providing every service. In April 1969 Richard Marsh (1928-2011), the latest minister of transport, stated the grant figures calculated for the line were as follows:

Table 13.2: 1969 subsidy calculations. The grant had to be re-assessed for each subsequent year.

Movement costs	£227,000
Terminal costs	£84,000
Track and Signalling	£391,000
Interest and Administration	£156,000
Total Costs	**£858,000**
Earnings	£223,000
Deficit	**£635,000**

He explained that earlier calculations had ignored the 'Interest and Administration'(10) charges and given earnings of £366,400; these had included the 'throughout earnings' of summer trains from locations as far afield as Plymouth, which had to be credited to the lines that they travelled over. Because of the benefit to the whole system of the summer trains the minister admitted 'we do of course take account to these earnings when deciding whether or not a line should be closed'.(11) In September 1969 he made his decision that the line should remain open as a grant-aided service, but the stations at Burton Agnes, Carnaby, Flamborough, Lowthorpe and Speeton should be closed as soon as possible; these closures came into effect from 5 January 1970. Arram was reprieved from the original list of Beeching closures.(2)

The economies suggested by Mr Fiennes in 1967, were either not fully implemented or took a long time to be carried out. The line has not been singled between Beverley and Bridlington,(12) but Bridlington to Filey was singled in 1973 with Filey to Seamer Junction not following until a decade later. The cost of manning the level crossings had risen to over £350,000 by 1980, but most of the work to reduce these costs was not carried out until the middle of the 1980s as shown in Appendix I : Signalling Table.

Table 13.3: Comparison of tickets issued for the stations that remain open. The figures are for outward journeys only and should generally be doubled for the total passengers handled at each station.

Station	**1911**(13)	**2004-5**(14)	**2009-10**(14)
Arram	4,804	1,033	1,759
Bempton	9,584	5,412	4,921
Beverley	167,616	293,364	290,849
Bridlington	124,951	186,356	200,797
Cottingham	114,909	104,461	99,650
Driffield	89,416	94,243	110,840
Filey	55,514	45,137	59,042
Hunmanby	19,602	6,743	10,270
Hutton Cranswick	16,513	18,141	16,733
Nafferton	20,177	12,101	13,950
Totals	**623,086**	**766,991**	**808,811**

The early 1960's idea that railways were an anachronism that should be exterminated as soon as possible is certainly rebutted by modern passenger usage (between 2002 and 2010 journeys increased nationally by over 40%). The figures for the outward journeys, in Table 13.3, show that the line is now carrying more passengers than it did 100 years ago, and certainly justifies the decision to retain it. The figures indicate that the larger stations have considerably increased their numbers, but the smaller stations, that remain, are generally not doing so well in comparison with 1911 (the stations that have been closed would have added 63,000 to the 1911 total in the table).

Despite disproportionate hikes in rail fares, in relation to salaries, the January 2012 cost of an annual, standard-class, season ticket from Bridlington to Hull was £1,884, about equal to the petrol cost alone for commuting by car for the 230 working days in the year. If we add tax, insurance, maintenance and depreciation, regardless of environmental issues, it still makes economic sense to 'let the train take the strain' instead of using this not very fast or enjoyable road.

Plate 13.1. A DMU runs in to Filey Holiday Camp station on 3 September 1977. Note that track had been lifted even before closure of the branch; this work was approved in 1974. (CJ Woolstenholmes / NERA Collection)

Endnotes:

1. *British Railways Yearbook; 1963 Edition*, pages 16-21. Since 1939 rail fares had increased at less than half the national rate of inflation, and this was the main cause of the increasing losses, not, at this stage, a huge downturn in traffic. With the loss only amounting to £2 per head of population per annum the cuts could have been less severe, allowing much more freight being retained on the railways to the greater benefit of the environment.
2. *The Reshaping of British Railways Parts 1 and 2*, 1963. The Report suggested that Arram, Burton Agnes, Carnaby, Lowthorpe and Speeton should be closed. Carnaby was the worst performer with no passengers joining and only one alighting during a two-day census in 1966. The others handled below 20 passengers per day; Arram was reprieved but Flamborough was added to the list.
3. East Yorkshire Archives, Beverley (EYA). Correspondence between town clerks, mainly Beverley and Bridlington, with BR and MOT about proposed closure in EYA BRBO/2/15/4/2641. Letter dated 7 September 1966 from divisional manager, Hull giving notice to local councils of impending closure.
4. *Ibid.* Minutes of meeting 24 February 1967.
5. *Ibid.* Letter from MOT dated 2 March 1967.
6. *Ibid.* Letter from Economic Planning Council dated 7 November 1966.
7. Author's observations.
8. EYA BRBO/2/15/4/2641. Bus and train comparison figures. Today the trains take the same time between Hull and Bridlington, but the buses now take 1 hr 45 mins. The Bridlington - Hull expresses took 37 minutes in the 1930s.
9. *Ibid.* Undated memo (probably early 1969) from local councils to Richard Marsh MP.
10. It was decided, during the subsidy negotiations, that each branch had to bear a proportion of the divisional, regional and BRB headquarters' costs.
11. EYA BRBO/2/15/4/2641. Letter Richard Marsh MP to Hon Richard Wood (MP for Bridlington) dated 17 April 1969. Figures for 1977 show that the earnings had reached £580,000 for 22.5 million passenger miles travelled.
12. The author was required to assess the track between Beverley and Bridlington, in 1970, with a view to retaining the line with the best rails and sleepers, but the singling idea was dropped when it was thought, with the more frequent train service between Hull and Bridlington, operating problems would occur.
13. NER statistics, NRM library.
14. Office of Rail Regulation statistics on station usage.

A Last Look at the Hull and Scarborough : an ex-Great Central Director's Day in Bridlington

No 62662 'Prince of Wales' passes Bridlington South on a 10-coach excursion from Wadsley Bridge (Sheffield) on 18 May 1959. (Neville Stead)

While the passengers enjoyed the delights of Bridlington the engine crew had to water and turn the locomotive, stable it on shed in order of departure, then maintain the fire in readiness for the return journey. No 62662 is seen below at the head of the middle row in front of the shed. (Neville Stead)

No 62662 makes its early evening departure for Wadsley Bridge. The locomotive would be withdrawn the following year. (Neville Stead)

Appendix I : Signalling Table
Hull & Scarborough Branch; Hull to Seamer Junction

Signal boxes in line order. b = before; c = circa; d = during. EP = Electro-pneumatic. GB = Gate Box. GF = Ground Frame. GW = Gate Wheel. IFS = Individual Function Switch. MH = McKenzie & Holland. MCH = McKenzie, Clunes & Holland. NX = Entrance / Exit.

Mileage		Name	Opened	Closed	Cabin Type and Location	Frame	GW / Levers	Remarks	Crossing
		Hull Station Yard [1]	b 1875	d 1887	n/k (Down)			Believed to be not the first cabin.	
	0m 286y	*Paragon Station* [2]	d 1887	11/12/1904	S1d (Up)	MH	- / 33	Resignalling work done in 7 stages.	None.
		Paragon Station [3]	11/12/1904	24/04/1938	S2 (Down)	MH EP	- / 143		
		Paragon Temporary [1]	11/12/1904	03/05/1905	n/k (Down)	MH	- / 30	Temporary signal box for stage work.	
	0m 532y	Park Street [1]	b 1875		n/k (Up)	MH	- / 46	Frame reduced to 39 by 1905.	
		Park Street [2]	24/06/1905	24/04/1938	S2 (Up)	MH EP	- / 179	Resignalling work done in 7 stages.	Bridged 1871.
		Paragon [3]	24/04/1938		LNE13 (Up)	OCS Panel		NX Panel from 1984.	
0m 39c		West Parade Junction [1]	d 1864	d 1875	n/k (Down)		? / ?		
0m 40.5c	0m 896y	West Parade Junction [2]	d 1875	17/04/1904	S1d? (Down)	Saxby	- / 32		Bridged 1884.
0m 46c	0m 1013y	West Parade Junction [3]	17/04/1904	29/03/1980	S2 (Down)	MH 16	- / 120		
		Bridlington Crossing [1]	d 1864	c 1874	n/k			Mileage not known.	
0m 59c	0m 1294y	*Victoria Crossing* [2]	c 1874	08/07/1945	S1a (Down)	Rly Sig Co	- / 20	New frame 1891.	None.
	1m 549y	Walton Street [1]	early 1886	22/06/1924	S1 wood (Down)	MH	+2 / 9		
1m 26c	1m 564y	Walton Street [2]	22/06/1924	29/03/1980	S4 (Up)	MH 16	+2 / 27	Power assisted gates and road traffic lights installed 1934.	Boom gates 01/12/1963.
							+2 / 20	Frame shortened 1963?	
		reduced to GB	31/03/1980	22/03/1987	S4		- / -	Cabin [2] demolished 19/04/1987.	
		Walton Street GB [3]	22/03/1987	16/07/1989 03/12/1989	Portacabin (Up)	IFS Panel	- / -	Attendance at crossing withdrawn December but Portacabin closed July and recovered 06/08/1989.	Barriers 09-16 July 1989.
		Cottingham Junction [1]	b 1864	d 1874	n/k (Up)		- / ?		
2m 12c	2m 247y	Cottingham Junction [2]	d 1874	17/08/1972	S1a (Down)	MH	- / 14		None.
2m 11.23c		*Cottingham South*				Stevens	- / 20	Steven's Frame relocked 1899.	
		[from 01/04/1927]				MH 16	- / 35	M&H No 16 of --/04/1906.	
3m 36.95c		Snuff Mill Lane	b 1909	29/10/1956				Temporary Block Post 1909, board signal. Originally a Public Crossing; reduced to an Occupation Crossing.	UWC.
3m 63.59c	3m 1399y	Thwaite Gates	c 1886	12/07/1984	S5 (Down)	MH 16	- / 9	New frame --/08/1906.	Barriers 26/02/1969.

Mileage		Name	Opened	Closed	Cabin Type and Location	Frame	GW / Levers	Remarks	Crossing
3m 77c		Cottingham Station	d 1874	d --/10/1906	S1s (Down)		- / n/k		None.
	4m 380y	Cottingham North [1]		d --/10/1906	n/k	MCH Dwarf	- / 9		
4m 17.20c	4m 378y	Cottingham North [2]	d --/10/1906	15/11/1987	S4 (Down)	MH 16	1 inc / 22	Additional lever added post 1936 pre 1955.	Boom Gates --/03/1963.
							1 inc / 23	Goods Facilities withdrawn 05/01/1970.	Barriers 08/11/1987.
4m 52.95c		Waterworks GF	--/06/1902	14/02/1966	OGF (Down)	NE 6"	- / 3		None.
							- / 2	GF replaced 1957.	
5m 15.38c		Moor	19/06/1900	26/08/1936	n/k (Up)	NE 6"	- / 6		None.
		Cottingham Moor						Renamed ?	
6m 50.89c	6m 1119y	Beverley Park Crossing [1]							
		aka *Park Crossing*	d 1874	d 1922	n/k (Up)		- / 4		
						MH 6"	+1 /11	New s/h frame 1909 + 1 lever wicket in separate frame?	
6m 50c approx		*Beverley Parks* [2]	20/07/1922	08/09/1984	S2 (Down)	MH 16	1 inc / 17	New Frame ordered 1922.	AOCR 09/09/1984. AHBC-X 04/08/1988.
7m 57.27c		England Springs Crossing						Board signal.	UWC.
8m 0.97c	8m 21y	Fleming Gates [1]	b 1874	d 1890					
		Fleming Gates [2]	d 1890	d 1924	S1a (Up)	MH 12 6"	1 inc / 12	New frame --/07/1890.	
		Flemingates							
		reduced to GB	d 1924	17/03/1985			1 inc / 4	1934 to GB but shown as GB in 1925 reduced for WW1? Frame reduced to 10 levers by 1925, and again in 1934 released by stn SB; demolished 06/10/1985.	Barriers installed 18/02/1968. RCB from 17/03/1985.
		Chantry Lane	d 1902?	d 1911?	(Down)	MH 11	1 / 5	Released by stn SB.	Closed.
		Grove Hill Crossing	d 1874	d 1911	(Up)		? / ?	Released by stn SB.	Diverted to Beverly stn.
		Beverley Station [1]	d 1877	d 1911	n/k (Down)	MH 12 6"	- / 17		
8m 15.77c	8m 347y	Beverley Station [2]	d 1911		S4 (Down)	MH 16	1 inc / 36		
		Beverley [BS]					- / 36	GW removed 29/10/1967 when barriers installed.	Barriers 29/10/1967.
							- / 20	Frame reduced on 17/03/1985.	
		Cherry Tree [1]	b 1877	d 1911	n/k (Up)	MH 12 6"	1 inc / 20		
8m 37.69c	8m 829y	Cherry Tree [2]	d 1911	17/03/1985	S4 (Down)	MH 16	2 / 29		
							- / 29	GW removed 18/09/1966 when barriers installed.	Barriers 19/09/1966.
							- / 24	Cabin demolished 02-06/10/1985.	CCTV.

Mileage		Name	Opened	Closed	Cabin Type and Location	Frame	GW / Levers	Remarks	Crossing
8m 62c	8m 1373y	Beverley Road Jct	14/03/1865		S0 (Down)	MCH Dwarf 6"?	- / 20	2-lever dwarf frame for wickets.	
		Beverley Junction					1 inc / 20		
		Beverley North		02/04/1985		MH 16	1 inc / 37	Cabin extended --/06/1910 and new frame fitted. Closed as Block Post 17/03/1985 but manned until 02/04/1985 by signalman supervising CCTV. Demolished 15/09/1985.	Lifting barriers 10-11/02/1974 CCTV from 02/04/1985.
11m 16.36c	11m 347y	Arram [1]	d 1874		S1s (Down)	MCH Dwarf 6"			
			ext 1910	20/06/1965		MH 6"	+1 / 19	Second-hand extended frame fitted --/11/1910.	
		reduced to Gate Box	20/06/1965	01/08/1984		IFS Panel	- / IFS	Goods facilities closed 04/05/1964.	
		Arram [2]	01/08/1984		(Up)	IFS Panel	- / IFS	Panel in station office.	AHBC-X 14/08/1988.
12m 77c		Lockington [1]	d 1874	d 1912	S1s (Down)	MCH Dwarf 6"	+1 / 10		
12m 74.77c	12m 1645y	Lockington [2]	d 1912	01/12/1985	S4 (Down)	MH 11	1 inc / 21		
							1 inc / 11	Goods facilities withdrawn 13/06/1960.	AOCR 01/12/1985, AHBC-X 23/10/1988.
13m 52.97c		Beswick Road Crossing						Board signal.	AOCR 01/12/1985, AHBC-X 23/10/1988.
14m 1.79c	14m 39y	Kilnwick	--/11/1874	n/k	S1s (Up)	MCH 6" Hook Cam and Soldier	- / 8		
		reduced to Gate Box	n/k	01/12/1985		LNER $3^3/_4$" GF	- / 6	GF renewed 11/1977. Demolished 03/06/1990.	AOCR 01/12/1985, AHBC-X 30/10/1988.
14m 44.64c	14m 982y	Watton Gates	--/08/1874	c 1916	S1s wood (Up)	MCH Dwarf 6"	- / 8	Closed for duration of WW1.	
		Watton Gates	c 1919	05/12/1921					
		Watton reduced to Gate Box	05/12/1921	01/12/1985		MH 16	- / 5	New Frame 1966; Key locks installed 1966 and board signal for Up dispensed with GF.	AOCR 01/12/1985 AHBC-X 30/10/1988.
16m 21c	stn	Hutton Cranswick [1]	d 1874	18/12/1907	S1s (Up)	MCH Dwarf 6"	1 / 10		
16m 19c	16m 418y	Hutton Cranswick [2]	18/12/1907	09/08/1987	S4 (Up)	MH 4? 6"	1 inc / 27	Second-hand frame of 1894 installed 1907. Goods facilities closed 10/08/1964.	
16m 18c		*Cranswick Level Crossing* [from 09/08/1987]					1 inc / 11	Frame shortened between 02/09 and 01/10/1983.	AHBC-X 09/08/1987.
		Hutton Cranswick GF	18/12/1907	14/05/1965	OGF (Down)	MH	- / 4		
16m 73c		Hutton Lane Level Crossing						Board signal.	
		Hutton						Renamed Hutton 09/08/1987.	AHBC-X 22/02/1989.

Mileage	Name	Opened	Closed	Cabin Type and Location	Frame	GW / Levers	Remarks	Crossing
18m 15c 18m 426y	Hutton Bank			n/k	NE Love Locks	- / 4	Hutton Bank and Hutton Grange are probably the same.	None.
18m 59 53c 18m 1265y	Hutton Grange	b 1889	½ye 06/1906	n/k (Down)			Cabin moved nearer to Driffield 1898.	None.
19m 26.34c 19m 579y	Driffield Junction *Driffield [D]* [from 12/04/1987]	21/09/1875		S1a (Down)	MH 6" MH 16 MH 16	- / 25 1 / 36 +1 / 3 + Panel	*aka Skerne Rd Crossing.* New frame 16-17/08/1938. From 12/04/1987.	Barriers installed 01/05/1966, MCB.
19m 33.92c	Driffield Station Gates	d --/12/1903	12/04/1987	S2 (Down)	MH 11	1 / 5	Demolished 19/04/1987.	RC MCB 12/04/1987.
19m 47c	Driffield Depots reduced to Gate Box	21/09/1875 18/04/1909	18/04/1909 04/09/1966	S1s (Down)	MH 6"	- / 14	*aka Eastgate South Crossing.*	Closed.
19m 54c 19m 53.65c 19m 1180y	Wansford Crossing *Wansford*	21/09/1875	12/04/1987	S1a (Down)	MH 6" MH 16	- / 17 1 inc / 47	New frame and extended 1909.	Barriers installed CCTV 12/04/1987.
19m1585y 20m 0.73c 20m 16y	Driffield North [1] Driffield North [2] *Meadow Lane Crossing*	21/09/1875 26/03/1909	29/03/1909 02/09/1935	(Down) S4 (Up)	MH 6" MH 16	- / 14 1 inc / 27	Crossing not worked from cabin.	UWC.
21m 46c stn 21m 44c	Nafferton [1] Nafferton [2]	 d 1907	d 1907 26/11/1989	S1s (Down) S4 (Up)	MCH Dwarf MH 16	+1 / 11 1 inc / 27		AHBC-X 26/11/1989.
21m 58c	Nether Lane Gates	d 1907	26/11/1989	OGF (Down)	MH ?	- / 5	Frame reduced to 2 levers.	AHBC-X 26/11/1989.
22m 09c	Black Carr Crossing		29/11/1965				Board Signal attendance withdrawn.	UWC.
23m 34c	Mingledale Crossing		13/08/1982				Board Signal attendance withdrawn.	UWC.
23m 64c	Lowthorpe	d 1874	20/10/1985	S1s (Up)	MCH Dwarf 6" 6" MH 16 MH 16	1 / 10 1 / 17 +1 / 16 +1 / 11	 SB raised to two storeys circa 1895. New frame 17/05/1939. Frame reduced Nos 12-16 removed.	AOCR 20/10/1985. AHBC-X 25/06/1989.
25m 10c	Harpham Crossing		10/03/1979				Board signal attendance withdrawn.	UWC.
25m 45c	Burton Agnes [1] Burton Agnes [2]	d 1874 09/03/03	09/03/1903 04/02/1990	S1s (Down) S1a (Up)	MCH Dwarf 6" MH 16 MH 16	1 / 11 1 inc / 35 1 inc / 13	GW outside frame. Spare levers removed between 1971 and 1983. Box demolished 1995. Goods facilities withdrawn 02/11/1964.	AHBC-X 04/02/1990.
	Thorneholme Crossing						Board signal attendance withdrawn.	UWC.
27m 24.80	Haisthorpe Crossing		29/11/1965				Board signal attendance withdrawn.	UWC.

Mileage	Name	Opened	Closed	Cabin Type and Location	Frame	GW / Levers	Remarks	Crossing
28m 56c stn								
28m 54c	Carnaby	d 1874	22/07/1990	S1s (Down)	MCH Dwarf 6"	- / 9		
					Saxby (s/h)	1 inc / 14	Cabin extended 1897.	
					MH 4 (s/h)	+1 / 20	New Frame --/07/1911.	Road re-aligned
							Demolished 28/10/1990.	and new
							Goods facilities closed 04/05/1964.	AHBC-X 23/07/1990.
30m 08c	Bessingby Junction	08/07/1903	--/07/1925	(Down)	MH 11	- / 25	Frame removed 1927; junctions removed 1928.	None.
	Bessingby Road Crossing	d 1874	d 1903	(Down)			Mileage n/k.	Bridged 1903.
30m 58c 30m 1286y	Bridlington South	--/10/1893		S1 mod (Down)	MH T bar	- / 50		
	Bridlington [BN]				?	- / 100	New Frame, cabin extended 1903.	None.
	[from 07/02/1998]				MH 16	- / 125	Frame extended, cabin extended 1912.	
					MH 16	- / 65	Frame shortened 25/11/1974.	
	Bridlington Station Crossing	d 1874	--/10/1893	n/k (Up)			Mileage n/k.	Bridged 1893.
30m 1736y	Bridlington GF [1]		d 1912		Stevens	- / 3		
30m 72c	Bridlington GF [2]	d 1912	16/05/1977	(Up)	MH Dwarf	- / 6		
					MH 20	- / 6	GF renewed 20/02/1940.	
31m 06c	Quay Crossing	d 1874	07/02/1998	S1 mod	MH 6"	2 inc / 18		
31m 05c	*Bridlington Quay*			(Up)	MH 16	2 inc / 59	Frame length in 1912 - new 1911 when cabin rebuilt.	
					MH 16	+2 / 55		
					MH 16	+2 / 42	Frame shortened probably 1942.	
					MH 16	0 / 40	GW removed 28-29/04/1973. Barriers installed.	Barriers 29/04/1973. CCTV controlled by Bridlington South.
	Sewerby Gates	n/k	06/01/1909			- / 1	External lever and board signal.	
32m 25c	*Sewerby*	06/01/1909	25/10/1987	S2 (Up)	MH 16	- / 7		
						1 / 8		AHBC 25/10/1987.
33m 27c stn	Marton			S1s (Down)	MCH Dwarf 6"	- / 10		
33m 31c	*Flamborough*	d 1874	01/01/1973		MH 6"	1 inc / 15	Cabin raised to two storeys when rebuilt in 1899	
	[from 01/07/1884]						and new frame installed.	
							Goods facilities closed 10/08/1964.	
	reduced to GB	01/01/1973	29/11/1987		MH 16	+1 / 16	New frame 29/03/1940.	AHBC
							Reduced to 6 levers + GW	29/11/1987.
							post 1979 and pre 1985.	

Mileage	Name	Opened	Closed	Cabin Type and Location	Frame	GW / Levers	Remarks	Crossing
34m 43c stn								
34m 41c	Bempton	d 1874	01/01/1973	S1a (Down)	MCH Dwarf 6"		Cabin extended at the north end by 6' in 1899? Goods facilities closed 10/08/1964.	
	reduced to GB	01/01/1973	25/04/1976		MH 16	- / 20	New frame 1919?	
	replaced by GF on platform	25/04/1976	17/01/1988	OGF	LNE GF	- / 6		Thence to AHB.
36m 15c	Buckton Lane Crossing		25/09/1983		None		Gate board abolished 14/05/1977. Key locks installed.	AOCR 25/09/1983, AHBC 19/03/1989.
37m 36c stn								
	Speeton [1]	d 1874	d 1913		MCH Dwarf 6"	- / 10		
37m 33c	Speeton [2]	d 1913	01/01/1973	S4 (Down)	MH 16	1 inc / 27		
					MH 16	1 inc / 16	Frame reduced 1964. Goods facilities closed 04/05/1964.	
	reduced to GB	01/01/1973	18/12/1988		MH 16	+1 / 7	Frame reduced again 01/01/1973.	AHBC 18/12/1988.
39m 30c	Speeton Lime Works	b 1877	b 1889	(Down)			Not shown in 1889 NER Appendix.	
41m 53c stn								
41m 51c	Hunmanby	d 1874	04/03/2001	S1 (Down)	MH 6"	- / 13	SB extended pre 1900?	
					MH 16	1 inc / 42	New frame --/11/1908.	
					MH 16	- / 16	Frame reduced 17/07/1983 floor plates removed, cut back to 16 levers on 01/01/1973. Goods facilities closed 10/08/1964.	AHBC-X 17/07/1983.
	Hunmanby GF							
41m 73c	Hunmanby Depot Crossing	d 1874	17/07/1983	OGF (Down)	MH 4" GF	- / 5	Frame 12/1908.	
	Sands Lane [from26/03/2000?]					- / 4	Reduced.	AOCL 17/07/1983, AHBC 26/03/2000?
	Filey Road Bridge	d 1886	d 1886	(Down)	Dwarf	- / 9	Mileage n/k.	
42m 40c	Royal Oak South	09/05/1947	01/10/1978	LNE (Down)	MH 16	- / 10		
44m 21c	Filey Holiday Camp	03/05/1948	03/09/1978	LNE (Down)	MH 16	- / 45	2m 48c from Hunmanby on branch.	
42m 70c	Royal Oak North	09/05/1947	03/09/1978	LNE (Down)	MH 16	- / 10		
	Driffield Crossing					- / 5	Same place as Royal Oak Crossing?	
43m 05c?	Royal Oak Crossing	d 1908?	12/06/1983	S4 (Down)	MH 16	- / 7	Key locks from 02/10/1955.	AHBC 12/06/1983.
44m 18c 44m 406y	Filey GF	n/k	10/05/1965	(Up)	MH 6"	- / 3	GF pre1890?	
44m 30c stn								
44m 777y	Filey [1]	d 1875	d --/02/1911	(Down)	MH 6"	1 inc / 20		
44m 35c 44m 775y	Filey [2]	d --/02/1911	24/06/2000	S4 (Down)	MH 16	1 inc / 37	Signal box demolished 03-04/03/2001. Goods facilities closed 10/08/1964.	AHBC CCTV- Radar.
45m 41c	Muston (Road Crossing)							
	Muston Crossing	d 1908	16/02/1986	S4 (Up)	MH 16	+1 / 7	Dismantled 15/03/1987 and re-erected on the Derwent Valley Light Railway as Murton.	AHBC 16/02/1986, monitored Filey.

Mileage	Name	Opened	Closed	Cabin Type and Location	Frame	GW / Levers	Remarks	Crossing
46m 41c stn	Gristhorpe	d 1875	13/03/1983	S1s (Down)	MCH Dwarf	+1 / 10	Gatewheel outside of frame	
46m 39c 46m 846y	reduced to GB	13/03/1983			MH 6" [s/h]	1 inc / 18	New frame 1910, (when cabin extended?). Key locks installed and gates made hand before 1967 but post 1957.	MCG.
46m 72c	Lebberston						Board signal abolished 08/06/1978.	MCG.
48m 19c	Cayton [1]	d 1875	22/04/1908	S1s (Up)	MH 4	+1 / 9	Gatewheel outside of frame .	
48m 18c 48m 405y	Cayton [2]	22/04/1908		S4 wood (Up)	MH 9	1 inc / 11	Second-hand frame of 1886 with No16 locking.	
	reduced to GB		24/06/2000		MH 16	- / 16	Probably became GB during WW1.	AHBC 24/06/2000.
49m ?c 49m 1293y	Seamer Carr	b 1898	d 1906			- / -		None.
50m 43c	Seamer Junction [1]	b 1872	d 1906	n/k (Up)	?	- / 21	39m 889y from York.	None.
50m 40c 50m 880y	*Seamer West* [2]	d 1906	10/04/2000	S4 (Down)	MH 16	- / 60		None.
York 38m 63c	*Seamer Junction* [from 1987]						39m 1388y from York.	
50m 71c stn	Seamer Station [1]	d 1874	b 1912	S1 (Up)	MH 6"	- / 14	39m 17c from York.	
	Seamer Station [2]	b 1912	10/04/2000	S4 (Up)	MH 16	1 / 33	Closed temporarily for refurbishment.	Bridged 1987.
	Seamer East [from 1933]							
	Seamer [*SR*] [3] temporary cabin	10/04/2000	05/11/2000	Portacabin (Up)	NX Panel		Temporary cabin.	
	Seamer [SR] [2] [reopened from 05/11/2000]			(Up)	NX Panel			
	Weaponess	post 1897			$6^1/_2$" York	- / 6	40m 17c from York; reported closed after 1939 season but referred to 1940 and 1944 in WONs.	None.
	Mere Crossing						Mileage n/k.	Bridged 1931.
	Musham Gates Crossing						Mileage n/k.	
	Scarborough Gasworks GF [1]	--/08/1874	--/10/1875	(Down)				
	Scarborough Gasworks Jct [2]	--/10/1875	--/08/1898	S1 (Down)	MH 6"	- / 9		None.
					MH 6"	- / 13	@ 1897.	
	Scarborough Gasworks [3]	--/08/1898	13/06/1965	S1 (Down)	MH 16	- / 45	41m 15c from York.	
						- / 80		
	Scarborough Washbeck [1]	--/06/1878	08/06/1908	S1 (Up)	MH 6"	- / 30	Frame dated 1887.	None.
	Scarborough Washbeck [2]	08/06/1908	17/05/1970	S4 (Down)	MH 16	- / 115	41m 888y from York.	
						- / 117		
	Scarborough Falsgrave [1]	--/06/1878	--/06/1885	(Up)		- / 40		None.
	Scarborough Falsgrave [2]	--/06/1885	--/06/1908	S1a (Down)	MH 8	- / 50		
	Scarborough Falsgrave [3]	--/06/1908	06/10/2010	S4 (Down)	MH 16	- / 120	41m 1395y from York.	
53m 63c stn	Scarborough Stn [1]	--/--/1885	02/07/1899	Spl	MH 11	- / 12		None.
	Scarborough Stn [2]	02/07/1899	22/10/1984	Spl (Down)	MH 11	- / 30	41m 1695y from York.	
					MH 11	- / 47	New frame in 1903.	
					MH 11	- / 36	Frame reduced.	

Index